PC Magazine®
Windows® XP Security Solutions

PC Magazine® Windows® XP Security Solutions

Dan DiNicolo

Wiley Publishing, Inc.

PC Magazine® Windows® XP Security Solutions

Published by
Wiley Publishing, Inc.
10475 Crosspoint Boulevard
Indianapolis, IN 46256
www.wiley.com

Published simultaneously in Canada

ISBN-13: 978-0-471-75478-7
ISBN-10: 0-471-75478-1

Manufactured in the United States of America

10 9 8 7 6 5 4 3 2 1

1B/RV/RR/QV/IN

For general information on our other products and services or to obtain technical support, please contact our Customer Care Department within the U.S. at (800) 762-2974, outside the U.S. at (317) 572-3993 or fax (317) 572-4002.

Library of Congress Cataloging-in-Publication Data

DiNicolo, Dan.
PC magazine Windows XP security solutions / Dan DiNicolo.
p. cm.
Includes index.
ISBN-13: 978-0-471-75478-7 (pbk.)
ISBN-10: 0-471-75478-1 (pbk.)
1. Computer security. 2. Microsoft Windows (Computer file) I. Title.
QA76.9.A25D565 2005
005.8—dc22
2005026406

About the Author

Dan DiNicolo is a freelance author, consultant, and trainer based in the snowy backwoods north of the 49th parallel. The author of a number of books and magazine articles related to computer security and networking, Dan is the holder of an alphabetic rash of technical certifications that mean nothing to anyone other than those holding or pursuing them. In his spare time Dan turns off his computer and attempts to interact with the real world, just like folks used to do in the good ol' days.

To Jessica, my pretty girl

Credits

ACQUISITIONS EDITOR
Katie Mohr

DEVELOPMENT EDITOR
Kelly D. Henthorne

TECHNICAL EDITOR
Todd Meister

PRODUCTION EDITOR
Kathryn Duggan

COPY EDITOR
Susan Hobbs

EDITORIAL MANAGER
Mary Beth Wakefield

PRODUCTION MANAGER
Tim Tate

VICE PRESIDENT AND EXECUTIVE GROUP PUBLISHER
Richard Swadley

VICE PRESIDENT AND EXECUTIVE PUBLISHER
Joseph B. Wikert

PROJECT COORDINATOR
Ryan Steffen

GRAPHICS AND PRODUCTION SPECIALISTS
Carrie Foster
Lauren Goddard
Denny Hager
Barbara Moore
Melanee Prendergast

QUALITY CONTROL TECHNICIANS
Amanda Briggs
John Greenough

PROOFREADING AND INDEXING
TECHBOOKS Production Services

COVER ILLUSTRATION AND DESIGN
Anthony Bunyan

Acknowledgments

A very special thank you to my editor Katie Mohr, the wonderful motivator and downright pleasant human being who made writing this book a pleasure. Thanks also to Kelly Henthorne and Todd Meister; I appreciate all of your hard work and especially your attention to detail. Thank you to my agent, Laura, for keeping on me to move beyond the idea stage with this book and put something concrete on paper.

An extra special thank you to both Mom and Flo for your support, with apologies for not being the best host with chapter deadlines looming.

Last but not least, thank you so much, Jessica. You make every day a most excellent adventure, and life just doesn't get any better than that.

Contents at a Glance

Contents

PC
MAGAZINE
www.pcmag.com

Part III Protecting Windows XP Against Internet Threats

PC
MAGAZINE
www.pcmag.com

Introduction

Once upon a time, viruses were considered the worst security-related ill that could befall a computer. My, how times have changed! Long gone are the days when simply installing an anti-virus program would protect your computer from the most dangerous threats making the rounds. Today, computer users connecting to the Internet need to protect themselves against a veritable army of security- and privacy-related threats including spyware, worms, phishing scams, and browser hijacks, to name but a few. In fact, venturing online without the right protection in place virtually guarantees that your computer will fall prey to the latest online ills, often in a matter of mere minutes.

Thankfully, all is not lost. Any computer—including the ones running Windows XP—can be easily secured to a high level if you know what you're doing, and that's why this Windows XP Security Solutions book exists. My goal is not to turn anyone into a computer security expert or to deconstruct computer security and privacy threats on a theoretical level. I'll gladly leave that to all of the technical junkies out there who enjoy spending their Saturday evenings analyzing computer log files. Instead, my primary motivation is to explain what the real security threats are and why you should care, and then outline the steps you need to take to ensure that both you and your Windows XP system remain properly protected. Whether your Windows XP system is already infected and you need to clean it up, or you want to ensure that you're adequately protected against future threats, this book provides the details you need to know.

Various studies have estimated that up to 90 percent of computers are infected by some security threat or another, so there's a very high possibility that yours is among those most at risk. Perhaps you're being inundated with pop-up windows every time you log on to Windows XP, or have noticed your computer doing "strange" things. It might be that you've managed to acquire some relatively harmless adware as a result of doing nothing more than surfing the Web. It's equally possible, however, that your PC has been compromised by spyware or a Trojan horse to the point where it can be remotely controlled without your knowledge. From anonymous users reading your e-mail messages to harvesting credit card details from your PC, the need to ensure that your computer is properly secured is more critical than ever before. It's not only your computer's security and privacy that's at risk—it's also your own.

I don't want to sound like Chicken Little and be the bearer of dire warnings about the sky falling, but computer security and privacy risks are very serious issues, and ones that deserve your immediate attention. This book isn't about making your Windows XP system perform faster, or tweaking it with a cool new look and feel. It's about taking the steps necessary to rid your system of any threats that may already be present and then ensuring that the potential for future security-related issues is minimized to the greatest degree possible. By the time you finish reading this book, you should be the proud owner of one very clean and secure Windows XP system, and have the ability to explain the dangers of not being properly protected to family, friends, and colleagues. If this book does help you to get your security issues sorted, I'd be thrilled to bits if you recommended it to others.

I've organized this book into seven main parts:

- **Part I, "Getting Down to the Business of Securing Windows XP":** Some of the most critical steps toward properly securing a computer are very basic in nature. In this section, you learn how to use Windows XP user accounts correctly, as well as implement and

maintain the elements that represent the foundation of any effective security strategy—specifically good, strong passwords. Along the way, you also become familiar with Windows XP's security-related tools and features, learning how they can be leveraged in your quest to not only eliminate existing security threats, but also prevent them from infiltrating your system again in the future.

- **Part II, "Making Surfing Safer":** The Internet is definitely a wild and wondrous resource, but surfing the Web today is a more risky activity than ever before. In this section you learn about how you can be exposed to security threats by doing nothing more than visiting an infectious Web page, and the ways in which you can secure Web browsers such as Internet Explorer to help reduce your exposure to these threats. Internet Explorer certainly isn't the only Web browser option out there, so you're also introduced to some of the so-called "alternative" browsers such as Mozilla Firefox. Additionally, you learn how parental control software can be used to keep your children safe when the venture online, or even help to ensure that workers aren't exposed to inappropriate content in corporate environments.
- **Part III, "Protecting Windows XP Against Internet Threats":** Ensuring that any Windows XP system is properly protected is a process that includes not only the operating system's built-in features and capabilities, but also the added help of a number of third-party security programs. In this section you learn more about protecting your Windows XP system with firewall, anti-virus, and anti-spyware software, along with ways to ensure your system is properly patched and protected with all of the latest Windows XP updates and Service Packs.
- **Part IV, "Messaging Your Way to E-mail Security":** E-mail is one of the most revolutionary communication methods ever invented, and today you would be hard-pressed to find an Internet user without an e-mail account. For all of its benefits, however, e-mail also has a dark side. Junk e-mail messages, often referred to as spam, aren't simply an annoyance—they are also a common carrier of threats that represent real risks to your security and privacy. Additionally, e-mail is an inherently insecure medium by default, leaving your messages open and exposed for any number of people to read without your knowledge. In this section you learn more about the ways in which you can effectively fight spam and reduce your exposure to related security risks, as well as how e-mail messages can be secured so that they cannot be read or tampered with as they travel over the Internet.
- **Part V, "Protecting Your Files":** Your personal files—be they documents, digital photos, or business-related databases—are arguably the most important objects stored on your computer. Although it's easy to assume that your documents are only valuable to you, the truth is that the information stored within them can be exceptionally valuable to both hackers and other users who share access to your Windows XP system. Unfortunately, few users take the steps necessary to ensure that their personal files are properly secured, putting both their personal security and privacy at an unnecessary risk. In this section you learn more about how to implement Windows XP's native file security features, as well as how to use techniques such as encryption to protect your sensitive files with industrial-strength security.
- **Part VI, "Securing Your Home Network":** There was a time when having a network in your home or office was something special, but that's no longer the case. Today, the availability of

high-speed broadband Internet connections and low-cost networking gear has converged to make the home network a reality for millions of users. For all of the sharing conveniences that a network provides, however, there are also many security concerns that need to be addressed, both on wired and wireless networks. In this section you learn more about securing Windows XP in network environments, including how to take the steps necessary to ensure that other users within range cannot connect to and "piggyback" on your wireless network and fast Internet connection.

- **Part VII, "Appendixes":** The appendixes provided with this book include details on reinstalling Windows XP securely should the need arise, along with catalogs of useful security programs and Windows XP-related Web sites.

Throughout this book you'll find a wealth of step-by-step instructions aimed at helping you to uncover and eliminate security threats that may already be present on your Windows XP system, along with others designed to help you prevent exposure to security and privacy risks in the first place. Along the way, I've done my best to provide practical and thought-provoking examples of the real dangers associated with different types of security and privacy threats. Although the individual chapters in this book can be used as standalone references for specific types of security risks, I ask that you consider each chapter within the context of an overall security solution for Windows XP. Keeping your system virus-free is in and of itself a good thing—however, a virus-free system that is riddled with spyware and other "holes" can never be considered secure. Security is a process, and to ensure a secure Windows XP system you need to give equal attention to everything from the quality of the passwords you choose to the way you lock down your wireless network. Neglect any one component, and your system will never be truly secure.

I've been writing about the need for PC users to pay more attention to Internet security risks for years now, and with the incredible popularity of Windows XP, I decided that the time was right to compile everything into a practical and easy-to-understand guide. I sincerely hope that you enjoy my writing style and find the chapters engaging, but I'll always be more concerned with you getting your Windows XP system properly secured. It is possible, and if you follow the steps outlined in this book, you can get the job done. After you do, take the time to explain the various security and privacy threats with which you're now familiar to friends, family members, and colleagues—the Internet can be a safer place, but getting there means improving security one PC at a time.

If you have any questions or comments, please feel free to contact me at the following e-mail address. I can't promise an immediate response, but I will do my best to get back to you as soon as possible. All the best, and may the Force be with you.

`dan@xpsecuritysolutions.com`
`www.xpsecuritysolutions.com`

Part I

Getting Down to the Business of Securing Windows XP

Chapter 1

Implementing User Accounts, Groups, and Logon Security

Securing your computer is in many ways like securing your home — you shouldn't rely on any one method to keep the outside world from getting in. Instead, you take a number of different measures that might include locking doors, installing an alarm system, and hopefully not alerting would-be attackers that lots of cool stuff is inside.

When it comes to securing Windows XP, you're given the choice of leaving the front door open or putting a lock in place. This door lock is known as a ***user account***, specifically a user account that includes a password. For a first line of defense in the quest to secure Windows XP and ensure user privacy, begin with user accounts.

This isn't to say that user accounts are strictly a security-related feature of Windows XP; they certainly have other reasons for being. However, user accounts are a key component toward changing your computer from being an open book to a secure fortress.

This chapter focuses on what user accounts are, the different types of accounts that exist, and how to create and configure them to ensure better system security. Along the way, you also learn about group accounts and the different user logon methods that can be used to control access to your Windows XP system.

Exploring User Accounts

When it comes to Windows XP, user accounts represent the foundation upon which all other security concepts and techniques rely. Quite simply, you can install any piece of "security" software — from firewalls and anti-virus programs to anti-spyware tools and encryption utilities — and your work is effectively all for naught if you do not implement user accounts correctly nor properly protect them. Most Windows XP users consider the user account logon process an annoyance, rather than a security feature. Unfortunately, neglecting or ignoring this essential security feature is the very reason why the majority of user desktop systems are insecure and vulnerable to an Internet's worth of security and personal privacy threats.

At the most basic level, a user account is nothing more than an object on a Windows XP system that represents a particular user. Made up of a username, and hopefully a password, user accounts represent the "credentials" that users need to supply to gain access to a Windows XP system. Beyond

simply identifying a user, a user's account dictates what tasks that person can perform on a computer, what files they have access to, and more. In a nutshell, user accounts are not an optional part of securing a Windows XP system — they're absolutely essential.

In a departure from previous versions of Windows aimed at home and small office users, Windows XP offers true user account security facilities in a way that cannot be easily ignored or dismissed. Although pressing the Esc key might have gotten a user past the Logon dialog box on a Windows 95 system, Windows XP offers much more robust and comprehensive logon security. As a matter of fact, the logon security capabilities of Windows XP are fundamentally the same as those used to secure servers running Windows 2000 Server or Windows Server 2003. In other words, Windows XP user account security offers a high level of protection for your system. If you're serious about your system's security and privacy, you'll want to take advantage of it.

The good news is that Windows XP makes it easy to create and manage user accounts via tools such as the User Accounts applet in the Control Panel (see Figure 1-1). Before you jump into creating any accounts, however, it's essential for you to understand the benefits that user accounts provide and important details on the different types of accounts that exist.

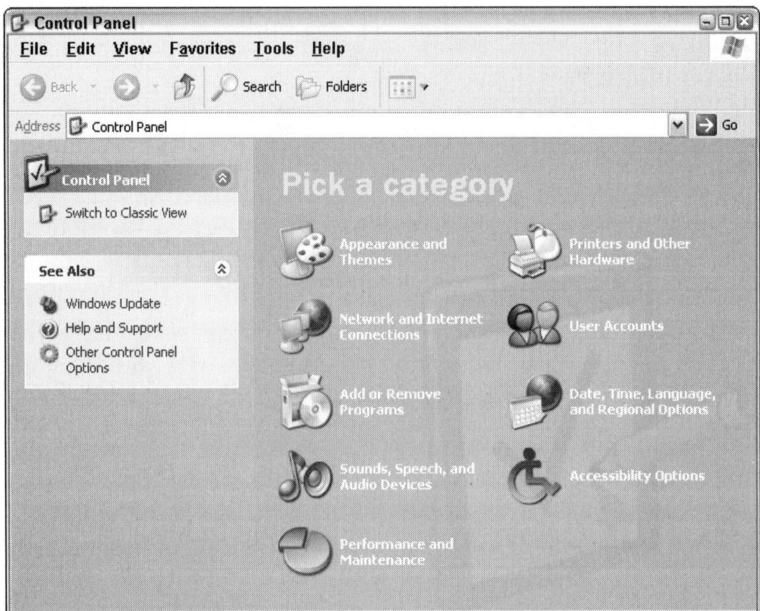

Figure 1-1: Click the User Accounts icon to create and manage user accounts.

Benefits of user accounts

Some user accounts are configured for general day-to-day use, including tasks like surfing the Web, working with e-mail, and playing games. Others are designed with system administration and configuration tasks in mind, including installing software and making changes to firewall settings. Ultimately, each person who uses a Windows XP system should be assigned their own personal user account, which provides the following benefits:

- A dedicated and customizable desktop environment
- A dedicated user profile where personal files, e-mail messages, and settings are stored
- The capability to control access to the desktop environment by adding a user account password
- The ability to secure personal files and folders, making them inaccessible by other users

Creating a dedicated user account for every person who uses a Windows XP system is not unlike setting up a number of Windows XP systems, in which each user has her own personal desktop environment. This model eliminates the hassles associated with older systems such as Windows 3.1, where users shared a common desktop and all related settings. In the world of Windows XP, having your own user account means being able to log on, set your desktop wallpaper image to something crazy or fun, and not having to deal with friends or family members who decide to change it. Your desktop can be neatly organized (recommended), or a complete mess (recommended only if you thrive in chaotic environments). Most important, having your own user account allows you to control which users can access your files and to what extent.

User account types

Although the idea of each user having their own dedicated account is a great, all user accounts are not created equal. There's a definite hierarchy in this part of the computing world, and Windows XP offers no exception. Some user accounts allow unrestricted access to every last bit of a Windows XP system, including files belonging to other users. Others limit what users can do while logged on, stopping them from carrying out common tasks such as installing software. When it comes to the security of your Windows XP system, creating user accounts is important; however, assigning appropriate user account types to various users is even more critical.

Windows XP includes five different types of user accounts:

- Computer Administrator accounts
- Limited accounts
- Standard accounts
- Guest accounts
- Special user accounts

Each of these user account types is examined in more detail in the following sections.

Note

In the world of Windows XP, a user is the person actually using the computer—you, your mom, dad, son, daughter, or friend. A user account is the object assigned to a user for the purpose of logging on. Some users will have only one user account, and others might have more than one user account—one for day-to-day use and another for system administration tasks.

COMPUTER ADMINISTRATOR ACCOUNTS

In the parallel universe that is Windows XP, one type of user account stands head and shoulders above the rest: the all-seeing and all-knowing *Computer Administrator account*. User accounts of this type have complete control over every element of a Windows XP system; users with this privilege level can literally do anything, up to and including actions that could irreparably damage a Windows XP installation.

A user configured as a Computer Administrator can do the following:

- Install and uninstall programs, hardware, and drivers
- Make system-wide configuration changes
- Create, delete, and manage all user and group accounts
- Read or open any file, including those belonging to other users
- Grant rights to or implementing restrictions on other users

One limitation is that the Computer Administrator cannot delete his account or change its type to Limited if it is the last Computer Administrator account on the Windows XP system.

Windows XP creates one Computer Administrator account by default (named Administrator) during its installation process. You might not even be aware that this account exists, as it's not displayed on the Welcome logon screen by default. This account is always present, however, and cannot be deleted.

The Computer Administrator user account type is supposed to work for the forces of good, not evil; however, this account type was never designed with normal, everyday, use in mind. As the list of its broad capabilities shows, Computer Administrators yield complete control over not only the Windows XP system itself, but also other users' accounts.

For this reason, regular users should never be granted Computer Administrator privileges. In fact, for security purposes alone, even the Computer Administrator should never log on to Windows XP with a Computer Administrator account unless he needs to perform configuration tasks that require this level of power. Unfortunately, many Windows XP systems run into security-related problems (such as infections by viruses and spyware programs) due to unnecessary or careless everyday use of the massive firepower the Computer Administrator account.

Toward the end of the Windows XP installation process, the installer is prompted to create at least one, and up to a maximum of five, additional user accounts for the people who will be using this computer (these accounts are above and beyond the default Administrator account that is always created). For reasons technically unknown (but almost certainly associated with making the system as easy to use as possible), Windows XP automatically makes each of these accounts a Computer Administrator.

Obviously, this is not a good thing. Although having each user account configured as a Computer Administrator means fewer restrictions for users (who can then do whatever they please), it also presents a very real security risk. Thankfully, all is not lost. You can change the type of any user account that you create, as you learn later in this chapter.

Caution

The decision as to which users should be granted Computer Administrator rights is ultimately up to you, but always keep system security in mind. Generally, any user with access to the Computer Administrator account should have an appropriate level of Windows XP knowledge. More importantly, they should be someone who can be trusted not to abuse or misuse the account's power. On some systems, every user may be responsible enough to be granted access to a Computer Administrator account to perform tasks such as installing programs. On others, the situation might dictate that only the owner of the PC has access to a Computer Administrator account. The bottom line is that on your computer, you get to choose who has access to Computer Administrator accounts, so choose wisely.

LIMITED USER ACCOUNTS

Unlike Computer Administrator accounts, *Limited user accounts* are designed for everyday personal use. Many people argue that these accounts are excessively restrictive because they stop users from carrying out common tasks such as installing hardware and software, changing security settings, and making system configuration changes. Indeed these statements are true, but they're also very much to the point — limited user accounts are designed to keep users from making potential harmful and dangerous changes to a system and by extension help to ensure a better-performing and more secure Windows XP system overall.

A user with a Limited account:

- Can add, change, or remove their user account password
- Can create a password reset disk for use in cases where their password is lost or forgotten
- Can make changes to their user desktop environment
- Can make their personal files private (except from the Computer Administrator)
- Can use software programs installed for all users
- Cannot make changes to system configuration settings or delete key files
- Typically cannot install hardware or software programs

Although Limited user accounts typically cannot install hardware and software, there are exceptions. On the hardware front, Windows XP systems do allow Limited users to plug in and use a variety of USB devices including pen drives, MP3 players, and the like. Most other hardware changes are restricted. As for software, Limited users can often install single-user programs that do not make any changes to system configuration settings, as is the case with many older programs designed for previous Windows versions; however, Limited users cannot install multi-user programs, or those that install new system services. Words such as "often," "typically," "many," and "most" are the name of the game here. The best way to see whether a program will install for a Limited user is to attempt the

installation. In some cases it may get the job done, but in others it will fail. Although the conveniences associated with being a Computer Administrator have appeal, everyday user accounts should always be of the Limited type if you're serious about securing your system. Unfortunately, going this route can lead to frustration (and even conflict) when one user wants to do something on a computer but is unable to due to restrictions imposed as a result of their Limited user status.

This is why the Computer Administrator account type exists, and there's nothing wrong with granting a responsible and trusted user the ability to use a Computer Administrator account if and when necessary. Later in this chapter, you learn how you can allow "trusted" Limited users to perform administrative tasks without leaving the safe confines of their everyday user account.

As a best practice, always try to follow what is known as the ***principle of least privilege*** when configuring security settings for any PC. This principle dictates that you give users only the minimum level of privilege that they require, and nothing more. Although the level of control that a particular user needs is open to debate (especially in their eyes), sticking to the least privilege maxim will help to ensure a more secure computer. In the case of user accounts, this means assigning all users Limited accounts for normal everyday use. Many viruses and spyware programs rely on the current user having administrator-level access to thoroughly infect systems and do their damage, so sticking with Limited accounts can help to mitigate potential risks. Suffice it to say that when it comes to Windows XP, user accounts, and security, less can actually be more.

Note

While Limited User accounts are the way to go for better overall system security, some popular programs refuse to work for users logged on with Limited accounts. A list of these programs can be found at `support.microsoft.com/default.aspx?scid=kb;en-us;307091`.

STANDARD USER ACCOUNTS

In the vast majority of cases, users running Windows XP on a home or small business network will have their systems configured as part of what is known as a ***workgroup***. This is the name that Microsoft gives to a collection of Windows computers connected to a network that is not centrally administered by a server running Windows 2000 Server or Windows Server 2003. Networks that include a Windows Server system dedicated to tasks like validating user logons are known as ***domains***.

Although both Windows XP Home and Windows XP Professional systems can both be members of a workgroup, only Windows XP Professional systems can be made members of a domain. This isn't surprising, considering that Windows XP Home is primarily designed with the home user in mind, while Windows XP Professional includes additional capabilities more geared toward business users.

When made a member of a domain network, Windows XP Professional systems include an additional user account type, the ***Standard user***. Standard users are fundamentally similar to Limited users in terms of what they're allowed to do, with one key exception — these users can install and remove software programs as long as the task in question doesn't affect other users. So, a Standard user could install a program for personal use but could not remove another program available to all users.

GUEST USER ACCOUNT

Along with Administrator, Windows XP also automatically creates a user account named Guest. As its name suggests, this account is meant for users without their own dedicated user account. Disabled by default (see Figure 1-2), the Guest account does not (and cannot) have a password assigned and has little in the way of powers beyond running installed programs.

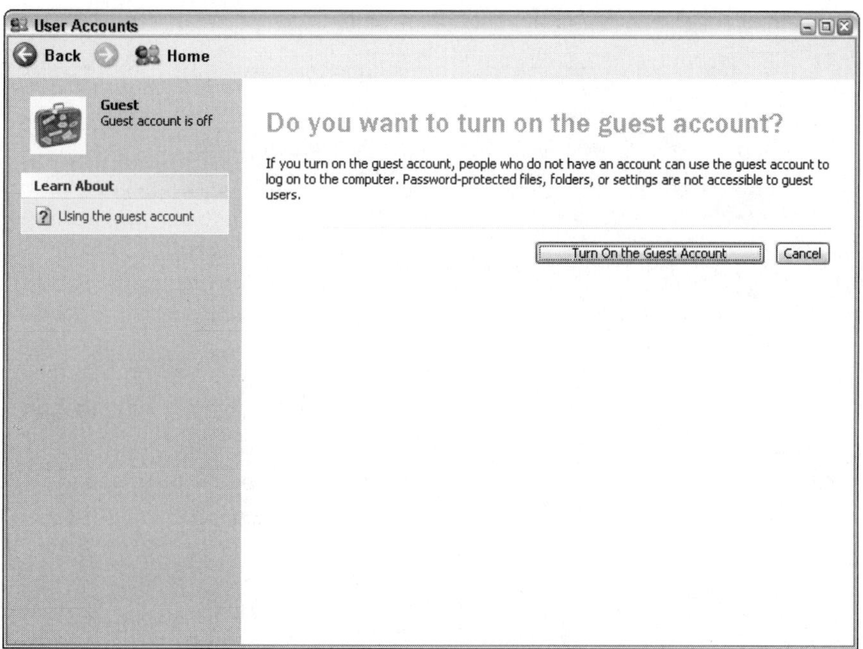

Figure 1-2: Windows XP's built-in Guest account is disabled by default.

The fact that the Guest account is disabled by default (and cannot be assigned a password) is a good indication that it represents a potential security risk. As a best practice, always leave the Guest account disabled and create Limited accounts for users who require occasional access to your Windows XP system. As you'll see later in this chapter, you can create a user account in less than a minute — well worth the effort from a security perspective.

SPECIAL USER ACCOUNTS

Although there's technically no such thing as "special" user accounts on a Windows XP system, you may encounter additional user accounts beyond the ones that you create. Rarely, programs will require a user account to be created in order to function correctly. Although these user accounts are typically hidden from view on the Windows XP Welcome screen, exceptions do exist.

The most common such event that you're likely to come across is a user account named ASP.NET Machine Account. If you happen to see an account by this name on your Welcome screen or in the User Accounts dialog box shown in Figure 1-3, don't panic. This user account is added to your system

after you have installed the .NET Framework, a component from Microsoft that's used to build and run Windows-based programs. If you're not sure how the .NET Framework got onto your system, it's possible that you downloaded it as part of visiting the Windows Update Web site, or because it was required by another program you were attempting to install. In any case, having the ASP.NET account configured on your system does not present any inherent security risk. If you're still bothered by it, however, you can remove the user account from your Welcome screen or completely disable it by following the instructions outlined later in this chapter.

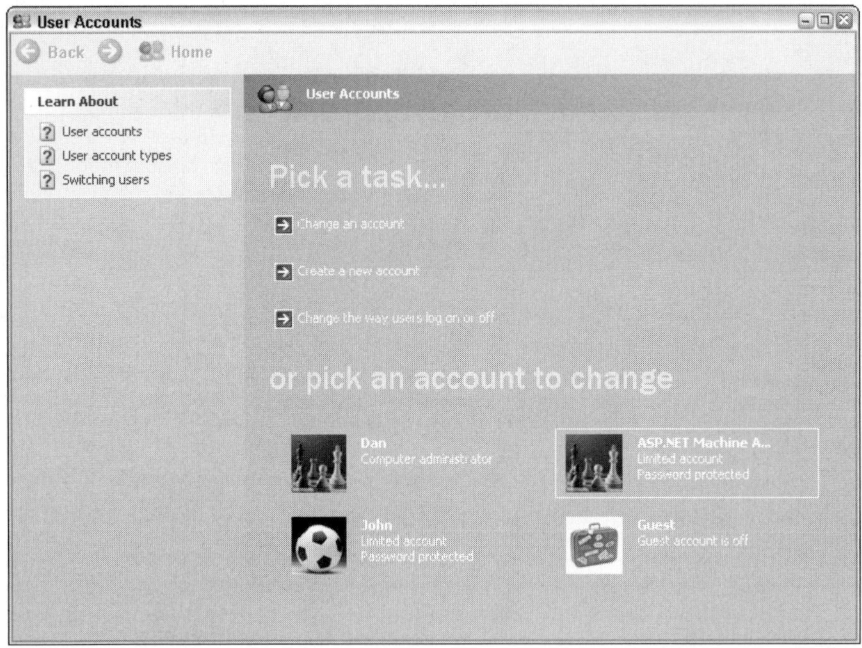

Figure 1-3: ASP.NET is a special user account created when you install Microsoft's .NET Framework.

Creating User Accounts

Now that you're familiar with user accounts and the different types that exist, it's time to get down to the business of actually creating them. As you'll soon see, creating user accounts couldn't be easier.

The primary tool used to create user accounts on both Windows XP Home and Professional systems is the User Accounts applet in the Control Panel. On Windows XP Professional systems, however, you also have the option of using the Computer Management tool to get the job done.

Creating user accounts in Control Panel

The User Accounts applet in Control Panel is the most intuitive and user-friendly tool for creating user accounts on a Windows XP system. Computer Administrators can use this tool to create accounts, as well as manage existing ones. Limited users can use the tool to manage settings related to their own account only.

Follow these steps to create new user accounts in Control Panel:

1. Click Start → Control Panel → User Accounts. The User Accounts Pick a Task screen appears.
2. Click Create a new account.
3. The Name the new account screen appears, as shown in Figure 1-4. In the field provided, type a name for the new account. This is the name that will appear on the Windows XP Welcome screen and on the Start menu. Click Next.

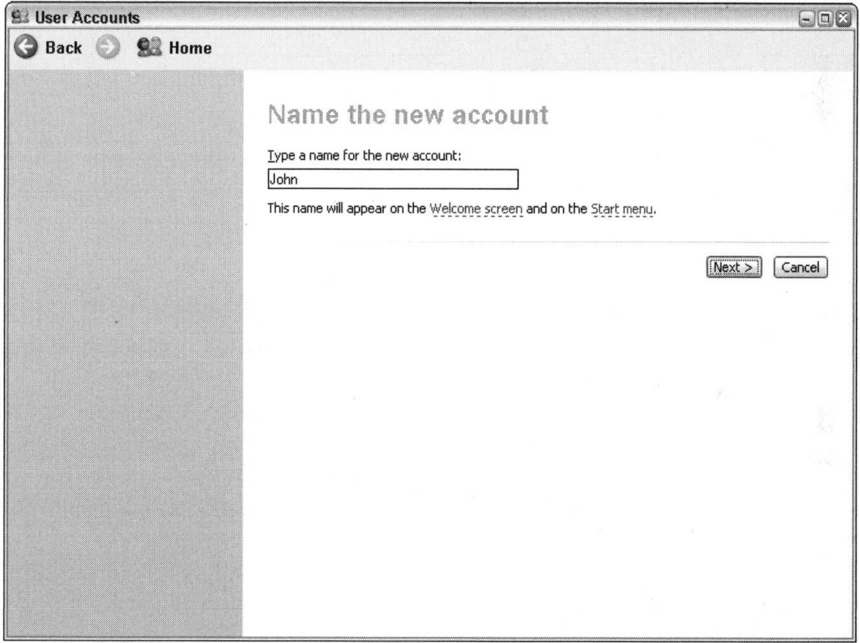

Figure 1-4: Supply the name for a new user account.

4. At the Pick an account type screen, select Computer Administrator or Limited (see Figure 1-5) and then click Create Account.

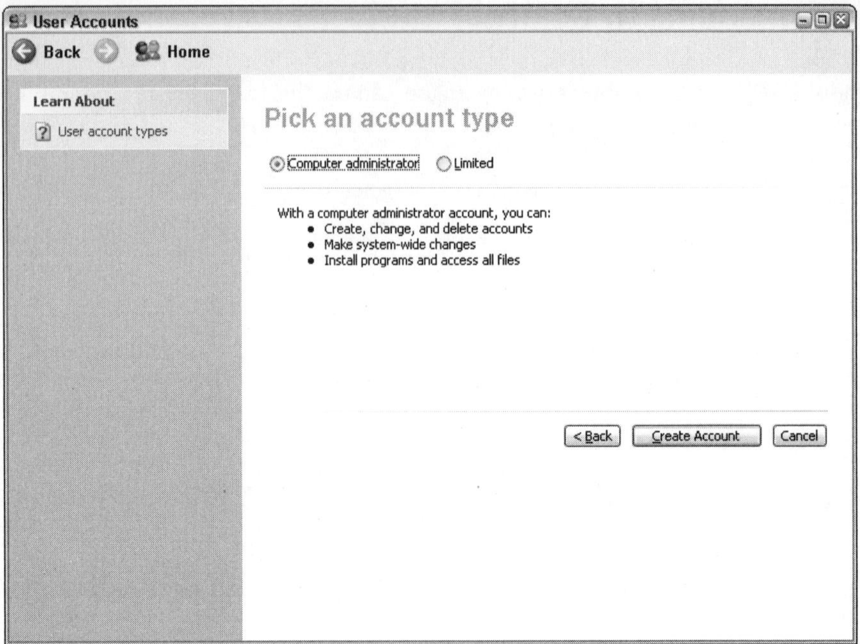

Figure 1-5: Select the new user account's type.

Creating user accounts with Computer Management

If you're running Windows XP Professional, you also have the option of creating and managing user accounts using the Local Users and Groups tool in the Computer Management MMC (Microsoft Management Console). Although not as user-friendly as the Users Accounts applet in the Control Panel, this tool often appeals to more advanced users who like the convenience of having access to many system configuration tools from within a single console window.

Follow these steps to create user accounts on a Windows XP Professional system using Computer Management:

1. Click Start, right-click My Computer, and click Manage.
2. At the Computer Management window, expand the Local Users and Groups folder by clicking on the plus sign (see Figure 1-6).
3. Right-click the Users folder and click New User.
4. In the New User window, enter a user name, full name, and description for the account.
5. Enter a password for the user account and then confirm it.
6. Click Create. A new user account is created to match the information you supplied.

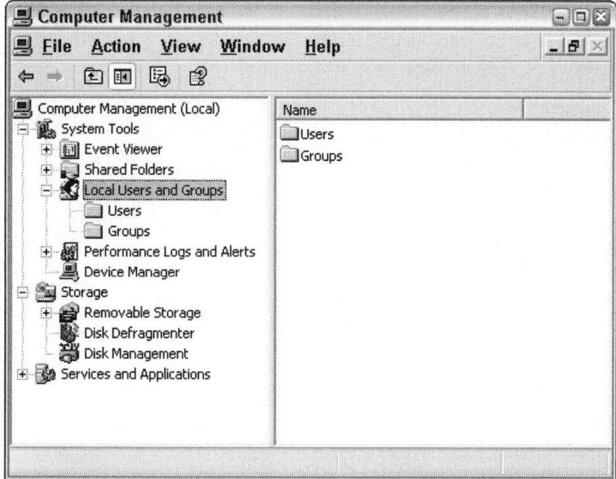

Figure 1-6: The Local Users and Groups tool is displayed in the Computer Management MMC.

Managing User Accounts

Creating user accounts is only part of the job of a Computer Administrator. After you create an account, occasionally you will need to manage it. Examples of security-related tasks associated with managing user accounts include the following:

- Changing account types
- Renaming accounts
- Adding, changing, and resetting passwords
- Disabling accounts
- Deleting accounts

Each of these tasks is explained in more detail in the following sections.

Changing user account types

As you're now aware, using a Computer Administrator account as your everyday user account is not recommended. Thankfully, the User Accounts tool in Windows XP makes it easy to change an account from one type to another, such as switching a Computer Administrator account to a Limited user, or vice versa.

Follow these steps to change a user account's type:

1. Click Start → Control Panel → User Accounts.
2. Click the user account name whose type you want to change.

3. Click Change the account type.
4. Select the type to which the account should be changed, as shown in Figure 1-7.

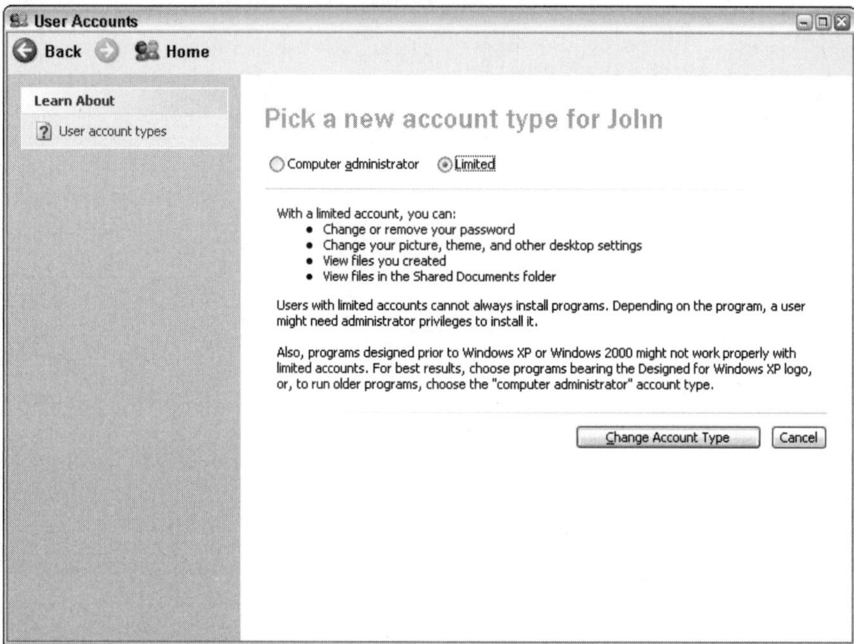

Figure 1-7: You can change an existing user account's type with the User Accounts tool.

5. Click Change Account Type.

Note

Only a Computer Administrator can change a user account's type. If the user whose account type is being changed is also logged onto the Windows XP system when the change is made, the new account type takes effect the next time the user logs on.

Renaming user accounts

Changing the name associated with an existing user account is significantly different than creating an account. When you rename an account, only the name is changed — the actual user account fundamentally remains the same. Accounts often are renamed in corporate environments to make the transition between a departing user and their replacement easier. If the account is renamed, the new user has the same rights and permissions as the old user, along with access to the old user's files and desktop environment. This is often preferable to creating an entirely new account and then configuring required rights and permissions manually. On a home PC, user accounts are typically only renamed when a user wants to change their onscreen display name.

Follow these steps to rename an existing user's account name in Control Panel:

1. Click Start → Control Panel → User Accounts.
2. Click the account you want to rename.
3. Click Change the name, as shown in Figure 1-8.

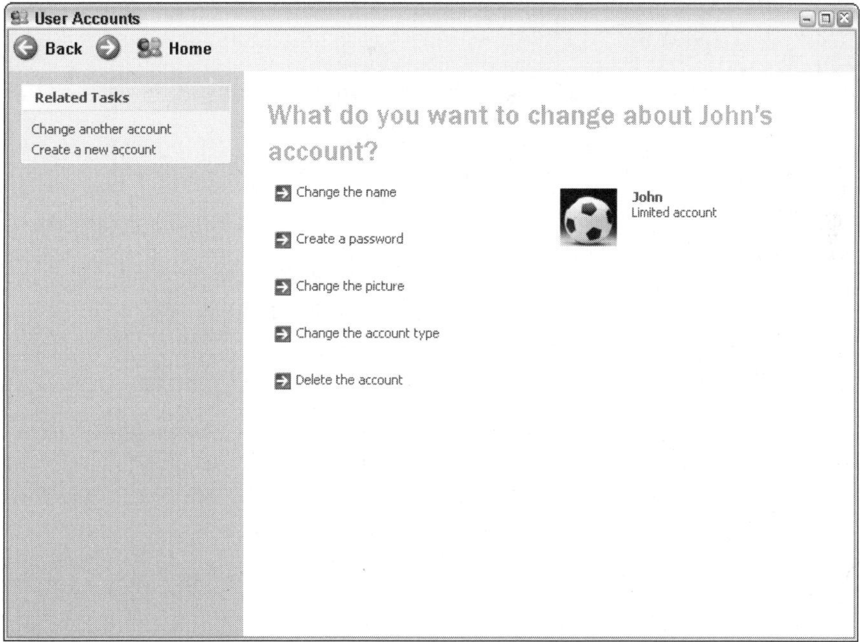

Figure 1-8: You can rename a user account.

4. Type a new name for the account and then click Change Name.

Tip

The built-in Administrator user account may be hidden from the Windows XP Welcome screen by default, but rest assured that hackers and others attempting to gain access to your computer know that it exists. Although you cannot delete this account, you can (and should) rename it to something less obvious. Choose a username for it that you'll remember and then assign it a sufficiently complex password. This isn't to say that changing the name of this account will keep a determined hacker out of your system, but it will foil less experienced users and make life a little more difficult for those in the know.

Managing user account passwords

Creating individual user accounts for every person that uses your Windows XP system is a great start, but it's only part of the story as far security is concerned. For user accounts to do anything more than act as a facility for separating user desktops and working environments, they must be assigned passwords. Every user should assign a password to their user account and, as a security/privacy precaution, be the only person who knows the password.

Follow these steps to add a password to an existing user account in Control Panel:

1. Click Start → Control Panel → User Accounts.
2. Click the name of the user account to which you want to add a password.
3. Click Create a password.
4. Enter the password for the user in the Type a new password box (see Figure 1-9).

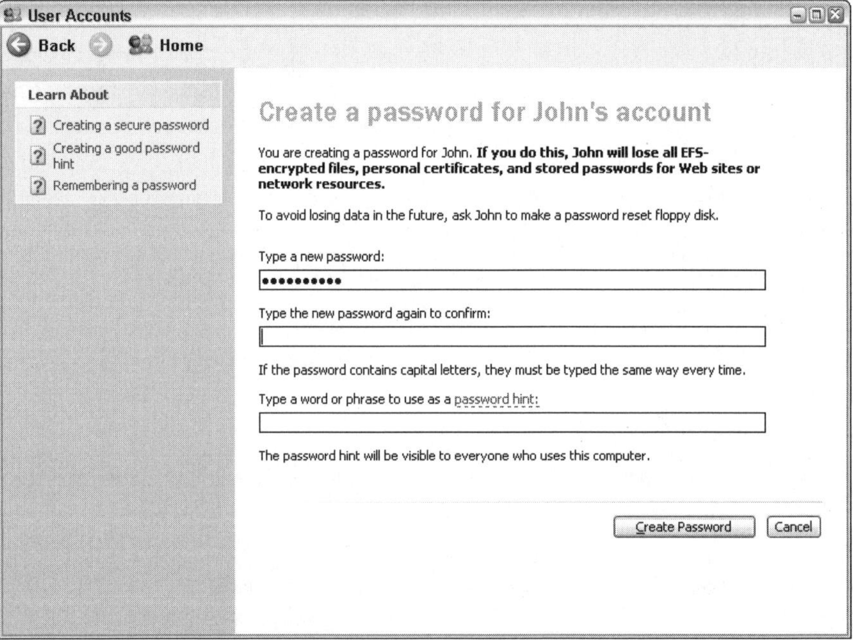

Figure 1-9: Adding a password to a user account is essential for system security.

5. Enter the same password again in the Type the new password again to confirm box.
6. Optionally, add a password hint in the Type a word or phrase to use as a password hint box.
7. Click the Create Password button.

Caution

Password hints exist to help you remember your password but are visible to all users from the Windows XP Welcome screen. If your hint is too obvious, other users may be able to guess your password. As a best practice, choose a password hint that makes sense to you but won't give your password away to others. Better still, don't configure a password hint at all.

Adding a password to your user account is an important step forward, but if you're serious about security, make a point of changing your password at least once every month or so. The User Accounts applet in Control Panel makes it easy to change (or even remove) the password associated with your user account.

Caution

Toward the end of the Windows XP installation process, you're prompted to create at least one personal user account. If you opt to create only one, Windows XP uses this Computer Administrator account to automatically log you on, bypassing the Welcome screen. This behavior occurs because you haven't configured a password for the account; however, Windows XP can also be configured to log you on automatically when you do have a password, via configuration changes to the Registry. Many third-party "tweaking" and customization tools make this easy, but it's definitely not a good idea from a system security standpoint. Such "tweaks" store your password in the Registry in plain text, and going this route effectively eliminates all of the security benefits associated with having a password in the first place.

Follow these steps to change the password associated with a user account in Control Panel:

1. Click Start → Control Panel → User Accounts.
2. Click the name of the user account whose password you want to remove or change.
3. To change the user account's password, click Change my password (if this is your account) or Change the password (if you are the Computer Administrator). Figure 1-10 shows the options on the administrator's screen.
4. Enter the new password for the user account, confirm it, and optionally add a password hint.
5. Click Change Password.

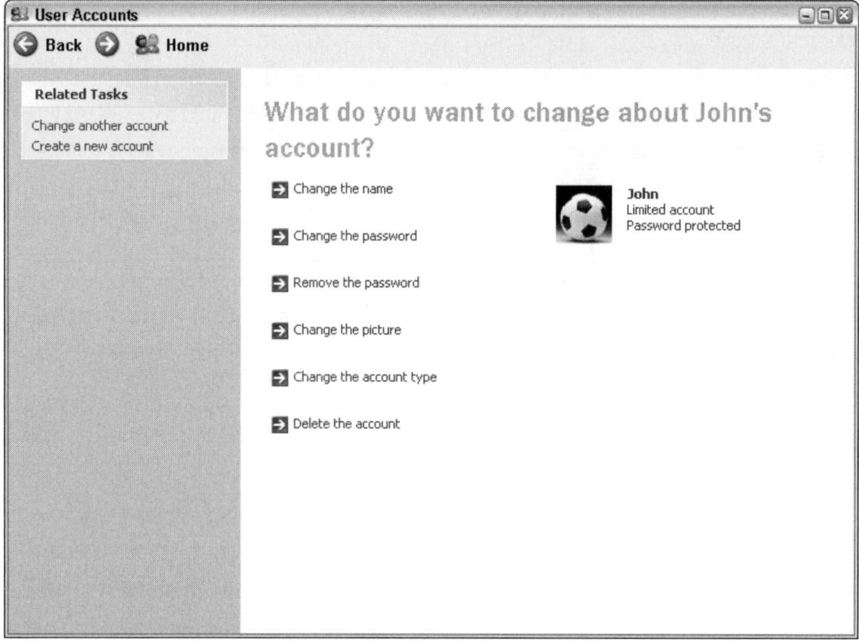

Figure 1-10: Changing your user account password regularly to enhance security.

Tip

Assigning a password to all user accounts is important, even if you're the only person using a computer. Any accounts left unprotected make easier for hackers, viruses, and spyware, and that's a risk not worth taking. Additionally, if your computer is ever lost or stolen, not having a password assigned gives others easy access to any personal data or files stored on your system.

Occasionally you may run into an issue where someone has forgotten the password associated with their user account and cannot log on. Should this happen, a Computer Administrator can reset their password by changing it using the User Accounts tool, or by using the Set Password option in the Computer Management MMC.

Follow these steps to reset a forgotten password using Computer Management:

1. Click Start, right-click on My Computer, and click Manage.
2. In the Computer Management window, expand the Local Users and Groups folder.
3. Click the Users folder and then right-click on the user account whose password you want to reset.
4. Click Set Password.

5. Read the warning message that appears with respect to the dangers associated with resetting user password (see Figure 1-11). Click Proceed to continue.

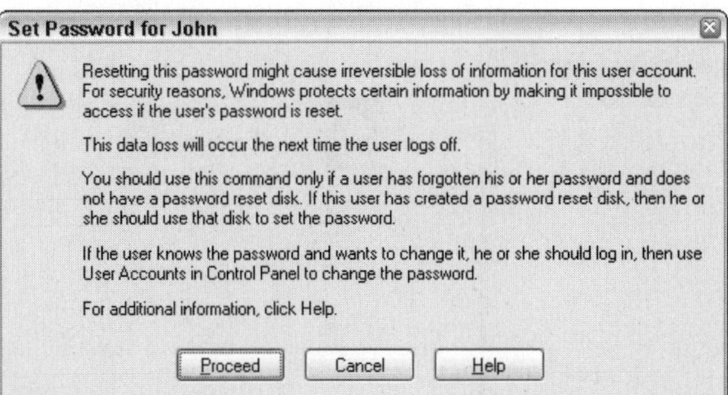

Figure 1-11: The warning message is presented when a Computer Administrator attempts to set another user's password in Computer Management.

6. Enter the new password, confirm it, and click OK.

Caution

As a general rule, do not add, change, or reset passwords for other user's accounts except during the original account creation process. If you add, change, or reset a password on their behalf (even with the best intentions) that user will lose access to her encrypted files, stored Internet certificates, and stored Web site passwords. Instead, have the user log on and add a password to their account using the User Accounts applet in Control Panel.

Understanding that users may forget their passwords, Windows XP allows all users to create a password reset floppy disk. This disk allows a user to log on and change his password without the need to worry about losing access to encrypted files and other stored settings. You'll learn more about creating a password reset disk in Chapter 2.

Disabling user accounts

Although it's not terribly common, you may encounter situations in which a person will not be using your Windows XP system for an extended period of time. In cases such as this, it makes good security sense to disable the account until it's needed again.

For a Windows XP Professional system, follow these steps to disable an existing user account using Computer Management:

1. Click Start, right-click My Computer, and click Manage.
2. At the Computer Management window, expand Local Users and Groups, and click the Users folder.

3. Right-click the user account you want to disable and click Properties.
4. Check the Account is disabled checkbox as shown in Figure 1-12 and then click OK.

Figure 1-12: Disabling a user account.

The User Accounts tool in Control Panel does not include an option to disable accounts (with the exception of the Guest account). As such, if you want to disable (or re-enable) user accounts on a Windows XP Home system, you need to use the Command Prompt to accomplish the task.

Follow these steps to disable or enable user accounts on Windows XP Home systems:

1. Click Start → All Programs → Accessories → Command Prompt.
2. To disable an account, at the Command Prompt, type `net user` *`username`* `/active:no` and then press Enter (see Figure 1-13), where *`username`* is the name of the account to be disabled.

```
C:\WINDOWS\System32\cmd.exe
Microsoft Windows XP [Version 5.1.2600]
(C) Copyright 1985-2001 Microsoft Corp.

C:\Documents and Settings\Dan>net user john /active:no
The command completed successfully.

C:\Documents and Settings\Dan>
```

Figure 1-13: Disabling a user account from the command line.

3. To enable a disabled account from the command line, issue the command `net user username /active:yes` and then press Enter.

Deleting user accounts

Creating individual user accounts is essential, but it's also important to delete user accounts that are no longer needed. If you believe that an account will be used again at some point in the future, disable it. If there's no chance that it will be again, deleting it is the more secure option.

Follow these steps to delete an existing user account in Control Panel:

1. Click Start → Control Panel.
2. Double-click User Accounts.
3. Click the user account name you want to delete.
4. Click Delete the account.
5. At the screen asking whether you want to keep the user's files, click Keep Files to save the contents of the user's My Documents folder to your desktop, or Delete Files to remove them, as shown in Figure 1-14.

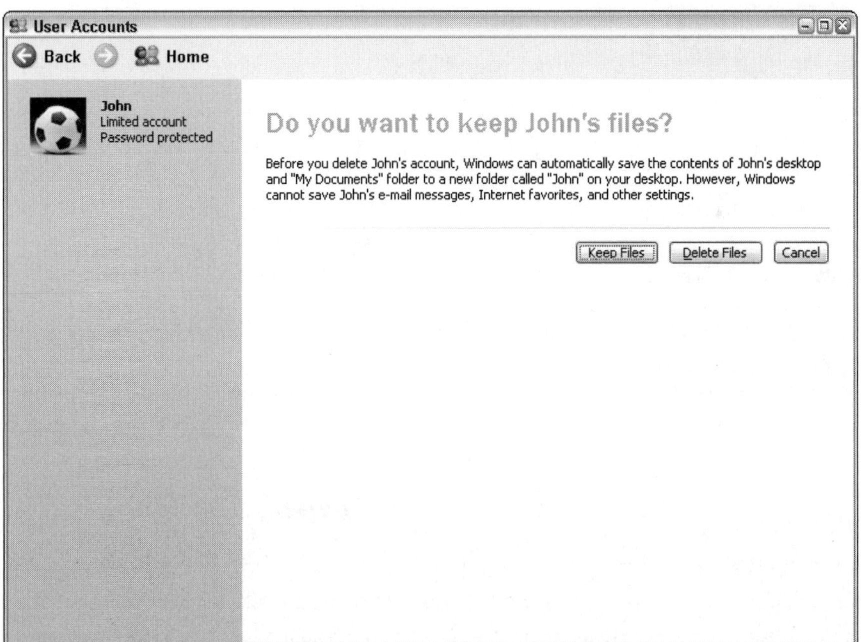

Figure 1-14: Options associated with deleting a user account.

6. When prompted, click Delete Account.

What's in a Name?

After deleting a user account, would a new user account of the same name not smell as sweet? When it comes to how Windows XP deals with user account names, the answer is actually no.

Imagine that your system includes a user account named Mike. When this user is created on a Windows XP system, it is assigned an identifier value known as a Security ID, or SID. A SID is a series of numbers that uniquely identifies a given security principal (user or group) on your system. Windows XP identifies different users and groups using their SIDs but names like "Mike," "Administrator," or "Guest" simply exist to help the mere humans keep things straight.

The reason this is important is that Mike isn't always necessarily Mike. For example, if you create a user account named Mike, delete it, and then create another user account named Mike, the two accounts are not the same. They may have the same name, and even belong to the same person. As far as Windows XP is concerned, however, you've created one unique account (with a unique SID), deleted it, and then created another unique account (with its own unique SID). In other words, if the old Mike account had been granted any rights or permissions, or been made a member of any groups, the new Mike account is not automatically granted the same levels of access or membership. Similarly, the new Mike may not be able to access the old Mike's files. When you attempt to delete a user account in Computer Management on a Windows XP Professional system, a message to this effect is displayed, as shown in the following figure.

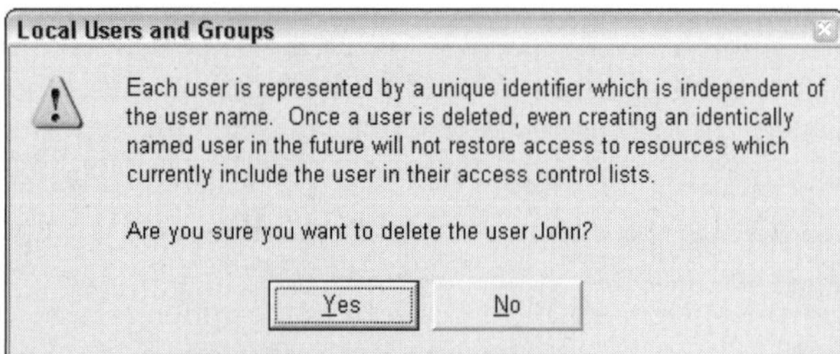

Warning message displayed when you attempt to delete a user account.

What it comes down to is this — deleting an account and then creating another with the same name does not the same user make.

Caution

When preparing to delete a user account, think carefully about whether there's any possibility that the user's personal files will be needed again in the future. The User Accounts tool asks whether you want to save the contents of the user's My Documents folder to your desktop, but all other files associated with the account (including e-mail messages) will be lost. Strangely, things work differently when you delete a user account using the Local Users and Groups tool in Computer Management on a Windows XP Professional system. In this scenario, when a user account is deleted, all of that user's personal files and settings are left untouched. Although the User Accounts tool offers to save the contents of a user's My Documents folder as part of deleting an account, you may want to save the user's e-mail messages, Internet Explorer Favorites, and other personal files. The easiest way to do this is to back up the user's profile folder prior to deleting the account. To do this, open My Computer and browse to the C:\Documents and Settings folder (your drive letter may be different, depending on how you installed Windows XP). Next, back up the folder bearing the user's name. With a saved copy of this folder, files and settings associated with the user can be restored at a later time should the need arise.

Understanding Group Accounts

Although user accounts provide the credentials (a unique username and password) that an individual uses to log on to a Windows XP system, group accounts exist for a slightly different purpose. As you may have guessed, a group is a collection of users, or more specifically, user accounts. On a Windows XP system, groups are used to grant (or deny) collections of users different rights to perform tasks, or permissions to access files and folders.

Windows XP includes a number of built-in groups by default, but Computer Administrators can also create custom groups to meet different needs. In a nutshell, groups exist to make life easier for system administrators — users with common needs can be placed into a group, and then that group can be assigned rights and permissions. When a user account is added to a group, it automatically inherits all of the privileges assigned to that group; therefore, instead of granting three different users the exact same level of access to a particular folder, an administrator could create a group, add the three users to it, and then assign the permissions for the folder to the group just once. If the group option sounds like more work initially, it is; however, after the group is created, adding rights or permissions to it again in the future becomes a great deal simpler that dealing with individual user accounts.

Exploring Windows XP's built-in groups

Windows XP Professional systems include nine different built-in groups by default, as shown in Figure 1-15.

Note

Windows XP Home does not provide access to the Local Users and Groups tool in Computer Management. As such, you can only modify group membership or create groups on Windows XP Professional systems. Additionally, group creation and management is limited to users with Computer Administrator accounts.

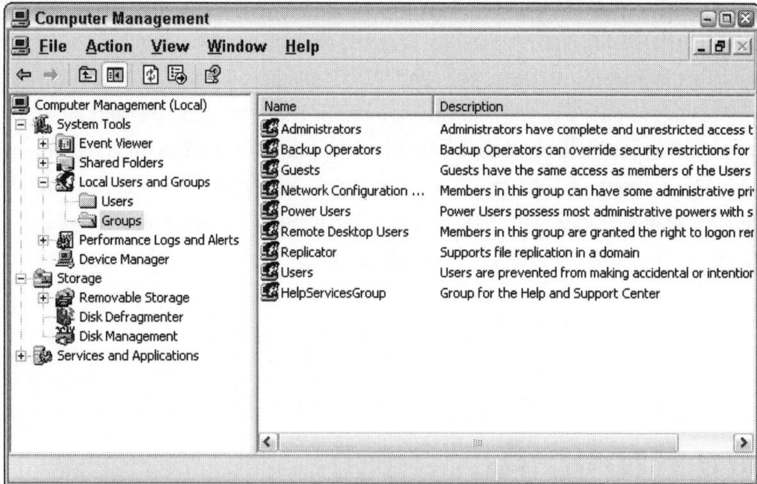

Figure 1-15: Windows XP's built-in group accounts.

Users accounts added to these groups automatically inherit the rights and capabilities associated with the group. Windows XP Professional's built-in groups include the following:

- **Administrators:** Membership in this group grants the user complete control over a Windows XP system. All Computer Administrator user accounts are members of this group.
- **Backup Operators:** Members of this group have the ability to back up and restore all user files, regardless of security restrictions.
- **Guests:** Members of this group are granted only basic access to a Windows XP system. By default, the Guest account is a member of this group.
- **Network Configuration Operators:** Members of this group have the ability to change network configuration settings, such as IP address settings.
- **Power Users:** Members of this group have more system access than Limited users, but less than Computer Administrators. Power users have the ability to install and remove most programs.
- **Remote Desktop Users:** Members of this group have the ability to log on to a Windows XP system remotely.
- **Replicator:** Members of this group are allowed to replicate files between systems in a domain network environment.
- **Users:** All user accounts created on a Windows XP system are members of the Users group.
- **HelpServicesGroup:** Members of this group can use the Help and Support center to remotely log onto and diagnose problems with a Windows XP system over a network.

Creating and managing groups with Computer Management

Windows XP Professional gives you the ability to add or remove users from group accounts, based on your specific needs. For example, you might want to add a user to the Backup Operators group to allow them to back up and restore files, or the Remote Desktop Users group to allow them to connect to and interact with your Windows XP system from another location. A user can be a member of multiple groups at the same time.

Follow these steps to manage the membership of an existing group on a Windows XP Professional system using Computer Management:

1. Click Start, right-click My Computer, and click Manage.
2. In the System Tools section, expand Local Users and Groups.
3. Click the Groups folder to view its contents. By default, Windows XP's nine built-in groups are listed.
4. Right-click the Administrators group and click Properties. The Members section of the General tab displays all user accounts that are currently a member of the Administrators group, as shown in Figure 1-16.

Figure 1-16: Members of the Administrators group.

5. Click the Add button.
6. At the Select Users windows, type the name of user you would like to add to the Administrators group and then click OK. If you're unsure of the exact username of the user you would like to add, click the Advanced button.

7. To view a list of all users and groups that can be added to the Administrators group, click the Find Now button.
8. When the list of user and group accounts appear, select the user account you want to add to the group and then click OK. Click OK again to close the Select Users window.
9. If you mistakenly add a user to the wrong group, click the user's name and then click Remove.
10. Click OK to close the group properties window.

Note

When you add a user to a group, the change takes effect the next time the user logs on.

Beyond its built-in groups, Windows XP Professional also allows you to create your own group accounts for the purpose of assigning users different rights and permissions collectively, rather than individually. These custom group accounts come in especially handy when you want more control over how users interact with different files and folders, a concept you'll learn more about in Chapter 12. For the time being, it's enough to be familiar with how group membership is managed and how group accounts are created on a Windows XP Professional system.

Follow these steps to create a new group on a Windows XP Professional system using Computer Management:

1. Right-click the Groups folder in Computer Management and then click New Group.
2. Enter a name for the group and an appropriate description, as shown in Figure 1-17.
3. Click the Create button. Your new group is added to the list of accounts.

Figure 1-17: Creating a new group account.

Although you can use the General tab in the properties of a group to add or remove members as shown earlier, you can also complete this task from the properties of a user account. To add a user to a group using this method, follow these steps:

1. Click the Users folder. Right-click a user account and then click Properties.
2. Click the Member Of tab. All groups that this user is a member of will be displayed.
3. Click the Add button.
4. At the Select Groups window, type the name of group you would like to add this account to, and click OK. If you're unsure of the exact name of the group, click the Advanced button.
5. To view a list of all groups that this user can be added to, click the Find Now button.
6. When the list of group accounts appears, select the group to add the user to and then click OK. Click OK again to close the Select Groups window.
7. If you mistakenly add a user to the wrong group, click the group name on the Member Of tab and then click Remove.
8. Click OK to close the user properties window.

Any groups that you create can also be deleted. Deleting a group does not delete user accounts that are members of the group.

Cross-Reference

You'll learn more about group accounts and how they can be used to control access to files and folders in Chapter 12.

Exploring User Logon Options

It's entirely possible that Windows XP was preinstalled on your new computer with a single, password-free user account already configured. If that was indeed the case, it's also possible that you've never actually seen the Windows XP Welcome screen.

Strange as it may sound, this logon screen only appears on Windows XP systems with at least two user accounts configured, or when you finally get around to adding a password to your single user account. As should now be crystal clear, implementing user accounts (complete with passwords) is a key and critical step towards securing Windows XP.

Although the Welcome screen is the logon facility with which most Windows XP users are familiar, other methods can be used to log on or supply your user credentials (the combination of your username and password) to access your system. The primary logon methods supported by Windows XP include the following:

- The Welcome logon screen, which is configured by default
- The classic Windows logon screen, which prompts for a username and password
- The Run As command, which won't log you on to your personal desktop environment but is a logon method all the same

Each of these Windows XP logon options is presented in more detail in the following sections.

Welcome screen/Fast User Switching

Windows XP is the first Microsoft operating system to introduce the concept of the Welcome screen as a user logon facility. When used, the Welcome screen allows users to access their personal desktop environment by clicking their username and then typing their password, assuming one is configured. If the password supplied is correct, the user is logged on and able to go about their business.

In conjunction with the Welcome screen, Windows XP also introduces a new feature known as Fast User Switching. Understanding that Windows XP systems are shared by multiple users in many households, Microsoft decided that it would be a great idea to allow user switching, a technique whereby one user can temporarily log off, leave programs running and files open, and allow another user to log on to the system, perhaps to quickly check their e-mail. When the second user has completed their tasks, they can log off completely, or choose the option to switch users. The original user can then select their username at the Welcome screen and continue with their work as if they were never interrupted.

Obviously, Fast User Switching can be a very good thing. It eliminates the hassles of requiring one user to save their work, close all programs, and log off completely to allow another user to gain access to the computer for a short period of time. Also, switching users is a much faster undertaking that the full logon/logoff process that requires user profiles to be loaded and unloaded.

Even with these benefits, Fast User Switching does have a downside, namely much higher resource consumption. When this feature is enabled, users have a tendency to leave their accounts logged on all the time, complete with running programs. Multiply that by three or four logged-on users, and it doesn't take long for all of a system's memory to be consumed and significant slowdowns to ensue.

Love it or leave it, the good news is that you have a choice in the matter. Although Fast User Switching doesn't present a security risk, you can disable it if you want to avoid the performance hit associated with having multiple users logged on simultaneously.

Follow these steps to disable Windows XP's Fast User Switching feature:

1. Open the Control Panel from the Start menu.
2. Click User Accounts.
3. Under Pick a task, click Change the way users log on or off.
4. At the Select logon and logoff options screen (shown in Figure 1-18), uncheck the Use Fast User Switching option. If your goal is to use Fast User Switching, you may receive a message stating that the option cannot be enabled if Windows XP's Offline Files feature is enabled. Disabling Offline Files will remedy the issue, if encountered.

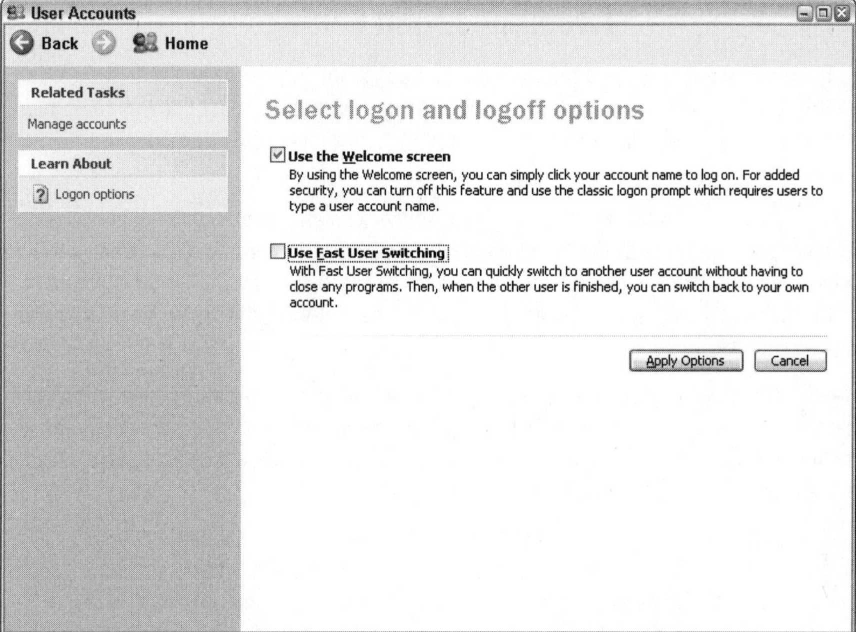

Figure 1-18: Disabling Fast User Switching.

5. Click Apply Options to save your changes.
6. Close the User Accounts and Control Panel windows.
7. Click Start and then click the Log Off button. When the Log Off Windows dialog box appears (see Figure 1-19), notice that the Switch User option is no longer available. Click Log Off.

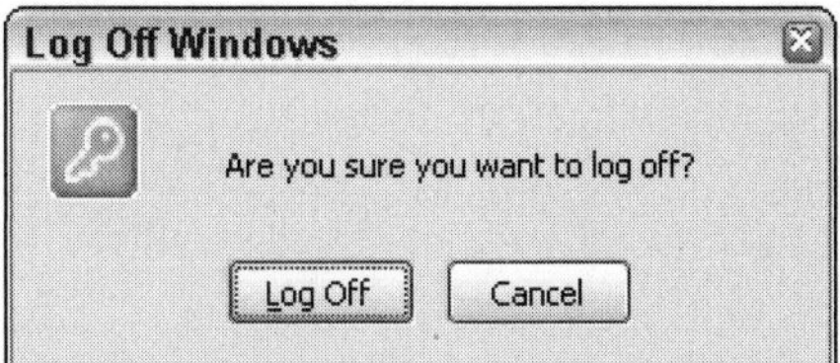

Figure 1-19: The Log Off Windows dialog box when Fast User Switching is disabled.

8. To log back on to Windows XP, enter your username and password and then click the green arrow button (or press Enter).

Tweaking Logon Settings

Most Windows XP users opt to use the Welcome screen to log on, if only because they're not aware that any other options exist. Truth be told, the Welcome screen is the most convenient logon environment for a multi-user Windows XP system, but it certainly is not the most secure option as far as user privacy is concerned.

Specifically, the Welcome screen automatically displays a list of all accessible user accounts on a system, with the exception of the built-in Computer Administrator account. Additionally, this screen also displays details about how many unread e-mail messages are waiting for other logged on users. Although this doesn't mean that one user can read another's e-mail, this behavior could be seen as infringing on other users' privacy.

Thankfully, the Windows XP Welcome screen (and the information it displays) can be controlled and customized. For example, you can opt to hide certain user accounts from being displayed, as well as do away with notifications about unread e-mail messages. All you need is a little help, which is available in the form of a free program download from Microsoft called TweakUI.

TweakUI is a Windows XP PowerToy, part of a set of different utilities that allow you to tweak and tune XP's behavior and get at settings that aren't normally accessible via Window's graphical configuration tools. While TweakUI provides access to no shortage of customizations (many of which will be examined throughout this book), the ones that are pertinent here are those in its Logon section, as shown in the following figure.

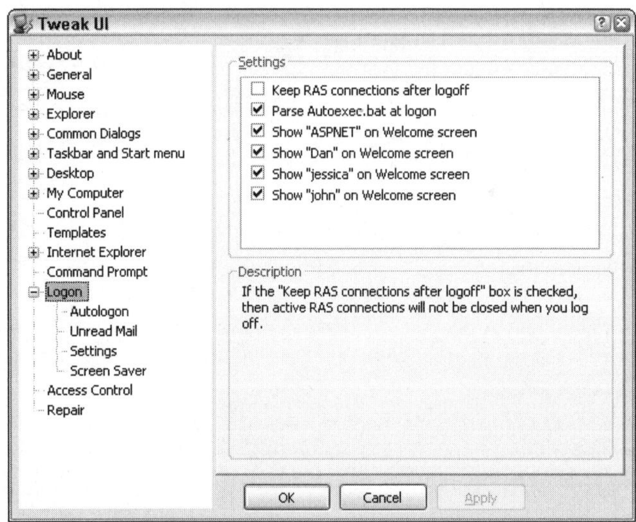

TweakUI allows you to customize a variety of Windows XP settings, including some related to system security.

Specifically, clicking the Logon item allows you to control which usernames are displayed on the Welcome screen. Uncheck the box next to a username, and it no longer appears (although it still exists). If you want to stop seeing the ASP.NET account installed with the .NET Framework, for example, this is a great way to go about it.

A bit of a quandary would seem to exist if you were to stop regular user's names from appearing on the Welcome screen. The fact of the matter is that the Welcome screen is not the be all and end all of the logon process. In fact, you can log on using any enabled account from the Welcome screen by pressing the Ctrl+Alt+Delete keyboard sequence. This displays the classic Windows logon dialog box, where you can enter username and password details.

To stop the Welcome screen from displaying notifications about unread e-mail messages, expand the Logon section in TweakUI and click Unread Mail. Unchecking the Show unread mail on Welcome screen checkbox stops Windows XP from displaying details about your unread messages, but this setting can also be applied to all user accounts on your system.

To download TweakUI for Windows XP, visit `www.microsoft.com/windowsxp/downloads/powertoys/xppowertoys.mspx`. Note that the latest version of TweakUI requires that your Windows XP system has at least Service Pack 1 installed.

Note

Only users with a Computer Administrator account can turn Fast User Switching on and off, and this feature cannot be disabled if more than one user is currently logged on to the computer. Additionally, while the Welcome screen is available when you boot a Windows XP system into Safe Mode, only Computer Administrator accounts are displayed and accessible — Limited users do not have access to a system running in Safe Mode.

Classic Windows XP logon

Windows XP's Welcome screen makes it easy for less experienced users to gain access to their user account — all they typically need to do is click their user name (which appears next to a fun little icon, of course) and enter their password. Although this method makes the entire logon process less frightening, it suffers from one serious security flaw, namely the fact that all user account names are displayed for the world to see. Worse still, the use of password hints can make determining the passwords associated with these accounts almost laughably simple.

With that in mind, any Windows XP owner who is serious about system security should consider passing on the Welcome screen logon in favor of the more secure classic Windows logon option. Although both perform the same basic user authentication process, the classic Windows logon screen doesn't suffer from the same rash of "helpfulness" that makes logging on from the Welcome screen not unlike a children's guessing game.

Follow these steps to disable the Welcome logon screen on a Windows XP system and use the classic Windows XP logon screen:

1. Open the Control Panel from the Start menu.
2. Click User Accounts.

3. Under Pick a task, click Change the way users log on or off.
4. At the Select logon and logoff options screen, uncheck the Use the Welcome screen checkbox. The Use Fast User Switching option will be disabled automatically, as it can only be used in conjunction with the Welcome screen.
5. Click Apply Options to save your changes.
6. Close the User Accounts and Control Panel windows.
7. Click Start and then click the Log Off button. When the Log Off Windows dialog box appears, click Log Off.
8. The Welcome screen has now been replaced with the Log On to Windows dialog box (Figure 1-20). To log back on to Windows XP, enter your password and then click OK.

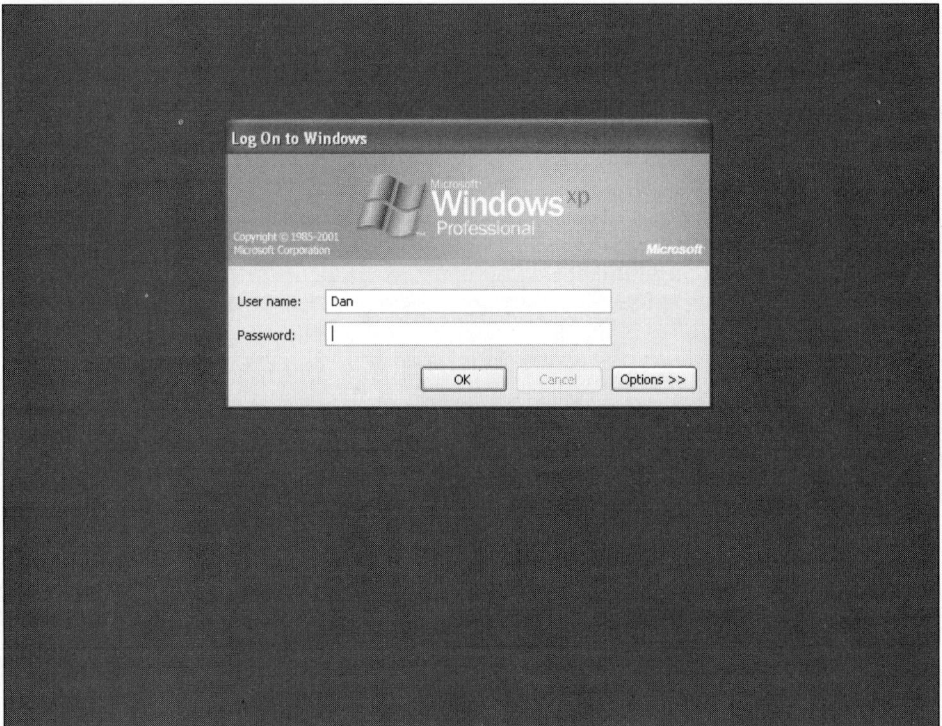

Figure 1-20: The classic Windows logon screen.

If you opt to use the classic Windows logon rather than the Welcome screen, you can add a little additional security into the mix by stopping Windows XP from displaying the name of the last user to logon to the system in the User name text box. Windows XP displays this name automatically, trying to save you from having to type in both your username *and* your password.

Unfortunately, as half of the information required to gain access to a Windows XP system, displaying a valid username automatically is not a good idea. With this information in hand, any malicious user who gains access to the computer needs only to guess or crack the account's password—typically not all that difficult a job. With this in mind, hiding the last username from appearing is a good security practice; typing this information adds a second or two to the logon process at most.

Note

See the related sidebar "Working with the Windows XP Registry" before attempting these steps.

Follow these steps to hide the username of the last person to log on to a Windows XP system:

1. Click Start → Run and then type Regedit.exe in the Open text box. Click OK.
2. In the Registry Editor window, browse to HKEY_LOCAL_MACHINE → Software → Microsoft → Windows → CurrentVersion → policies → system.
3. In the right pane, double-click `dontdisplaylastusername`, as shown in Figure 1-21.

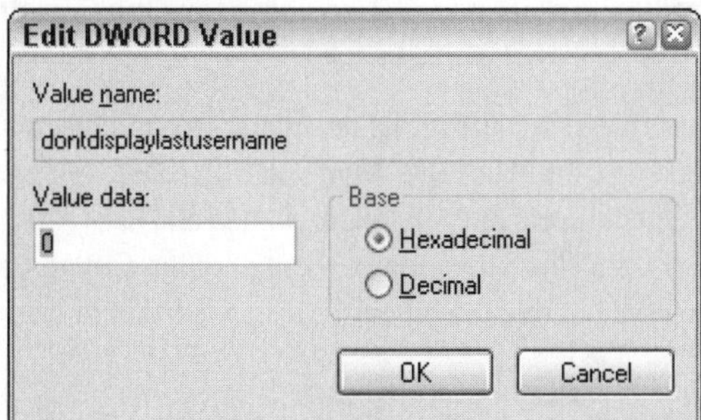

Figure 1-21: Disabling display of the last username.

4. Change the Value data field from 0 (which displays the last username) to 1 (which means that the last username will not be displayed). Click OK.
5. Close the Registry Editor window and reboot Windows XP for the changes to take effect. When the Log On to Windows dialog box appears, the Username field should now be empty. To log back on to Windows XP, enter your username and password and then click OK.

Working with the Windows XP Registry

Back in the olden days, operating systems like MS-DOS stored all user and system configuration settings in what amounted to glorified text files. Things changed with the release of Windows 95, when a new centralized configuration database known as the Registry was introduced.

Windows XP continues to use the Registry as its primary storage database of user and system settings, but the vast majority of users never interact with the Registry directly. This is because Windows XP provides graphical tools that act as intermediaries for common configuration changes. For example, a user who wants to change his screen settings uses the Display applet in Control Panel, which in turn makes the necessary changes to the Registry.

In cases where Windows supplies a graphical or command-line tool for making configuration changes, it should be your primary choice. Quite simply, the Registry is a dangerous place where making any incorrect changes can affect system stability or even render it completely unable to boot. If you visit the Microsoft Web site and see Registry changes suggested, you'll always find accompanying warnings on the potential dangers of the undertaking.

Although there's no question that editing the Windows XP Registry can be dangerous, there are still times when you'll need or want to edit it directly — if only because no suitable graphical or command line tool exists to get the job done. With several Registry-related changes outlined in this book, it's important that you be familiar with the steps used to back up and restore portions of the Registry, should the need arise.

The primary tool used to edit the Registry is known, quite simply, as Registry Editor. To open this tool, click Start→Run, type Regedit.exe in the Open text box, and click OK. What you'll be presented with is what appears to be a folder hierarchy, complete with all sorts of crazy folder names and contents, as shown in the following figure. Note that the Registry is a "live" database of configuration settings, so you'll never be prompted to save your changes. This is but one reason why it's so important to be careful.

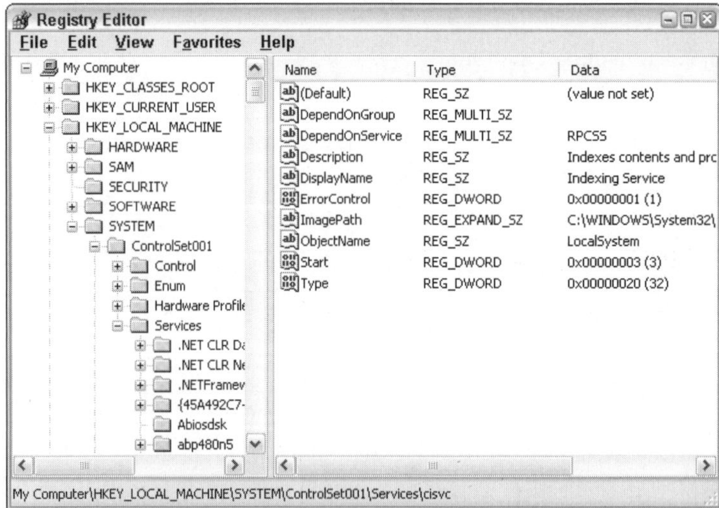

Windows XP's Registry Editor is used to make changes to Registry settings.

Prior to adding, deleting, or editing any Registry setting, right-click the folder (known as a "key" in Registry-speak) where the change will be made. If you click Export, you'll be prompted to save the key's contents to a file with a .REG extension. Save this file to an appropriate folder as a backup. If you want to take a look at the contents of the file out of curiosity, just right-click it and select Edit to open it in Notepad.

Should you need to restore the Registry settings saved in a .REG file, all you need to do is browse to the file and double-click it. You'll be presented with a message asking you to confirm that you want to add the contents of the file to the Registry. After you click OK, the Registry key in question is overwritten with the backed up settings.

You can also back up the entire Registry, but this is a longer and somewhat more arduous process. The Backup utility included with Windows XP is capable of getting this done by selecting the option to back up an object known as System State. For details on using Windows Backup to get the job done, visit `support.microsoft.com/kb/308422/`.

Run As

Earlier in this chapter you were led to believe that a way existed for a Limited user to perform tasks requiring the powers of a Computer Administrator—without the need to log off and back on, no less. Well, it's actually true, the product of a Windows XP feature known as Run As.

Run As is a feature available on both Windows XP Home and Professional systems that allows you to open a program or install software by supplying alternate user account credentials for that particular task only. For example, imagine that you're logged on with your Limited user account, and need to install a new piece of software. Rather than log off and then log on with a Computer Administrator account to complete the task, you can use the Run As command to open the program's installer file. As part of doing this, you'll be prompted to supply the username and password associated with an account allowed to carry out such a task, in this case a Computer Administrator.

Assuming that you've supplied a valid username and password, the installation process (and that particular process only) will proceed as it normally would for a Computer Administrator. When it's done (the installation is complete, or the program that you opened is closed), the privileges associated with the account used with the Run As command effectively disappear until you use it again.

Follow these steps to open or install a program using the credentials of another user account via the Run As feature:

1. Click Start → My Computer.
2. Browse to the program file or shortcut that you wish to open using another user's credentials.
3. Right-click the file and then click Run as.
4. When the Run As dialog box appears, click The following user, as shown in Figure 1-22.
5. Enter the name of the alternate user account in the User name field.
6. Enter the password associated with the user account in the Password field.

Figure 1-22: The Run As window.

7. Click OK. The program opens and functions according to the rights and privileges associated with the user account information supplied.

8. Complete the required task(s) and then close the program. Your privilege levels are again those associated with the account you originally used to log on to Windows XP.

An alternate version of Run As is available to those who prefer working from the Windows XP Command Prompt, in the form of the `runas.exe` command. The basic syntax of the command is:

```
runas /user:username program
```

Username is user account name that will be used to launch the program or shortcut file specified. After this command is entered, you're prompted to supply the user's password, as shown in Figure 1-23. For a complete breakdown of switches and settings associated with the `runas` command, enter `runas /?` at the Command Prompt.

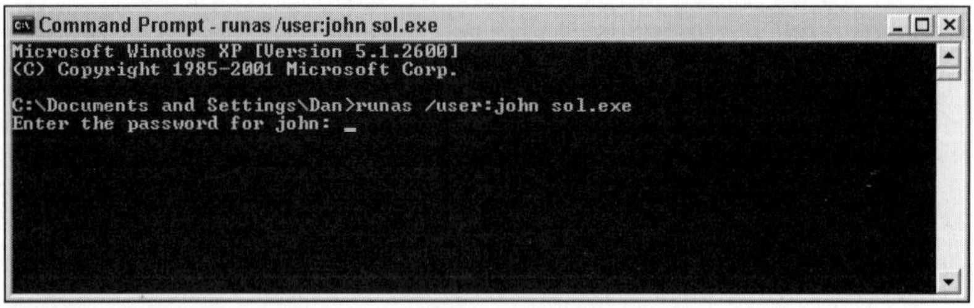

Figure 1-23: Using runas.exe from the Command Prompt.

Tip

The Run As command makes it practical for everyone to use a Limited user account for day-to-day business on a Windows XP system; however, if you use the command frequently it can be difficult to keep track of which credentials have been used to open a certain program or process. Rather than guess or need to dig through process details in Task Manager, consider downloading and installing PrivBar. This add-on toolbar for Windows Explorer and Internet Explorer displays the username and privilege level (for example, member of Administrators) associated with the user that opened the program. With this toolbar installed, you'll never be in the dark about the powers associated with a particular Explorer or IE window. For details on installing and configuring PrivBar, visit blogs.msdn.com/aaron_margosis/archive/2004/07/24/195350.aspx.

Using Run As with Windows Explorer

Although the Run As command works perfectly with just about any EXE file or shortcut you need to launch, it does not function as you might expect with Windows Explorer. In fact, if you try to launch Windows Explorer with the Run As command, what you'll find is that exactly nothing appears to happen.

In fact, something does happen, but you don't see it. Windows Explorer is not only a tool for browsing for files and folders, but also the Windows XP shell process that supplies you with your desktop, Start menu, and more. By default, Windows XP does not allow two versions of Windows Explorer to run under different user credentials at the same time. So, when you use the Run As command to open Explorer.exe as a different user, the system sees that Windows Explorer is already running, and closes the newer process, sight unseen.

This default behavior is somewhat annoying, especially because Windows Explorer is such a powerful tool for system administration — it provides the capability to launch and install programs, access Control Panel tools, and more. Thankfully, it is possible to get around the issue by following these steps:

1. Log on to Windows XP system using your Computer Administrator account.
2. Click Start → My Computer.
3. Click Tools → Folder Options.
4. Click the View tab.
5. Scroll down the list of Advanced settings, check Launch folder windows in a separate process as shown in the figure, and click OK.

Continued

Using Run As with Windows Explorer (Continued)

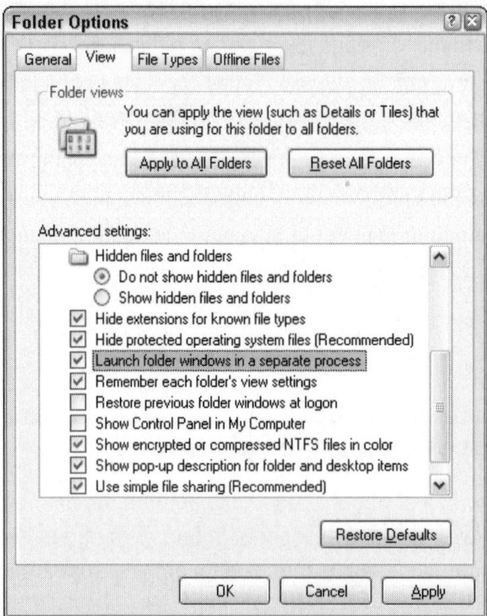

Configuring Windows XP to launch folder windows in a separate process.

6. Log off and then log back on with your Limited user account.
7. Use the Run As command to open Windows Explorer, specifying the username and password of your Computer Administrator account.

After completing these steps, you can now open Windows Explorer under the credentials of your Computer Administrator account while logged on with your Limited account.

Summary

The security of any Windows XP system is only as good as the security associated with its user accounts, groups, and logon settings. Keep the following points in mind when it comes to maximizing the security of your system:

- Each user should have a personal user account.
- Every user account should have a password configured.
- A user's everyday user account should always be of the Limited type.

- Only trusted users should be granted access to a Computer Administrator account. Even with this access, this account should not be used for everyday tasks.
- User accounts that will not be used for an extended period of time should be disabled.
- Users accounts that are no longer needed should be deleted.
- It's important to be familiar with Windows XP's built-in groups, the capabilities they assign to members, and how to create new groups if required.
- For better security, use the classic Windows logon screen (with the last username hidden) rather than the Welcome screen.
- Use the Run As command to perform administrative tasks when required.

Chapter 2

Implementing Password Security

Although user accounts are the foundation upon which secure Windows XP systems are built, the security they provide is only as good as the passwords that protect them. In fact, one could make a compelling argument that implementing user accounts with weak passwords is the same as not having any security at all. Part of the issue revolves around the fact that most users opt for simple passwords that are easy to remember, but people and their bad password habits are not the only culprits. Windows XP must share part of the blame, with a myriad of hacking tools and password recovery programs available to crack and reset even the most secure and complex passwords under the right conditions.

User accounts represent one of the first lines of defense on a Windows XP system, but the need for good password practices hardly ends there. If you use the Internet, chances are that you have a myriad of different usernames and passwords configured to access different Web sites. Although some of these may not represent a security risk, such as the one used to access the members area of your favorite gardening Web site, others may be associated with services where rock-hard security is essential, as with online banking. Unfortunately, most users not only use weak passwords but also compound the issue dramatically by using the *same* weak password for different user accounts.

If you're serious about security (and hopefully that's why you're reading this), you'll want to be absolutely sure that the passwords you use are actually capable of protecting your accounts. This chapter explains how to select good passwords, how to test their strength, and the importance of switching them up regularly as serious threats like spyware proliferate. Along the way, you'll also learn how to configure Windows XP to enforce password and account lockout policy settings on users, how to get some help when it comes to remembering passwords, and how logon security can be completely compromised with the right tools and techniques. Finally, this chapter takes a dip into other types of system passwords and security measures that can be used to protect your PC, explaining why even strong passwords may not provide enough protection when another user (or hacker) has physical access to your computer.

Password Security

Passwords have always presented of one life's great quandaries. On the one hand you can select different complex passwords for each and every one of your user accounts, but what good is a strong password if you can't remember it? On the other hand, using similar (or even the same) weak passwords for

every account virtually assures that you'll never forget it, but offers the equivalent of no real protection at all. The bottom line is that all user accounts passwords must be complex to offer a high degree of protection; however, it's equally important for you to be able to remember your passwords. The good news is that striking this balance is not as difficult as most people make it out to be, although it does require a little effort and dedication on your part.

Selecting good passwords for user accounts involves three primary steps:

- Choosing good, strong, passwords
- Avoiding common password mistakes
- Changing your passwords frequently

Each of these steps is looked at in more detail in the following sections.

Choosing good passwords

It's a question for the ages — what makes a password good and strong? The answer isn't all that difficult, but there is definitely a formula of sorts involved. A strong password should ***always***:

- Be composed of at least seven characters at an absolute minimum. The longer the password, the better, and Windows XP supports user account passwords up to 127 characters in length.
- Include both uppercase and lowercase letters.
- Include numbers.
- Include at least one (but preferably a few) special characters such as ` ~ ! @ # $ % ^ & * ( ) _ + - = { } | [ ] \ : " ; ' < > ? . / , spaces, and so on. Alt-characters (those that require you to press down the Alt key and use number keys to access special non-ASCII characters) are also valid and a great option to increase password security.

If you follow these suggestions, your password will be very difficult to guess. Going above and beyond the suggested minimums, however, makes for an even stronger password, one that will be exceptionally difficult for even the most advanced hacking tools to compromise. In other words, an 18-character password that includes both upper- and lowercase letters, a couple of numbers, and a few different symbols should keep your account well protected from malicious users commandeering even the latest and greatest hacking tools.

Although the complex 18-character password sounds great in theory, it's not hard to imagine how difficult it can be to remember, especially if chosen randomly. The password Y6we)+Av*f6jJcvsI45 is certainly strong, but it will do you little good if you can never remember it.

One of the easiest ways to create a strong password is to make it a derivative of something you'll remember. For example, if you often find yourself daydreaming about bass fishing, consider a password like NxtGR8*Trp4~Bas5. Loosely, this would translate to something you could remember, such as "next great (fishing) trip for bass." Every element of an industrial-strength password is there: upper- and lowercase letters, a few numbers (replacing similar-looking or -sounding letters), and a couple of symbols thrown in for good measure. Remembering a password like this is surprisingly easy after typing it a few times, especially if it's related to something you're interested in or looking forward to.

Common password mistakes

If you follow the advice about creating good passwords, you're already on the right track. However, there are still a few common password pitfalls that you'll want to avoid.

A strong password should *never*:

- Include any part of your username or full name, as well as names of friends, family members, places, and pets that would be easy for others to guess
- Include personal information like your birthday, phone number, address, tax identification number, or other potentially sensitive personal/family/business information
- Be the same (or similar) to any other password you use
- Be composed of regular English-language words, phrases, or acronyms

Caution

Hackers know that most people use weak passwords, usually ones based on personal information. The sad reality is that far too many users rely on easily guessed details (child and pet names, favorite sports team, and so on) to protect even their most confidential user accounts. If you've fallen into this common trap, don't panic. Instead, make a point of changing all your passwords to strong, secure alternatives today.

Additionally, to keep your passwords strong, you should never:

- Share your passwords with anyone, including friends and family
- Use the same or similar password for different user accounts
- Write your passwords down in a way that it will be accessible to other users
- Use the same password for any extended period of time

Caution

Never provide a password when asked for it by others or share it with friends. Passwords are similar to the PIN numbers associated with bank or credit cards, and should be treated in the same way. If you ever feel like any of your passwords have been compromised, change them immediately.

You may feel as though you've come up with a suitable and brilliantly strong password, but it never hurts to take it for a test drive. Although there are many different programs designed to test password strength, you can also gauge the strength of your passwords on the SecurityStat.com Web site. This site includes a tool that allows you to input your proposed password and then "scores" it against a number of password best practices.

To test a proposed password with this tool, follow these steps:

1. Click Start → Internet Explorer (or open your preferred Web browser).
2. In the Address bar, type `www.securitystats.com/tools/password.php` and then press Enter.
3. Enter a variation of your proposed password in the textbox on this page. Don't use the exact password that you intend to use, but rather one that is similar. For example, if the password you want to test is NxtGR8*Trp4~Bas5, enter something such as MjtFG4*Rto3#Das9.
4. Click Submit. The password will be analyzed and then rated as shown in Figure 2-1. If necessary, use the suggestions provided on this page to help you create a stronger alternative password.

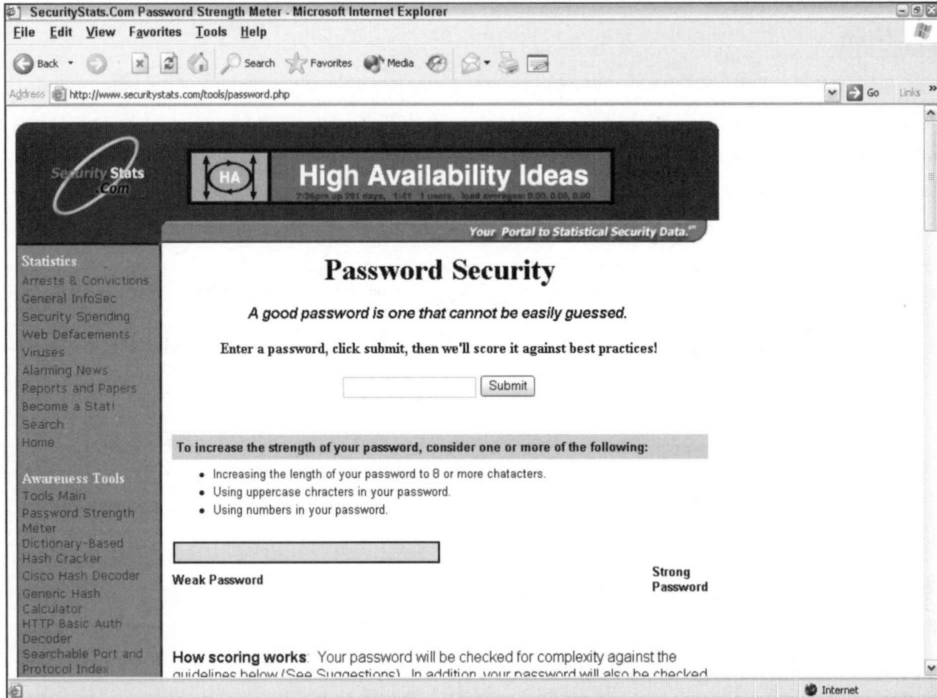

Figure 2-1: The Password Strength Meter is a free testing tool available at SecurityStats.com.

Cross Reference

You'll learn more about protecting against virus threats in Chapter 8, and fighting spyware and related issues in Chapter 9.

Are You Being Watched?

Perhaps the most common reason why many users don't take password security as seriously as they should is that they don't believe that anyone would be interested in their personal information or communications. In other words, their computer (or their online user accounts) contains nothing of intrinsic value to others.

Unfortunately, these users are amongst the primary targets for hackers, spyware programs, and viruses. Every PC contains useful information about its users, from details such as credit card numbers to private e-mail messages. Ultimately, this information can be used for purposes as malicious as identity theft, blackmail, and spying, to more innocent activities such as displaying targeted onscreen advertising messages.

These issues have become especially prevalent of late with the wildfire-like spread of spyware programs and dangerous viruses. Many of these pests are designed to steal personal information from your PC and then forward it to servers on the Internet without your knowledge. Others are even more dangerous because they install programs that allow others to access and control your PC remotely or capture each and every one of your keystrokes, making everything you type potentially accessible to hackers or other malicious third parties.

It's been estimated that up to 90 percent of all home and small office computers are infected by spyware and other similar exploits. If even a very small percentage of these systems have dangerous remote control programs or keystroke loggers installed, that's very bad news indeed. If you suspect (or know) that one or more of these pests has infected your computer, it's important to completely remove them and then immediately change the passwords associated with all of your sensitive user accounts. If you don't, you're running the risk that someone out there on the Internet may already have complete access to some or all of your user accounts.

Changing passwords regularly

Creating strong passwords for your user accounts is critical but so too is not letting them get "stale" as a result of prolonged use. As a general rule, make a point of changing all important user account passwords regularly, say once every 30 to 90 days. Changing your passwords more frequently helps to improve overall user account security; using the same passwords for extended periods increases your risk exposure. Later in this chapter you'll learn how to configure Windows XP Professional systems with password policy settings to enforce more secure user account password practices.

Note

After they feel comfortable with a password, most users will go to great lengths to avoid changing it. Perhaps human nature is to blame, but think of the process as being similar to eating your vegetables or taking your vitamins. Even though some may not taste all that appealing to begin with, they're good for you. The same can be said for passwords — changing frequently may seem like a terrible pain, but you'll be better off (security-wise) in the long run. At the end of the day, the pain associated with a serious breach of your personal privacy is much worse than the brief pinch experienced when the time to change passwords arrives.

Windows XP Passwords

Here a password, there a password, everywhere a password! There's simply no shortage of user accounts that you'll need to work with as the owner of a Windows XP system, each protected with a different password. In some cases, you'll be responsible for choosing and assigning passwords for these accounts; in others, third parties such as your ISP will assign them to you. Regardless of the manner in which they're obtained, all passwords are important, and it's largely up to you to both remember them and ensure they're properly secured.

The primary types of account passwords that you'll need to deal with on a Windows XP system include the following:

- User account passwords
- Web site passwords
- E-mail and Internet service passwords
- File security passwords

User account passwords

As you learned in Chapter 1, Windows XP includes the capability to separate and secure the working environments of different users with user accounts. When protected by a strong password, your user account represents the first line of defense towards securing your files and improving your personal privacy.

On a Windows XP system, user account passwords are stored in a protected part of the Registry known as the Security Accounts Manager (SAM) database. Instead of storing actual passwords in this database, Windows XP first creates a one-way mathematical hash value of individual passwords and then stores these hashed values in the SAM database. This database is protected by a system startup key stored on the hard drive and then decrypted/encrypted as a part of the system startup/shutdown process.

The one-way hash function used to store user passwords is technically not reversible, but that doesn't mean it offers perfect security. A number of tools and utilities make it possible for a hacker with access to the SAM database to compromise its security and then access another user's account. You'll learn more about these types of software later in this chapter.

The password storage facilities in Windows XP are far from perfect, but this isn't an excuse not to protect user accounts with strong passwords. Many of the tools designed to crack or detect user account passwords rely on brute-force cracking methods, where thousands of different words (including the entire contents of English-language dictionaries) are used in an attempt to "guess" their way into a system. When you configure strong passwords for your Windows XP user accounts, this cracking process becomes exceptionally difficult, to the point where the work associated with the undertaking is usually not worthwhile. Unless a hacker's motives are personal, most will not invest the time and effort required to hack a well-secured system. Quite simply, there's just no shortage of other low-hanging fruit (improperly secured systems) out there for them to take advantage of.

As the owner of a Windows XP system, it's a safe assumption that you'll also be its primary administrator. From a security standpoint, it's up to you to educate other users on the importance of configuring a strong user account password, as well as changing it regularly. If you're running Windows XP

Professional, there is some help to be had on this front. By implementing policy settings, you can actually enforce strong user password requirements, ensuring that all users have no choice but to get with the program. You learn more about Windows XP's password policy settings later in this chapter.

Lock, Then Walk

Although often looked at as nothing more than yet another cool way to personalize a user's desktop environment, screen savers actually have an important security function that shouldn't be overlooked. All screen savers can be password protected, meaning that after a certain amount of idle time has passed and the configured screen saver kicks in, the user's password will need to be entered again to get back to their Windows XP desktop.

It may seem more hindrance than help, but password protecting a screen saver serves an important security function. Consider the case where you initially log on to Windows XP and then step away to refill your coffee mug. Assuming that you don't log off or select the option to switch users, any person could sit down at the computer, and have full access to your e-mail, personal files, and so forth — they're literally using the computer logged on as you, after all.

As a best security practice, configure Windows XP to prompt for the user's password when exiting the screen saver. To do so, click Start → Control Panel → Display → Screen Saver (if Control Panel is running in Category view, click Start → Control Panel → Appearance and Themes → Choose a screen saver instead). Next, choose your preferred screen saver from the drop-down list, and check the On resume, password protect box, as shown in the following figure. If you're using the Windows XP Welcome screen to log on, this value reads On resume, display the Welcome screen.

Configuring a password-protected screen saver.

Continued

Lock, Then Walk (Continued)

You probably don't want the screen saver kicking in after your computer has only been idle for a minute or two, so set the Wait value to a more appropriate value such as 10 or 15 minutes.

After a password protected screen saver kicks in, the computer is "locked" if you're using the classic Windows logon screen. When the mouse is moved or a key is pressed, the current user is prompted for their password, as shown in the following figure. At this point, only the current user can log back on to their desktop. For cases where a user forgets to log off and another person needs to use the computer, a computer administrator can unlock the system. This isn't a concern if you're using the Welcome screen, which will be displayed when the system is resumed. From here, the existing user (or another user, if Fast User Switching is enabled) can log on as they normally would, no administrative intervention required.

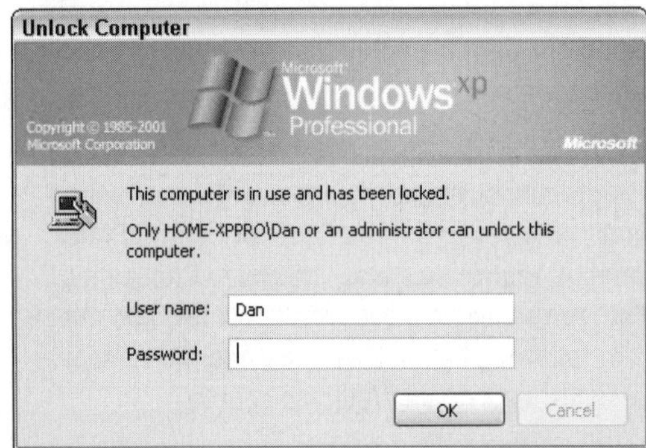

The Unlock Computer window appears when you try to resume activities on a system with a password-protected screen saver enabled.

Have each user password protect their screen saver to ensure that their user account remains properly protected, even when a refill is the priority of the moment.

Web site passwords

Although most people only have to worry about remembering the details of a single Windows XP user account, Web sites user account present another issue entirely. Needed for everything from entering the "members area" of some sites to accessing Web-based e-mail, it doesn't take long for these accounts to add up at an alarming rate.

In many cases your e-mail address serves as your username on these sites, but it's usually up to you to select a password. Some sites do enforce password policies (such as requiring a minimum password length of 6 characters), but most don't make the requirements very tough — they're too afraid to enforce strict password requirements, lest they scare away or frustrate a potential member.

Even in cases where a site does allow you to select a weak password, it's important to take the high road and choose a good strong password. This is obviously more critical for some sites — there's no denying that an online banking user account is more important than the one used to access the member's area of a gardening Web site — but treating all user accounts as being "important" is a good idea, even if only as part as developing better password habits.

Later in this chapter you learn how password management software can make the process of implementing good user account password security much easier.

Caution

Never use the same password for different Web site user accounts. Many people sign up for a new Web site user account, provide their e-mail address (typically required) and then configure the same password for the new site as they use to protect their e-mail account. Effectively, this is the same as sending the new site your e-mail username and password, which in turn gives them all the information they would need to log on to your e-mail account. If you have done this in the past when creating Web site user accounts, change the password associated with your e-mail account immediately as a precaution.

Read My Fingerprint

Imagine logging on to Windows XP or your favorite Web site by doing nothing more than touching your finger to a special scanning device. If it all sounds a little too high-tech or sci-fi, look out — the technology that makes it all work is already here and is probably for sale at a computer retailer near you!

Fingerprint scanning is a biometric technology that relies on the fact that like snowflakes, every fingerprint is unique. Because your fingerprints can be used to uniquely identify you, they can also be incorporated in a process whereby touching your finger to an appropriate "reader" device serves the same function as typing in your unique username and password.

Microsoft has already designed a number of different devices that incorporate fingerprint readers, including keyboards, mice, and dedicated USB scanners. The software included with these products stores scanned images of your fingerprints, and associates these them with your Windows XP user account. After the software has the information it needs, you can use the fingerprint scanner to log on to Windows XP, or as an alternative method of logging on to password-protected Web sites.

Although these devices are relatively inexpensive, even Microsoft warns that they should not be used as a logon method for sensitive Web sites, such as those used for online banking. This is somewhat disconcerting from a security perspective, so you may want to hold off giving your PC this particular dose of biometrics for the time being.

Microsoft hasn't release any retinal scanning products yet, but you'll probably want to keep an eye (no pun intended) on biometric technologies nonetheless. Eventually, scanning may replace (or at least become a key component of) all secure logon processes. For more information on Microsoft's line of fingerprint reader products, visit `www.microsoft.com/hardware/mouseandkeyboard/productlist.aspx?fprint=yes`

E-mail and Internet service passwords

Some passwords are easier to forget than others, especially when Windows XP helps by "remembering" them for you. Such is typically the case with user accounts assigned to you by your Internet Service Provider (ISP). For example, if you use a dial-up or DSL-based Internet connection, your ISP likely supplied you with a username and password that must be used to connect to their service. After initially configuring these settings in Windows XP, however, you can save the information such that you don't have to type the password manually each time you log on.

The same is usually true of the e-mail account details assigned by your ISP. This user account (which gives you access to your e-mail Inbox) is usually configured once in an e-mail program such as Microsoft Outlook or Outlook Express, with the password again remembered for future reference. Having the program remember the username and password associated with your account saves you the trouble of having to re-type your password each and every time you want to check for new messages.

In some cases an ISP will allow you to choose passwords for these accounts, but many simply assign them to you. Although the username and password combination that you use for dial-up or DSL access typically cannot be changed, the password associated with your user account usually can. Many service providers give you access to a dedicated support Web site from which you can change your e-mail account's password, as well as other account details. Check your ISP's Web site to see whether you can change details like your password online. If you can, configure strong passwords for your e-mail accounts, and change them regularly.

File security passwords

Last but certainly not least, many programs include the capability to secure files, folders, and even entire disks with a password. A great example is the password protection that can be incorporated into a Zip file, where the correct password must be supplied to open the file and get at its contents. Similarly, many encryption programs use individual passwords as the "key" to encrypt and decrypt files.

The major difference between user account passwords and those used to secure files is that file passwords are sometimes shared with other users. For example, you might password protect a file that you send to another user, and that user will need to supply that same password to open the file. If sharing a file in this way is your goal, come to an agreement with the other user as to a suitable password in advance; never use one of your own personal passwords, which would ultimately need to be shared with the other user.

Cross-Reference

Public key encryption is a better option for securely exchanging files with other users. You learn more about encryption and other methods of securing files, folders, and disks in Chapter 13.

Implementing Password and Account Lockout Policies

Convincing users to apply passwords to their user accounts is sometimes tough, but getting them to configure good strong passwords is even more of a challenge. Even after you've explained their importance and outlined the potential dangers of choosing a weak password, most users will still opt for a basic or familiar password that they have no trouble remembering. Even worse, some users will configure a password in short term and then remove it once they get tired of typing it in.

Understanding that old habits die hard, Windows XP Professional includes the capability to configure policy settings that enforce password requirements on all system users. For example, you can configure settings that control how often passwords must be changed, how long they must be, and even force users into selecting a reasonably strong password. As you've already learned (by the fact that users can log on without a password), no such policy settings are enabled or enforced by default. If you want to get your system's security situation under control, however, the configuration of Password Policy settings is an absolute necessity.

Note

Password and Account Lockout Policy settings cannot be configured on Windows XP Home systems. These capabilities are limited to Windows XP Professional systems only.

Windows XP's primary Password Policy settings include:

- **Enforce password history:** Dictates the number new and unique passwords a user must use before they can go back to using an older password. The higher this number, the better.
- **Maximum password age:** Controls how many days a user can use their current password before being forced to change it. The default value is 42 days, but shorter time periods are obviously more secure.
- **Minimum password age:** Controls how many days a user must use their current password before they're allowed to change it. Effectively, this setting stops users from getting around settings like Enforce password history by immediately changing their password a number of times until they can get back to using their previous (and perhaps preferred) password. By default, users are allowed to change their password immediately. Consider setting this value to a few days or more.
- **Minimum password length:** Dictates the minimum number of valid characters in a user's password. Seven would be a good start, but 15 or higher is definitely more secure.
- **Password must meet complexity requirements:** Controls the characteristics that make a user's password valid, including character requirements.

Note

If you enable the Password must meet complexity requirements policy setting, user passwords must be at least six characters long, cannot contain their real name or username, and must include at least three of the following four elements: uppercase letters, lowercase letters, numbers, and symbols. The password Mydoghasfleas would not meet these complexity requirements, but the password My&do6hasFlea5 would.

Password Policy settings offer an excellent first step towards enforcing some basic rules and requirements in the user password arena; however, it's equally important to ensure that your Windows XP system can guard against hacking attempts. For example, under Windows XP's default configuration, any person can try to log on with another user's account an unlimited number of times by attempting to guess their password. If you implement password complexity requirements, this certainly makes the challenge more difficult, but it's still better to be safe than sorry.

Windows XP Professional systems address the issue with Account Lockout Policy settings. In a nutshell, these policy settings allow you to dictate how many incorrect logon attempts can occur before an account is finally locked. If you are locked out, an account cannot be used to log on to your Windows XP system until a computer administrator unlocks it, or a preconfigured period of time has passed.

Windows XP's Account Lockout Policy settings include the following:

- Account lockout duration: Dictates the number of minutes that an account remains locked out until it is unlocked automatically. If set to a value such as 5, a user could attempt to log on again 5 minutes after being locked out (enough time to take a break, and perhaps remember their password). If set to 0, accounts are locked out until unlocked by a computer administrator.
- Account lockout threshold: Controls the number of failed logon attempts before a user's account is locked out. When set to 0, user accounts are never locked out.
- Reset account lockout counter after: Dictates the number of minutes that must pass before the account lockout threshold value is reset to 0.

The Reset account lockout counter after setting can be a little confusing. The purpose of resetting the Account lockout counter is to ensure that incorrect logon attempts don't add up over time. For example, if you set the Account lockout threshold to 3, then 3 incorrect logon attempts will lock out the account — regardless of whether they all happened over the last minute, or cumulatively (say 3 individual times) over the course of the last 6 months. Configure the Reset account lockout counter to a value such as 30 minutes to ensure that incorrect logon attempts don't accumulate towards a lockout days or weeks from now. Every user will forget or mistype their password occasionally!

Caution

After Account Lockout settings are configured to lock out accounts on a Windows XP Professional system, these settings are enforced for all users, including computer administrators. The only exception is the built-in Administrator account, which cannot be locked out. Don't forget the password (and potentially the new username) that you've applied to this account. If all other user accounts get locked out, you'll need to be able to log on with this account to unlock them.

Configuring Password Policy settings

Security-related policy settings are configured using the Local Security Policy MMC on a Windows XP Professional system. Only users with Computer administrator accounts can use and make configuration changes with this tool.

Follow these steps to configure password policy settings on a Windows XP Professional system:

1. Click Start → Control Panel.
2. In the left Control Panel menu, click Switch to Classic View.
3. Double-click Administrative Tools.
4. Double-click the Local Security Policy shortcut.
5. In the Local Security Settings window, expand Account Policies.
6. Click the Password Policy folder (Figure 2-2) to view the default policy settings.

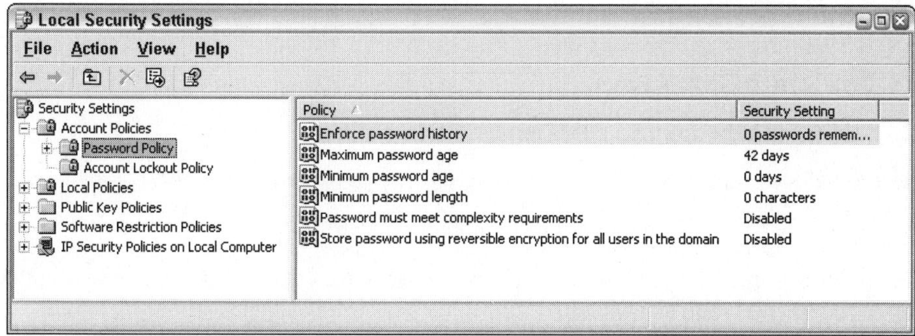

Figure 2-2: Password Policy settings.

7. Double-click Enforce password history to open its properties window (Figure 2-3). Select the number of user passwords to be remembered and then click OK.

Figure 2-3: Enforce password history Properties window.

8. Double-click Maximum password age, select an appropriate value in days, and click OK.
9. Double-click Minimum password age, select the minimum number of days that a user must user a given password before changing it, and click OK.
10. Double-click Minimum password length, select a minimum length for user password (such as 8), and click OK.
11. Double-click Password must meet complexity requirements, click Enabled, and click OK.
12. Close the Local Security Settings window.

Follow these steps to test your new password policy settings on a Windows XP Professional system:

1. Click Start → Control Panel.
2. Double-click the User Accounts applet.
3. Click your username and then click Change my password.
4. At the Change your password screen, enter your current password.
5. In the Type a new password box, type a password that does not meet the new policy requirements, such as testpass.
6. Enter the testpass password again in the Type the new password again to confirm box.
7. Click Change Password. The User Accounts dialog box appears (Figure 2-4) stating that your password does not meet the configured password policy requirements.
8. Enter a new password that does meet your new password policy requirements and then click Change Password.

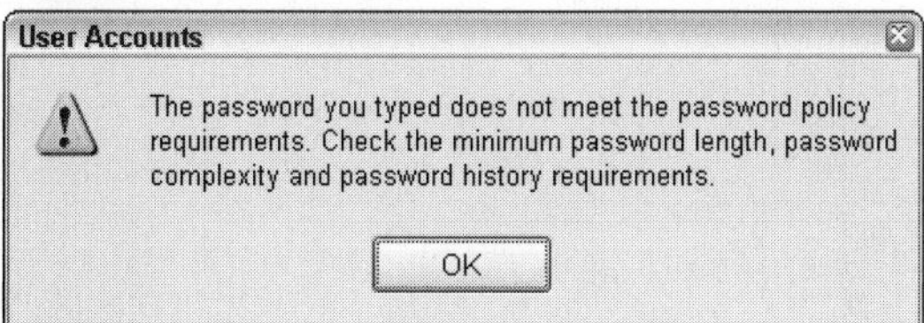

Figure 2-4: Message displayed when a password doesn't meet policy requirements.

Configuring Account Lockout Policy settings

Similar to Password Policy, Account Lockout Policy settings are configured using the Local Security Policy tool, which is only accessible to Computer administrators.

Follow these steps to configure account lockout settings on a Windows XP Professional system:

1. Click Start→Control Panel.
2. In the left Control Panel menu, click Switch to Classic View.
3. Double-click Administrative Tools.
4. Double-click the Local Security Policy shortcut.
5. Click the Account Lockout Policy folder (Figure 2-5) under Account Policies to view the default policy settings.

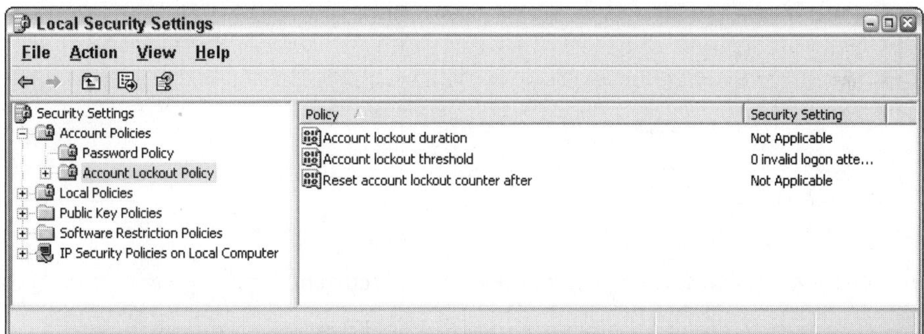

Figure 2-5: Account Lockout Policy settings.

6. Double-click Account lockout threshold and then configure the number of invalid logon attempts (for example, 3) that can be attempted before an account is locked out (Figure 2-6). Click OK.

Figure 2-6: Account lockout threshold.

7. After the Account lockout threshold is configured, the Suggest Values window opens to suggest settings for the remaining Account Lockout Policy settings. Click OK.
8. Double-click Account lockout duration, and type 0 in the Account is locked out for box. When set to 0, accounts are locked out indefinitely, as shown in Figure 2-7. Click OK.

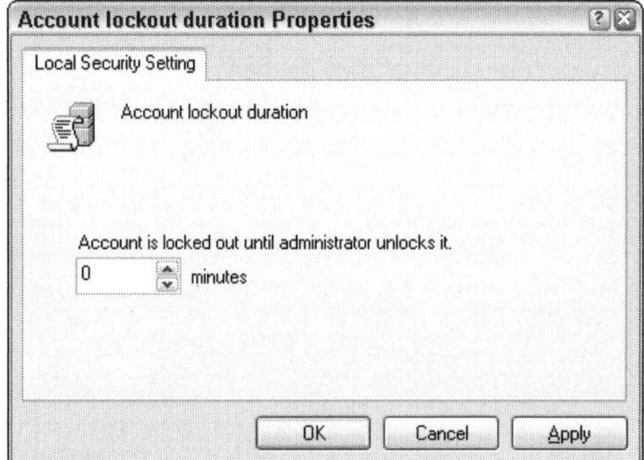

Figure 2-7: Account lockout duration.

9. Close the Local Security Policy window and log off.

Follow these steps to test your new account lockout policy settings and unlock a locked user account:

1. Attempt to log on to another user's account using an incorrect password until you reach the configured Account lockout threshold.
2. After this number of failed attempts has been reached, the Logon Message dialog box (Figure 2-8) appears, stating that the account has been locked. Click OK.

Figure 2-8: Message displayed when a user account is locked out.

3. Log on with your Computer administrator account.
4. Click Start, right-click My Computer, and click Manage to open the Computer Management MMC. User accounts cannot be unlocked via User Accounts in Control Panel.
5. Expand Local Users and Groups and then click on the Users folder.
6. Double-click the locked out user account.
7. On the General tab (Figure 2-9), uncheck the Account is locked out checkbox and then click OK.

Figure 2-9: A locked out user account.

8. Close the Computer Management MMC.

Tracking Logon Attempts

Implementing Account Lockout Policy settings is one easy way to track whether someone has been trying to log on to your Windows XP system as another user. Assuming that the user in question hasn't simply forgotten their username and password combination (you'll have to ask them), chances are good that another person has been playing a password guessing game with the account in question.

A suspiciously locked out account provides a good initial clue that something may be amiss, but there is another way to gather more information on logon attempts. The tool you need for this purpose is the Security log in Event Viewer, which automatically logs details of all successful and failed user logon attempts on both Windows XP Home and Professional systems.

To check the contents of your system's Security log, following these steps:

1. Click Start, right-click My Computer, and click Manage. The Computer Management MMC opens.
2. Expand Event Viewer and then click Security. Successful events are listed with a key icon, while failed events are designated with a lock, as shown in the following figure.

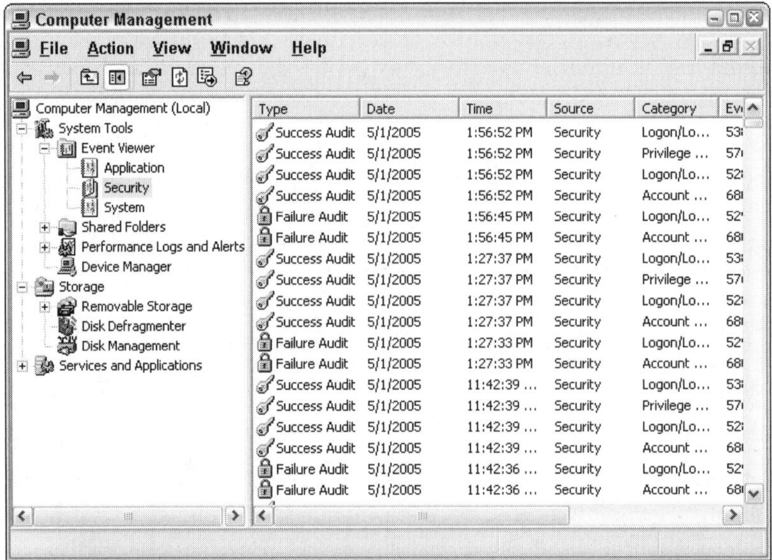

Reviewing events in Windows XP's Security log.

3. In the Category field look for events of the Logon/Logoff type. Double-click a Failure Audit event of this type to view details about the event, as shown in the following figure.

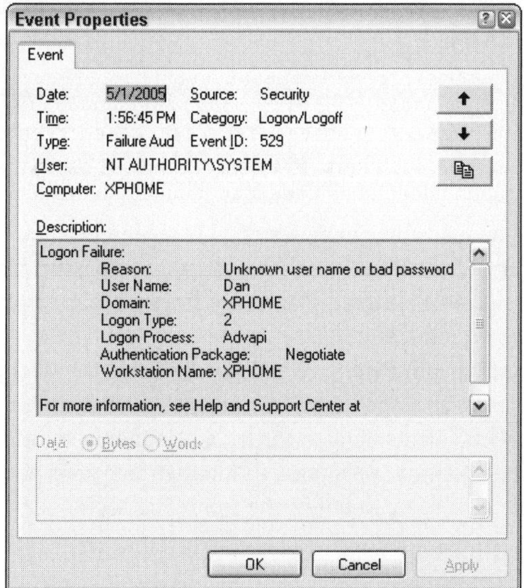

Reviewing the details of an event in Windows XP's Security log.

In the case of a failed logon attempt, the Description section lists details including the user account associated with the logon attempt, the reason the logon failed, and the time at which the event occurred. Although this obviously won't show you which person attempted to log on as this user, the time at which the event occurred should make narrowing things down a little easier.

As a general rule, take some time to browse through your system's Security log at least every couple of weeks, even if nothing appears to be amiss. You may not find anything suspicious, but it's better to keep an eye open for potential issues rather than to assume that everything is perfectly fine.

Note

To turn on, use, or configure settings related to Event Viewer's Security log, you must be logged on with a Computer administrator account. On a Windows XP Home system, security-related events are added to the Security log automatically, and these settings cannot be changed. On a Windows XP Professional system, events that should be recorded in the Security log can be configured using the Local Security Policy or Local Computer Policy tools, both of which are explored in more detail in Chapter 3.

Storing Passwords Securely

Remembering one strong password can be tough, but trying to remember 10 or more good passwords can be next to impossible. Between user account, Web site, Internet service, and file encryption passwords, it's not uncommon for the average user to have anywhere between 15 and 20 username and password combinations to remember.

Certainly, forgetting a required password can be a frustrating experience — it represents one of the main reasons why most users opt for the easy way out (using very simple and similar passwords) if given the chance. As you're now aware, however, this is an extremely bad idea from a security perspective, and increases risks to your personal privacy dramatically.

Thankfully, help is close at hand. On the logon user account front, Windows XP includes a helpful feature that virtually ensures you'll never be locked out if you happen to forget your password. For all other user accounts (those for Web sites, e-mail accounts, and so forth), a reasonable solution can be found in form of secure password management software, programs that remember your passwords for you. Both of these helpful tools are looked at in more detail in the following sections.

Password reset disk

Understanding that users may occasionally forget their passwords, Windows XP allows users to create a special floppy disk that can be used to reset user account passwords should they be lost or forgotten. Known as a password reset floppy disk, each user on your Windows XP system should create one as a precaution, just in case they ever forget their password.

After a password reset disk has been created, any user that has forgotten their password can use their personal disk to reset their password, should the need arise. One key benefit is that users who reset their password by using this floppy disk do not lose access to their encrypted files, stored Internet passwords, and certificates, as they would if a computer administrator reset their password in Control Panel or using the Computer Management tool.

Follow these steps to create a password reset disk for your Windows XP user account:

1. Click Start → Control Panel.
2. Click User Accounts.
3. Click your username.
4. In the Related Tasks menu in the upper-left corner, click Prevent a forgotten password.
5. At the Welcome to the Forgotten Password Wizard screen (Figure 2-10), click Next. If your computer does not include a removable disk drive (for example, a floppy disk drive), you will be prompted with a dialog box informing you that you cannot use this feature.

Figure 2-10: The Forgotten Password Wizard.

6. Insert a blank, formatted floppy disk into Drive A: and then click Next.
7. At the Current User Account Password screen, type your current password and then click Next.
8. After the disk creation process is 100% complete, click Next and then click Finish.

Caution

After you create a password reset disk for your user account, label it appropriately (but not too obviously) and store it in a safe place. Anyone with physical access to your Windows XP system and this floppy disk can log on using your username and change your password to whatever value they please.

Follow these steps to reset your user account password using your password reset disk:

1. At the Welcome screen, click your username and then press Enter. When the Did you forget your password balloon appears (Figure 2-11), click use your password reset disk.

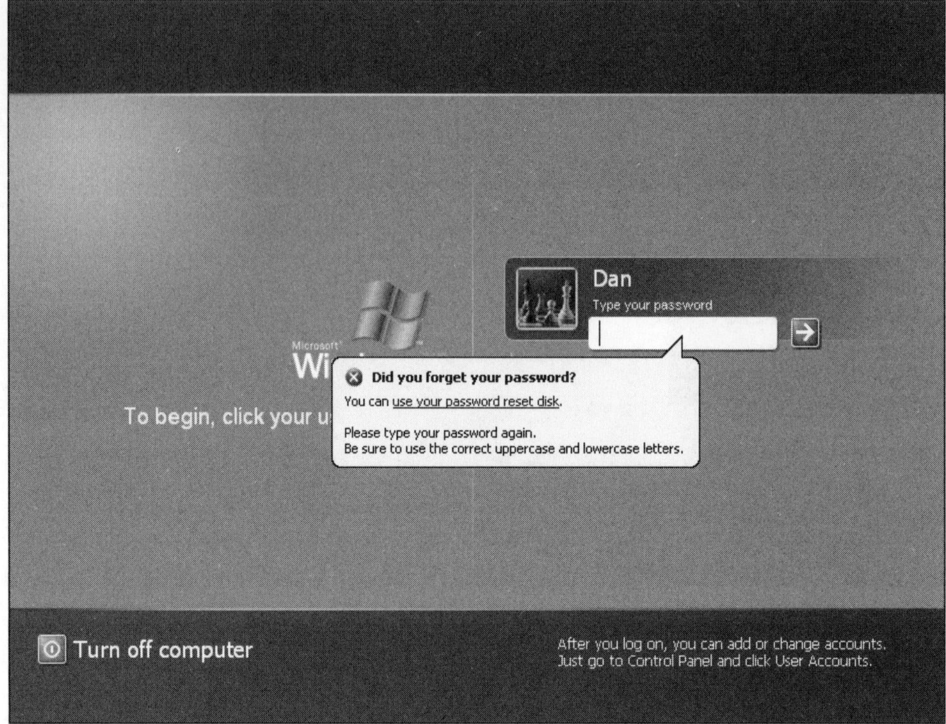

Figure 2-11: Options when an incorrect user password is supplied.

2. When the Welcome to the Password Reset Wizard screen appears, click Next.
3. Insert your password reset disk in Drive A: and then click Next.
4. At the Reset User Account Password screen (Figure 2-12), enter and confirm a new password for your user account and then click Next.
5. Click Finish to complete the wizard.
6. Log on to Windows XP using the new password for your account.

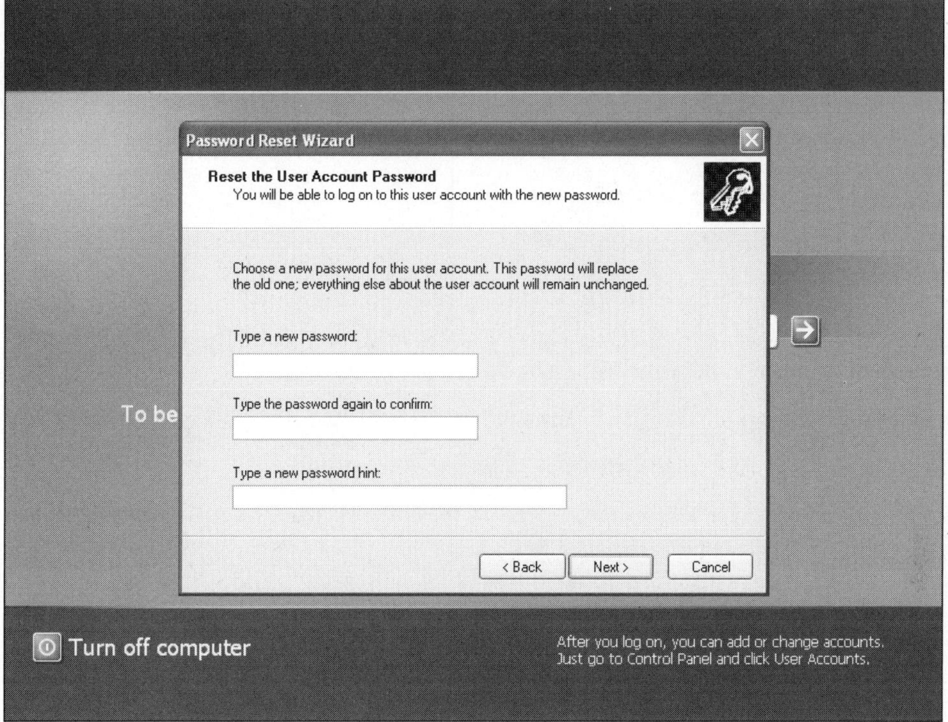

Figure 2-12: Reset your user account password by using a password reset disk.

Password-management software

Instead of dealing with the frustration of trying to remember username and complex password combinations for different Web sites, you may want to consider employing the help of a password management program. These programs are designed to help you create a username and password database for different Web sites and services, remembering logon details for you.

A good password management program allows you to store all sorts of username and password combinations, and protect the contents of its database with strong encryption. In most cases, these programs allow you to configure a master password, which must be entered before you can use, add, or change the user account settings it stores.

One great example of such a program is Access Manager 2 from Citi-Software. This program (free for personal use) offers comprehensive password management capabilities, complete with strong encryption protection. It can be downloaded from `www.accessmanager.co.uk`.

After installed, you should begin by configuring a strong master password for the Access Manager database. After that's done, you can begin adding username and password combinations for everything from Internet dial-up and e-mail account settings to Web site passwords and even password-protected documents.

You can use Access Manager to protect just about any username and password combination that you need to remember. You can't use the program to log on to Windows XP (you'll need to log on to

Windows XP to open it), but it certainly does make life easier on the password front. In fact, it can be the perfect tool if you're really having trouble dealing with all those different complex passwords. Access Manager remembers every individual complex password for you, and all you need to remember is the program's master password.

Follow these steps to add a master password and Web site logon passwords to Access Manager:

1. Double-click the Access Manager 2 shortcut icon on your desktop.
2. When the Logon screen appears, click OK.
3. Click Tools→Set Master Password.
4. Enter a strong password in the Enter New Password textbox. Use the Password Strength section as a guide to how strong your password is.
5. Enter your strong password again in the Confirm New Password textbox, and click OK.
6. To add a new password to Access Manager, click the New icon.
7. In the Title textbox type a descriptive name for the entry, such as Hotmail password.
8. Type your username in the Username textbox.
9. Type your password in the Password textbox, or click the Generate Password button to create a strong password for this account. Note that if you use this feature, you need to change your password to this value on the associated Web site.
10. In the Document textbox, type the Web address associated with this username and password combination, for example www.hotmail.com.
11. Select a password type from the Type drop-down menu, for example, E-mail account (Figure 2-13).
12. Click OK to create the account.

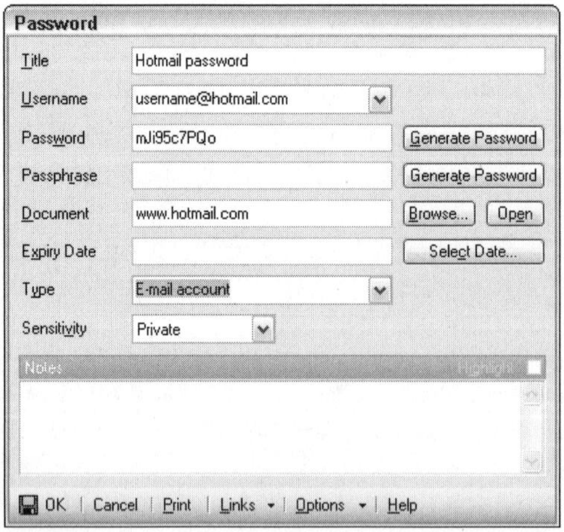

Password
Title Hotmail password
Username username@hotmail.com
Password mJi95c7PQo Generate Password
Passphrase Generate Password
Document www.hotmail.com Browse... Open
Expiry Date Select Date...
Type E-mail account
Sensitivity Private
OK | Cancel | Print | Links | Options | Help

Figure 2-13: Adding user account information in Access Manager.

Follow these steps to log on to a Web site using a password stored in Access Manager:

1. Click the entry you want to open in the Access Manager window to select it (Figure 2-14).

Figure 2-14: Selecting an account entry in Access Manager.

2. Click View → Open Document. Internet Explorer or your preferred Web browser opens to the configured site address.
3. In the Access Manager window, click the contents of the Username field and drag it to the Username textbox in Internet Explorer. Your username should now appear in this field.
4. Click the password field in Access Manager and drag it to the Password textbox in Internet Explorer. The series of asterisks representing your password appear.
5. Press Enter or click OK to log on to your account.

Caution

If you lose or forget the master password associated with your Access Manager database, you will not be able to decrypt or gain access to your saved user accounts and passwords.

Strong Passwords to Go

Although storing and protecting your passwords on one computer with a free program such as Access Manager may do the trick, perhaps you're a little more mobile. If you regularly log on to different computers at different locations, you may want to consider a portable solution to the complex password issue.

In this case, portable comes in the form of a password management program offers support for USB keychain or pen drives. These portable memory devices work with some password management programs, acting as an encrypted storage location for your usernames and passwords. With everything you need to access your logon details stored on a pocket-sized device, you can access them from any PC with an accessible USB port.

The Professional version of Access Manager 2 offers support for USB storage devices, giving you instant access to your password database from any computer with Microsoft's .NET Framework installed. The free version of Access Manager can be upgraded to Professional for a small fee.

Another program that gets the job done is RoboForm Portable, available from `www.roboform.com/removeable.html`. This inexpensive program not only securely stores your usernames and passwords on a USB device, but also includes the capability to store your Web site bookmarks and personal details used to automatically fill out Web-based forms. That's secure, mobile, and handy.

Password Cracking and Recovery

In a perfect world, every user account would be protected by a strong password that was changed frequently and never forgotten. Tools such as Windows XP's password reset disk and third-party password management programs can be a big help, but it's still entirely possible that you may one day encounter a situation where you cannot gain access to your Windows XP system due to a forgotten password.

Forgetting the password associated with a Limited user account isn't a terribly big deal, even when you don't have its password reset disk handy. In the worst-case scenario, you can log on with a Computer administrator account, change the password in question, and log on normally.

The forgotten password issue really rears its ugly head when none of the passwords associated with Computer administrator accounts can be remembered. Without administrator-level access to a Windows XP system, you won't be able to accomplish much in the way of configuration tasks, and that's obviously not a feasible situation in the longer term. Chances are good that you'll need to install new software or make changes to system settings eventually.

Fortunately (or unfortunately, depending on whether your trying to keep the bad guys out or let yourself in), a number of tools and utilities are available that make it possible to reset user account passwords on a Windows XP system. Some of the more popular free and commercial tools used to recover Windows XP passwords include:

- Offline NT Password and Registry Editor, a free Linux-based bootable disk that can be used to reset passwords (Figure 2-15) available from `home.eunet.no/~pnordahl/ntpasswd/`.

- LC 5 (the latest iteration of the popular L0phtCrack tool), a commercial password scanning, auditing, and recovery tool for both Windows and UNIX systems available from `www.atstake.com/products/lc/`.
- Locksmith (included in ERD Commander 2005), a wizard-based commercial tool that allows you to reset the Windows XP Administrator password, available from `www.winternals.com/products/repairandrecovery/erdcommander2002.asp?pid=erd`.

```
****************************************************************************
*                                                                          *
*  Windows NT/2k/XP Change Password Utility / Registry Editor / Boot disk *
*                                                                          *
*  (c) 1998-2004 Petter Nordahl-Hagen. Freely noncommercial distributable *
*  See docs & license file on floppy for more info on license and credits *
*  Linux kernel & utilities (c) lots of people, freely distributable     *
*  Encryption library by the OpenSSL project                              *
*  Thanks to EZ for bootfloppystuff                                       *
*                                                                          *
* DISCLAIMER: THIS SOFTWARE COMES WITH ABSOLUTELY NO WARRANTIES!          *
*             THE AUTHOR CAN NOT BE HELD RESPONSIBLE FOR ANY DAMAGE       *
*             CAUSED BY THE (MIS)USE OF THIS SOFTWARE                     *
*                                                                          *
* NOTE: The 'chntpw' binary contains cryptograhic algorithms,             *
*       like DES and others, which may be illegal to re-export            *
*       from your country.                                                *
*                                                                          *
* More info at: http://home.eunet.no/~pnordahl/ntpasswd/                  *
* Email       : pnordahl@eunet.no                                         *
*                                                                          *
****************************************************************************
* Floppy build date:  Thu Mar 3 21:21:13 CET 2005

Loading vmlinuz......._
```

Figure 2-15: Offline NT Password and Registry Editor.

Most of the programs designed to recover or reset passwords on a Windows XP system require physical access to the computer in question. Through the use of a bootable floppy disk or CD, these tools load their own operating system environment (usually based on Linux or the Windows installation sequence), and complete their password reset magic from within.

Although the ability to reset or recover a Windows XP administrative password can certainly be helpful, it also brings to light a potential security risk. In the hands of a malicious user, these same password recovery tools could be used to gain Computer administrator access to your Windows XP system. Of course, this requires the user to have physical access to your PC, as well as the ability to boot the computer from its floppy disk or CD drive. Thankfully, you can put additional security features in place to restrict this type of access, as outlined later in this chapter.

Implementing Additional Password Security Options

Protecting your user accounts with strong passwords is critical. As you've now learned, however, any person with physical access to your computer can potentially bypass even the most complex logon passwords using any one of a number of password cracking or recovery utilities.

To use these various tools, a person not only needs physical access to your computer but also the ability to start your system with a bootable CD or floppy disk. Unfortunately (from a security perspective), the default BIOS settings on most computers are configured such that your system will first attempt to boot from a floppy disk, then a bootable CD, and finally your hard drive. This means that any user who inserts a bootable disk can potentially get past any of the Windows XP security settings you've implemented, with the right tools.

Thankfully, all is not lost. The current BIOS settings on your computer may allow the system to be booted from a floppy disk or CD, but you can change these settings. Furthermore, you can protect your computer with different BIOS passwords to restrict BIOS configuration changes, and even require a password for the Windows XP boot process to start. In the following sections you learn more about the different passwords that can be implemented to control what users can do when they have physical access to your Windows XP system.

BIOS passwords

When you start your computer, an onscreen message appears that lists the key (or key combination) that must be pressed to access your system's BIOS configuration settings — usually something such as F1, F2, or the Delete key; this differs depending on the make and model of your computer, as well as the type of BIOS is has installed. You may be prompted with a message pressing this key to enter the BIOS, System Setup, System Configuration Settings, or similar.

Tip

If you're having trouble accessing or configuring your computer's BIOS settings, Wim's BIOS Page is an excellent reference site, found at `www.wimsbios.com`.

Your computer's BIOS won't be secured in any way by default, and that's potentially dangerous if you're worried about someone making configuration changes to your PC. In fact, if left unprotected, a user could seriously damage your system or render it virtually unusable by changing BIOS settings alone. Worse thing, they could implement BIOS passwords before you do, locking you out of your own system.

Although their names may differ slightly depending on the manufacturer, almost every BIOS can be protected by two different passwords:

- A supervisor password, which must be entered in order to change BIOS configuration settings.
- A user password, which must always be entered before the computer launches into any main boot process.

Figure 2-16 shows the BIOS Password configuration screen for a computer with a common Phoenix BIOS.

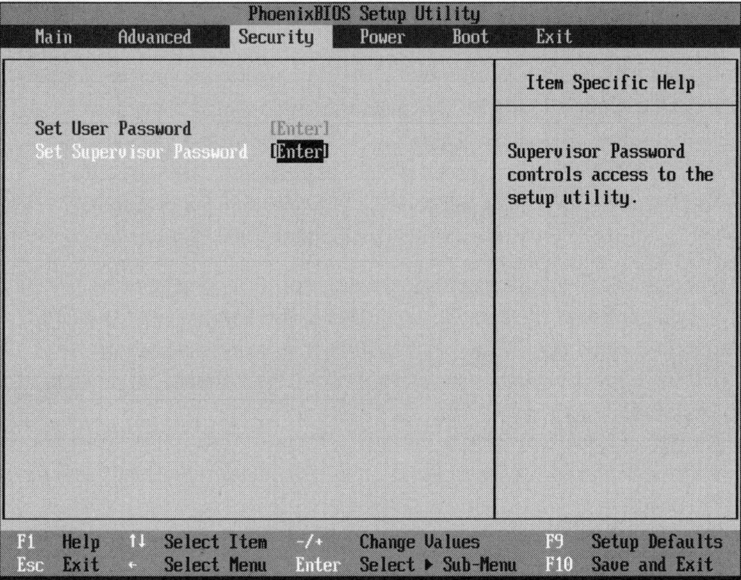

Figure 2-16: BIOS Security configuration screen.

The exact steps to configure user and administrator passwords for a BIOS differ by manufacturer, but is generally similar to the following:

1. Reboot your computer. Watch for the onscreen message that lists the key you need to press to enter the BIOS. Press this key when the message appears. If it passes you by and the Windows XP boot process begins, reboot and try again.
2. When the BIOS configuration screen appears, look for a section marked Passwords or Security. When found, enter a password for Supervisor access.
3. Enter a User password if that's your preference. If you do enter a User password, keep in mind that any user attempting to start your computer needs to know and supply this password to boot into Windows XP.
4. Even with a User password in place, the default BIOS configuration allows any user who knows the password to boot from a floppy disk or CD. If you're concerned about this, look for a section in your BIOS marked Boot or Main. You should find settings that allow you to configure the order in which your computer attempts to boot, usually something along the lines of A:, D:, C: — meaning your floppy drive first, CD drive second, hard disk third. You can usually change the order of this list to make your hard drive the first boot device in the list, or even remove the other options completely.
5. Press the appropriate key sequence to save your new BIOS settings (usually ESC, then Y for yes).

Evading BIOS Passwords

If you do happen to lose or misplace BIOS configuration passwords and cannot boot your system or change BIOS settings, there may still be hope. Many BIOS manufacturers configure "backdoor" passwords that can be used to access and change configuration settings should the need arise. Some PC vendors (such as Dell) can also help you to reset the BIOS password for your computer if you call their technical support line and can provide the necessary details about your system. Utilities that claim to be able to crack BIOS passwords can also be found on the Internet.

Although it again depends on the specific BIOS used, BIOS passwords can also sometimes be circumvented or erased by removing and then replacing a computer's CMOS battery, or by shorting the jumper pins on the motherboard that control CMOS memory. Of course, you should not rely on either of these methods as an alternative to remembering your password. Furthermore, attempting such changes might result in physical damage to your PC.

Caution

If you do opt to configure BIOS passwords, it's imperative that you remember them or your PC could be rendered unable to boot. If necessary, write these passwords down and store them in a safe place.

Hard disk passwords

In addition to BIOS passwords, many laptops include a feature that allows you to configure a hard drive password. Although fundamentally similar to a BIOS User password, it's actually more complex. When a hard drive password is configured, a user cannot boot from or access the drive without this password. Even if the hard drive is physically removed from the laptop and installed in another computer, the password is still required for access; erasing CMOS memory or other BIOS-like techniques cannot circumvent it.

A hard drive password certainly appears to be a secure ways to protect your computer, but proceed with caution. If you forget this password, your only real option is to replace the drive, or employ the services of a dedicated (and potentially very expensive) hard disk recovery service in an attempt to crack or reset the password.

However, if your laptop's hard drive includes extremely sensitive information that you cannot risk another user gaining access to, you may want to consider configuring this option. If you system includes the capability to configure a hard drive password, the setting is usually configured from the same BIOS screen as User and Supervisor passwords.

Syskey password

As you learned earlier in this chapter, the Windows XP SAM database stores hashed copies of user account passwords, and encrypts the database for extra protection. By default, the system key (also known as the startup key) used to encrypt the database is also stored on the computer. As an added security feature, you can export this key to a floppy disk that must be inserted each and every time you attempt to boot Windows XP. Alternatively, you can leave the startup key on the hard disk, and assign it a password that must be supplied towards the end of the Windows XP boot process.

Obviously either of these methods can be used to add yet another layer of security to the Windows XP startup process; however, if this floppy disk is created and lost (or if you assign a password and forget it), it's unlikely that you'll be able to gain access to your system. Although some of the tools designed to recovery passwords claim to be able to bypass or reset this password, they should not be relied upon as a backup method.

The tool used to change how the startup key is stored or protected on a Windows XP system is called Syskey, and can run by any Computer administrator user account.

Follow these steps to run the Syskey utility on a Windows XP system:

1. Click Start → Run.
2. Type **syskey.exe** in the Open textbox and then click OK.
3. At the Securing the Windows XP Account Database window, click Update.
4. If you want to protect the system key with a password, click Password Startup (Figure 2-17), enter and confirm your password, and click OK. Alternatively, to store the system key on a floppy disk, click Store Startup Key on Floppy Disk, click OK, and insert a blank disk when prompted.

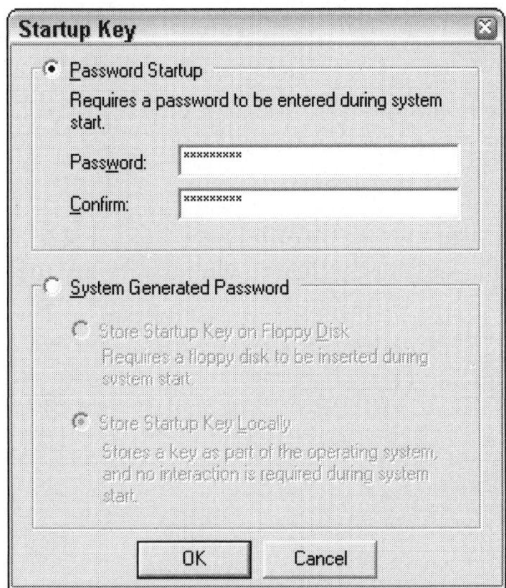

Figure 2-17: Configuring a startup password with Syskey.

5. When the Success dialog box appears, click OK.

Let's Get Physical!

Even if you use the strongest user account passwords and implement multiple layers of password security, no computer is ever 100 percent secure (in a true computer security sense) if other people can gain physical access to it. The best you can do when attempting to secure your Windows XP system is implement the strongest security settings available and then ensure that physical access to the computer is restricted to users (to the greatest extent possible) that you know and trust. If this side of things does have you worried, however, you'll want to explore some of the different options that can be used to better secure the physical aspects of your computer.

If your Windows XP system is a desktop computer, you may want to look into locking cases that require an actual key to gain access to internal components such as hard drives, CMOS batteries and so forth. Of course, that won't stop a thief for picking the computer up and walking away with it.

This is especially true with laptop computers, where theft tends to be a far too common issue. A variety of vendors supply cable locks that can be used to fasten both laptop and desktop PCs to a fixed option, but you shouldn't rely on these as more than a temporary barrier to theft. They may keep a laptop safe in a public location, but they're no match for a set of good bolt cutters. To address this issue, some cable locks include piercing alarms that are triggered when cut or moved; other manufacturers provide complete system replacement insurance if your computer is stolen while locked down. That may provide some comfort on the financial front but doesn't address the fact that someone else may now have access to your personal files and e-mail messages.

Of course, don't forget the old tried-and-true battle horse of physical security—the locked door. Sometimes the most simple security techniques are also the most effective.

Follow these steps to boot a Windows XP system protected by a startup password:

1. Restart your Windows XP system.
2. Toward the end of the boot process, the Windows XP Startup Password dialog box appears (Figure 2-18). Enter the startup password that you configured with the Syskey tool and then click OK.

Figure 2-18: Entering a startup password.

3. After the startup password is accepted, log on to Windows XP normally.

Caution

If you choose to store the Windows XP Startup key on a floppy disk, be sure to make a copy of this disk and store it in a safe place in case the original is ever lost or stolen. Without it, you will not be able to log on to your Windows XP system.

Summary

The security of any Windows XP system is only as good as the passwords used to protect it. Keep the following points in mind when it comes to managing user account and other system passwords:

- Create strong passwords that are at least seven characters long and include uppercase and lowercase letters, numbers, and symbols.
- Never include your username, real name, or other personal details in passwords.
- Assign every user account a unique password.
- Change passwords regularly.
- Change any password that may have been compromised immediately.
- Personal user account passwords should never be shared with friends, family, or other users.
- Educate other users on the importance of implementing strong passwords and changing them regularly.
- Use Password Policy and Account Lockout Policy settings to improve user account security on Windows XP Professional systems.
- Review the contents of the Event Viewer Security log periodically.
- Have every Windows XP user create a password reset disk.
- Consider using password management software to securely store details for different user accounts.
- At a minimum, add a BIOS supervisor password to your system.

Chapter 3

Using Built-In Tools and Settings to Improve Windows XP Security

Question anyone with even a basic awareness of computer security and privacy issues about the most important tasks toward securing a Windows XP system, and you're almost certain to be lectured on how critical it is to have both firewall and anti-virus software installed. Although there's no denying that the protection offered by firewalls and virus protection programs is absolutely necessary, the processes involved with properly securing a Windows XP system go far beyond these essential basics. To secure any Windows XP system to a high level, you need to take advantage of capabilities offered by both third-party security programs and the built-in tools and settings provided by Windows XP.

No shortage of useful and powerful tools and settings are at the disposal of all Windows XP users. Even tools and options that aren't specifically designed with security-related functions in mind can prove powerful allies in the war to keep your Windows XP system locked down and protected. As a Windows XP user who is serious about security, understanding the arsenal of defensive tools at your disposal is simply essential; although you may not use every available utility or setting on a regular basis, it's important to know what Windows XP can and can't do before you start looking elsewhere for your security solutions.

In this chapter, you learn more about the native tools and settings that will help you in your quest to create the most secure Windows XP system possible. From disabling unnecessary (and potentially risky) operating system services to using the power of policy to implement user and computer restrictions, Windows XP really can help to get the job done. The biggest issue, however, is finding and knowing how to take advantage of many of the not-immediately-obvious security features in Windows XP — the very reason why this chapter exists!

Managing Windows XP Services

Every Windows XP system loads a number of background services during the startup process to provide a variety of operating system-related functions. Although many of these services must be running to perform common day-to-day user tasks, a number of services are typically not required by most

users and can actually represent a security risk if left enabled. Thankfully, Windows XP provides a way for you to control the specific services that run on your system, and selectively disable those that you don't need or use.

Some of the Windows XP services that are started by default but that may present a security risk include:

- **Internet Information Services.** This service is not installed by default, but is present on your system if you've installed any IIS-related component (such as Windows XP's built-in Web or FTP server) on a Windows XP Professional system. If you find this service running and you're not currently using IIS capabilities, disable it.
- **Messenger.** Not to be confused with the popular MSN Messenger program, this Messenger service is designed to allow networked computers and users to communicate with dialog-style onscreen message boxes. Unfortunately, spammers commonly use the Messenger service to send spam-like messages to your desktop. If this service is running on your system, you should disable it. After Windows XP Service Pack 2 is installed, the Messenger service is disabled by default.
- **Netmeeting Remote Desktop Sharing.** This service allows remote users to connect to your desktop and interact with it using the Netmeeting program. If you're not using Netmeeting, disable this service.
- **Remote Desktop Help Session Manager.** This service is a key component of Windows XP's Remote Assistance feature that allows users to connect to others' Windows XP systems in a bid to offer (or receive) s remote control-style support. If you are not using Remote Assistance, disable this feature.
- **Remote Registry.** This service allows users to connect to the Registry on other Windows XP systems from over the network. By disabling this service, remote users will not be able to connect to your computer's Registry for other networked computers.
- **Routing and Remote Access.** This service is designed to allow Windows XP to perform router-related functions. It is typically not required in home or small office environments, and should be disabled.
- **SSDP Discovery Service.** This service functions in coordination with the Universal Plug and Play service, and can represent a serious security risk to your PC. If you plan to disable Universal Plug and Play for security purposes, disable the SSDP Discovery Service as well.
- **Telnet.** This service allows Windows XP Professional systems to be managed remotely from a command-line interface. If you are not using Telnet sessions to manage your Windows XP Professional system, disable this service.

- **Universal Plug and Play.** This service relates to the Universal Plug and Play standard (not Windows XP's hardware-detection Plug and Play feature), a service that allows different types of networking devices to interconnect and communicate seamlessly. Unfortunately, the Universal Plug and Play service can also represent a serious security risk, and should be disabled if it's not being used.

The number of services present on a given Windows XP system depend both on the edition of Windows XP you're running, as well as the programs you have installed on your computer. Many programs add their own Windows XP services as part of their installation process, and these services are required for the program to function correctly.

Note

Disabling services that present a potential risk is always a good idea from a system security perspective, but can also have performance benefits. Every service running on a Windows XP system consumes resources like memory, regardless of whether it's being used or not. By disabling unused services, you can often improve Windows XP's performance significantly. For details on Windows XP's built-in services and recommendations on which ones you can potentially disable to improve performance, see the Services Guide for Windows XP available at `www.theeldergeek.com/services_guide.htm`.

The easiest way to reduce the risks associated with running unnecessary or potentially dangerous Windows XP services is to simply disable them, which effectively stops them from starting automatically when Windows XP loads. The tool used to manage service settings on a Windows XP system is the Services MMC, which allows you to start, stop, pause, resume, and restart individual services as necessary, or selectively enable or disable services as required. Any service that you disable for security reasons can always be re-enabled at a later time, if necessary.

Follow these steps to disable Windows XP services that may present a security risk:

1. Click Start → Control Panel → Administrative Tools → Services. The Services MMC appears, as shown in Figure 3-1.
2. To stop a particular service, scroll down to the service name, right-click, and select Stop. The service is now stopped (as shown by lack of a Started status message in Figure 3-2) but will restart again automatically the next time Windows XP loads if no further action is taken.
3. To stop a service from starting automatically when Windows XP loads, it must be disabled. Right-click the service name and then click Properties to open the service's Properties window to the General tab.

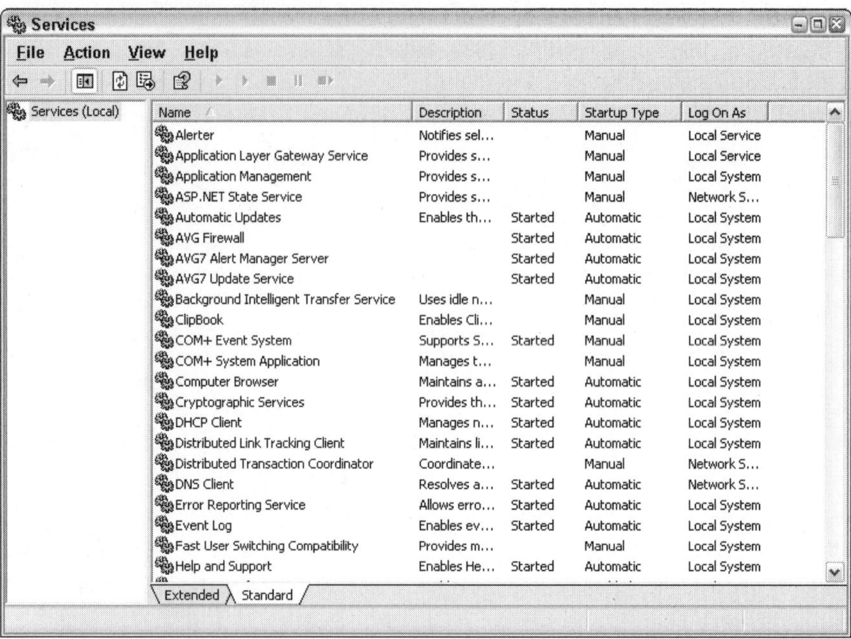

Figure 3-1: The Services MMC displays the status of services installed on a Windows XP system.

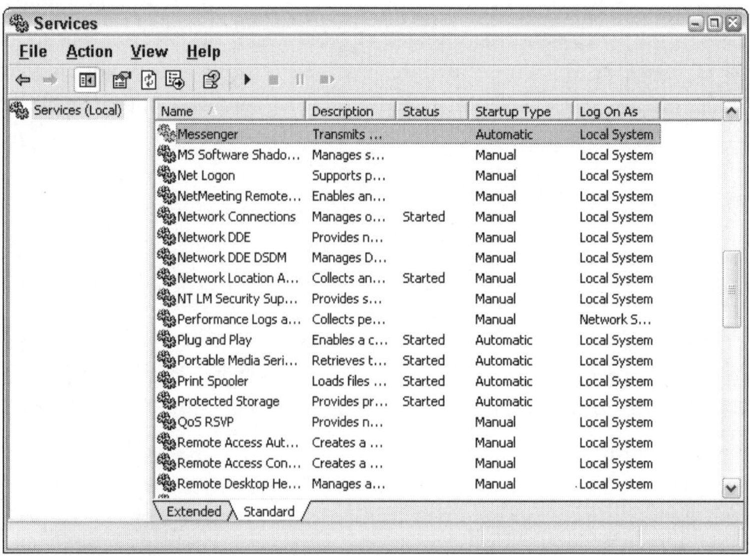

Figure 3-2: A stopped service (Messenger) is still configured to start automatically along with Windows XP.

4. In the Startup type drop-down list, select Disabled (as shown in Figure 3-3) and then click OK. The service is now stopped and disabled such that it will not start automatically the next time Windows XP loads.

Figure 3-3: Disabling the Messenger service.

Spam of a Different Sort

One of the more intrusive and annoying types of spam that Windows XP users have had to contend with is the direct result of Windows XP's Messenger service. This service has nothing to do with the popular MSN Messenger instant messaging program, but rather a Windows XP feature that allows onscreen messages to be sent between users and computers on a network. Looking for a way to get their message across to large numbers of users almost instantly, spammers and other online marketers have taken to sending them using the Messenger service, which is enabled and started by default on Windows XP systems that don't yet have Service Pack 2 installed. An example of a message received via the Messenger service is shown in the following figure.

An example of an onscreen message received via Windows XP's Messenger service

Continued

Spam of a Different Sort (Continued)

If you receive spam messages of this type, your Windows XP system is not properly secured — a firewall would automatically block any such messages received, for example. As far as dealing with Messenger service spam, you have three options — install personal firewall software (or enable Windows Firewall), disable the Messenger service completely, or install Windows XP Service Pack (which disables the Messenger service as part of the installation process).

Messenger service spam isn't dangerous in the same manner as malware or viruses, but the details these messages contain might lead you to believe that something is wrong with your system, or even persuade you to visit a potentially infectious Web site.

Exploring Running Processes with Task Manager

Every program and service that runs on a Windows XP system does so in the context of what is known as a process. If you open Microsoft Word, for example, the WINWORD.EXE process runs until you close the program. Similarly, every time you open a new Internet Explorer browser window, another instance of the IEXPLORE.EXE process starts up. Sometimes a program runs many processes simultaneously, and it's also not unusual for Windows XP to use a single process to carry out many different tasks.

From a user's perspective, a running program is generally considered to be one that they can visually "see" onscreen. For example, when you click the shortcut to open Internet Explorer, a new browser window opens, and the program is obviously running. Not every process that runs on a Windows XP system does so in a visual manner, however. Many programs and processes are designed to run silently in the background, doing their thing without the need for any user interaction whatsoever.

Unfortunately, most users don't recognize that there are a number of processes working away in the background on their Windows XP system. Some of these processes are absolutely required for Windows XP to function. Others may be related to programs you've installed, which start automatically along with Windows XP. Still others may be silently tracking your online activities, capturing personal details from your computer, or even using your Windows XP system as a gateway for sending spam e-mail messages. These more malicious processes are usually referred to as malware or spyware, but can also be the result of infections by viruses, worms, and Trojan Horses.

Outside of relying on the capabilities of anti-virus and anti-spyware programs to detect rogue programs, you can also use Windows XP's Task Manager tool to review all processes running on your system — including the good, the bad, and the ugly. By reviewing the list of running processes in Task Manager, you can determine exactly what's running on your computer and the amount of resources that are being consumed on a process-by-process basis. The names of different running processes are especially valuable from a security perspective — if you think that malware or another pest might be infecting your Windows XP system, an unrecognizable or unusual running process name may provide the clue that something is amiss. Ultimately, a Web search for the process name will help you to determine whether it's legitimate and necessary or a security risk that needs to be addressed.

Follow these steps to review running processes with Task Manager on a Windows XP system:

1. Right-click the Windows XP Taskbar and click Task Manager on the shortcut menu.
2. When the Task Manager window opens, click the Processes tab, as shown in Figure 3-4. This tab displays all processes on your Windows XP system that are currently running, and includes details about their memory and CPU usage.

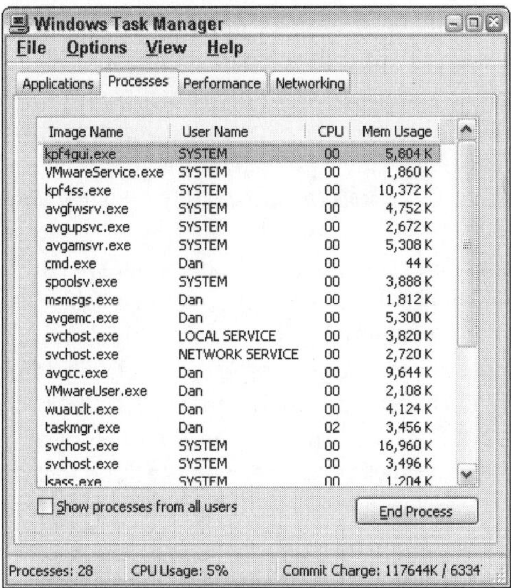

Figure 3-4: Task Manager's Processes tab displays information on all running processes, including those running quietly in the background.

3. To close a process that you believe to be a security risk (see the Tip below for details on determining whether a process is dangerous or not), click the process name and then click End Process. When the Task Manager Warning window appears, click Yes to end the process.

Tip

When reviewing running processes in Task Manager, notice that their image names are often fairly cryptic, for example svchost.exe. This can make it very difficult to determine whether a running process is a legitimate process, or something that represents a security risk like malware or a Trojan Horse. When in doubt about the purpose of a process, fire up your Web browser and head to `www.processlibrary.com`. The ProcessLibrary.com Web site allows you to search for Windows processes by name in a quest to determine the real deal behind unfriendly process image names.

Reviewing the Security Event Log

To help keep Computer administrators abreast of potential issues, Windows XP tracks a number of security-related events in its Security log. This log file, which is accessible via the Event Viewer MMC snap-in, is configured to audit a variety of different "success" and "failure" events that serve to record security-related issues that have occurred on a Windows XP Home or Professional system. Any user with a Computer administrator account has the ability to view and manage the contents of the Security log file.

The Security log in Event Viewer is a great resource for a number of reasons. It provides detailed information about potential security violations, such as failed user logon attempts. As an example, if one user was trying to log on with another's account by attempting to guess their password repeatedly, the Security log would list each failed logon attempt, including username, date, and time details—invaluable information as part of trying to trying to determine who made the logon attempt. Similarly, an entry is added to the Security log every time that a user logs on successfully, allowing you to determine which users have been using your Windows XP system, and when.

Beyond simply tracking logon events, the Security log also records details about system events (the time on the computer's clock being changed), changes to system policy settings (such as File and Printer sharing being enabled), and the use of administrative privileges. Not every event recorded in the Security log is one that requires action on your part, but having access to detailed information about security-related events that have occurred is certainly useful. In its default configuration, Windows XP's Security log will store up to 512 KB of event information and then overwrite older entries when this file size is reached. This can happen quickly, so it's generally a good idea to periodically save and then empty the contents of the Security log, and/or configure it with a larger maximum size. You learn more about configuring Security log settings shortly.

The Security log in Event Viewer contains two primary types of events:

- **Success Audits**. Identified by a "key" icon, success audits display information about a security-related event that was successful, such as a user logging on to Windows XP successfully.
- **Failure Audits**. Identified by a "lock" icon, failure audits are used to display information about a security-related failure, such as a user being unable to log in as a result of specifying an incorrect username or password.

On a Windows XP Home system, you cannot change the security event categories that are logged. On a Windows XP Professional system, however, logging for security event categories (both success and failure events) can be configured via Local Security Policy. You learn more about Local Security Policy later in this chapter.

Follow these steps to review entries in the Event Viewer Security log:

1. Click Start → Control Panel → Administrative Tools → Event Viewer.
2. When the Event Viewer MMC opens, click Security to view events in the Security log, as shown in Figure 3-5.

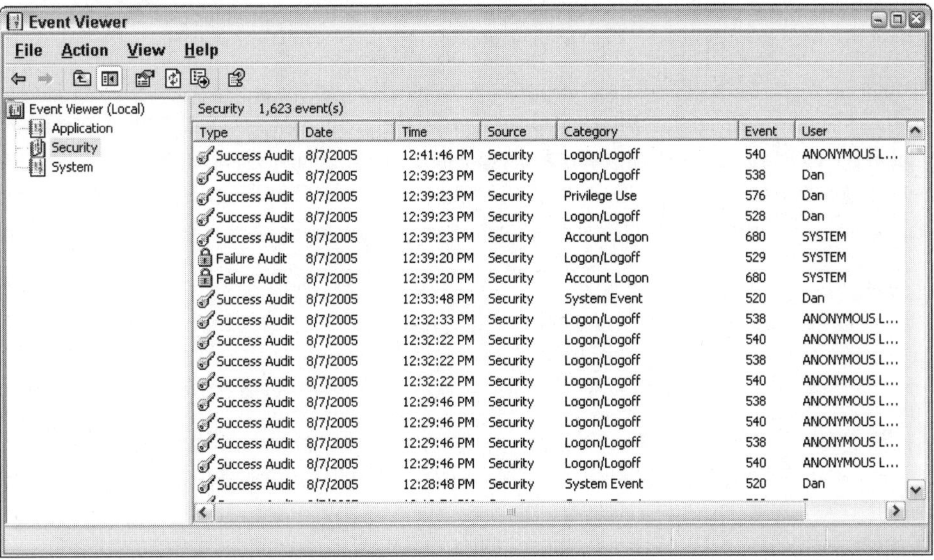

Figure 3-5: The Security log in Event Viewer.

3. Double-click a Security log entry to view its details. The example shown in Figure 3-6 is a Failure Audit event in the Logon/Logoff category that was logged as a result of user Dan trying to log on with an incorrect password.

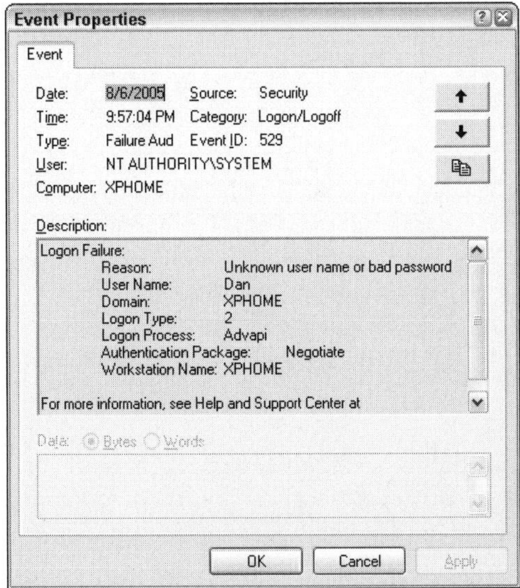

Figure 3-6: Reviewing the details of a failed logon attempt in the Security log.

Tip

Although the Properties window for a specific event includes many useful pieces of information, problems can often be difficult to decipher due to the technical nature of the information provided. If you find yourself unable to determine what a logged security event actually means, try performing a search on the Microsoft Help and Support Web site (`support.Microsoft.com`) for the item's Event ID number (for example, Event ID 529). Alternatively, you can try searching for details on the EventID.net Web site, available at `www.eventid.net`.

Follow these steps to configure Security log settings:

1. Click Start → Control Panel → Administrative Tools → Event Viewer.
2. Right-click Security and then click Properties. This opens the Security Properties window to the General tab, as shown in Figure 3-7. Configure new Security log settings as per your personal preferences.

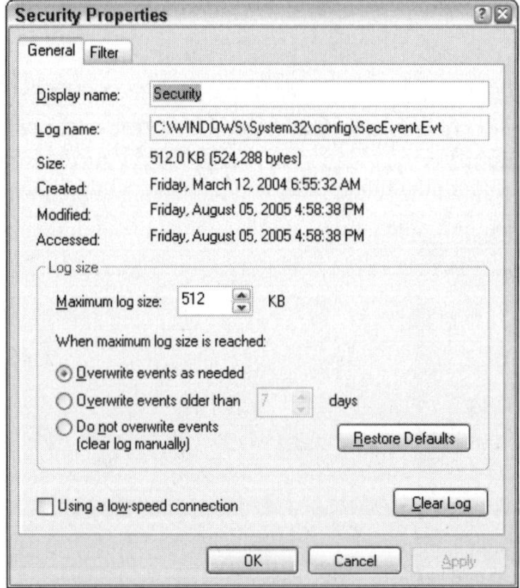

Figure 3-7: Configuring settings for the Security log.

3. To save the contents of your Security log, right-click Security in Event Viewer and then select Save Log File As. Browse to an appropriate folder, give the file a descriptive name, and click Save.
4. After the Security log file has been saved, you can safely empty the active log by right-clicking Security and selecting Clear all Events (and then Yes when prompted to confirm the action).

Note

Windows XP's Event Viewer also includes both System and Application logs. The System log is where operating system-related errors, warnings, and information events are logged; the Application log is used to store events related to programs installed on your system. Both are valuable sources of troubleshooting information. As a best practice, you should also consult Event Viewer's System and Application logs for potential issues every time you review the contents of your Security log.

Using Windows Security Center

After Windows XP Service Pack 2 (or higher) has been installed you'll find a new applet in the Control Panel named Security Center. Windows Security Center is a new Windows XP tool designed to help keep users informed about the status of different security-related programs and settings, and alert you in cases where a component might be misconfigured, out-of-date, or disabled. Specifically, Windows Security Center is design to keep you informed as to the status of firewall software, the Automatic Updates feature, and your anti-virus program.

When you open the Windows Security Center tool in Control Panel, details on the status of all three items is provided. From a security perspective, the status of each of these items should always be "On." In cases where an item is set to anything other than On, details about the potential dangers of your current setting and recommendations will be provided.

Even if you never open the Security Center applet in Control Panel, this tool still keeps you informed about potential security threats related to your firewall, anti-virus program, and the status of Automatic Updates by displaying warning icons and balloon messages on your taskbar. An example of such a message is shown in Figure 3-8.

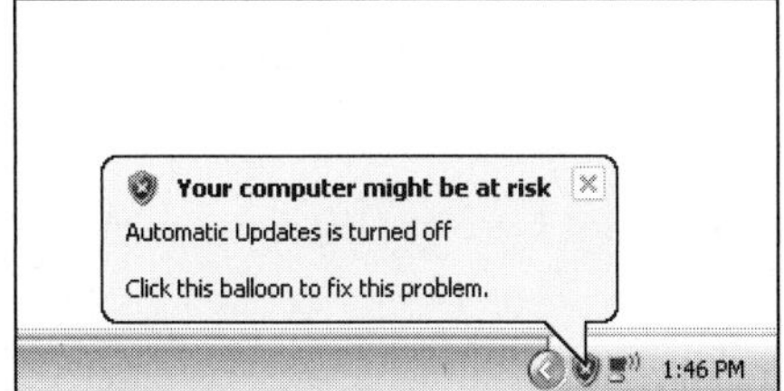

Figure 3-8: Security Center taskbar message displayed when Automatic Updates have been turned off.

Follow these steps to open and review Windows Security Center settings:

1. Click Start → Control Panel → Security Center. The Windows Security Center window opens as shown in Figure 3-9.

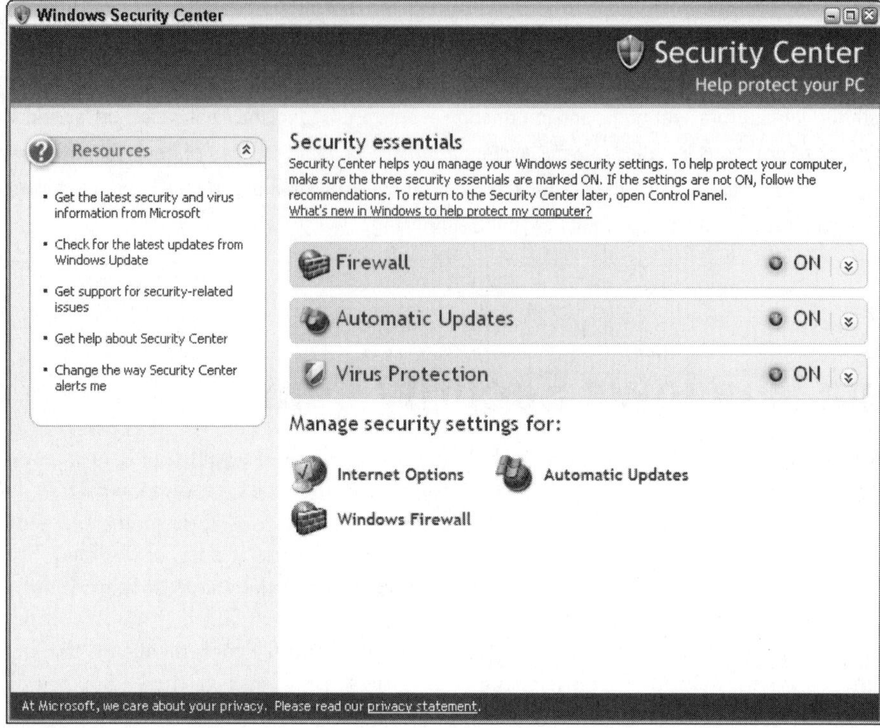

Figure 3-9: The Windows Security Center tool is installed on systems running Service Pack 2 (or higher).

2. Review the status information in the Firewall, Automatic Updates, and Virus Protection sections. If any of these items are not set to On, click the arrows next to the status message to view additional information, as shown in Figure 3-10.

Cross-Reference

You learn more about Windows Security Center and its firewall, anti-virus, and Automatic Updates monitoring features in Chapters 6, 7, and 8.

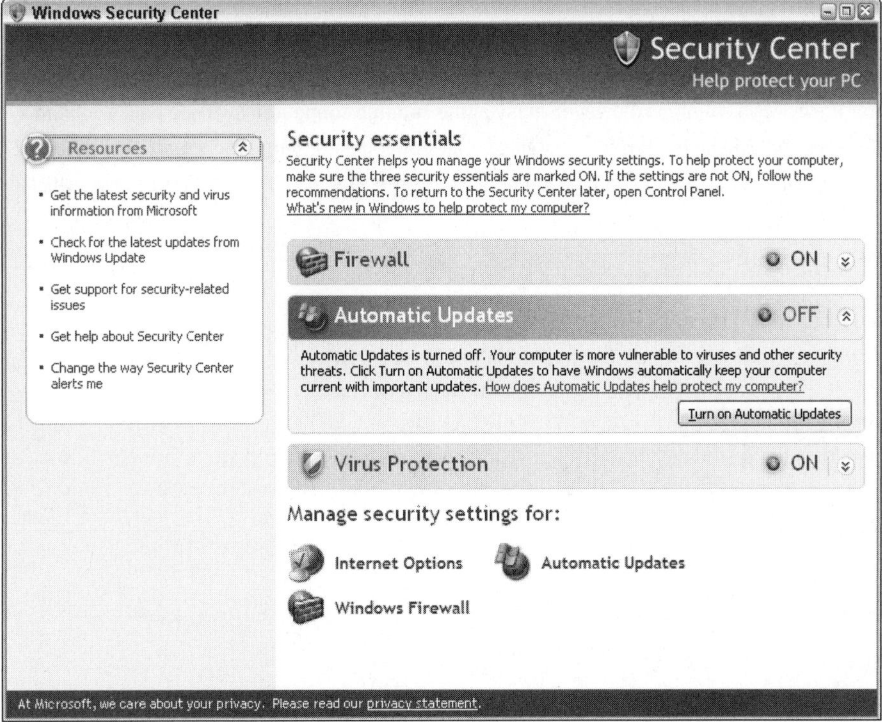

Figure 3-10: Reviewing the status of problem items in Windows Security Center.

Configuring Local Security and Policy Settings

One of the most powerful ways to control the configuration of a Windows XP system is via the configuration of what are known as "policy" settings. In general terms, Windows XP's policy settings allow you to delve beyond the standard configuration options found in areas like Control Panel for the purpose of implementing more advanced or restrictive settings. Some of these configurable settings allow you to control the ways in which Windows XP communicates; others impose limitations on the actions that all users can perform. Ultimately, Windows XP's policy settings offer more power to administrators looking for greater flexibility and control over who uses their system and how.

The ability to configure policy settings via a graphical interface is available on Windows XP Professional systems only, accomplished by using the Local Security Policy and Local Computer Policy MMC snap-ins. In the following sections, you learn more about configuring both Local Security Policy and Local Computer Policy settings on a Windows XP Professional system.

Note

Policy settings cannot be configured on Windows XP Home Edition systems using the Local Security Policy and Local Computer Policy MMC snap-ins; however, many of the settings configured by these policy-related tools can be implemented on Windows XP Home systems by way of editing the Registry directly. For details on implementing policy settings by making changes to the Registry, visit `www.j79zlr.com/gphome.php`.

Local Security Policy

Windows XP Professional allows you to configure a variety of security-related settings via the Local Security Policy MMC. This tool is designed to give you more control over advanced options and settings that aren't typically accessible through Windows XP's "standard" graphical tools. The majority of users generally don't need to delve into these settings to ensure a secure system, but they do offer Windows XP administrators who want a higher level of control over their system a way to exercise it. The Local Security Policy MMC interface is shown in Figure 3-11.

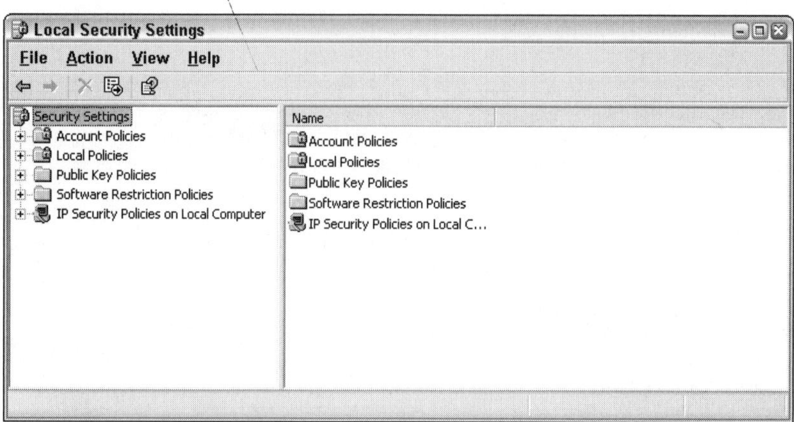

Figure 3-11: The Local Security Policy MMC.

The broad categories of settings that can be configured using the Local Security Policy tool include:

- **Account Policies.** As you learned in Chapter 2, Account Policies allow you to control and configure settings related to user password requirements and account lockout settings. Settings found in the Account Policies section are amongst the more commonly configured on a Windows XP system.

- **Local Policies.** Configurable Local Policies on a Windows XP system include settings related to auditing, user rights assignments, and security options. Auditing settings give administrators greater control over the types of events that are recorded in Windows XP's Security log. User rights assignments allow an administrator to assign advanced capabilities to users and groups, such as the right to back up files and folders. Security options allow you to control things like the status of the Guest account, how users can interact with removable media, and the ways in which a Windows XP system allows network communications to occur.
- **Public Key Policies.** The Public Key Policies section of the Local Security Policy MMC allows you to configure settings related to Windows XP Professional's native file encryption feature, the Encrypting File System (EFS). You learn more about configuring EFS-related settings in Chapter 13.
- **Software Restriction Policies.** The Software Restriction Policies section of the Local Security Policy MMC is designed to allow administrators to define more (or less) restrictive settings that relate to who can use installed software programs on the Windows XP, and to what extent.
- **IPSec Policies.** IPSec is an encrypted communication protocol used to protect communications on a TCP/IP network. The IPSec Policies section allows an administrator to define secure communications rules and parameters that should be used when Windows XP tries to exchange data with other IPSec-aware operating systems.

Follow these steps to review local security policy settings on a Windows XP Professional system:

1. Click Start → Control Panel → Administrative Tools → Local Security Policy.
2. In the Local Security Policy MMC window, expand the local policy categories to view their contents.
3. To view the configurable options for a policy setting, double-click a policy setting to open its Properties window, as shown in Figure 3-12.

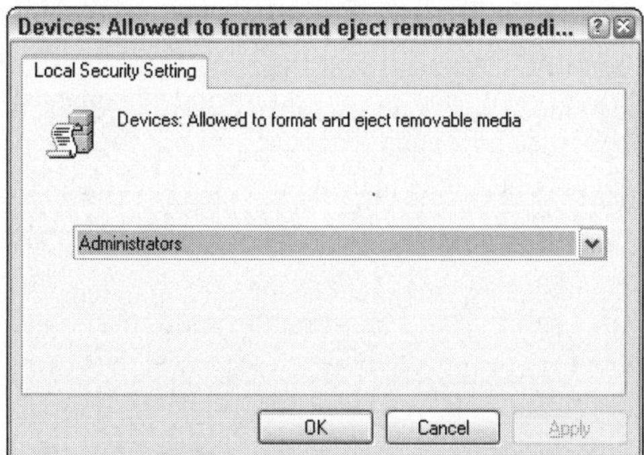

Figure 3-12: Reviewing the properties of a Local Security Policy setting.

Caution

Many of the configurable settings available in the Local Security Policy MMC are advanced and should never be altered unless you're absolutely clear about what the setting does, and the repercussions of making changes to it. As a general rule, very few of Windows XP's policy settings need to be changed as part of ensuring a secure home or small office computer.

Local Computer Policy

If you've ever used a Windows computer in a larger corporate environment, you may already be familiar with the idea behind computer policies. From a user's perspective, computer policies are usually seen as a set of restrictions that have been implemented to stop them from changing the configuration of their PC. For example, in some companies users are not allowed to change their wallpaper picture or settings; in others, they cannot save files or folders to their desktop. In effect, bigger companies use computer policy "restrictions" to maintain a consistent Windows desktop environment. Although sometimes frustrating for users, implementing computer policy settings typically leads to a more stable desktop environment, which in turn leads to lower user training and support costs.

As you might imagine, implementing computer policy settings on a network with a thousand (or many more) Windows XP Professional systems running would be a daunting task if each PC needed to be configured individually. For this reason, networks that are configured into what is known as a Windows "domain" can use capabilities included with Windows 2000 Server or Windows Server 2003 to centrally configure policy settings once and then have them apply to all client systems in the domain, including systems running Windows XP. When configured in this way, the process of deploying computer policy settings is accomplished by what is known as Group Policy.

In effect, the settings that can be configured via the Local Computer Policy MMC on a Windows XP Professional system are the same ones that can be deployed via Group Policy on a larger Windows network. The only real difference is that deploying settings to Windows XP clients via Group Policy requires a network running at least one Windows Server 2003 (or Windows 2000 Server) computer running Microsoft's Active Directory service. For cases where a network doesn't include such a server, the Local Computer Policy tool allows you to configure these same policy settings on a Windows XP Professional system, albeit one computer at a time.

Although there's no denying that Local Computer Policy is a powerful Windows XP feature, you should always be selective about the settings you choose to enable, especially on a home computer. Implement settings that are too restrictive, and users may not be able to perform the basic actions that they need or want to, often leading to frustration or even a sense that your Windows XP system doesn't function correctly. If you do opt to enable any Local Computer Policy settings, try to do so in a way that attempts to strike a balance between usability and reasonable restrictions—your goal should always be to ensure a consistent and well-functioning Windows XP system, not one that is so restrictive as to almost be unusable.

Examples of common User and Computer settings that can be configured using the Local Computer Policy MMC snap-in include user desktop settings (hiding or displaying certain elements), Control Panel settings (allow access to Control Panel or blocking it completely), System settings (allowing users to make certain types of configuration changes), Windows Component settings, and more. If you can think of a useful computer- or user-related configuration setting, chances are that there's a Local Computer Policy setting that can be used to make it happen.

There are literally hundreds of different Local Computer Policy settings that can configured to control how users interact with a Windows XP system — far too many to cover here. The best way to gather more information about Local Computer Policy settings is to browse through the Local Computer Policy MMC interface and review configurable options. If you want to know more about what a particular setting does, right-click it and click Properties. The Explain tab in the Properties of an object provides a detailed overview of the setting and the impact that implementing it has on users of your Windows XP system, as shown in Figure 3-13.

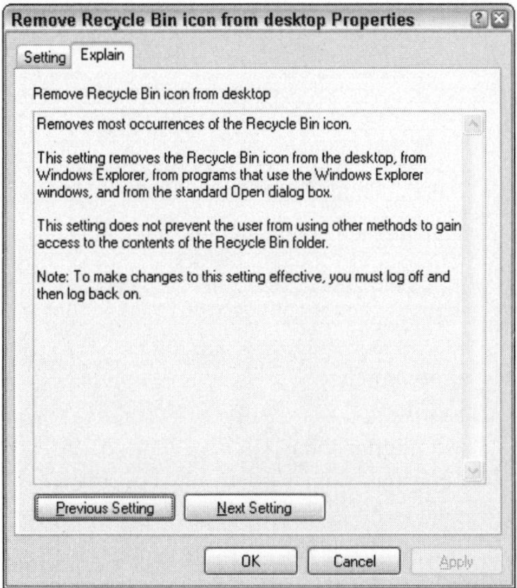

Figure 3-13: Reviewing the Explain tab in the Properties of a Local Computer Policy setting.

Almost all of Windows XP's configurable Local Computer Policy settings support three different configuration options. These include:

- **Not Configured.** This is the default option for most Local Computer Policy settings — when set to this value the policy setting is ignored.
- **Enabled.** When set to Enabled, the function outlined in a Local Computer Policy setting is enforced. If you're ever in doubt about what enabling a given setting actually does, always consult the Explain tab for details.
- **Disabled.** Results vary when a Local Computer Policy setting is configured to the Disabled setting. In some cases, disabling a setting results in the opposite action of the one suggested in the policy's name being taken. In others, the setting is simply disabled. Always consult the Explain tab in the properties of a Local Computer Policy setting prior to disabling it — it's always important to determine exactly what the repercussions of making this change will be.

In addition to the three basic setting outlined in the previous list, many Local Computer Policy settings allow you to configure additional advanced options, which vary from setting to setting. For example, when you set the Offer Remote Assistance policy item to Enabled, additional configuration options are exposed as shown in Figure 3-14.

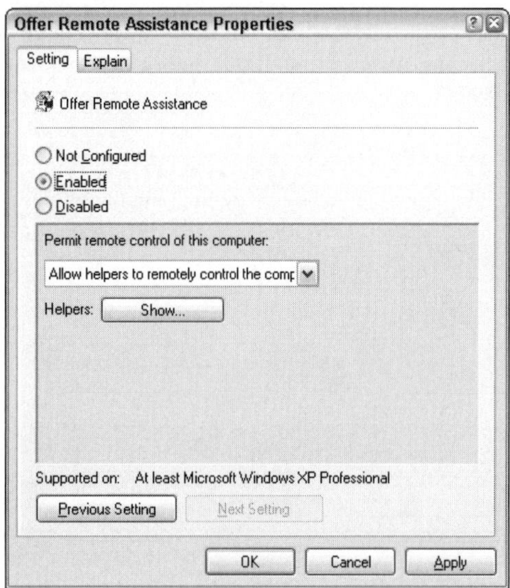

Figure 3-14: Some Local Computer Policy settings include additional configuration options once enabled.

Follow these steps to review and configure group policy settings on a Windows XP Professional system:

1. Click Start → Run. In the Open textbox, type mmc.exe and press Enter. An empty MMC window opens.
2. Click File → Add/Remove Snap-in.
3. At the Add/Remove Snap-in window, click Add.
4. At the Add Standalone Snap-in window, click Group Policy (as shown in Figure 3-15), and click Add.
5. When the Select Group Policy Object window appears, click Finish. Close the Add Standalone Snap-in window and then click OK at the Add/Remove Snap-in window.
6. Expand Local Computer Policy → User Configuration → Administrative Templates → Desktop. A list of user desktop-related configurable policy settings appears, as shown in Figure 3-16. In this case, the State of all settings is Not Configured.

Figure 3-15: Adding the Group Policy snap-in to manage Local Computer Policy settings.

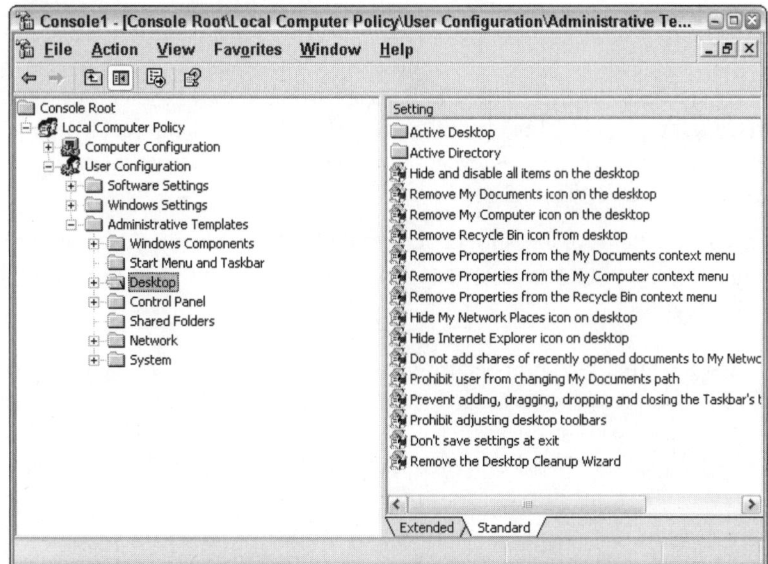

Figure 3-16: Reviewing user desktop configuration settings.

7. Double-click a setting such as Remove Recycle Bin icon from Desktop to open its Properties window, as shown in Figure 3-17.

Figure 3-17: Reviewing the Properties of a Local Computer Policy setting.

8. If you want to enable the setting (which in this case would remove the Recycle Bin icon from all users' desktops), click Enable and then click OK. If you later decide that you want to undo this action and return the Recycle Bin icon to user desktops, change the state of the setting back to Not Configured.
9. If you did enable the Remove Recycle Bin icon from Desktop setting, close the Local Security Policy MMC and return to your desktop. The Recycle Bin icon should no longer be visible on the desktop.

Most of the settings configured via Local Security Policy are implemented immediately; however, there may sometimes be a short time lag between the time that settings are configured and their actual implementation. In some cases, you may need to log off and then back on for user-related settings to take effect or even restart Windows XP for computer-related policy changes to be implemented.

Caution

Use caution when configuring restrictive Local Computer Policy settings on a Windows XP Professional system. The settings that you configure with the Local Computer Policy MMC apply to all users, including Computer administrators. If you configure settings that are too restrictive, you may actually stop all users (including administrators) from being able to undo the changes.

Summary

Windows XP includes a variety of built-in tools and settings that can be used to help improve system security. Keep the following points in mind when using built-in tools and settings to secure your Windows XP system:

- Disable all unnecessary services on your Windows XP system, especially those that represent a possible security risk.
- Use the Processes tab in Task Manager to determine which programs and background processes are running on your Windows XP system. Unknown or unfamiliar processes could be malware or other programs that represent a security risk.
- Review the Security log in Event Viewer regularly to check for potential security issues that might need to be addressed or to gather information on past events.
- Periodically open the Security Center applet in Control Panel to check the status of your firewall, Automatic Updates, and your anti-virus program. Address issues as they're discovered, and keep an eye on Windows XP's taskbar for Security Center warning icons and messages.
- Review Local Security Policy and Local Computer Policy settings on a Windows XP Professional system to determine whether implementing any of these settings will help you to better secure and protect your system. Always exercise caution when implementing these settings, however, because all configured settings impact all users, including Computer administrators.

Part II

Making Surfing Safer

Chapter 4

Securing Your Web Browser

It comes as a surprise to many new users that the Internet isn't limited to the World Wide Web and e-mail facilities alone. Although a great deal of Internet real estate exists beyond these components, it's hard to argue that the Web isn't the "face" of the Internet. In fact, the vast majority of users rely on one particular program — their Web browser — to access every facet of the Internet. From using Web-based e-mail services to browsing Usenet newsgroups via specialized Web sites, there are few corners of the Internet that one cannot reach via a Web browser such as Internet Explorer.

As handy and ubiquitous as the Web browser may be, its popularity has made it an increasingly popular target for hackers, crackers, and other shady organizations in the online world. As the capabilities of Web browsers have grown beyond accessing simple HTML-based Web pages, so too have the risks associated with using browsers as an interface to the Internet. The experiences offered to the Web surfers of today are much more "dynamic" in nature, allowing them to interact with sites in a variety of new and exciting ways. The drivers behind these innovations include technologies such as Java, scripting languages, ActiveX, and the like. Unfortunately, many of the same technologies and features that make surfing the Web a more interesting and dynamic experience for the Web surfers of today are the same ones putting the browsing public at a more serious security and privacy risk than ever before.

And so the time has come where every Internet user — and (arguably) especially those who use Internet Explorer — needs to give serious consideration to the security of their Web browser. From malware threats like spyware and browser hijackings to the privacy risks associated with tracking cookies, there's just no shortage of security and privacy threats that can find their way onto your Windows XP system via your Web browser.

In this chapter you learn more about the need for Web browser security, and how to implement it using the most popular Web browser around — Windows XP's native Internet Explorer (IE). You also learn why many people are looking beyond IE to many "alternative" Web browsers as suitable (and often safer) substitutes in their quest to surf the Web with a higher degree of system security and personal privacy.

The Need for Web Browser Security

Back in the day, there were few risks associated with surfing the Internet — you would fire up your Web browser (probably Netscape Navigator at the time), enter a Web page address, and press Enter. Your browser would request the page from the Web server specified, after which the page and

supporting elements like images and sounds would be sent back for display in your browser window. The whole arrangement was very exciting (at the time), but didn't offer much in the way of an interact experience.

This lack of interactivity on the Web didn't last very long. Programmers and corporations soon realized that what people really wanted was a media-rich and interactive Web experience. Unfortunately, most users' Internet connections were still relatively low at the time — 56.6 kbps dial-up connections were considered to be fast, and connections as slow as 14.4 kbps were not uncommon. The speeds at which users could reliably (and affordably) connect to the Internet seriously limited what Web sites owners were realistically able to offer on their Web sites from a content perspective.

As you are now likely well aware, things on the speed front quickly changed — high-speed technologies such as DSL, cable, wireless, and satellite Internet now make it possible for users to connect to the Internet at speeds often hundreds of times faster than those associated with traditional dial-up. When high-speed and relatively affordable Internet connections reach users' homes, the notion of a vastly superior and interactive Web surfing experience became a reality.

Ultimately, the growth in high-speed Internet connections has brought rise to a whole slew of new and dynamic Web technologies. Many sites use scripting, Java, and ActiveX technologies to allow you to play games via your Web browser. Others allow you to customize the look and feel of sites to match your own personal preferences. Still others allow you to access and interact with your home computer's Windows desktop from a Web browser at a remote location. The future of the Web and the ways in which users will be able to interact with sites (and each other) will only be limited by the programming skills and imaginations of those creating new and dynamic Web sites.

Unfortunately, many of the same technologies that have given rise to the cool and interesting capabilities of the Web of today have also been employed for the forces of evil (so to speak). In fact, in many cases users need to do nothing more than visit a Web site programmed to include malicious code to find their computer infected by threats like Trojan horses, spyware, relentless pop-up advertising windows, and even "cookies" that track their every move on the Internet for (primarily) market research purposes. In effect, the hacking, cracking, and general "bad guy" communities online have taken advantage of the "usability" features of Web browsers to infect and infest computers with a wide variety of objects that present very real risks to the security and privacy of Internet users.

Perhaps the worst thing about browser-based threats is that as a user, you really don't need to do anything more than click on a (seemingly) harmless link or open the wrong Web page to end up with a computer rife with security and privacy threats. Unfortunately, these browser-based threats tend to sneak by not only anti-virus software packages, but also personal firewall programs. With an estimated 80 to 90 percent of all computers infected by some form of malware (aka malicious software), the security and privacy risks to the Web surfers of today are both very real and incredibly common. With that in mind, it's absolutely imperative that you take the steps necessary to configure your browser such that the threats posed by Web-based pests don't put the security of your PC and your own personal privacy at risk.

Securing Internet Explorer

As the native Web browser included with Windows XP (as well as previous Windows versions), it's little surprise that Internet Explorer (IE) is the most popular Web browser in use on the Internet. Where once Netscape Navigator was surfer's browser of choice, IE has firmly established its dominance amongst the Web surfing public — be it for better or worse.

As the most popular Web browser in use, Internet Explorer has also become the prime target for all manner of security-related threats. This is especially true of malware objects that have found their way onto the majority of Windows XP systems by way of Internet Explorer's (historically) lax security settings. With support for all major Web-scripting languages, "interactive" components such as ActiveX controls, and it own Java virtual machine, Internet Explorer has arguably been the perfect vehicle for malware developers looking for a way to infect and infest Windows users' PCs. Effectively, those aiming to compromise the security of Windows systems took Internet Explorer's focus on usability and used it to as a gateway to compromise system security and user privacy.

Thankfully, Microsoft has recently made a newfound commitment to system security and has made a number of improvements to Internet Explorer via new security features and improved default settings included when Windows XP users install Service Pack 2. If you haven't done so already, you should install the latest Windows XP Service Pack, if only to address the security risks associated with running earlier iterations of Internet Explorer.

Cross-Reference

For details on installing the latest security updates and Service Packs on your Windows XP system, see Chapter 7.

To its credit, Internet Explorer is a highly configurable Web browser that includes a number of helpful and effective security-related features and components. These include the capability to do the following:

- Divide Web sites into different Web content zones and apply different security-related settings to each.
- Configure privacy options globally or for individual Web sites.
- The capability to control access to broad categories of Web sites based on their contents.
- Prevent browser pop-up windows and manage add-on components designed to extend the capabilities of Internet Explorer (once SP2 or higher is installed).

Each of these Internet Explorer security and privacy features is explored in more detail in the following sections.

Configuring IE zone security settings

One of the most powerful security features available in Internet Explorer is the ability to categorize Web sites into what are referred to as "Web content zones." Internet Explorer includes four of these zones, three of which can be customized to include the sites you specify. The benefit of this zone-based approach is that different zones can be configured to different levels, applying a set of configurable security settings to all sites that are members of the zone. Ultimately, this allows you to place Web sites with a high potential risk factor into a zone with very restrictive security settings and to place sites you consider safe into zones with more permissive settings.

Internet Explorer's four Web content zones include:

- **Internet.** The Internet zone is the default Web content zone in which all sites not specifically added to other zones are considered to reside. In effect, this makes all Web sites part of the Internet zone unless otherwise configured. The default security level assigned to sites in the Internet zone is Medium.
- **Local intranet.** The Intranet zone is a special zone used to designate all Web sites that reside on your private network. For example, if you have a Web server running on a computer on your home network, it would be considered part of the Local intranet Web content zone. The default security level assigned to sites in the Local intranet zone is Medium-low.
- **Trusted sites.** The Trusted sites zone is a manually configured list of Web sites and domains that you explicitly trust. For example, you might add your bank's Web site address to this list, as well as others like the address of your Webmail provider, preferred online news sources, and other trusted sites you visit frequently. The default security level assigned to the Trusted sites zone is Low.
- **Restricted sites.** The Restricted sites zone is a manually configured list of Web sites and domains that you do not trust. All less-secure browsing features are disabled when you visit a site on this list. The default security level assigned to the Restricted sites list is High.

Internet Explorer allows you to assign one of four different pre-configured security levels for any of its Web content zones or define your own custom settings. The four pre-configured security levels that can be assigned to Web content zones include:

- **Low.** This is the least secure level that can be configured for a Web zone but also the most functional. Minimal safeguards and warning prompts are provided at this level, and most types of content from sites are downloaded and run without issue. This level should never be assigned to the Internet zone.
- **Medium-low.** This security zone level is effectively the same as the medium level, but with fewer prompts. Most types of content are downloaded and run without issue, although unsigned ActiveX controls are not downloaded. This level is most appropriate for the Local intranet zone.
- **Medium.** This security zone level tries to strike a reasonable balance between browsing functionality and security. This level prompts the user before potentially unsafe types of content are downloaded, and never downloads unsigned ActiveX controls. This setting is most appropriate for the Internet zone.
- **High.** This security zone level is the most restrictive from a security standpoint, but also the least functional. All less secure features are disabled at this level in a bid to stop dangerous content from infecting or impacting your system. This setting is most appropriate for the Restricted sites zone.

Although the pre-configured security level settings address typically meets the needs of most users, custom level settings can also be assigned to any zone. To define custom level settings for a zone, select the zone's icon and then click the Custom Level button. This opens the Security Settings window, as shown in Figure 4-1.

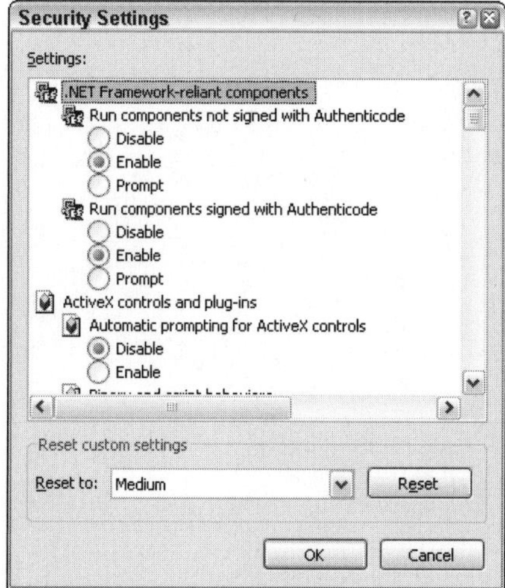

Figure 4-1: Configuring custom security settings.

When you configure custom settings for a Web content zone, the ability to choose a new security level via the slider tool is disabled; however, you can return to any site's default settings (and regain access to the security level slider) at any time by selecting the zone in question and clicking the Default Level button.

As a general rule, you should never need to change the security level settings associated with a given Web content zone after Windows XP Service Pack 2 (or higher) has been installed. Instead of changing a zone's security level, add specific Web sites to a suitable Web content zone. For example, add a site that you trust (such as google.com, for example) to your Trusted sites list, and add potentially dangerous sites (such as coolWebsearch.com) to your Restricted sites list. These sites then inherit the security settings applied to its "parent" zone.

Follow these steps to add a Web site to your Trusted sites list:

1. Click Start → Internet Explorer → Tools → Internet Options → Security.
2. On the Security tab (as shown in Figure 4-2), click Trusted Sites and then click the Sites button.
3. In the Trusted sites window, enter the address of the trusted Web site in the Add this Web site to the zone textbox, as shown in Figure 4-3. Click Add.
4. Add additional sites to the Trusted sites zone as necessary and then click OK once complete.

Figure 4-2: Internet Explorer's Security tab.

Figure 4-3: Adding a Web site to the Trusted sites Web content zone.

Cross-Reference

Certain anti-malware programs, such as Microsoft AntiSpyware, prompt you any time that a new site is added to your trusted sites list for security purposes. You learn more about Microsoft AntiSpyware in Chapter 9.

Web sites can be added to your Restricted sites list in exactly the same manner others are added to the Trusted Sites zone; however, the process of individually adding each and every site that might be considered dangerous would be a huge undertaking. Thankfully, a utility named IE-SPYAD2 can do all of the dirty work for you. IE-SPYAD2 is a tool that adds a comprehensive list of Web sites and domain names associated with online advertisers, marketers, and malware developers to IE's Restricted sites list. This tool is free, and the list is updated with new site and domain details on a regular basis.

Note

IE-SPYAD2 is a version of the tool that adds entries to Internet Explorer's Restricted sites list for all users of the same computer. The IE-SPYAD tool can be used to add entries for the current user only if so desired.

Follow these steps to add a comprehensive list of potentially problematic Web sites to Internet Explorer's Restricted sites list by installing IE-SPYAD2:

1. Click Start → Internet Explorer, or open your preferred Web browser. Browse to `netfiles.uiuc.edu/ehowes/www/resource.htm`.
2. Scroll down to the Download section of the page and click the link to download ie-spyad.exe. Save the file to an appropriate folder location when prompted.
3. Double-click the ie-spyad2.exe file. This is a self-extracting ZIP archive that extracts the program's file to a new folder named C:\ie-spyad2. Extract the files to this location.
4. Click Start → My Computer and browse to the C:\ie-spyad2 folder. To add the list of sites to Internet Explorer's Restricted sites list, double-click the install.bat file. This opens the IE-SPYAD2 Install/Uninstall Utility window, as shown in Figure 4-4. Press the 2 key to install IE-SPYAD2 and then press the 1 key to confirm. After the process is complete, the SUCCESS message appears.
5. To confirm that IE-SPYAD2 added sites to Internet Explorer's Restricted sites list, click Start → Internet Explorer → Tools → Internet Options → Security → Restricted sites → Sites. The Web sites list in the Restricted sites window should now list hundreds of Web site addresses and domain names, as shown in Figure 4-5. In some cases, this list may not appear to be populated due to the way in which Internet Explorer displays Restricted sites when system-wide changes are implemented. Even when sites added using IE-SPYAD2 are not displayed, users are still blocked from accessing them. To remedy this issue, you can install IE-SPYAD for each individual Windows XP user instead of using IE-SPYAD2.

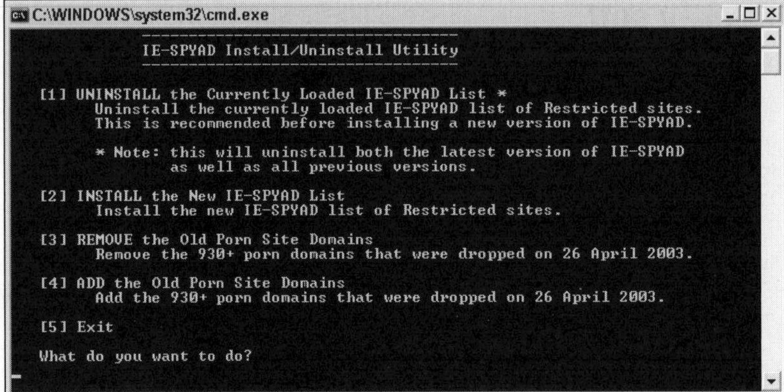

Figure 4-4: Installing IE-SPYAD2 to add sites to Internet Explorer's Restricted sites Web content zone.

Figure 4-5: Reviewing the contents of Internet Explorer's Restricted sites list after installing IE-SPYAD2.

Cross-Reference

Protecting your Windows XP system from the dangers associated with malware objects is not a matter of configuring Web browser security settings alone. Every Windows XP system should also have a suitable anti-malware program installed to remove malware threats as they're discovered, or better still prevent them for finding their way onto your PC in their first place. You learn more about the techniques and programs used to fight malware threats in Chapter 9.

Configuring IE privacy settings

The ability to completely block access to potentially dangerous Web sites by adding them to the Restricted sites Web content zone is great and certainly helps to improve Internet Explorer (and by extension Windows XP) security when used correctly; however, you also need to give some serious thought to your personal privacy when surfing the Web — specifically about whether the sites your visit should be able to identify you, and the types of information that those sites should be allowed to collect. A banner ad displayed on a Web page may seem harmless enough, but it's not uncommon for online advertisers to place a special file (known as a "cookie") on your computer to track the sites you visit for marketing and/or research purposes.

Internet Explorer includes three main features to help improve your personal privacy online. These include:

- Configurable privacy settings that allow you to control how your computer deals with cookies. Cookies are files created by Web sites (and stored on your computer) that often contain information about your personalization preferences for Web sites, but can also include username and/or e-mail address information. It's important to recognize that the vast majority of cookies are not malicious — they're often required to visit secure sites such as those associated with online banking, for example.
- Privacy alert messages that appear when you attempt to access a site that doesn't meet the privacy criteria you've configured.
- The ability to view a Web site's P3P privacy policy. Many Web sites now include P3P documents that outline exactly how they use any information that they collect when you access the site, or details stored in their cookies.

Follow these steps to configure Internet zone privacy setting in Internet Explorer:

1. Click Start → Internet Explorer → Tools → Internet Options → Privacy.
2. The Privacy tab displays details of the current security level, as shown in Figure 4-6. Use the slider to configure a higher security level according to your preferences. As a general rule, the Internet zone's privacy settings should be set no lower than Medium.
3. If you don't feel that any of the Privacy tab's pre-defined settings meet your needs, you can also click the Advanced button to define custom settings as shown in Figure 4-7.

Note

Understanding how Internet Explorer's privacy settings evaluate Web sites before allowing or denying cookies, most of the major online advertising and marketing entities have designed sites such that their cookies will be allowed even if you configure Internet Explorer's privacy option to the High setting. If you absolutely want to ensure that your computer does not receive cookies from a certain Web site or online advertiser, block its address on the Per Site Privacy Actions screen accessible via the Sites button on the Privacy tab.

Figure 4-6: Internet Explorer's Privacy tab.

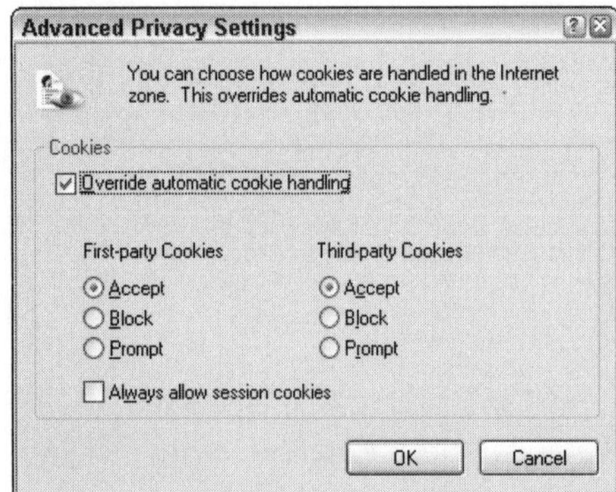

Figure 4-7: Configuring Advanced Privacy settings.

Follow these steps to allow or deny cookies from a particular Web site:

1. Click Start→Internet Explorer→Tools→Internet Options→Privacy.
2. Click the Sites button. At the Per Site Privacy Actions screen, enter the Web site address or domain name from which you want to allow or deny cookies in the Address or Web site textbox.
3. With the Web site address or domain name entered, press the Block or Allow button. This adds the site to your Managed Web sites list, as shown in Figure 4-8. Click OK when all allowed or blocked sites have been added.

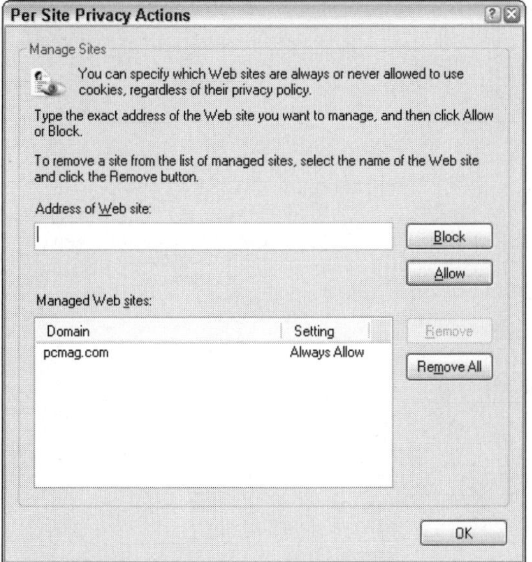

Figure 4-8: Blocking cookies from a Web site.

Caution

If you configure Internet Explorer's privacy settings to block all cookies, you may not be able to access secure Web sites that require your computer to accept cookies to function. To block most cookies, configure your Web browser to use the "High" privacy setting and then click the Advanced button to add individual Web sites or domains for which cookies should always be allowed, such as your online banking Web site.

Follow these steps to view a Web site's privacy policy settings:

1. Click Start → Internet Explorer. Browse to a Web site of your choice. The Web site visited in this example is the P3P Public Overview Web page at www.w3.org/P3P/.
2. Click View → Privacy Report. This opens the Privacy Report window, as shown in Figure 4-9.
3. Click the address of the Web site in this list and then click Summary to view the Privacy Summary document for the site, as shown in Figure 4-10. This summary provides key details on how the site collects and users information about its visitors.

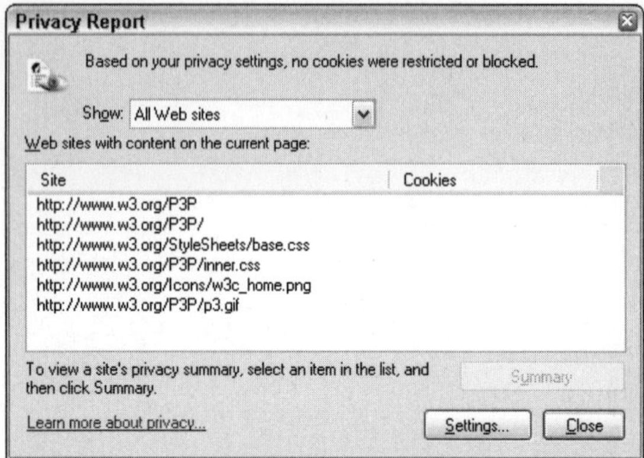

Figure 4-9: Internet Explorer's Privacy Report window.

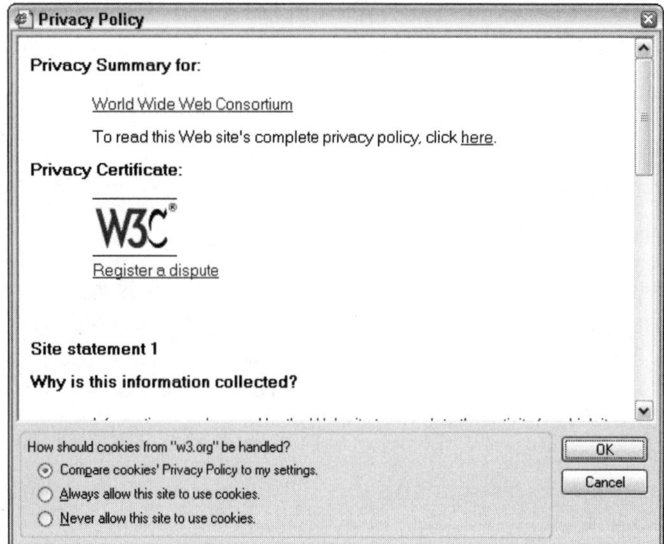

Figure 4-10: Reviewing a Web site's Privacy Summary.

Note

Although it would be great if every Web site published Privacy Policy information, the vast majority of sites still do not — in other words, it's not unusual to visit a Web site with Internet Explorer and then receive a "Could not find a privacy policy for" message when you select the View → Privacy Report menu option. For more details about Privacy Reports and the P3P project, visit `www.w3.org/P3P/`.

Managing access to Web content

As great a resource as the Web is, it certainly contains no shortage of potentially offensive content. From sites that include inappropriate language and violent content to those that contain materials of a sexually explicit nature, even a basic Web search can lead you to pages that many people would find inappropriate.

To help address this issue and give you more control over the types of Web sites that users of your Windows XP system can access, Internet Explorer includes Content Advisor settings. These settings (which are effectively disabled by default) allow you to control the types of content that user can gain access to according to defined levels. For example, you could configure Content Advisor settings to allow users to access Web sites that contain "mild" expletives, while denying them access to sites containing graphic depictions of sex, violence, or nudity.

To control access to potentially offensive Web sites, Internet Explorer's Content Advisor feature relies on what are known as content "ratings." By default, Internet Explorer includes the built-in ratings capability supplies by the Internet Content Rating Association (ICRA, formerly known as RSACi); however, ratings from other Internet rating systems can also be installed to better meet your specific content filtering needs.

Note

A great example of an alternate rating system is the one provided by SafeSurf, a rating system design for (and by) parents to help them control how their children can access the Internet. For more details on the SafeSurf rating system and enabling it with Internet Explorer, visit `www.safesurf.com`.

Beyond simply filtering out potentially offensive content, Internet Explorer's Content Advisor settings also allows you to define lists of approved sites (ones that will never be subject to filtering settings), and protect settings with a supervisor password to ensure that other users cannot make changes to the filtering settings that you've configured.

Follow these steps to configure Content Advisor settings in Internet Explorer:

1. Click Start → Internet Explorer → Tools → Internet Options → Content.
2. On the Content tab's Content Advisor section, click Enable.
3. On the Ratings tab (shown in Figure 4-11), click one of the category listings (such as Language) and then adjust the slider to specify the types of content in that category that users should be allowed to see.
4. Click the Approved Sites tab as shown in Figure 4-12. If you add a site's address in the Allow this Web site textbox and click Always or Never, the setting you choose applies to the site, regardless of the settings configured on the Ratings tab.

Figure 4-11: Configuring Content Advisor Ratings in Internet Explorer.

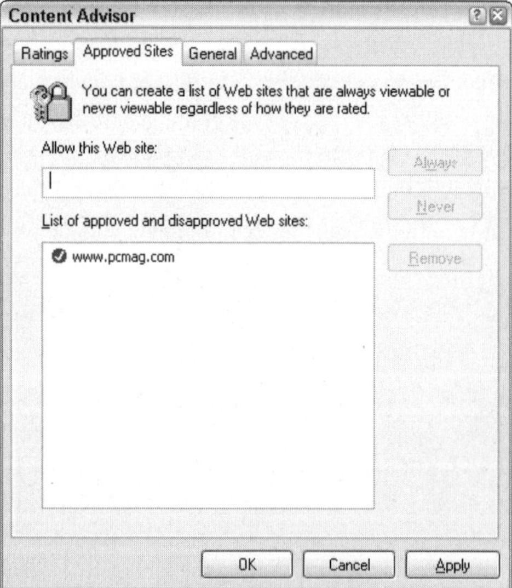

Figure 4-12: Configuring Approved Site setting in Internet Explorer.

5. Click the General tab as shown in Figure 4-13. Configure settings in the User options section according to your preferences and then click the Create password button in the Supervisor section to configure a password that needs to be entered when you want to make changes to Content Advisor settings or allow users to access a restricted Web site.

Figure 4-13: Configuring general Content Advisor settings.

Cross-Reference

Internet Explorer's Content Advisor settings can help you regulate what users can access on the Web, but these capabilities are usually no match for dedicated content filtering (aka parental control) programs. You learn more about content filtering programs in Chapter 5.

Service Pack 2 Internet Explorer security enhancements

One of the easiest ways to improve the security of Internet Explorer is to install Windows XP Service Pack 2 (SP2). SP2 adds a number of new security-related features and capabilities to Internet Explorer, making it less susceptible to threats such as malware and providing you with more control over how your browser will respond when the sites you visit attempt to download elements like files or ActiveX controls.

Many of the security enhancements added to Internet Explorer by SP2 are behind-the-scenes in nature and require little in the way of user interaction; however, three new features are more visible and configurable, and you should be familiar with them:

- The ability to manage Internet Explorer add-ons
- A new integrated pop-up window blocker
- The new information bar that informs you when a site tries to download a file, install an ActiveX control, or display a pop-up window on your PC

Each of these features is explored in more detail in the following sections.

MANAGING BROWSER ADD-ONS

One of the most powerful features of Internet Explorer is that users have the ability to extend and enhance its capabilities by installing any of hundreds of different third-party browser add-ons. For example, if you install Adobe's Acrobat Reader software, its browser add-on component makes it possible to open and view PDF files from within the Internet Explorer browser window. Other add-ons are designed to add useful features to your browser by way of installing new toolbars. A great example of such an add-on is the Google toolbar, which provides the ability to perform Internet searches without the need to visit the Google Web site first and allows you to highlight the term you've searched for in a resulting page, making it easier to find the information for which you're looking.

Although there's no denying that the ability to add a wide range of new features and capabilities to Internet Explorer is a very powerful option, not all browser add-ons are designed to be helpful. In fact, many Internet Explorer add-ons have more malicious intents in mind such as monitoring your Web surfing activities, collecting personal information about you, or even displaying annoying pop-up ads. In some cases, these add-ons quietly hide in the background and go about their business in an almost completely transparent manner. In others, they add their own dedicated toolbar to your Internet Explorer window, and appear as though they allow you to perform some useful function (like performing and saving Web searches).

It can be difficult to determine whether a browser add-on is legitimately useful or malicious in nature, and sometimes even tougher to figure out which add-ons are actually installed and running on your system. The appearance of a new toolbar (that you didn't purposely install) in Internet Explorer is usually a sign that malware or some other pest has found its way onto your PC. Thankfully, the Manage Add-ons feature added to Internet Explorer after SP2 is installed can help you to determine which add-ons are present on your system, while allowing you to selectively enabled, disable, or even update individual items.

To view the Internet Explorer add-ons installed on your system, click Tools→Manage Add-ons. The Manage Add-on window (as shown in Figure 4-14) displays a list of all browser add-ons that have been installed, displaying information about the add-on's name, publisher, status, and file details.

Some add-ons are fairly easy to recognize, such as the Shockwave Flash Object — if this is present in your browser, you almost certainly installed the Macromedia Flash plug-in to be able to view Flash-based Web sites. The origin or purpose of other objects may be more difficult to determine, especially in cases where a long number such as {9819CC0E-9669-4D01-9CD7-2C66DA43AC6C} (a number known as a CSLID), is shown as the add-on name. To enable or disable an add-on, simply click its name and select the appropriate option from the Settings section of the Manage Add-ons window, as shown in Figure 4-15. As a general rule, you should disable any add-on that you don't recognize or feel completely comfortable with until you can gather more information about any potential threats that it may pose. If you find that you've disabled a legitimate tool that you want or need to use, you can always re-enable it from the Manage Add-ons window as a later time.

A great resource to help you determine whether an Internet Explorer add-on is legitimate is the CLSID / BHO List / Toolbar Master List available at the CastleCops Web site at `castlecops.com/CLSID.html`. You can use this site to search for browser add-ons by name or CSLID number. When the name or CLSID is found, this site displays details about the add-on, including whether it's a legitimate tool or one that represents a security/privacy threat to your PC (as if often the case with add-on malware objects).

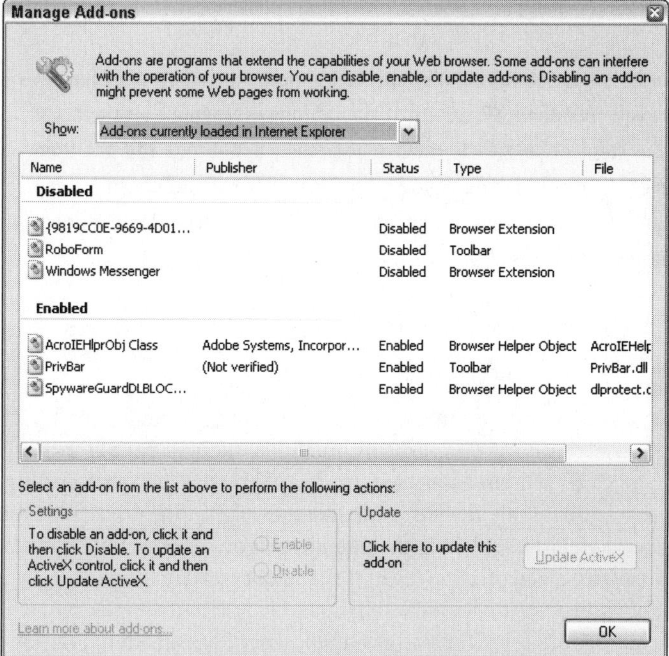

Figure 4-14: Internet Explorer's Manage Add-ons window.

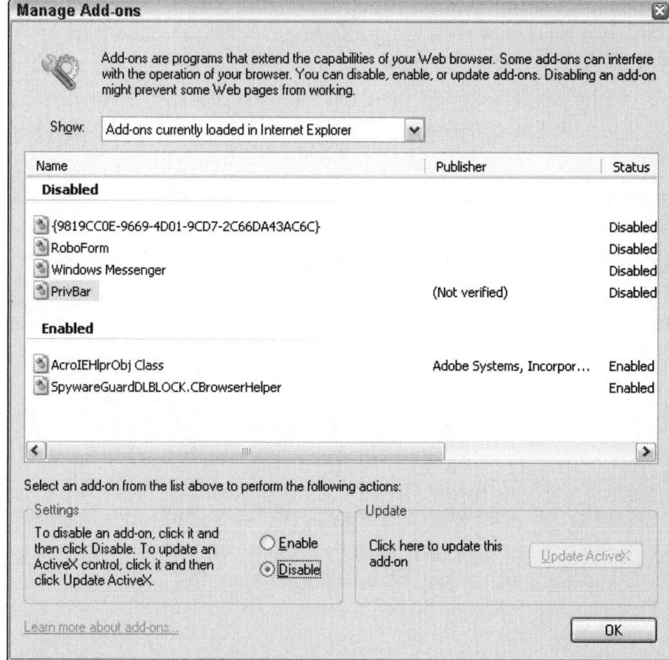

Figure 4-15: Disabling a browser add-on.

Cross-Reference

Internet Explorer's capability to manage add-ons is helpful, but it's important to note that simply disabling an add-on doesn't completely remove it from your Windows XP system. It may no longer present a viable threat while disabled, but you should still take the steps necessary to remove potentially dangerous add-ons from your computer by uninstalling them complete (using Add or Remove Programs in Control Panel) or employing the services of an anti-spyware program. You learn more about dealing with malware-related threats (including malicious Internet Explorer add-ons) in Chapter 9.

BLOCKING POP-UP WINDOWS

Internet marketers and advertisers are always dreaming up new ways to gain exposure for their various products and services on the Internet. Although advertising methods such as banner ads are now widely accepted (and basically expected) as a necessary evil on free Web sites, ads that pop-up in their own smaller browser windows are still largely reviled. In some cases, these pop-up ads are no more than an annoyance, easily dismissed by simply closing the offending browser window. In other cases, however, the onslaught of pop-up ads is relentless — even if you close one such window, two more may appear in its place.

The pop-up windows that close "cleanly" are a legitimate (although generally considered annoying and intrusive) form on online advertising, and can be easily controlled. If you install Windows XP Service Pack 2, for example, Internet Explorer can be configured to block all pop-up windows from opening or to allow pop-ups from certain Web sites only. A number of third-party Internet Explorer add-ons also include pop-up blocking capabilities, such as the Google and Yahoo! toolbars. The pop-up blocker you choose to use is largely a matter of personal preference — for the most part, they all perform the same basic function. If you do have SP2 installed, you can enable the pop-up blocker in Internet Explorer by clicking Tools → Pop-up Blocker → Turn On Pop-up Blocker. After turned on, you can head to Tools → Pop-up Blocker → Pop-up Blocker Settings to configure pop-up blocker settings, as shown in Figure 4-16.

A pop-up blocker may put an end to the annoyance that is pop-up advertising, but it's important to recognize that this capability offers little in the way of any security-related functionality. For example, if your Windows XP system is infected by malware designed to display pop-up windows as part of its programming, simply blocking the pop-up doesn't mean that your computer is any more safe or secure. In fact, chances are good that the malware component (now sans pop-ups) is still doing its thing silently in the background while continuing to represent a security and privacy threat to you and your PC.

Although there's no denying that pop-up blockers are a helpful solution to an annoying problem, always keep in mind that these tools are designed to stop an annoying behaviour, not remove or prevent security threats from your PC. Similar to sweeping dirt from a floor under a rug, don't rely on a pop-up blocker to "solve" what may actually be the signs of a bigger problem such as a spyware infection. As annoying as they may be, a relentless onslaught of browser pop-up windows is one of the best clues that something more dark and dangerous may be lurking on your PC.

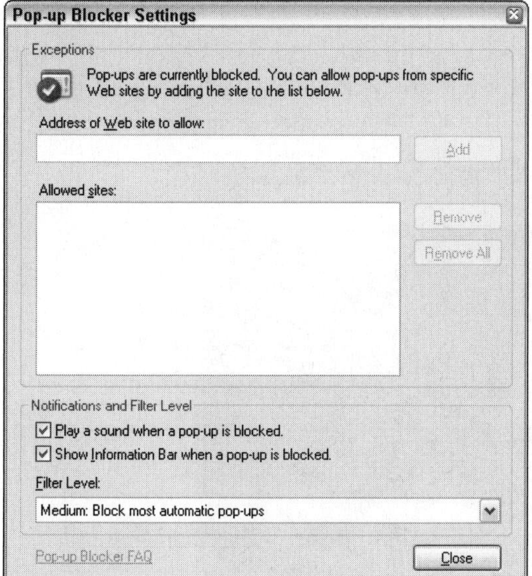

Figure 4-16: Configuring Internet Explorer's Pop-up Blocker settings.

THE INFORMATION BAR

Installing SP2 also adds a new feature to Internet Explorer that is similar to one originally introduced in Microsoft Outlook. The Information Bar is a visual feature that appears just below Internet Explorer's Address bar for the purpose of displaying information about downloads, blocked pop-up windows, potential security risks, and more. For example, if you have turned on Internet Explorer's pop-up blocker and a site attempts to launch a pop-up window, the Information Bar appears and displays a message alerting you to the fact that a pop-up was blocked, as shown in Figure 4-17.

The Information Bar is designed to keep you informed about potential risks encountered while surfing the Web with Internet Explorer. Whenever this bar appears, you can click the message it contains to display a shortcut menu with additional options, such as allowing the stated action or configuring related settings. An example of this shortcut menu is shown in Figure 4-18.

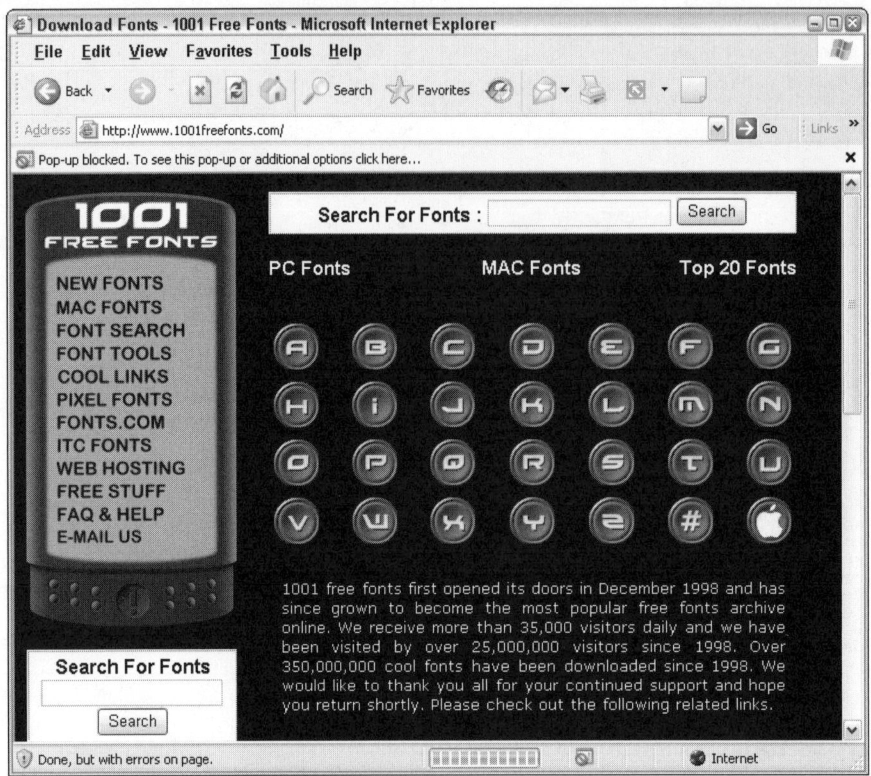

Figure 4-17: Internet Explorer's Information bar.

Ultimately, the Internet Explorer's new Information Bar feature helps you keep informed about potential security risks to your PC as you browse the Web. It's important to note, however, that the Information Bar is just that — a feature that provides you with information about potential risks but one that also leaves you in control of the actions taken as a result of the details provided. The Information Bar does not stop you from downloading a potentially dangerous file or ActiveX control if you explicitly tell it to allow the action — in other words, keep an eye on the details that the Information Bar provides, read the messages you encounter carefully, and make an informed decision on how you want to proceed.

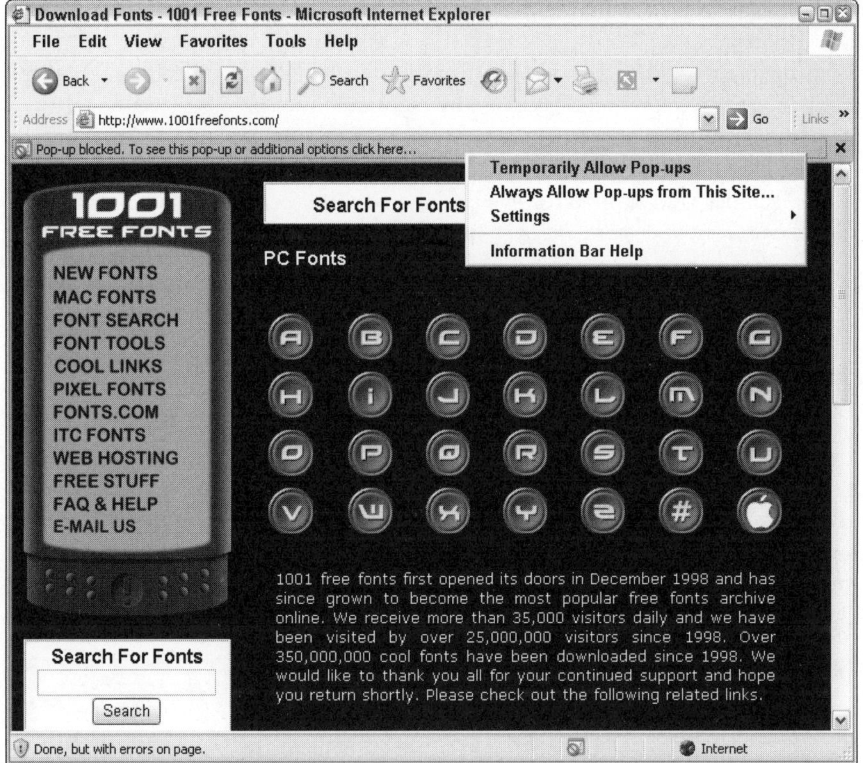

Figure 4-18: An example of the shortcut menu that appears when you click Internet Explorer's Information Bar.

Using "Alternative" Web Browsers

Prior to the release of Windows XP Service Pack 2, a number of security vulnerabilities led security and media organizations to recommend that users stop using Internet Explorer and switch to a "safer" Web browser. There's no denying that many of the more recent browser-related exploits specifically targeted Internet Explorer (especially as a result of its scripting-, Java-, and ActiveX-related capabilities), but there is no rock-solid guarantee that other Web browsers are not being targeted by malware developers, or that they won't be in the future.

Regardless, increasing numbers of users are making the switch to "alternative" Web browsers every day. Internet Explorer was the obvious choice for most users (as it is already included with Windows XP); however, a number of third-party Web browsers exist. Users who make the switch to these browsers typically sacrifice little in the way of browser functionality, and are often zealous in supporting them — as an alternative to what they perceive as the "dangers" of Internet Explorer, regardless of how safe (or unsafe) it may actually be when properly secured.

Some of the most popular "alternative" Web browser programs include:

- **Firefox.** This open-source Web browser has firmly entrenched itself as a viable alternative to Microsoft's Internet Explorer and has a rapidly expanding user base (see Figure 4-19). Some of this browser's key features include "tabbed" browsing (where a single browser window can be used top open multiple Web pages, each on their own tab), integrated Google search facilities, and support for live bookmarks and RSS feeds. Firefox is available as a free download from `www.mozilla.org/products/firefox/`.
- **Netscape.** Once the undisputed king of Web browsers, Netscape's popularity waned as Internet Explorer's feature set advanced and surpassed it year ago. The latest versions of Netscape have vastly improved, and users are once again returning to it as an alternative to Internet Explorer. You can download the latest version of the Netscape Web browser from www.netscape.com.
- **Opera.** Opera is another popular alternative browser that includes features such as tabbed browsing, integrated search and password management tools, and advanced customization features. Billed as "The Fastest Web Browser on Earth," an ad-supported version of Opera can be downloaded from www.opera.com. The ad-free version is available for purchase on the site for just under $40.

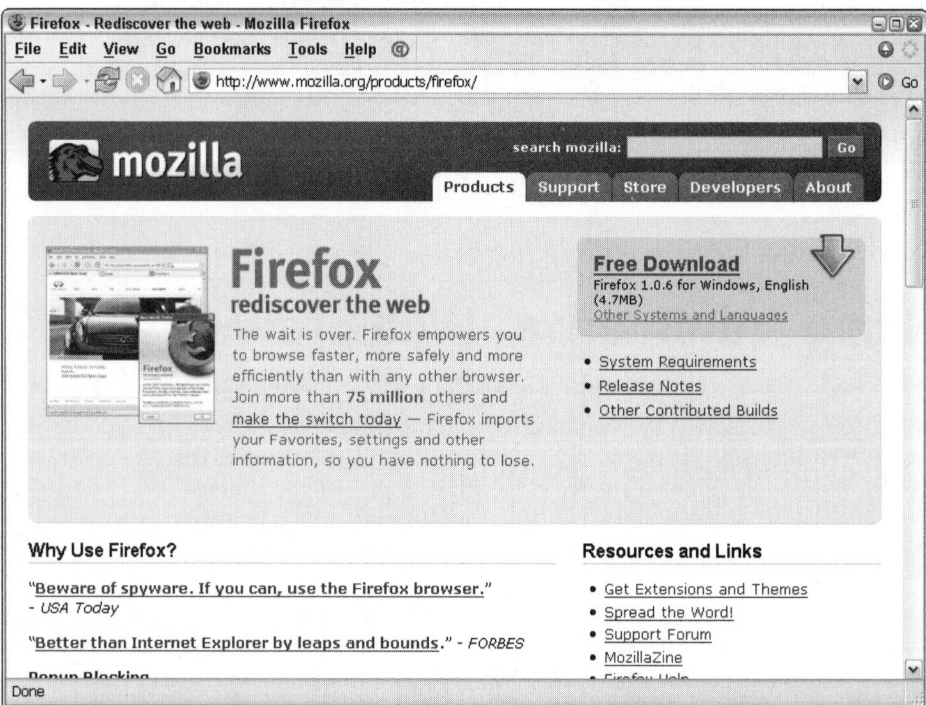

Figure 4-19: The Firefox Web browser is an increasingly popular alternative to Internet Explorer.

Regardless of whether you intend to switch from Internet Explorer to an alternative browser permanently, it's well worth your time to download at least one of these programs to explore them further. Using a different Web browser does entail a slight adjustment period, but some of their advanced features and capabilities make them worth taking for a test drive.

Caution

No program or Web browser will ever offer complete or absolute security. Internet Explorer certainly receives it fair share of bad press, but vulnerabilities have been discovered in other Web browser programs as well. To review both old and new security issues discovered in Internet Explorer and competing products in more detail, visit the Secunia Advisories Web site at `secunia.com/advisories/`.

Summary

Web browsers such as Internet Explorer are amongst the most popular and oft-used tools on any Windows XP system. Unfortunately, a number of security and privacy threats can impact a Windows XP system without proper browser security settings configured.

Keep the following points in mind when it comes to securing your Web browser:

- If you haven't done so already, install Windows XP Service Pack 2 to take advantage of new (and more restrictive) Internet Explorer security settings.
- Add Web sites to Web content zones to define the security parameters that should apply to sites you visit frequently.
- When configuring Web content zone settings, never configure lower settings than those recommended by Internet Explorer. More restrictive settings are always more secure, but may impact browsing functions.
- Install a tool such as IE-SPYAD2 to add hundreds of Web sites known to be dangerous to Internet Explorer's Restricted sites Web content zone.
- Configure appropriate Internet Explorer privacy settings to control the amount of information about your browsing habits that will be shared with online marketers, advertisers, and Web site owners.
- Explore Internet Explorer's Content Advisor settings as a method of controlling the types of content that you and other users can view on the Web.
- Disable any unknown or suspicious looking browser add-ons immediately — these are often malware programs or components.

- Use Internet Explorer's built-in Pop-up Blocker to stop advertising pop-up windows from appearing. Understand, however, that blocking pop-ups does nothing to address underlying security risks that may exist, such as malware infections.
- Consider using an alternative Web browser such as Firefox or Netscape if you're concerned abut the security and privacy risks associated with Internet Explorer. Although there are no guarantees that other Web browsers are more secure, you may find that an alternative browser better meets your Web surfing (and security) needs.

Chapter 5

Restricting Access to the Internet

The Internet has revolutionized the way in which we obtain information. Once upon a time, learning about the finer points of perennial gardening or the architecture of ancient Greece almost certainly meant taking a trip to the local library and digging through card catalogues in a quest to find books on the subject. Today, you can simply fire up your Web browser, perform a keyword search, and gain access to thousands of pages of information on just about any subject imaginable. If information is power, the Internet certainly flexes more than its fair share of muscle.

As great a resource as it may well be, the Internet also has a large and dangerous dark side. There are literally millions of Web pages devoted to pornography. Tens of thousands of computers are connected for the purpose of swapping pirated software, music, and videos. Scores of Web sites are dedicated to spreading messages of hate and intolerance, and even promoting violence. It's literally the best and worst of society mixed together in a never-ending maze of information, delivered directly to your desktop. That's the same desktop that your children may be using to chat with a friend, or to research a subject to complete their homework.

You would be hard-pressed to find a teenager who hasn't used the Internet, and many kids are now hopping online at ages as young as six. It sounds scary, but the vast majority of children are accessing the Internet without direct supervision and with no real restrictions or controls in place. This not only leaves them exposed to a wide variety of sensitive information, but also makes it easily accessible. Where the top shelf of the magazine rack at your local variety store may be just out of reach, gaining access to even more explicit content on the Internet is never more than a click away.

Unfortunately, the dangers of the Internet don't begin and end with shady content. There are some very questionable people online as well, with hundreds of reported cases of adults hanging out in Internet chat rooms attempting to "befriend" young users. These adults typically pose as minors themselves, attempting to engage children in explicit conversations or arrange real-life meetings. Ultimately, the Internet has the ability to put children in harm's way on a number of fronts.

Thankfully, as is not lost. The Internet can be a safe and secure resource with the right approach. Technology can provide part of the solution, but it does not offer a complete answer — ensuring that they use the Internet safely also means educating your children about potential dangers, and giving thought to how you monitor their online activities. In this chapter, you learn about some of the key dangers that children face online, and methods that can be used to help mitigate these risk. This includes some practical tips for parents of children venturing online, an explanation of how content filtering software can help keep your Windows XP system "clean," and a look at why restricting access to the Internet isn't a solution for just kids anymore.

Keeping Children Safe Online

In a perfect world, the Internet would automatically shield children from contact with questionable content and dangerous people. Unfortunately, nobody exercises complete control over the online world in any centralized manner. What is considered illegal in one country may not even be considered an issue in another. Although a myriad of laws and regulations exist for the purpose of enforcing the "rules" in different jurisdictions, the Internet is not bound by geography. If a certain type of content is disallowed on Internet servers located in the United States, the owner can easily make the switch to a server in another country with more relaxed laws. To the Internet user, the physical location of a particular Web site really doesn't make a difference — it's just another site, accessed by clicking yet another link.

Ultimately, what this means is that you cannot rely on anyone else — from lawyers and politicians to Web site owners — to keep your children safe online. Hopefully things will be different in the future, but that's not the case right now. Today, keeping your children out of harm's way on the Internet is a responsibility left almost solely in your hands. Don't ignore the dangers or pretend they don't exist — if you have a computer with Internet access in your home, it's up to you to ensure that your children (and potentially their friends) aren't being exposed to inappropriate materials or dangerous people online.

Understanding online risks and dangers

Any reasonable parent would agree that they don't want their child reading pornographic, hateful, or violent magazines. Similarly, they would almost certainly never allow their child to have personal conversations with a complete stranger, or arrange to meet someone they don't know at the local mall. In the "real world," most parents go to great lengths to teach their children the differences between right and wrong, and educate them about the dangers and risks that they'll encounter in everyday life. Unfortunately, almost all of these important messages pertain to the physical world only — interactions with real objects, people, and places.

For better or worse, the Internet is basically an electronic mirror of the physical world, and children need to be educated about online risks and dangers. What good is teaching your children not to talk to strangers if they believe that the risk applies only to people on the street, not "happykid93," an otherwise anonymous chat buddy that they met on the Internet? Clearly, the potential dangers associated with chatting up a nameless and faceless person on the Internet are at least as great as doing the same with some random person walking down the street.

Realities in the physical and online worlds can be strikingly similar, but most parents are at a relative disadvantage when it comes to warning their kids about the dangers on the Internet. In a nutshell, many children are better versed (from experience) in the ways of the Internet than their parents. Be this as it may, it's important for parents to understand the risks that children face in the online world, and then come up with appropriate solutions to ensure that their children remain safe and protected.

Some of the key risks and dangers that children face on the Internet include:

- **Online predators.** Adults posing as children or teens represent a very real threat to child safety online. These "predators" (as they've come to be known) tend to hang out in Internet chat rooms geared towards a younger audience, posing as minors themselves. Many seek to befriend children in the hope of gaining their trust, and sometimes arranging

a "real life" meeting. Although the number of adults engaged in predator-like activities is extremely small, the threat they pose is very real. Unfortunately, many younger Internet users simply take their online chats and correspondences at face value, never considering that someone might not be who they claim to be.

- **Access to pornography and other objectionable content.** It's almost impossible to use the Internet for any extended period of time without coming into contact with objectionable materials such as pornography, hate literature, or worse. By its very nature, the Internet is home to all manner of content, including the good, the bad, and the ugly. Finding these materials is no more difficult than performing a simple search on sites such as Google or Yahoo!. Compounding the issue is the fact that children can easily stumble upon these materials without purposefully seeking them out.
- **Disclosing personal information.** There are laws in place to stop Web sites from gathering personal information from Internet users under 13 years of age without parental permission, but there's little that actually stops children from submitting their information online. Some sites use the information they collect to "market" to children; others use it for demographic purposes. Regardless, it's never a good idea for children to submit their name, address, or contact details online. This information can be used for a myriad of purposes, some of which might put your child in harm's way.
- **Misunderstanding sources.** The Internet is a wonderful research tool, literally overflowing with information. Alas, along with the myriad of excellent learning resources available online, there are also an astonishing number of sites containing incorrect and misleading information, not to mention outright lies. Younger Internet users may have trouble distinguishing whether what they've read is true or false, and whether a source is even reliable—you can't believe everything that you read, and that's especially true on the Internet.

Practical tips for parents

Getting children to understand and appreciate the risks associated with using a resource like the Internet isn't always easy. The following sections outline some practical tips for parents looking for ways to help improve the online safety of their children.

TALK THE TALK

Educating children about anything starts with a discussion, and there's arguably no better way to help keep your children safe on the Internet than by sitting down and having a chat about the potential dangers and risks associated with using the Internet.

A great way to start is by asking your child about how they use the Internet right now. Do they surf the Web frequently? Do they use instant messaging programs, e-mail, and perhaps a Web camera to communicate with friends? Do they download songs in MP3 format from file sharing services or play online games? An important part of helping to protect your children against online risks involves understanding how they use the Internet as a resource.

After discussing how they currently use the Internet, talk to them about some of the risks and dangers to which they may be exposed. Ask them about their own experiences, and even those of their friends. Remind them that even though the Internet may not seem "real" in a physical sense,

there actually are people using the Internet in different ways, and that not everyone is actually who they claim to be. Most importantly, try to instill in your child that the same rules that apply to keeping safe in the physical world also apply on the Internet.

Finally, take some time to discuss the ways in which your child is allowed to use the Internet. For example, if you don't want them hanging out in Internet chat rooms, let them know. Similarly, you might want to broach issues such as your feelings on pornography, hate literature, and the like. Come to a reasonable agreement on what you will (or will not) allow when it comes to them using the Internet. Of course, this agreement may vary greatly depending upon your own thoughts, feelings, and beliefs, not to mention the age and needs of your children.

Tip

For some great advice related to understanding online dangers and explaining them to your children, see the US Department of Education's "Parents Guide to the Internet", accessible online at `www.ed.gov/pubs/parents/internet/index.html`. The document is a little dated (it was originally released in 1997), but it contains excellent advice for parents looking for ways to ensure that their children remain safe on the Internet.

LOCATION, LOCATION, LOCATION

Back in the old days, parents purchased PCs for their children with thoughts of a glorified typewriter in mind — in other words, it would be an "educational" tool to aid in completing their schoolwork. However, computers have very much become the ultimate entertainment center, especially with the growth of high-speed Internet connections. From chatting with friends online to playing games and even watching movies, there's no shortage of things for a PC- and Internet-connected kid to do.

When thought of as a "study" tool, most parents will gladly agree to locate a PC in a child's bedroom, or another "quiet" area in the home. This makes sense in cases where the PC actually is being used for educational purposes, but it also makes monitoring a child's Internet activities very difficult. If your (or your child's) PC is located in a private area, keeping an eye on what your children are doing online can be difficult, if not next to impossible.

With that in mind, you may want to consider where you place your home computer(s) a little more carefully. If you want to keep the "temptation" of venturing into the darker corners of the Internet minimized, few things help more than setting up the Internet-connected computer in a high traffic area. If you have more than one PC in your home, you may want to consider connecting only those in "public" areas to the Internet, leaving the rest disconnected to act as glorified typewriters.

USE PARENTAL CONTROL SOFTWARE

Discussing online dangers and keeping an eye on their surfing habits can go a long way towards making the Internet a safer place for your children; however, even kids with the best intentions can wander into the unknown out of curiosity, and monitoring Internet usage could be a full time job on its own. Thankfully, you don't have to go it alone — help is available in the form of content filtering programs, sometimes referred to as parental control software.

As the names suggest, parental control or content filtering programs are designed to put you in control over what your children can and cannot do online. For example, these programs typically

allow you to block all access to all pornographic Web sites at the click of a button. This ultimately stops users from attempting to visit known adult Web sites, or search for related terms. When an attempt to access blocked or filtered sites is made, most parental control programs display an error message and log the attempt to a file that can be referenced at a later time.

Beyond simply blocking content, parental control programs typically allow you to configure times when Internet usage is allowed, and even control which programs can be used. For example, you might decide that your children should only be allowed to access the Internet between 6:00 and 8:00 in the evening and even then cannot use access Internet file sharing or instant messaging programs. In the meantime, you could allow all other users to access the Internet without restrictions.

Ultimately, parental control programs put you in control over how your children access the Internet, and to what extent. If you do choose to go this route, consider letting other users know that the software is installed, and exactly what it does and does not allow. Nobody likes to feel as though their activities are being monitored or watched; however, if the situation has been discussed and everyone knows that the filtering software is present, all users are certain to think more carefully about where they attempt venture online. Parental control software is explored in more detail in the following section.

Note

If Internet Explorer is your preferred Web browser, you may already be familiar with the Content Advisor feature accessible under Tools → Internet Options → Content. This feature uses a rating system developed by the Internet Content Rating Association (ICRA) to help you control access to sites that include references to nudity, sex, violence, or coarse language. Although using Internet Explorer's Content Advisor settings can help to control access to certain Web sites with objectionable content, this feature is not nearly as comprehensive as using a content filtering program to monitor and control online activities. For more details on Content Advisor and its configuration, visit `www.icra.org/faq/contentadvisor/setup/`.

Restricting Internet Access Using Parental Control Software

When it comes to controlling how children and other users of a Windows XP system access the Internet, few solutions offer as great a degree of flexibility and power as parental control (aka content filtering) programs. These software packages typically include the capability to:

- **Restrict access to different types of Internet content by category, or by defining your own custom filters.** Most parental control programs allow you to block access to all pornographic Internet content by enabling a single filter. Where a particular built-in category doesn't meet your exact needs, you can typically allow or deny access to other types of content by specifying keywords or Web site addresses.

- **Control access to the Internet using different communication methods and program types.** This feature allows you to block access to an instant messaging or file-sharing program while allowing users to surf the Web with a browser such as Internet Explorer.
- **Control the times at which Internet access is allowed or denied.** Most parental control programs provide a feature whereby you can specify a schedule so that access to the Internet is only allowed at certain times of the day, on certain days of the week.
- **Log users' Internet activity, including the Web sites that they've attempted to access and the contents of instant messaging conversations.** Logging and reporting features are an important part of all parental control packages, keeping parents informed of all Internet activity or attempts to access restricted Web sites.
- **Enable content filtering for all users, or only certain users.** Most parental control software packages include the ability to enable content filtering for certain users only, thus allowing other users to access the Internet without restrictions.

A number of different parental control programs are available for Windows XP, with each offering similar (but slightly different) combinations of features and capabilities. Some of the more popular parental control software packages include:

- **CYBERsitter.** CYBERsitter combines excellent Web filtering features with the capability to control access to instant messaging tools, FTP sites, file sharing programs, and even USENET newsgroups. It includes the capability to filter e-mail messages based on their content, configure a schedule to control when Internet access is allowed, and control which Windows XP user accounts should have their online activities filtered. Available from www.cybersitter.com, CYBERsitter costs approximately $40.
- **ContentProtect.** Available from `www.contentwatch.com`, ContentProtect costs approximately $30. ContentProtect stands out from many other content filtering programs because of its excellent reporting features and dynamic filtering capabilities.
- **NetNanny.** Available from `www.netnanny.com`, NetNanny costs approximately $40. NetNanny extends on the basic filtering capabilities found in similar tools by including the capability to block access to online games.

Note

This chapter uses CYBERsitter 9.0 to demonstrate the features and configuration of a parental control software package for Windows XP. CYBERsitter has consistently ranked at or near the top of PC Magazine's reviews. You can find recent reviews of different content filtering programs at `www.pcmag.com/article2/0,1759,1618808,00.asp`. Of course, you should download trial versions of different content filtering programs to determine which program best meets your specific needs and requirements.

Follow these steps to install CYBERsitter and configure the program's Internet options:

1. Open Internet Explorer or your preferred Web browser and then download the CYBERsitter installation package from www.cybersitter.com/trialreq.htm. Double-click the downloaded Setup2k.exe file to begin the installation process.
2. At the Welcome screen, click Next.
3. At the Important screen, click Next.
4. At the License Agreement screen, click Next.
5. At the Installation Notes screen, click Next. After the installation process is complete, click Finish.
6. When CYBERsitter opens for the first time, you're prompted to choose your Internet connection type, as shown in Figure 5-1. Click the appropriate option, enter your primary e-mail address, and click Close. This closes the CYBERsitter window but leaves the program running and active in the background.

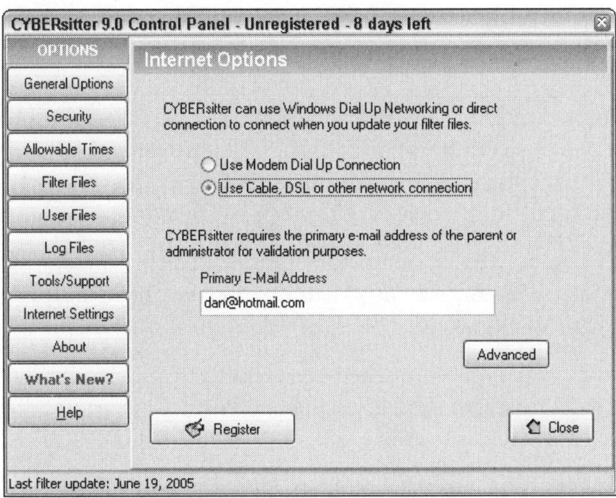

Figure 5-1: CYBERsitter's Internet Options screen.

CYBERsitter includes a broad array of configurable options to address different content filtering needs. The program's default configuration offers a fair degree of protection, but you should review all of CYBERsitter's settings to ensure that access to different types of Internet content is allowed or denied as per your specific needs and preferences.

Many of CYBERsitter's key configuration settings are accessed from the program's General Options screen, as shown in Figure 5-2.

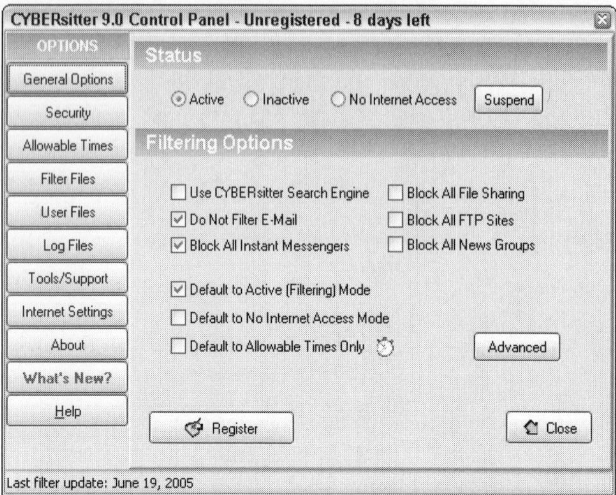

Figure 5-2: CYBERsitter is capable of filtering access to a wide variety of Internet content and programs.

Setting found on the General Options screen include:

- **Status.** Use the Status section to control whether CYBERsitter is Active (filtering content), Inactive (disabled and not filtering content), or set to disallow Internet access completely by selecting the No Internet Access option. CYBERsitter can also be temporary disabled by clicking the Suspend button and configuring a time period after which filtering will again be active.
- **Use CYBERsitter Search Engine.** This option automatically redirects all attempts to visit search engine Web pages to CYBERsitter's family-friendly search engine. Unfortunately, this option is not compatible with Windows XP.
- **Do Not Filter E-mail.** When this option is unchecked, CYBERsitter automatically scans all incoming and outgoing e-mail messages for inappropriate content. This feature does not work with HTML-based e-mail services such as Hotmail or Yahoo! Mail.
- **Block All Instant Messengers.** When this option is selected, communication via instant messaging programs such as Yahoo! Messenger or MSN Messenger is blocked.
- **Block All File Sharing.** Use this option to block access to file sharing programs such as Kazaa, Morpheus, and BearShare. P2P file sharing services are rife with pornography and pirated software, music files, video, and more.
- **Block All FTP Sites.** Select this option to block users from connecting to all FTP sites for the purpose of uploading or downloading files. FTP servers are commonly used to exchange the same types of files as those found on file sharing services. Many FTP sites are legitimate, and access to FTP is necessary if users are maintaining a Web site, need to download updates to certain programs (for example, anti-virus software), and so forth.
- **Block All News Groups.** USENET newsgroups are yet another common source of pornography and pirated software, music, and video files. Select this option to prevent

users from accessing USENET newsgroups altogether. Although USENET newsgroups can be a source of questionable materials, newsgroups still remain one of the best technical- and community-based resources on the Internet.

- **Default to Active (Filtering) Mode.** Select this option to have CYBERsitter start with content filtering enabled.
- **Default to No Internet Access Mode.** When this option is selected, CYBERsitter starts with Windows XP and does not allow users to access the Internet.
- **Default to Allowable Times Only.** When this option is selected (also configurable from the Allowable Times section), you can configure a schedule that dictates the times and days of the week where Internet access is allowed.
- **Advanced.** Click this button to specify ports that should (or should not) be filtering Internet traffic in a manner similar to a firewall. You learn more about firewalls, ports, and their configuration in Chapter 6.

After configuring your preferred settings on the General Options tab, click the Security button on CYBERsitter's left menu, as shown in Figure 5-3.

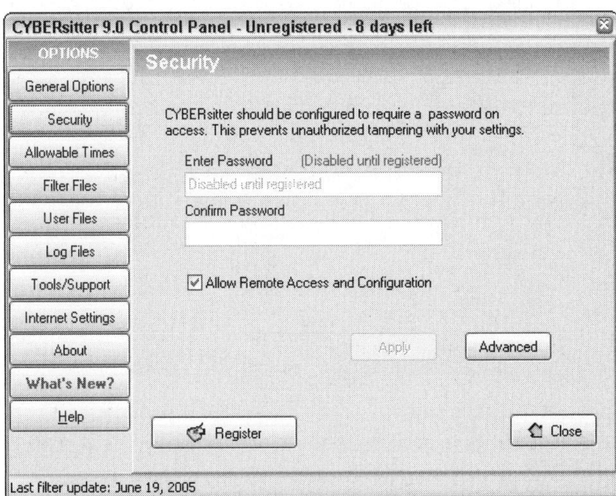

Figure 5-3: Password-protect CYBERsitter to stop other users from accessing and changing its configuration settings.

The Security screen allows you to configure the following settings:

- **Password.** When you enter a password for CYBERsitter, the configuration of the program cannot be changed until this password is entered. Always configure a password to stop other users from changing CYBERsitter's settings. It's worth noting that the ability to password protect settings is not available in the trial version of CYBERsitter.

- **Allow Remote Access and Configuration.** When this option is selected, CYBERsitter settings can be managed and maintained from a remote location or another computer on your network using the CYBERsitter Remote Control program. This feature is also not available in the trial version.

The majority of CYBERsitter's more powerful security settings are accessible by clicking the Advanced button in the Security section. This opens the Advanced Security Options window, as shown in Figure 5-4.

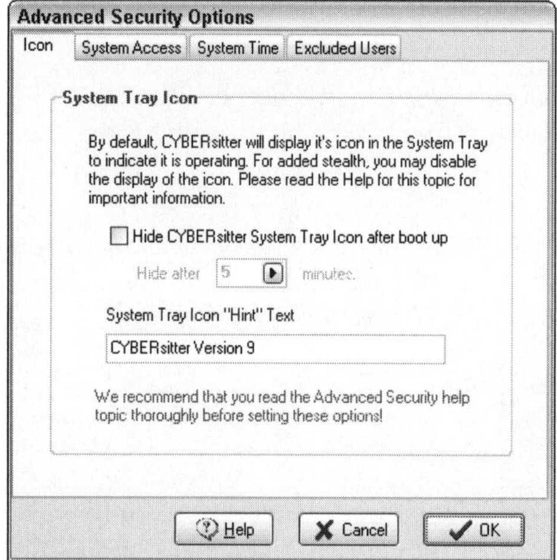

Figure 5-4: CYBERsitter's Advanced Security Options window gives you more granular control over the program's configuration.

Settings found in this window include:

- **Icon.** Use settings on the Icon tab to control whether the CYBERsitter icon is displayed on the Windows XP taskbar. If you select the option to hide the icon, CYBERsitter is effectively working in "stealth" mode, hiding its presence from other users. To configure CYBERsitter settings when its icon is hidden, click Start ➝ Run type cyb2k.exe, and press OK to open the main program window.
- **System Access.** Configure settings on the System Access tab to prevent users from editing the Windows XP Registry, using Control Panel tools, changing Internet access settings, and even opening the Task Manager program. Disabling access to these items helps to ensure that users cannot circumvent CYBERsitter's features by changing system settings.
- **System Time.** Configure settings on the System Time tab to stop users from changing Windows XP time settings in an attempt to bypass "allowable times" restrictions.

- **Excluded Users.** The Excluded Users tab allows you to configure a list of Windows XP user names for which Internet access should not be filtered for CYBERsitter. For example, if you want content filtering enabled for all user accounts except your own, add your Windows XP username to this list.

CYBERsitter filters Internet content in a number of different ways but primarily by blocking access to words and Web sites that could lead to the viewing of objectionable materials. The Filter Files section contains a list of default and optional content types that can be filtered, as shown in Figure 5-5.

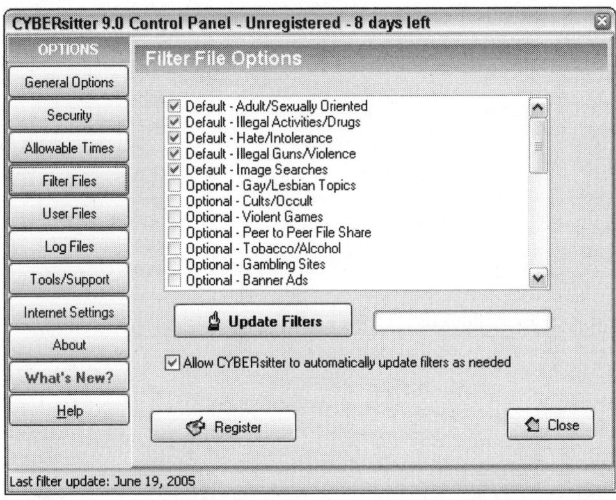

Figure 5-5: CYBERsitter blocks all objectionable content types by default, but can be configured to block a variety of different content types via its optional filters.

As installed, CYBERsitter blocks access to "Default" items only. This includes the most common types of objectionable content, such as that deemed pornographic, hateful, illegal, and so on. However, CYBERsitter also allows you to block access to a whole slew of different content types to better meet your needs. For example, you could choose to block access to all sites related to wrestling, or those that include an online chat component. Simply check the box next to a filter setting to block access to Internet resources dedicated to that particular subject area. Figure 5-6 illustrates what users see in their Web browser if they attempt to access the ESPN Web site when sports-related content is being blocked.

Figure 5-6: Message displayed when a user attempts to access a filtered Web site.

Note

Your Web browser may not display the exact message shown in Figure 5-6 when CYBERsitter blocks a site or a user's attempt to search for a forbidden term — a blank Web page or one bearing the message "The page cannot be displayed" may appear instead. If you haven't informed other users that content filtering software has been installed, they may interpret these screens as meaning that something is wrong with the Internet connection or Windows XP.

Understanding that its built-in content filters won't always meet your particular needs, CYBERsitter also allows you to configure more specialized filter settings from its User Files section. You can use the Bad Sites, Words, and Phrases tab (shown in Figure 5-7) to configure a custom list of items that should be blocked. If you want to shield others from visiting bowling Web sites, for example, you could simply add the word [bowling] to this list. To block access to a specific Web site you would enter its address instead.

Conversely, there may be Web sites that are blocked by one of CYBERsitter's filters, but to which you still want to allow access. For example, if you wanted to block access to all sports-related Web sites but still always allow access to sports.yahoo.com, you could configure the Always Allowable Sites tab as shown in Figure 5-8.

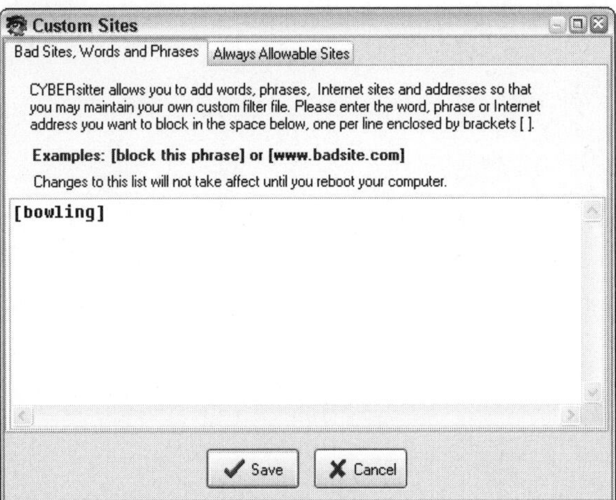

Figure 5-7: If CYBERsitter's built-in content filters don't meet your specific needs, you can configure your own custom filters.

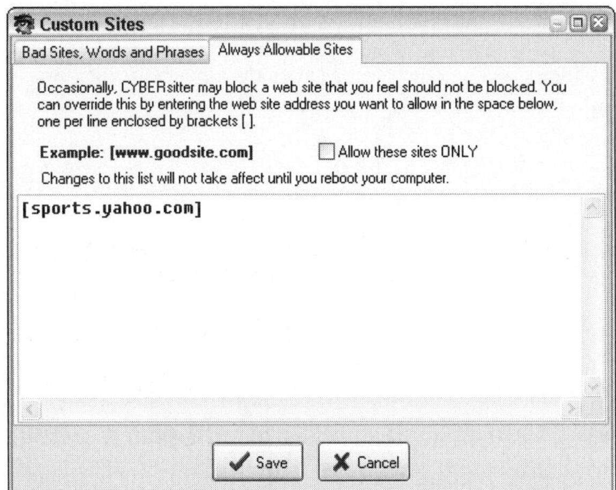

Figure 5-8: CYBERsitter allows you to configure individual Web sites as "always allowable" to prevent them from being blocked by its content filters.

Although real-time content filtering helps to ensure that children or other users of your Windows XP system cannot access objectionable content, you might also be interested in tracking what users have attempted to access on the Internet, even if the attempt was blocked.

CYBERsitter includes advanced logging features for just this purpose. By default, the program logs all Internet-related actions attempted by users to what it terms a "violation log." Logging settings are configurable from CYBERsitter's Logging and Reporting screen, as shown in Figure 5-9.

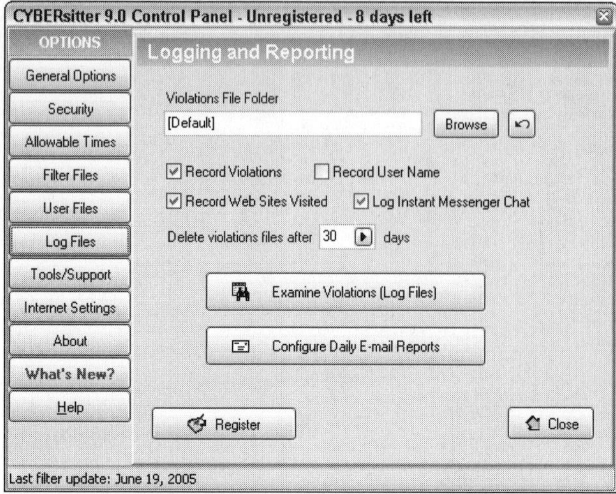

Figure 5-9: CYBERsitter's Logging and Reporting screen.

Configurable settings and options on the Logging and Reporting screen include:

- **Record Violations.** When this option is selected, CYBERsitter saves details about all content filter violation attempts to its log file.
- **Record User Name.** Check this box to record the Windows XP user name of the person who was logged on to the system when a violation attempt occurred.
- **Record Web Sites Visited.** When this option is selected, all Web sites that users attempt to visit are recorded to the violation log file.
- **Log Instant Messenger Chat.** When checked, entire conversations that take place using an instant messaging program such as MSN Messenger are recorded to the log file.

CYBERsitter can be configured to record a wide variety of information for reporting purposes, but the details contained in its violation log are useful only if you review the log regularly. CYBERsitter's Logging and Reporting screen includes two options for the purpose of reviewing its violation log file:

- **Examine Violations (Log Files).** When you click this button, the Open dialog box appears, allowing you to choose which log file you'd like to view. By default, CYBERsitter creates a new log file every day, named using the convention YYYYMMDD.log. An example of a CYBERsitter violation log file is shown in Figure 5-10.
- **Configure Daily E-Mail Reports.** Click this button to configure settings (as shown in Figure 5-11) that have CYBERsitter automatically e-mail the previous day's violation log file to you every day. This file can be attached to the e-mail message in plain text or in a password protected Zip file.

```
C:\WINDOWS\system32\Logs\Net\20050620.log
Open  Print  Help  Exit
06/20/05 01:28:34 PM    Dan     ACCESSED        http://www.mls.ca/
06/20/05 01:28:37 PM    Dan     ACCESSED        http://www.mls.ca/map.aspx
06/20/05 01:28:40 PM    Dan     ACCESSED        http://www.mls.ca/presentation/print.css
06/20/05 01:28:42 PM    Dan     ACCESSED        http://www.mls.ca/presentation/CobrandCSS/cobra
06/20/05 01:28:44 PM    Dan     ACCESSED        http://www.mls.ca/presentation/javascript/commo
06/20/05 01:28:46 PM    Dan     ACCESSED        http://www.mls.ca/presentation/javascript/deepm
06/20/05 01:29:00 PM    Dan     ACCESSED        http://toolbarqueries.google.com/search?client=
06/20/05 01:29:00 PM    Dan     ACCESSED        http://www.mls.ca/favicon.ico
06/20/05 01:29:01 PM    Dan     ACCESSED        http://www0.mls.ca/favicon.ico
06/20/05 01:32:23 PM    COMMENT CYBERsitter opened from system tray
06/20/05 01:41:41 PM    Dan     ACCESSED        http://www.2000trainers.com/rss.xml
06/20/05 01:41:41 PM    Dan     ACCESSED        http://www.2000trainers.com/rss
06/20/05 01:41:41 PM    Dan     ACCESSED        http://www.2000trainers.com/rss/
06/20/05 02:41:43 PM    Dan     ACCESSED        http://www.2000trainers.com/rss.xml
06/20/05 02:41:43 PM    Dan     ACCESSED        http://www.2000trainers.com/rss
06/20/05 02:41:43 PM    Dan     ACCESSED        http://www.2000trainers.com/rss/
06/20/05 03:27:11 PM    Dan     FILTERED        MONSTER.COM
06/20/05 03:27:11 PM    Dan     BLOCKED http://www.monster.com/
06/20/05 03:27:11 PM    Dan     FILTERED        MONSTER.COM
06/20/05 03:27:11 PM    Dan     ACCESSED        http://www.safe-site.com/
06/20/05 03:27:12 PM    Dan     ACCESSED        http://toolbarqueries.google.com/search?client=
06/20/05 03:27:12 PM    Dan     ACCESSED        http://www.safe-site.com/favicon.ico
06/20/05 03:27:12 PM    Dan     IGNORED http://aws-beta.amazon.com/onca/xml?Service=AlexaWebInf
06/20/05 03:27:20 PM    COMMENT CYBERsitter opened from system tray
06/20/05 03:32:27 PM    ACCESSED        http://www.google.com/
```

Figure 5-10: CYBERsitter creates new violation log files daily that list users' Internet activities.

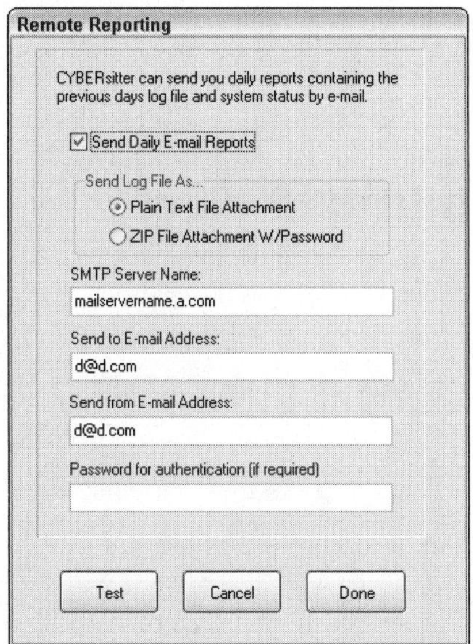

Figure 5-11: CYBERsitter can be configured to send violation log files to you as a daily e-mail report.

In addition to its real-time content filtering capabilities, CYBERsitter also includes a tool called System Snooper, accessible from the program's Tools and Support screen. This tool allows you to scan your system's hard drive looking for evidence of recent Internet activities where objectionable

material may have been viewed or accessed. Figure 5-12 displays the System Snooper window; note that after the scanning process is complete, you can double-click any item to open it and view its contents.

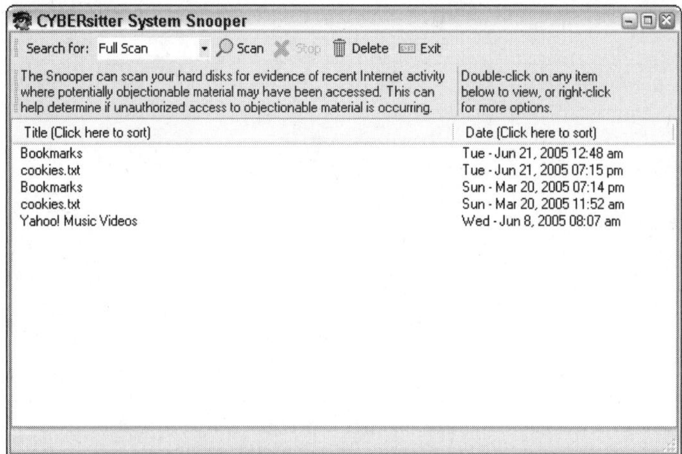

Figure 5-12: CYBERsitter's System Snooper tool helps you to search for and sort through potentially objectionable content present on your computer.

Using Content Filtering in Business Environments

You might think that just children need to have their online activities regulated and monitored, but that's not the case. Almost all large companies — and increasingly, smaller companies as well — use some type of content filtering software to stop employees from venturing to all corners of the Internet on company time.

In the business world, content filtering is implemented for two main reasons. The first is an attempt to help reduce inefficiency — it's been estimated that Internet-surfing employees cost American companies billions of dollars annually in lost productivity. The second is to mitigate the potential for litigation and lawsuits resulting from workers being exposed to objectionable content on company premises.

The degree to which a company filters its employees' Internet activities varies greatly from one company to the next. Some filter all non-work-related sites; others selectively block only objectionable materials such as pornography, hate literature, and "illegal" content. Given the popularity of Web-based e-mail and instant messaging programs, many companies block access to these services as well or limit their use to certain times of the day only (for example, at lunch hour or break times).

Where standalone content filtering programs (such as CYBERsitter) are an ideal solution for implementing control over a small number of computers, businesses typically install server-based filtering programs that work in conjunction with proxy servers to control employee Internet access in a centralized manner. For details on popular content filtering programs that work with proxy servers like Microsoft's Internet Security and Acceleration (ISA) Server, see `www.isaserver.org/software/ISA/Content-Security/`.

Summary

The Internet can be a dangerous place, particularly for children. From objectionable content to shady users, the potential risks to users are as real as there are in the physical world. Keep the following points in mind when it comes to restricting access to the Internet:

- The Internet has a dark side, one that can put children in harm's way. Educate children about the potential dangers they face online, and monitor their Internet activities.
- Consider installing parental control software to ensure that children cannot access objectionable content on the Internet. These programs also give you more control over when users can access the Internet and the types of software they can use while online.
- If you do opt to install parental control software, protect its configuration with a password, and review its log files and reports regularly.
- Content filtering software isn't for children only. If you run a business that gives employees access to the Internet, consider installing content filtering software to avoid having objectionable content accessible to users, and to help increase employee productivity.

Part III

Protecting Windows XP Against Internet Threats

Chapter 6

Protecting Windows XP with a Firewall

There's little question that the Internet is one of the most valuable resources of our time. It's not only a reliable and effective communication facility but also an invaluable research tool. As a global "network of networks," the Internet is very much a community, complete with elements that are both good and bad. Although the vast majority of Internet users are honest folks trying to making use of a great resource, there also exists a large (though relatively small, percentage-wise) group of people online who would like nothing more than to compromise the security of your PC for their own gains.

These malicious users are the hackers, crackers, and script kiddies that represent the "enemy" to millions of legitimate Internet users worldwide. Unfortunately, you have little choice but to ensure that your computer is protected from these users and their threats. The number sounds almost unbelievable, but it's been estimated that an unprotected and unpatched computer is typically compromised less than 20 minutes after being connected to the Internet. From infecting your computer with viruses and spyware to installing "remote control" programs, the risks associated with leaving your PC unprotected are very real. In the same way that you lock your car doors when parking in a public location, you need to lock down your PC when venturing online.

In the case of computers connected to the Internet, the "lock" in question is a firewall. Although the capabilities of different firewalls vary, the primary role of a firewall is to act as the gatekeeper between your computer and the Internet. A firewall allows you to control what level of access (if any) Internet users have to your PC, and potentially which programs and services on your computer can gain access to the Internet. Quite simply, without the protection of a firewall, your PC will quickly end up being a revolving door of incoming and outgoing traffic, remaining exposed to an Internet's worth of security and privacy threats.

In this chapter you learn more about how a firewall works to protect your PC from the dangers of the Internet, and how some can be used to control what leaves your computer destined for the online world. You also are introduced to the benefits, limitations, and configuration of different software firewalls, including Windows XP's native Windows Firewall. Finally, you learn about the tools and techniques that can be used to test firewall security, helping you to ensure that your chosen firewall solution is actually providing the levels of protection that it should be.

Understanding the Role of a Firewall

At the most basic level, a firewall is a software program that acts as a security intermediary between your computer and a network like the Internet. The job of the firewall is to inspect all packets sent and received by your PC and then decide whether to allow or disallow them based on its configured rules. When a certain type of traffic is allowed by the firewall (for example, packets sent and received by an instant messaging program), communication occurs in the same manner as if no firewall were in place at all. If another type of traffic were denied, however, communication attempts using that method would fail—the firewall would intercept the packets, compare them to configured rules, and then determine that the communication attempt should not be allowed, discarding the packets in the process.

Ultimately, a firewall puts you in control over which traffic is allowed to enter your PC and which traffic is allowed to leave. In their default configuration, most firewalls allow all communication attempts originating from your PC to go on their way unencumbered—assuming that since the request came from your computer, its "good" traffic and should be allowed to proceed. Conversely, almost all firewalls are configured to deny all connection attempts to your PC originating from the Internet by default—in other words, the firewall protects your computer from being connected to by Internet users unless you tell it to do otherwise. This default setup ensures that you can access the Internet in whatever way you choose, while stopping all outside users from connecting to your PC.

Although this firewall setup appears perfectly reasonable at first glance, the security risks associated with the Internet today actually make it less than optimal. In the following sections you learn more about how firewalls control inbound and outbound traffic, and why each of these traffic directions needs to be carefully considered when it comes to ensuring that your firewall provides adequate security.

Inbound filtering

Inbound filtering is the term used to describe how a firewall deals with unsolicited traffic that it receives from the Internet. Unsolicited traffic is a connection attempt that does not correspond to any request that originated from your computer. In other words, if you fire up your Web browser and make a request to view a certain Web page, the information that the Web server sends back to your system is not unsolicited—you made the request, and the Web server simply replied. In the eyes of a firewall, an unsolicited connection attempt is where an Internet user or computer attempts to connect to your PC without you doing a thing. A remote user attempting to connect to File Transfer Protocol (FTP) server software installed on your PC would be an example of an unsolicited request. In its default configuration, a firewall typically denies these types of requests.

Of course, there may be times when you actually want Internet users to be able to connect to your computer. For example, you may want to play an online multi-player game, or exchange files over an instant messaging session. For times where you do want another user to be able to connect to your PC for these reasons, you can configure a firewall to allow the action. Doing this is sometimes referred to as "opening a port," "acting as a server," or "configuring an exception." In the case of an online game, you may need to configure your firewall to open the ports used by the game to allow your competitor to connect to your PC. As part of doing this, you would be telling the firewall to continue blocking all incoming connection attempts, except those required to play the game.

Inbound filtering is as close to a universal firewall feature as you'll find. With no additional configuration necessary, a firewall will block all incoming connection attempts by default and then only allow certain types of traffic through based on the rules you configure. Ultimately, inbound filtering is what stops any user on the Internet from connecting to your PC without your permission. When a firewall is not installed and enabled, no inbound filtering takes place, meaning that Internet users can connect to available services on your PC without any intermediary keeping an eye on things.

Outbound filtering

Where inbound filtering is designed to control which traffic originating from the Internet can enter your PC, outbound filtering controls which traffic can leave your computer destined for the Internet. By default, most firewalls are configured to allow all traffic leaving your computer to access the Internet without restriction — the basic assumption being that you made the request, and know what you're doing.

The ability to access anything on the Internet may seem great at first glance, but the ability to filter outbound traffic is important for a number of reasons. You may actually want to restrict access to what users of your computer have access to online. For example, perhaps you want to allow all users to be able to surf the Web and send and receive e-mail messages but want to block them from using the computer to connect to file sharing services. If your firewall supports outbound filtering, you can control and restrict the types of traffic that leave your PC.

Although the ability to control inbound traffic is imperative, implementing a firewall that includes outbound filtering capabilities has become particularly important from a system security perspective. This is particularly true at a time where an estimated 80 to 90 percent of all PCs are infected by viruses and/or spyware. If a virus infects your computer, it may try to use your PC and Internet connection to infect other systems. Similarly, many spyware programs are designed to collection information (such as files, personal details, and even credit card numbers) from your computer and then send it off to a server on the Internet. Unless you have a firewall installed that is capable of outbound filtering, these pests can use your Internet connection without restriction, silently connecting to the Internet without your knowledge.

Firewalls that support outbound filtering implement the feature in a few key ways. Some work at the "port" level, allowing or denying traffic based on its type. For example, you could configure this type of firewall to disallow outbound FTP connections. Other firewalls function at a program or service level, allowing you to specify exactly which programs should be granted access to the Internet. With this type of firewall, you could allow a program such as Outlook Express to access the Internet, but deny a file-sharing program from connecting online.

Ultimately, a firewall that supports both inbound and outbound filtering capabilities offers the best protection for your PC. As with any security feature, however, the capability of a firewall to protect your system is dependent upon it being configured correctly.

Configuring Windows Firewall

When Windows XP was first released, its built-in firewall component was known as Internet Connection Firewall (ICF). This firewall feature was not enabled for any network or dial-up connections by default, leading to a situation whereby most Windows XP systems were left unprotected. Things changed when Windows XP Service Pack 2 was released — installing it replaced ICF with the new Windows Firewall, which is automatically enabled to protect all network connections by default.

Cross-Reference

For details on keeping Windows XP updated and protected by the latest Service Packs and security patches, see Chapter 7.

Unfortunately, Windows Firewall (like ICF before it) offers inbound filtering capabilities only. In other words, Windows Firewall completely lacks the capability to filter or control Internet-bound traffic. Although it does a good job of protecting your PC from connection attempts by Internet users, it does nothing to stop viruses or spyware already installed on your computer from using your Internet connection to infect other computers or send off your personal information to third parties.

Its lack of outbound filtering capabilities makes Windows Firewall a suitable firewall option only in cases where you're absolutely sure that your computer is both 100 percent virus- and spyware-free. If either type of pest infects your computer, Windows Firewall allows them to access the Internet without impunity, putting both your security and privacy at risk.

Having said that, using Windows Firewall to protect your PC is still a better option than not using a firewall at all. For this reason, the configuration of Windows Firewall and its settings is explored in more detail throughout this section. A third-party firewall that offers both inbound and outbound filtering capabilities, however, is definitely a better option towards helping to ensure a more secure PC.

Cross-Reference

You learn more about protecting your computer against spyware in Chapter 8, and about dealing with viruses and related threats in Chapter 9.

Along with "upgrading" ICF to Windows Firewall, installing Service Pack 2 added a new security tool to Windows XP's Control Panel. Known as Windows Security Center, this tool was designed to help keep you informed on the current status of your computer's firewall, virus protection, and operating system updates. On the firewall front, Windows Security Center outlines whether Windows Firewall is on, or if another third-party firewall is installed and enabled. In cases where all firewall components have been turned off, Windows Security Center displays a warning message in its program window, and also alerts you via a Security Center icon and message box on your Taskbar, as shown in Figure 6-1.

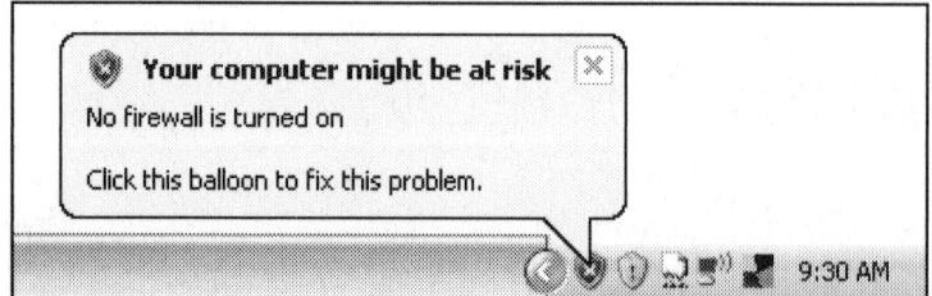

Figure 6-1: Notification message from Windows Security Center when no firewall is protecting a Windows XP system.

Follow these steps to check the status of Windows Firewalls in Windows Security Center:

1. Click Start → Control Panel → Security Center. The current status of your Firewall is listed as shown in Figure 6-2.

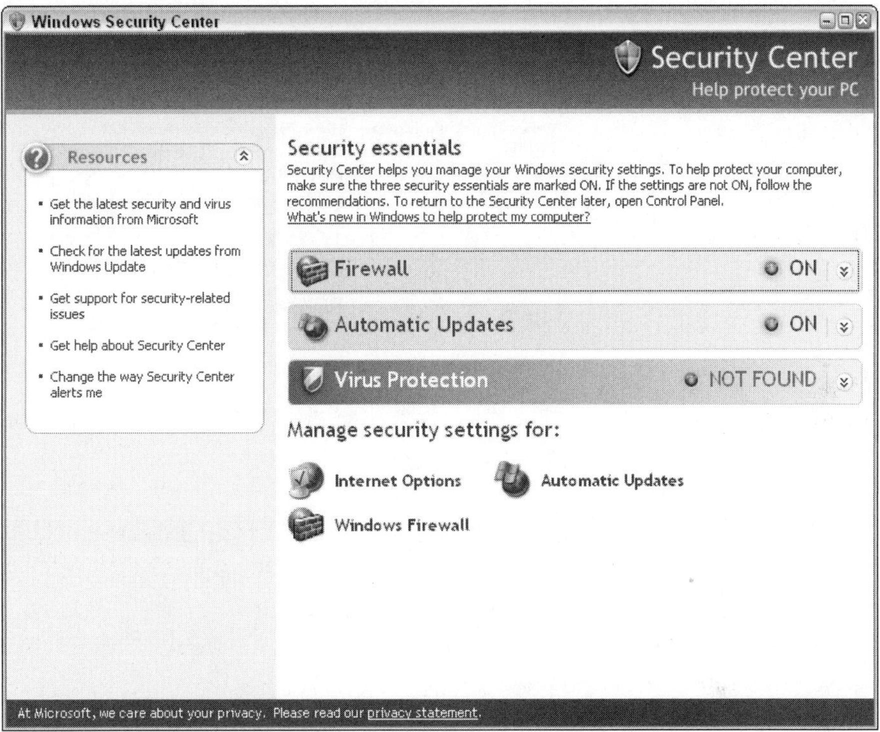

Figure 6-2: Viewing firewall status information in Windows Security Center.

2. If the status message for your Firewall reads Off (Figure 6-3), click the Recommendations button.

3. On the Recommendation window (Figure 6-4) click Enable now. Windows Firewall is now enabled for all network and dial-up connections.

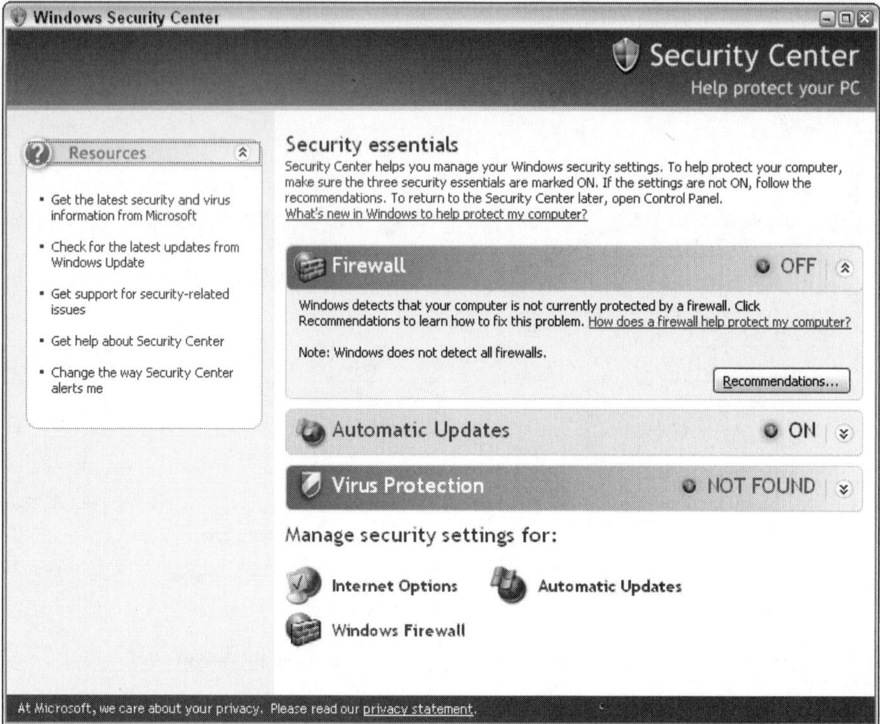

Figure 6-3: Windows Security Center displays information about the current status of your firewall, Automatic Updates, and virus protection.

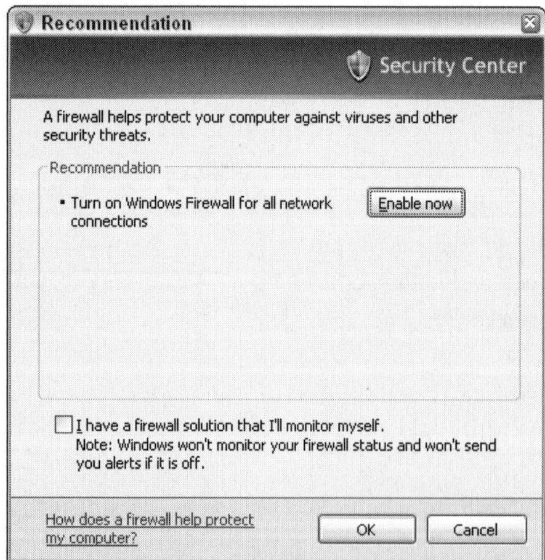

Figure 6-4: The Security Center Recommendation window.

4. Click Close at the Windows Security dialog box and then click OK.

Note

Use Security Center to periodically check the status of your firewall, along with the status of Automatic Updates and Virus protection.

When Windows Firewall is turned on, it is enabled for all network connections present on your Windows XP system by default. This includes all:

- Network card connections, such as Local Area Connection objects
- Dial-up connections, such as those created to connect to your Internet Service Provider or a VPN
- IEEE 1394 (FireWire) connections

To quickly gauge whether a connection is being protected by Windows Firewall, click Start → Control Panel → Network Connections. All connections protected by Windows Firewall are listed as "Firewalled" as shown in Figure 6-5.

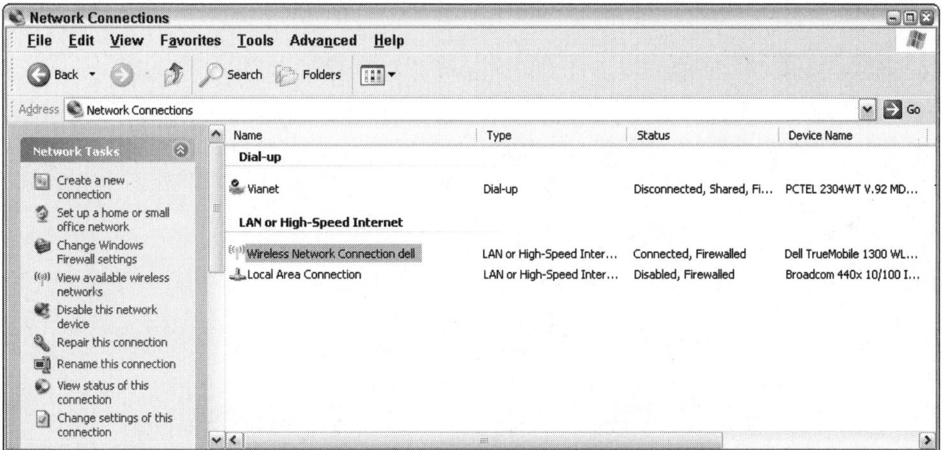

Figure 6-5: Network and dial-up connections protected by Windows Firewall are listed as "Firewalled" in the Network Connections Status column.

Note

If you don't see the Status column when you open Network Connections, select View → Details.

Although leaving all connections protected by Windows Firewall is generally a safe default option, you may not want certain connections protected by a firewall, such as one that connects to other computers on your home network only. Windows Firewall can be selectively enabled or disabled for different connections if necessary.

Follow these steps to enable or disable Windows Firewall for a specific connection:

1. Click Start → Control Panel → Network Connections.
2. Right-click on a network or Internet connection and click Properties.
3. Click Advanced → Settings.
4. At the Windows Firewall window, click Advanced. In the Network Connection Settings section (Figure 6-6), check or uncheck the boxes next specific network or dial-up connections to enable or disable Windows Firewall for that connection. When complete, click OK.

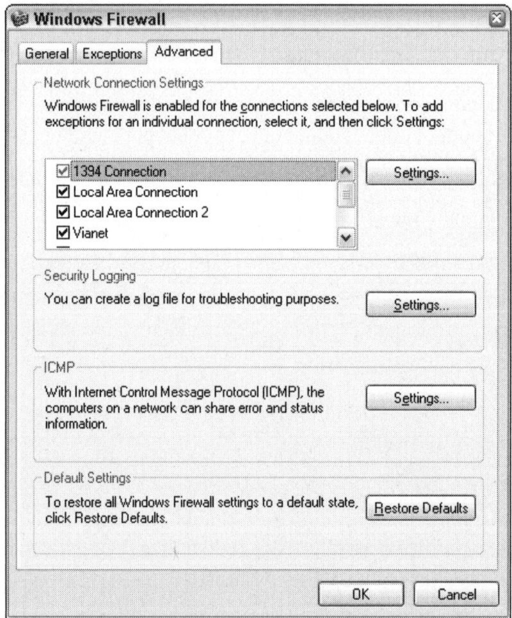

Figure 6-6: The Windows Firewall Advanced tab.

Caution

Never completely disable or turn off the firewall being used to protect your Internet connection — doing so puts your Windows XP system at serious risk.

The Windows Firewall Advanced tab also allows you to configure the following options:

- **Exceptions for individual network and dial-up connections.** In the same way that Windows Firewall can be enabled or disabled for a specific connection, program "exceptions" can also be configured on a connection-by-connection basis. Configuring an exception for a program is the equivalent of allowing inbound connections, through Windows Firewall, that allow outside users to connect to and communicate with a particular program. You learn more about configuring exceptions later in this section.
- **Security logging settings.** Windows Firewall logs all allowed and denied incoming connection attempts to your computer in a log file by default. This log can be used as a reference to determine if outside users have attempted to connect to your computer, and whether the connection attempt was successful or dropped. Logging can be selectively enabled or disabled for different network connections.
- **ICMP settings.** ICMP is the protocol used by troubleshooting and diagnostic programs such as Ping. Windows Firewall can be configured to respond to ICMP packets received from other users or to discard these packets when they're received.

Follow these steps to configure advanced settings for Windows Firewall:

1. Click Start → Control Panel → Windows Firewall → Advanced.
2. In the Security Logging section, click Settings.
3. In the Log Settings window, ensure that both the Log dropped packets and Log successful connection options are checked, as shown in Figure 6-7. Note that all Windows Firewall activity is logged to a file named pfirewall.log in the C:\Windows folder by default. Click OK.

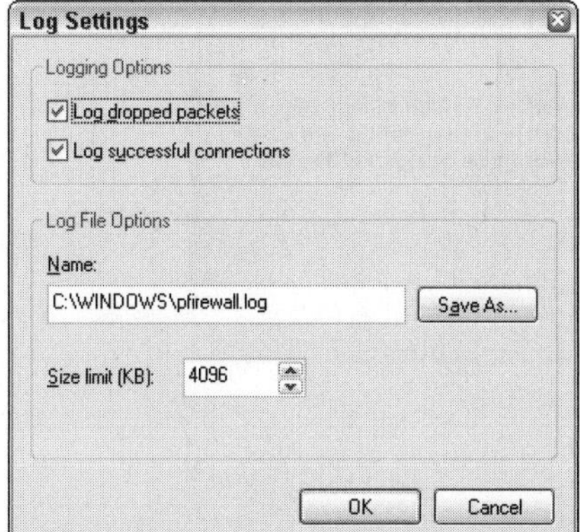

Figure 6-7: Configuring Windows Firewall log settings.

4. In the ICMP section, click Settings. By default, Windows Firewall is set to Allow incoming echo requests (pings) as shown in Figure 6-8. If you prefer that Windows Firewall discard all ping requests, uncheck this box. Click OK.

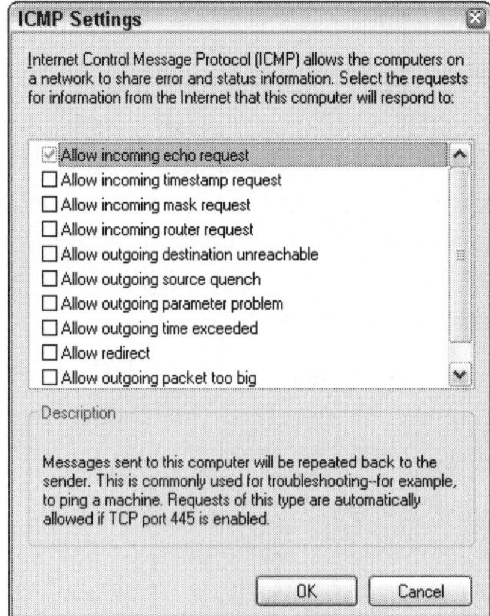

Figure 6-8: Configuring Windows Firewall ICMP settings.

5. If you ever change the configuration of Windows Firewall settings and want to return to its original default settings, simply click the Restore Defaults button in the Default Settings section. When the Restore Defaults Confirmation dialog box appears (Figure 6-9), click Yes.

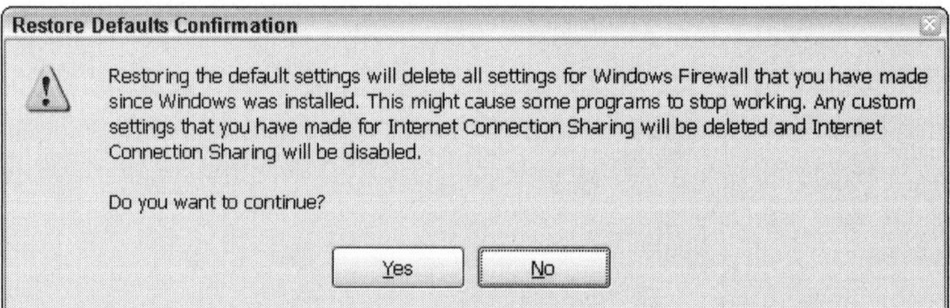

Figure 6-9: Restoring Windows Firewall's default settings.

6. Click OK to close the Windows Firewall window.

Note

Windows Firewall's logs can be difficult to decipher due to the large (and fairly cryptic) information they contain. To make the process of reviewing the Windows Firewall log file easier, use a third-party log reading tool such as the Windows XP Log Reader, available from `www.winxpcentral.com/windowsxp/fwlog.php`.

If you're running Windows Firewall and want to allow incoming connections to a certain program or service on your computer, you need to configure an exception. In simple terms, you can think of exceptions as a statement that says "block all incoming connections, with the following exceptions." So, if you want to allow a user to connect to your computer for the purpose of offering remote assistance, you need to configure an exception for Remote Assistance. Similarly, if you want to allow Internet users to connect to an FTP server installed on your Windows XP system, you need to configure an exception for FTP connections.

Exceptions can be configured with Windows Firewall by doing the following:

- **Specifying the program that external users will connect to.** For example, if you had FTP server software installed and wanted users to be able to connect it, you could simple specify an exception for the FTP server program. Windows Firewall will then open the necessary ports to allow incoming connections automatically.
- **Specifying the communication port used by a program or service.** When programs are capable of accepting incoming connections, they are often said to be "acting as a server." Any program capable of "acting as a server" listens for connection attempts on what are known as TCP or UDP ports. A "port" is simply a unique number used by a particular service — for example, an FTP server program listens for incoming connection attempts on TCP port 21; a Web server listens for connections on TCP port 80 by default. Windows Firewall allows you to open communication ports to allow incoming connections to reach your computer correctly. For cases where you need to open ports on your firewall to allow incoming connections (as is often the case with online multi-player games), consult the program's documentation for details on the correct port(s) to open.

As part of configuring an exception to allow incoming connections, Windows Firewall also allows you to configure what is known as a "scope." A scope is simply a way of defining (more specifically) who is allowed to make use of an exception. Scope options include:

- **Any computer.** This option, selected by default, makes the exception accessible to all computers, including all users on the Internet.
- **My network (subnet) only.** This option makes the exception accessible to all computers on your private network only. For example, Windows Firewall automatically creates and enabled an exception for the File and Printer Sharing service, but limits the "scope" of this exception with this option. Ultimately, this ensures that other computers on your home network can connect to the protected computer for the purpose of sharing files or printers, but stops Internet users from being able to do so.

- **Custom list.** This option allows you to specify the unique IP address (or addresses) of computers that should be allowed to connect via the exception. For example, if you plan to use an exception to play a multi-player game with only a few friends, you should select this option and enter your friends' IP addresses. By selecting this option, only the addresses listed will be able to connect to the exception, stopping all Internet users from being able to connect through the exception's opening in your firewall.

Follow these steps to configure an exception for Remote Assistance with Windows Firewall:

1. Click Start → Control Panel → Windows Firewall → Exceptions. The Windows Firewall Exceptions tab lists a checkbox next to all programs and services that it is not blocking from accepting incoming connections, as shown in Figure 6-10.

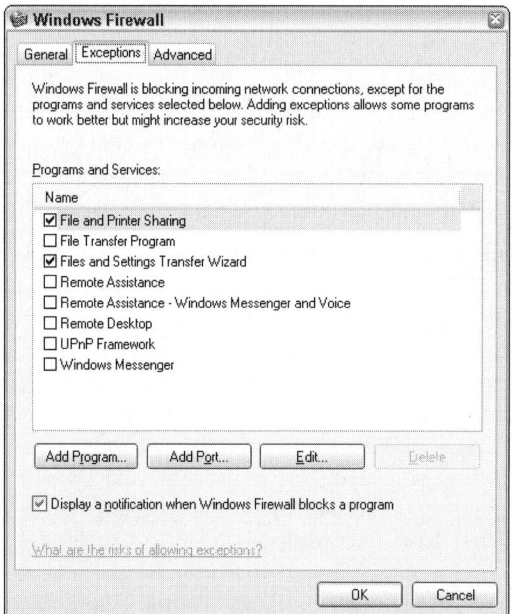

Figure 6-10: The Windows Firewall Exceptions tab.

2. To allow another user to connect to your Windows XP system for the purpose of providing help via Remote Assistance, check the box next to Remote Assistance, as shown in Figure 6-11.

3. With the Remote Assistance option selected, click the Edit button.

4. At the Edit a Program window, click the Change scope button. By default, Windows XP allows incoming Remote Assistance connections from any computer, as shown in Figure 6-12.

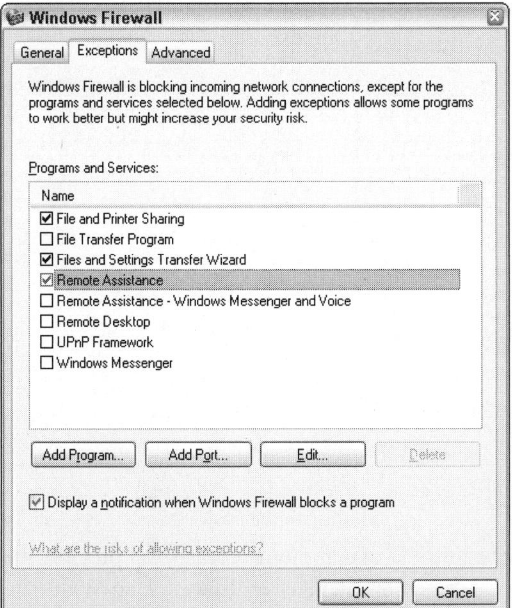

Figure 6-11: Configuring an exception in Windows Firewall to allow incoming Remote Assistance connections.

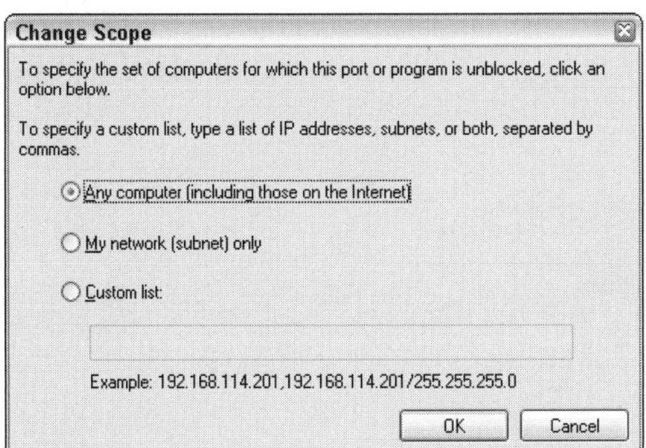

Figure 6-12: Reviewing the scope associated with an exception.

5. Click Custom list and then enter the IP address of the user who will connect to your computer to offer Remote Assistance. If configured as shown in Figure 6-13, only the user with the IP address 24.10.10.10 would be allowed to connect to your computer through Windows Firewall, and connections originating at all other IP addresses would continue to be blocked.

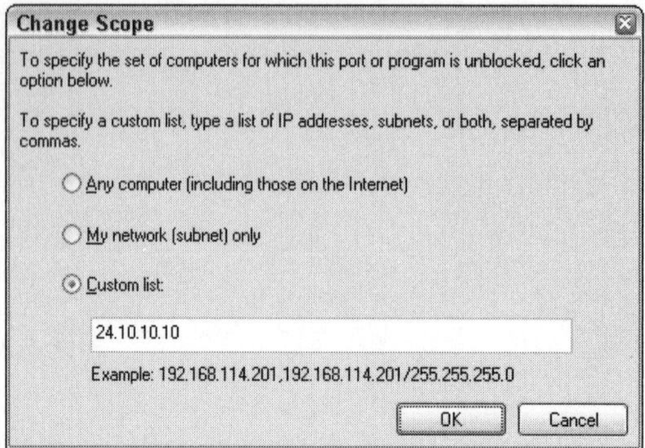

Figure 6-13: Changing an exception's scope to allow connections from a single IP address only.

6. Click OK three times to save your changes and exit Windows Firewall.

The Windows Firewall Exception tab lists a number of commonly configured program and service exceptions in its list by default. This list is far from comprehensive, however, so Windows Firewall provides the capability to add new custom exceptions for programs or services not on this list.

Follow these steps to add an exception for a specific program, such as an online multi-player game:

1. Click Start → Control Panel → Windows Firewall → Exceptions.
2. Click the Add Program button and then click on the name of the program in the Programs list (as shown in Figure 6-14), or click the Browse button to specify the path to a program not included on the Programs list.

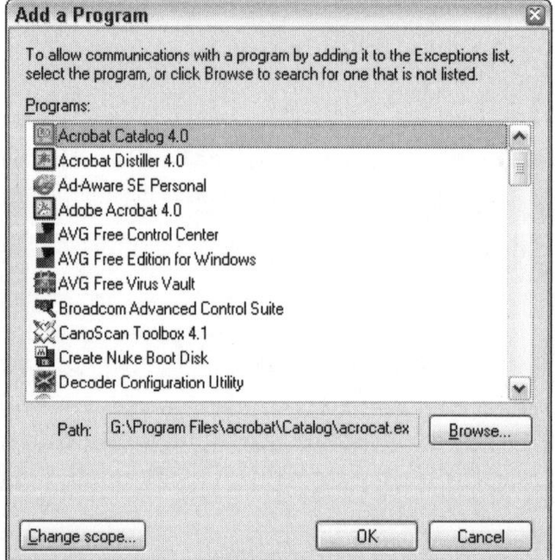

Figure 6-14: Adding an exception for a program.

3. Click the Change scope button to limit who can connect via this exception, or click OK to implement the exception for all users. After complete, the exception appears checked on the Exceptions tab, as shown in Figure 6-15.

Figure 6-15: Reviewing the exception created for a new program.

4. Click OK to close Windows Firewall.

Note

You can also add Windows Firewall exceptions by specifying the TCP or UDP port number on which a particular program accepts incoming connections. The port numbers that need to be configured are typically listed in the program's user manual; however, you can also find an updated list of common port numbers online at `www.iana.org/assignments/port-numbers`.

Windows Firewall allows you to configure exceptions manually, but it also prompts you for a decision every time that a new program that wants to accept incoming connections is opened. Ultimately, the Windows Firewall dialog box that appears prompts you to select whether the program should be allowed to "act as a server."

Internet Connection Firewall (ICF)

Prior to the release of Service Pack 2, Windows XP systems included a firewall component known as Internet Connection Firewall (ICF). Unlike Windows Firewall, ICF was not enabled by default, leaving all network and dial-up connections with the security protection of a firewall. It was only after ICF was enabled manually that a specific connection started to block incoming connection attempts.

While installing Service Pack 2 (as outlined in Chapter 7) and taking advantage of Windows Firewall is a better option than using ICF, ICF should still be enabled for your Internet network or dial-up connection if you don't have SP2 installed.

Follow these steps to enable ICF for your Internet network or dial-up connection:

1. Click Start → Control Panel → Network Connections.
2. Right-click the network or dial-up connection used to connect to the Internet and then click Properties.
3. Click on the Advanced tab.
4. Check the Protect my computer and network by limiting or preventing access to this computer from the Internet box, as shown in the following figure.

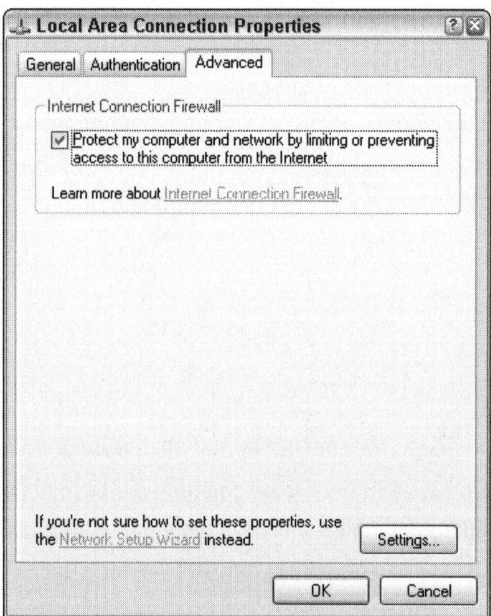

Enabling Internet Connection Firewall on a Windows XP systems prior to Service Pack 2.

5. Click OK.

Similar to Windows Firewall, ICF monitors incoming connection attempts only, and does nothing to police the traffic that leaves your PC, destined outbound for the Internet or other computers on your network.

Follow these steps to allow or deny an exception when a program (Skype is used in this example) you open requests it:

1. Click Start → All Programs → Skype → Skype.
2. When the Windows Security Alert dialog box appears (as shown in Figure 6-16), click Keep Blocking or Unblock.

Figure 6-16: The Windows Security Alert message appears when a new or unknown program attempts to configure itself to allow incoming connections.

3. If you choose the Unblock option, a new exception is configured for the program in Windows Firewall.

Although exceptions are required any time that you want to allow outside users to make an incoming connection to your computer through Windows Firewall, they should also be disabled when they're no longer required (even if only temporarily). By disabling an exception, you stop users from making inbound connections to your PC, which is a more secure option — especially when the program or service in question is not being used. To disable an exception, simply uncheck the box next to its name on the Exceptions tab in Windows Firewall.

Implementing Third-Party Firewall Software

Windows Firewall completely lacks outbound filtering capabilities, and for that reason alone you should strongly consider making the switch to third-party firewall software that includes both inbound and outbound filtering capabilities. Some of the more popular personal firewall software packages available for Windows XP include:

- **Kerio Personal Firewall.** Available from `www.kerio.com`, Kerio Personal Firewall comes in both paid and free-for-personal-use editions.

- **McAfee Personal Firewall Plus.** Available from www.mcafee.com, McAfee Personal Firewall Plus costs approximately $40 after a free 30-day trial period.
- **Norton Internet Security.** Available from www.symantec.com, Norton Internet Security costs approximately $50 after a free 15-day trial period.
- **Sygate Personal Firewall.** Available from www.sygate.com, Sygate Personal Firewall comes in both paid and free-for-personal-use editions.
- **ZoneAlarm.** Available from www.zonelabs.com, ZoneAlarm comes in both paid and free-for-personal-use editions.

All of the personal firewall packages in the preceding list offer both inbound and outbound filtering capabilities, including in the free-for-personal-use editions, as applicable. The paid versions of each program tend to include a variety of advanced and value-added security features, such as virus scanning, privacy tools, cookie management capabilities, and more.

Every personal firewall product for Windows XP functions in a slightly different manner, and includes different features and capabilities; however, some of the key features of personal firewall software packages for Windows XP include the capability to:

- Allow or deny specific programs or services from making outbound or receiving inbound connection attempts. A single program can be configured as allowed to make outbound connections and not to receive inbound connections, or a combination thereof.
- Have the firewall alert you every time a new program attempts to access the Internet. When a program attempts to access the Internet for the first time, an onscreen message appears alerting you to the action. You are prompted to allow or deny the program, and can typically select an option to have the firewall "remember" your choice, avoiding additional prompts for that specific program or service in the future.
- Alert you whenever an outside user attempts to make a connection attempt to your PC. Most firewall programs alert you with an onscreen message any time that an outside user attempts to connect to your PC. Not only does the message provide you with details such as the IP address of the remote user, but also the specific port to which the connection was attempted. Some firewalls even let you know about specific security exploits that relate to the connection attempt, helping to keep you well informed about potential threats. Onscreen alert messages can typically be turned off if you don't want to be informed of every connection attempt, with details stored in a log file for future reference instead.
- Enable different security settings for programs attempting to communicate on your home network or the Internet. For example, you might configure your firewall such that file and printer sharing inbound connection attempts from other computers on your home network are always allowed, while those originating from the Internet are always denied. In some firewall programs, your home network is referred to as the "trusted" zone.
- Allow incoming or outgoing connections by TCP or UDP port numbers, ranges of IP addresses, and more.

Note

Kerio Personal Firewall is used for demonstration purposes throughout this section. It is arguably no more or less able than any of the other personal firewall packages available for Windows XP, but it has an excellent reputation for providing solid inbound and outbound filtering capabilities, including in the free-for-personal-use version. You can download Kerio Personal Firewall from `www.kerio.com/us/kpf_home.html`.

Follow these steps to install and configure Kerio Personal Firewall:

1. Double-click the Kerio Personal Firewall installation file (kerio-pf-4.1.3-en-win.exe in this example) to begin the installation process.
2. At the Choose Setup Language screen, select your preferred language from the drop-down list and then click OK.
3. At the Welcome screen, click Next.
4. At the What's New screen, click Next.
5. At the License Agreement screen, click I accept the terms in the license agreement, and click Next.
6. At the Destination folder screen, click Next.
7. At the Initial Firewall Setting screen, click Advanced (Learning mode), as shown in Figure 6-17. Selecting this option ensures that you'll be prompted to make a decision every time a new program or service attempts to access the Internet for the first time. Click Next.

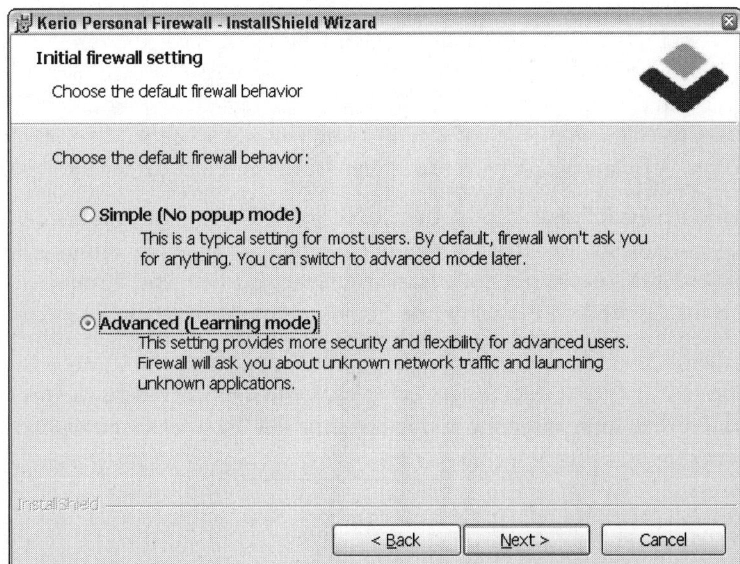

Figure 6-17: Specifying the initial firewall setting for Kerio Personal Firewall.

8. At the Ready to Install the Program screen, click Install. When the installation process is complete, click Finish.
9. Click Yes to restart your Windows XP system and then log on with your user account.
10. At the New network interface or network IP address dialog box (Figure 6-18) you are prompted to confirm whether the interface specified is connected to a "trusted" network. If this network interface is connected to your home network, click Yes, it is; otherwise, click No, it isn't.

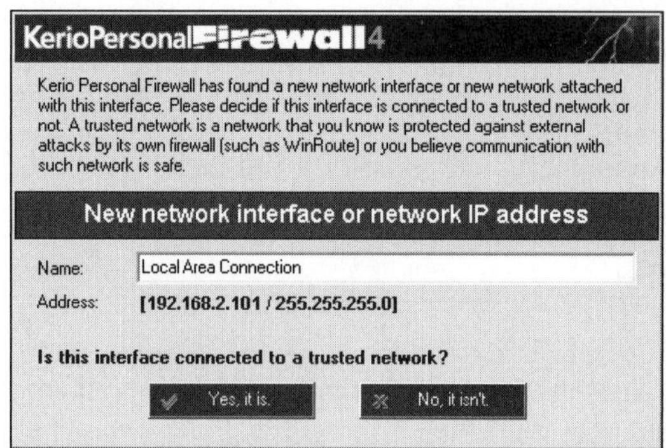

Figure 6-18: Designating your network connection and IP address as part of a trusted network.

11. Double-click the Kerio Personal Firewall icon on your taskbar to open the main program window.
12. Click the Network Security tab, as shown in Figure 6-19, to view the current status of different programs and services on the Application tab. This tab lists whether programs are services are allowed inbound (In) or outbound (Out) access to your trusted network and the Internet. A green checkmark designates the action is always allowed; a yellow question mark means that you'll be prompted with an onscreen message when an attempt to perform that action occurs. A program or service that is denied access is marked with a red X icon.
13. By default, Kerio Personal Firewall configures itself such that you'll be prompted to make a decision when any program or service attempts inbound or outbound communication for the first time. To test this capability, click Start → Internet Explorer and browse to a Web site. The Outgoing Connection Alert (Internet) box appears, as shown in Figure 6-20.
14. To allow Internet Explorer to always connect to the Internet, check the Create a rule for this communication and don't ask me again checkbox and then click Permit. This prevents Kerio Personal Firewall from alerting you the next time that Internet Explorer attempts to access the Internet.

Figure 6-19: Reviewing the status of programs and services in Kerio Personal Firewall.

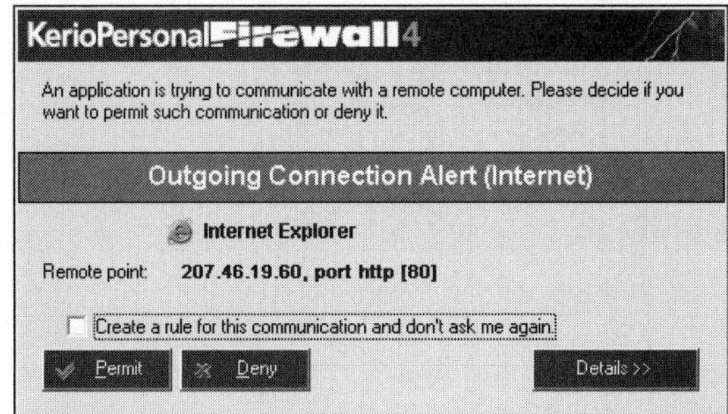

Figure 6-20: Kerio Personal Firewall displays alert messages when new programs or services attempt to make outgoing connections.

Note

Some Windows XP processes must be granted outbound access to your Trusted Network or the Internet in order for outbound communications to function correctly. For example, Generic Host Processes for Win32 Services is used by Windows XP to determine the IP address associated with a name like `www.pcmag.com`,

using DNS. If this service is not granted outbound access, you will not be able to connect to Web sites by name. If you're ever in doubt about the purpose (or safety) of a particular program or service that requests outbound access, search for it on Google or by using the online Process Library at www.processlibrary.com.

Follow these steps to allow or deny inbound or outbound access to a program or service already listed on the Application tab in Kerio Personal Firewall:

1. Double-click the Kerio Personal Firewall icon on your taskbar to open the main program window.
2. Click the Network Security tab.
3. Right-click the current configuration for a process in a particular direction to change the setting for that program or service. For example, right-click the settings that permits Internet Explorer to communicate outbound onto the Internet, as shown in Figure 6-21. Use the shortcut menu that appears to change the setting to Permit, Deny, or Ask, based on your preferences.

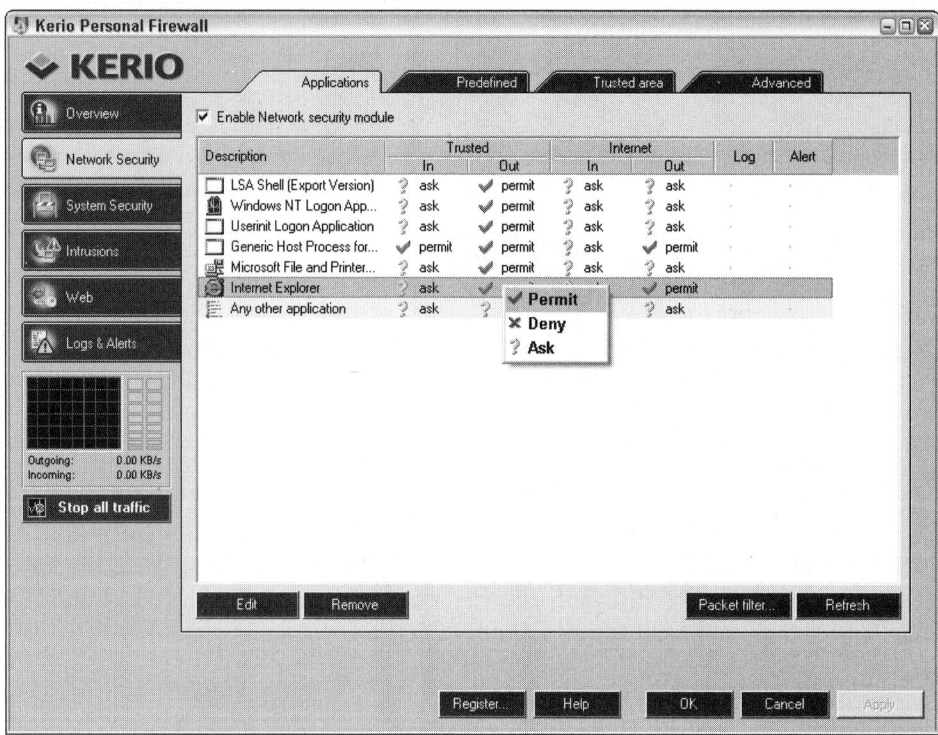

Figure 6-21: Changing connection settings for programs or services with Kerio Personal Firewall.

4. Alternatively, double-click the name of a program or service on this list to edit its settings, as shown in the Connection settings window shown in Figure 6-22.

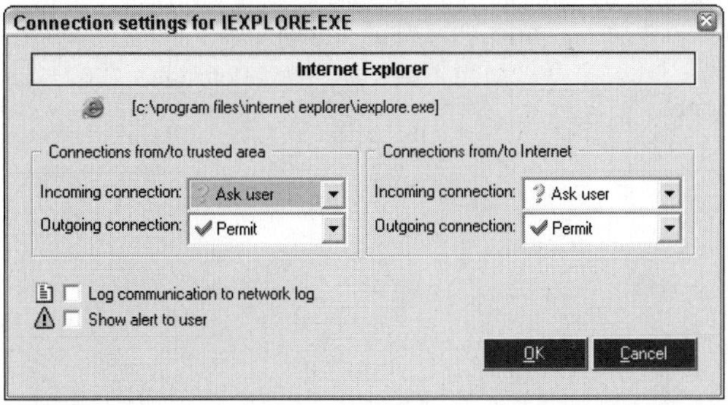

Connection settings for IEXPLORE.EXE
Internet Explorer
[c:\program files\internet explorer\iexplore.exe]
Connections from/to trusted area
Incoming connection: Ask user
Outgoing connection: Permit
Connections from/to Internet
Incoming connection: Ask user
Outgoing connection: Permit
Log communication to network log
Show alert to user
OK
Cancel

Figure 6-22: Changing connection settings for a particular program or service with Kerio Personal Firewall.

Beyond configuring inbound and outbound connection settings for different programs and services, Kerio Personal Firewall allows you to configure a wide range of advanced security settings that can be used to better protect your Windows XP system. Some of the more popular options include:

- The capability to password-protect the configuration of your firewall. When password-protection is enabled (from Overview → Preferences → Enable password protection), only a user who supplies the correct password can change the firewall's configuration settings.
- The capability to stop all inbound and outbound traffic instantly by clicking the Stop all traffic button.
- The capability to control whether certain programs and services are allowed to start at all, and whether a particular program has the capability to launch another. To configure permission settings that control whether a particular program is allowed to run on your system, browse to System Security → Applications.
- The capability to configure custom rules that allow or deny certain types of inbound or outbound traffic under Network Security → Applications → Packet filter.

All of the personal firewall packages available for Windows XP include different advanced features and capabilities. Prior to settling on any one particular firewall, test some of the alternatives available to determine which best meets your needs. You may find that you prefer one firewall's interface to another's, or deem one easier to use than the rest. As one of the most important pieces of software installed on your computer, it's imperative that you pick a firewall package that you feel comfortable with — there's nothing worse than "fighting" with a program that you find annoying or hard to use.

Hardware Firewalls

If you're the proud owner of a broadband (DSL, cable, or satellite) Internet connection and a home network, you're probably using a hardware router of some sort to share your Internet connection. Home routers come in both wired and wireless varieties, and ultimately act as an intermediary between your home network and the Internet. An example of a hardware router designed for home users is shown in the following figure.

A Linksys hardware router.

Besides allowing you to share your broadband Internet connection amongst computers on your home network, these devices also include an integrated firewall component, leading many people to refer to them as a "hardware" firewall.

By default, the firewall components of these routers behave in a manner similar to Windows Firewall. They deny all incoming connection attempts from Internet users by default, but allow all outgoing traffic to find its way onto the Internet, unrestricted. This tends to be the best default option for inexperienced users, who want the security protection that a firewall provides in stopping Internet users from accessing their network, but still want to be able to surf the Internet without restriction.

Unlike Windows Firewall, however, a hardware firewall will typically allow you to control not only what can enter your network, but also what can leave it destined for the Internet. For example, imagine that you want to restrict access to the Internet such that only Web surfing and sending e-mail messages is allowed. With a hardware firewall, you could configure rules that would allow only these types of outbound Internet access, and restrict all others, as shown in the following figure. The ability to configure these types of rules is especially helpful if your goal is to stop users on your network from accessing file sharing services, online multi-player games, or even instant messaging chats.

Some hardware firewalls even allow you to "schedule" rules such that they only apply during certain times of the day. For example, you might configure your firewall with a scheduled rule that would deny all Internet access from 3:00 to 8:00 in the evening and then allow complete access from 8:00 to 10:00 in the evening. If you're looking for a way to keep the kids from surfing when then should be doing their homework, this technique works perfectly. Making things better still is the ability to apply rules to certain PCs only, ensuring that other computers still have unrestricted access as required.

Certainly, a hardware firewall is a powerful device, and can offer great protection when correctly configured; however, you shouldn't expect your hardware firewall to alert you to configuration issues or settings in the same manner as a software firewall. Additionally, you may occasionally run into programs when attempting to run both a hardware and software firewall on the same network. For example, if you have a hardware firewall in place and have Windows Firewall enabled on your

Windows XP system at the same time, you may occasionally run into problems. Amongst the most common is the situation where you want to allow inbound access into your network by an Internet user, perhaps to play an online game. Configuring an exception for the game in Windows Firewall would not be enough—you would also need to open the appropriate ports on your hardware firewall to allow traffic through, or it would never reach your Windows XP system.

Consult your router's user manual for more details on configuring its firewall features and settings. For details on allowing inbound access through your hardware firewall, you can also consult the step-by-step instructions available online at `www.portforward.com`.

Testing Your Firewall

After you have firewall software installed, it's important to test it (at least occasionally) to be sure that it is providing appropriate and adequate protection for your Windows XP system. Two primary methods are used to test firewall security:

- **Port scans.** A port scan tests the inbound security of your firewall by scanning through ranges of TCP and UDP port numbers in an attempt to determine whether individual ports are open (allow incoming connections), closed (block incoming connections), or stealth (don't even appear to exist as far as Internet users are concerned). The information provided by a port scan helps you ensure that you haven't left certain ports open by accident, and also helps you understand how outside users "see" your system when it's connected to the Internet. Hackers commonly use port scanners to determine which ports are open on a computer. For example, a hacker might perform port scans against thousands of IP addresses to see whether a particular vulnerability is installed on any computers. By testing your own firewall with a port scanner, you gain access to the same types of information used by hackers and can then configure your firewall with appropriate settings to mitigate any potential risks to your PC. A number of Web sites allow you to perform free port scans from your Web browser, including Shields UP!! (`www.grc.com/x/ne.dll?bh0bkyd2`), Broadband Reports (`www.dslreports.com/scan`), AuditMyPC (`www.auditmypc.com`), and others.
- **Outbound security tests.** A few different utilities are capable of testing the outbound filtering capabilities of your firewall by attempting to access your Internet connection without your knowledge. The basic idea is that you download and such a tool, which attempts to connect to the Internet by bypassing your firewall's outbound security settings. If your firewall catches the attempt (by alerting you to the fact that a new program is attempting to access the Internet), the test has passed. If you are not alerted to the connection attempt and the tool is able to communicate over the Internet successfully, the outbound security test has failed. Outbound security tests are particularly important as part of ensuring that your firewall will not allow spyware programs and other threats to connect to the Internet undetected if they've found their way onto your system. Two of the more popular tools used to test outbound firewall security include FireHole (available from keir.net/firehole.html) and Firewall Leakage Tester (available from `grc.com/lt/leaktest.htm`).

Follow these steps to test the security of your firewall via an online port scan:

1. Click Start → Internet Explorer, or open your preferred Web browser.
2. In the Address bar, type **www.grc.com/x/ne.dll?bh0bkyd2** and then press Enter.
3. Read through the agreement information on the Shields UP!! Web page and then click Proceed.
4. In the Shields UP!! Services section (Figure 6-23), click Common Ports. This option scans your system in an attempt to determine the status of ports to which Internet users commonly try to connect.
5. When the scanning process is complete, a result (including a Passed or Failed message) appears, as shown in Figure 6-24. In the case of the system used in this example, the test failed because the scanned computer replied to a "ping" issued by the port scanner, verifying the system's existence; however, the port scan also showed that all common ports are running in "stealth" mode.

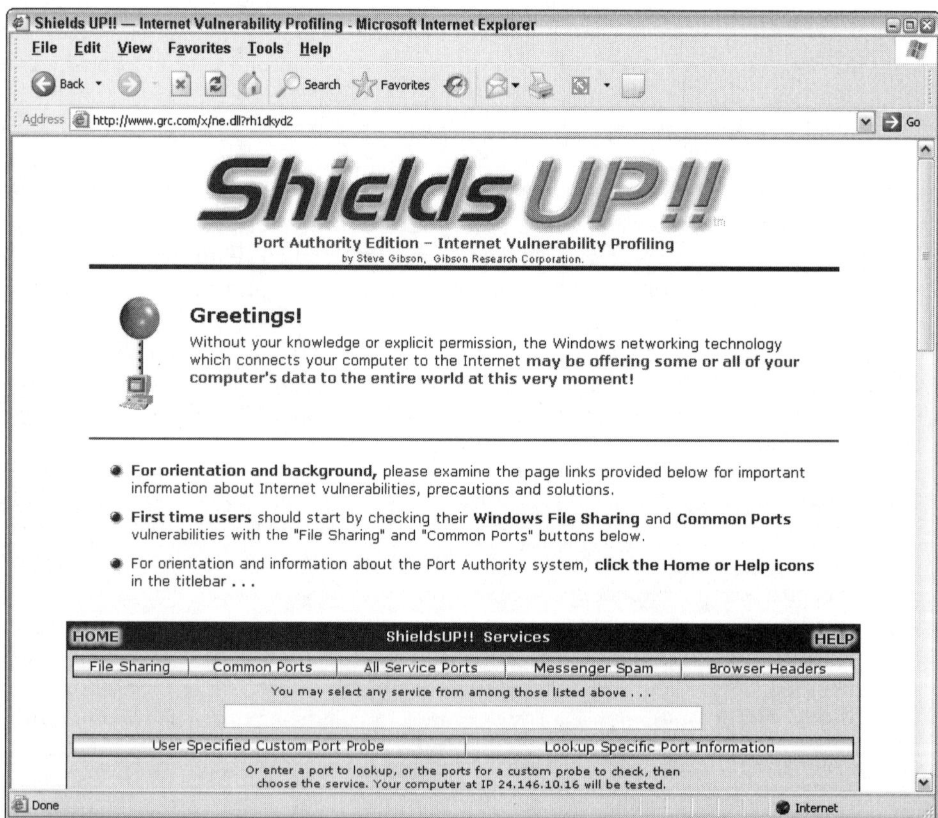

Figure 6-23: Testing your firewall with the Shields UP!! port scanning Web site.

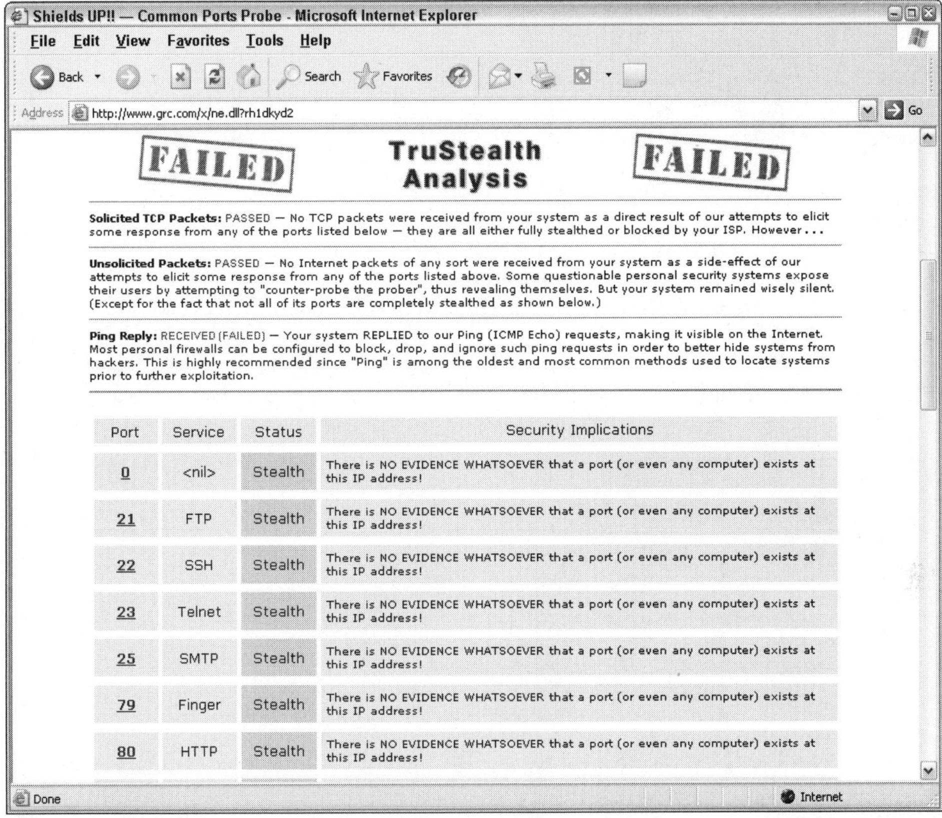

Figure 6-24: The results from a Shields UP!! port scan.

Caution

The port scan outlined in the previous example scanned "common" port numbers only. If you believe that other inbound connection ports on your firewall many be open, complete a scan of All Service Ports with Shields UP! (which tests your system's first 1056 ports) or a scan of all 65,000+ ports with the Firewall test tool at `www.auditmypc.com`.

Follow these steps to test the outbound security of your firewall using the LeakTest testing tool:

1. Download firehole.exe from grc.com/lt/leaktest.htm.
2. Double-click leaktest.exe to open the tool and then click OK.
3. At the Ready to Test screen (Figure 6-25), click the Test for Leaks button.

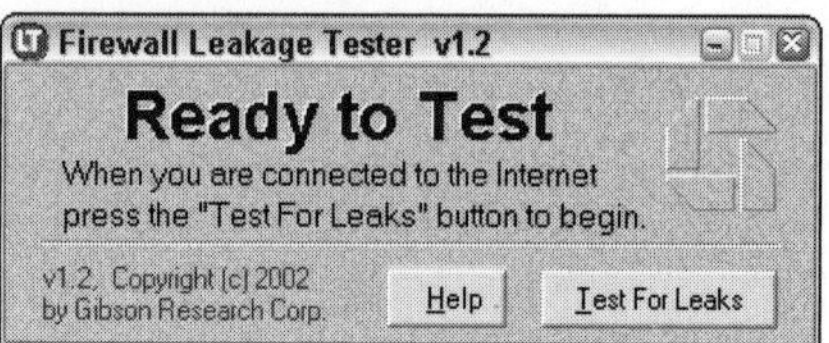

Figure 6-25: Firewall Leakage Tester is a basic tool to test the outbound security of your firewall.

4. Read the instructions provided on the First Time Help screen and then click OK.
5. If your firewall did nothing to stop LeakTest from connecting to the Internet, the Firewall Penetrated! message shown in Figure 6-26 is displayed.

Figure 6-26: Message displayed when your firewall fails the outbound connection test.

6. If your firewall alerted you to the fact that LeakTest was attempting to access the Internet and you denied the action, the Unable to Connect message shown in Figure 6-27 is displayed.

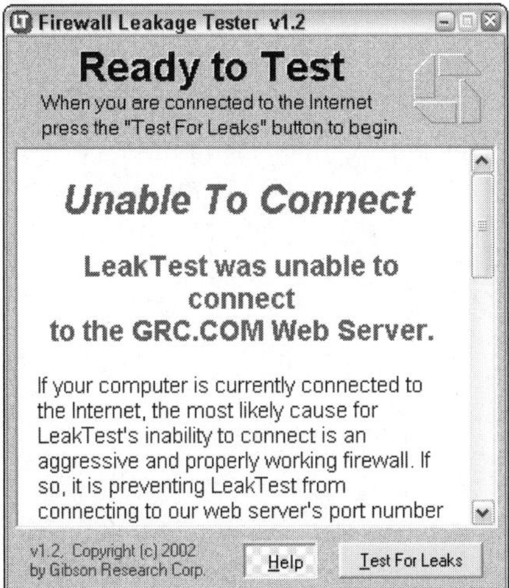

Figure 6-27: Message displayed when your firewall passes the outbound connection test.

Summary

When it comes to protecting a Windows XP system that connects to the Internet, arguably no single component is as important to the process as a firewall. Keep the following points in mind when it comes to protecting your Windows XP system with a firewall:

- A firewall should never be considered an "optional" component on a Windows XP system. Every Windows XP system connected to the Internet should have firewall software installed and enabled, and preferably a package that supports both inbound and outbound filtering.
- Windows Firewall is the native firewall component included with Windows XP systems that have at least Service Pack 2 installed. Windows Firewall is enabled for all connections automatically, but lacks outbound filtering capabilities.
- When you need to allow incoming connections from Internet users, do not disable your firewall. Instead, configure an "exception" or rule for the program or service to which external users need to connect. When these inbound connections are no longer required, disable their associated exceptions or rules.
- Consider installing a personal firewall software package on your Windows XP system rather than relying on the capabilities of Windows Firewall (or even the firewall in your

broadband router). With the proliferation of virus and spyware threats on the Internet, it's more important than ever before to use a firewall that not only supports both inbound and outbound filtering but also alerts you to suspicious connection attempts as they occur.

- Periodically test the security of your firewall using online port scanners and outbound testing utilities. Doing so helps to ensure that you haven't mistakenly left a port open or exception enabled that could be used to compromise the security of your Windows XP system.

Chapter 7

Keeping Windows XP Patched and Protected

If you've ever purchased a new car, you might be familiar with the concept of a "factory recall." In the automotive world, recalls occur when a flaw is found in a component, typically one that could impact the overall safety of the vehicle. When it's discovered, manufacturers issue a factory recall to all of the current owners of the specific make and model in question, allowing them to have the component replaced — typically at no charge.

In the world of operating systems such as Windows XP, processes similar to factory recalls also occur from time to time. For example, a new security flaw might be discovered that could allow another user to connect to your Windows XP system, or remotely issue commands to make changes to its configuration. When these issues are discovered, Microsoft works to determine the cause of the problem and then creates and issues a free "fix" that you can download and install to correct the issue. Unlike a factory recall, Microsoft doesn't ask you to bring your PC in for repairs; instead, they provide you with the necessary details and "tools," and ask you to fix it yourself. In the world of Windows XP, these tools are software programs known as security updates and Service Packs.

Ultimately, you (and you alone) are responsible for ensuring that your system is adequately patched and protected from the latest security threats. If your Windows XP system is properly updated, it's usually much less susceptible to the latest viruses, worms, and other security issues. Leave your system unpatched, however, and you run the risk of becoming a hacker's new best friend.

Thankfully, Windows XP allows you to keep your system updated against the latest security threats in a variety of different ways. In this chapter you learn more about the functions of security updates and Service Packs, as well as the three primary options that can be used to keep your Windows XP system updated and protected.

Windows XP Security Updates

It has been estimated that Windows XP was programmed using somewhere in the ballpark of 40 million lines of code. That's a mammoth undertaking, to be certain, and one in which hundreds (if not thousands) of different programmers, analysts, and managers played a role.

Given the scope of such a project, it's not surprising that everything from small to more serious flaws are identified in Windows XP from time to time. Some of these flaws are pose no real security risk, and are addressed at a later time. Others are more serious and demand immediate attention, resulting in the release of what are often referred to as "patches," "hotfixes," or "updates."

In the world of Windows, security issues discovered after the initial release of an operating system such as Windows XP are addressed by way of fixes known as security updates and Service Packs. Both of these methods of addressing security issues are explored in more detail in the following sections.

Security updates

A security update is a fix designed to address a single security issue on a Windows XP system. Sometimes referred to as patches or hotfixes, security updates are periodically released, as required. When new and potential exploits are discovered, a team of programmers at Microsoft works to develop an update that addresses the issue and then distributes the updated code in such a way that it can be installed just like any other program.

Security updates for Windows XP are normally released once a month (typically on the second Tuesday). Some months pass without as much as a single Windows XP update; another might include five or more. In cases where the security risk is particularly time-sensitive, such as where infection from a new virus or worm is spreading rapidly, Microsoft may release a security update within hours of the news.

To help users understand the risk associated with a given issue, each security threat is assigned what is known as a "severity rating." As a general rule, you should apply all updates marked as "Critical" or "Important" as soon as possible. Those with a rating of "Moderate" or "Low" don't present as serious a risk, but could potentially impact your Windows XP system.

Microsoft distributes security updates in a few different ways, each of which is explored later in this chapter.

Caution

Microsoft will never send you security updates as an attachment to an e-mail message. If you receive messages claiming to be updates from Microsoft, do not open the attachment, because it almost certainly contains a virus or similar threat. Microsoft does have a security notification system, but its e-mail messages alert you only to the fact that updates have been released and provide a link to their Web or FTP site. For more details on Microsoft's software distribution policy, see `www.microsoft.com/technet/security/bulletin/info/swdist.mspx`.

Service packs

Where a security update is a patch designed to address a single security issue, a Service Pack is a comprehensive collection of updates that is bundled together as one large package. As a general rule, a Service Pack will include all security updates that preceded it, along with other minor fixes and feature improvements that have nothing to do with security at all. In this way, installing a Service Pack is effectively the same as updating to a more feature-rich and secure version of Windows XP.

In addition to including all updates that preceded their release, Service Packs are also cumulative— Service Pack 2 (the most recent release at the time of writing) includes all updates originally included with Service Pack 1. In other words, you can jump straight to installing Service Pack 2, even if you don't currently have Service Pack 1 installed.

Updating Windows XP to the latest Service Pack version is highly recommended from a security perspective. If you choose not to install the latest Service Pack, your system could be missing one or more critical security updates, leaving it at risk.

Caution

The Internet is rife with tales of how the latest Service Pack or security update managed to render a user's Windows XP computer unable to boot or perform some other function. Although there's no doubt that some of these stories are true, most bad Service Packs experiences are a result of users not following instructions or not properly determining the preparedness of their system. Prior to installing any Service Pack, you should always back up of your personal files. Additionally, check developers' Web sites to ensure that any programs you rely upon will function after the Service Pack is installed. For details on some of the different ways that a Service Pack can be uninstalled (if necessary), visit `support.microsoft.com/kb/875350`.

Depending upon how Windows XP was originally installed on your computer, you may already have the most recent Service Pack installed. Follow these steps to determine which Service Pack (if any) is currently installed on your Windows XP system:

1. Click Start → Control Panel.
2. Click Switch to Classic View (if necessary).
3. Double-click the System applet. In the System section of the General tab, your system's Windows XP edition will be listed, along with it's current Service Pack version (if applicable), as shown in Figure 7-1.

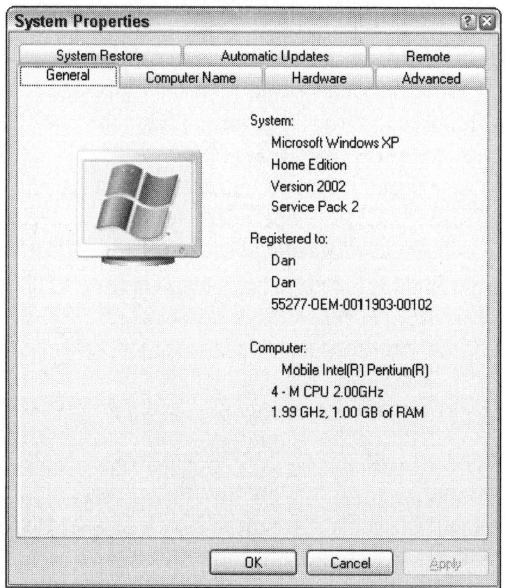

Figure 7-1: Use the System applet to determine which Service Pack has been installed on a Windows XP system.

Windows XP Update Options

To satisfy the needs of different Windows XP users in home and office environment, Microsoft makes security updates and Service Packs available via a number of different distribution mechanisms. Windows XP systems can be updated to include the latest security updates and Service Packs using three primary methods:

- Visiting the Windows Update Web site
- Using Windows XP's Automatic Updates feature
- Manually downloading and installing updates

Each of these methods is explored in more detail in the following sections.

Using Windows Update

When it was first developed, the Windows Update Web site heralded an exciting new innovation in the world of distributing important patches and updates. Prior to Windows Update, any user who wanted to apply the latest updates had to seek them out on the Microsoft Web or FTP site and then download and install the necessary files. Unfortunately, there was no easy way to identify which updates has already been installed, or whether any critical updates were missing. As a result, a large percentage of systems were left unpatched, making them vulnerable to a wide variety of security threats.

With the release of the Windows Update Web site, Microsoft found a way to address the challenges associated with keeping systems updated while making the process easy enough for inexperienced users. All a user needed to do was open the site in Internet Explorer, select the option to scan for updates, and use the scan results to determine which updates should be downloaded and installed. Unfortunately, this method still relied upon users taking the initiative to visit the site to scan for updates. As such, many systems continued to remain unpatched.

Today, the Windows Update Web site remains a popular way to obtain the latest security updates and Service Packs for Windows XP and previous Microsoft operating systems, as well as other updates (for example, driver files) that have little to do with system security. Ultimately, the Windows Update Web site offers a popular alternative for users who want to control which updates are installed on their Windows XP system and when the update process take place.

Follow these steps to check for available updates on the Windows Update Web site:

1. Click Start → Internet Explorer. Internet Explorer is the only browser that works correctly with the Windows Update Web site.
2. In the Address box, type **http://www.windowsupdate.com** and then press Enter. The Windows Update Welcome screen appears, as shown in Figure 7-2. If this screen does not appear, you may need to download and install Internet Explorer add-ons, in which case the Windows Update Web site walks you through the process.
3. To scan for, download, and install critical security updates only, click the Express Install (Recommended) link.

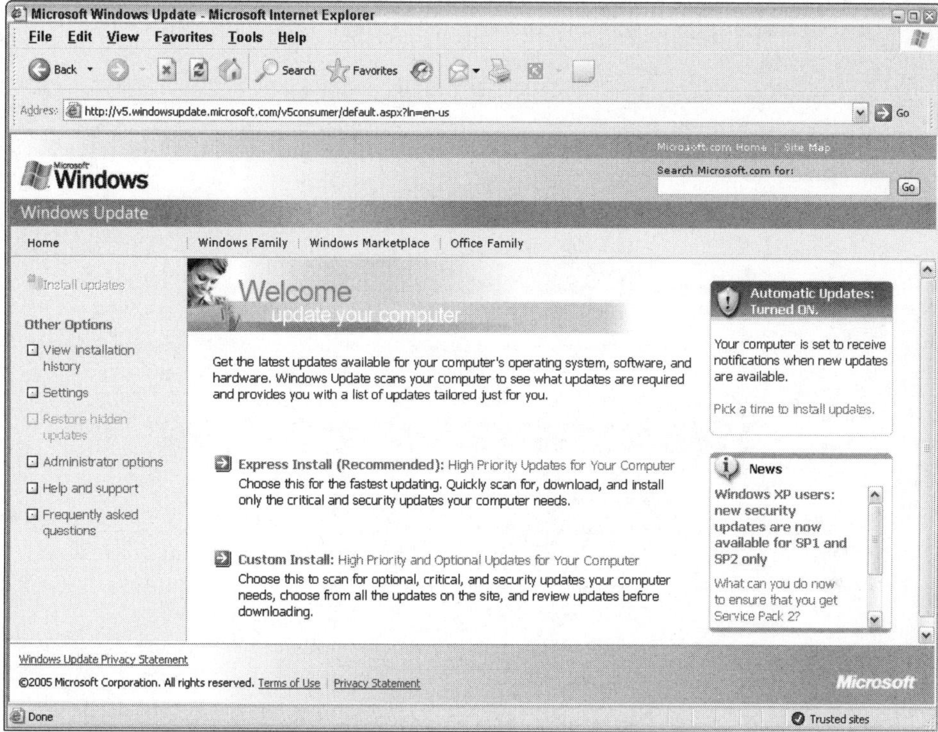

Figure 7-2: The Windows Update Web site.

4. After the scanning process is complete, the Express Install screen lists all high priority updates for your system, as shown in Figure 7-3. Click Install.

5. When all updates have been downloaded and installed, the Installing Updates window will let you know. In some cases, you are prompted to reboot to complete the installation process, as shown in Figure 7-4. If this is the case, click Restart Now.

Tip

If you want to stop other users (for example, other administrators) on your Windows XP system from using the Windows Update Web site to download and install updates (presumably in favor of an alternate option like Automatic Updates), open the Registry Editor and browse to `HKEY_LOCAL_MACHINE\Software\Microsoft\Windows\CurrentVersion\Policies\Explorer`. If the Explorer folder is not already present, right-click Policies and select New → Key; name the key Explorer, and click it to view its contents (it will be empty at this point). Next, create a new DWORD called NoWindowsUpdate and set the value to 1. If you do this, users attempting to update your system will receive a message stating that network policy settings prevent them from using the Windows Update Web site.

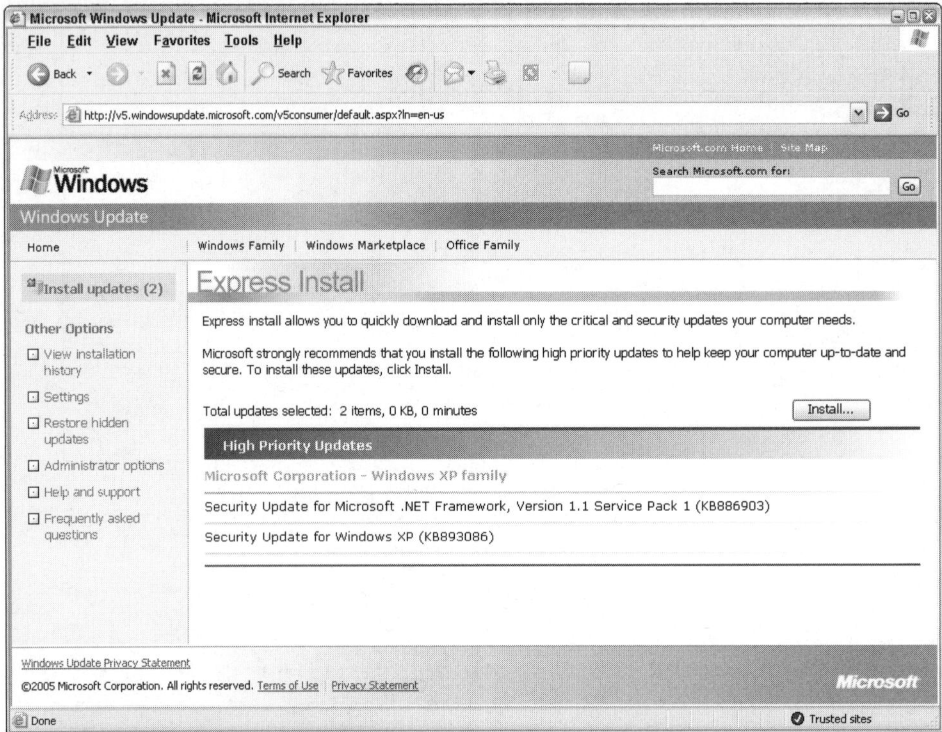

Figure 7-3: Installing updates using the Windows Update Web site.

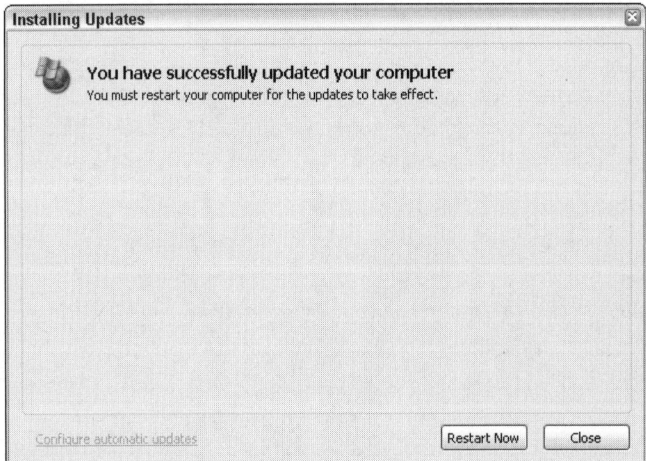

Figure 7-4: After updates are successfully installed, you may be prompted to restart your computer.

Noncritical Updates

The Express Installation option on the Windows Update Web site provides the easiest way to keep your computer updated with the latest security updates and Service Packs if you prefer to be in control of how (and especially when) updates are applied.

The Express option on the Windows Update Web site may be recommended, but selecting the Custom Installation option also has benefits. Where the Express option focuses on important security updates (which all users should apply) only, the Custom option includes updates for programs, relevant driver files, and more. For example, this option may enlighten you to the fact that a new and improved driver is available for your modem or video card, or that different add-ons or feature packs have been released for programs such as Windows Media Player.

After selecting the Custom option and allowing it to complete a scan, you are provided with a list of all pertinent updates available for your system, categorized into sections named high priority updates, optional software updates, and optional hardware updates, as shown in the following figure.

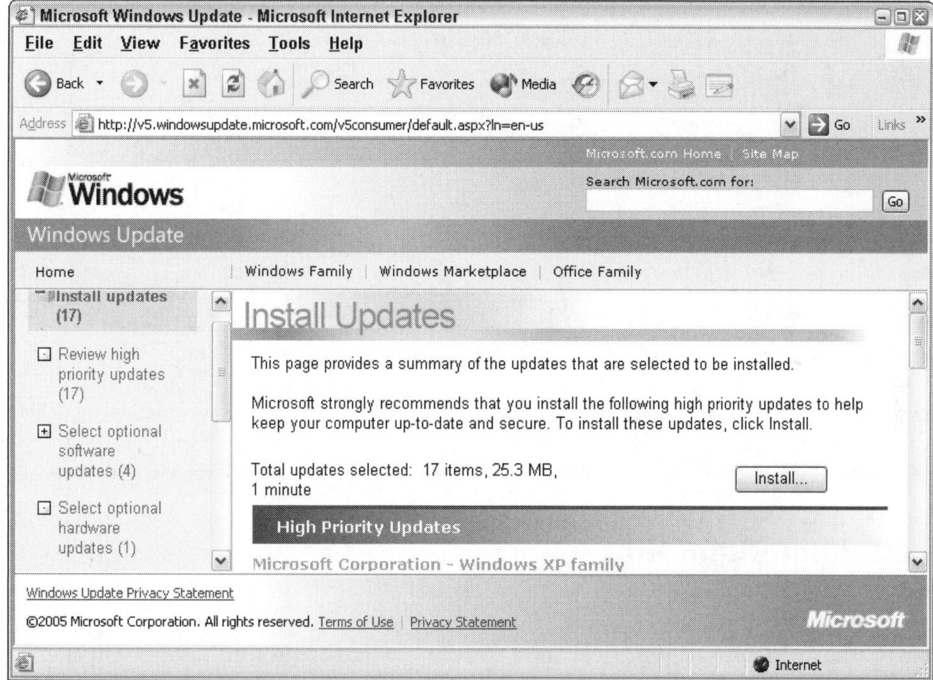

Reviewing available updates after completing a custom scan at the Windows Update Web site.

To select an item, simply check the box next to its name. After you've checked all those you want to download, just click the Install button to download and install the updates.

Continued

Noncritical Updates (Continued)

Along with the capability to download and install non-critical updates, the Windows Update Web site also includes the View installation history feature, as shown in the following figure.

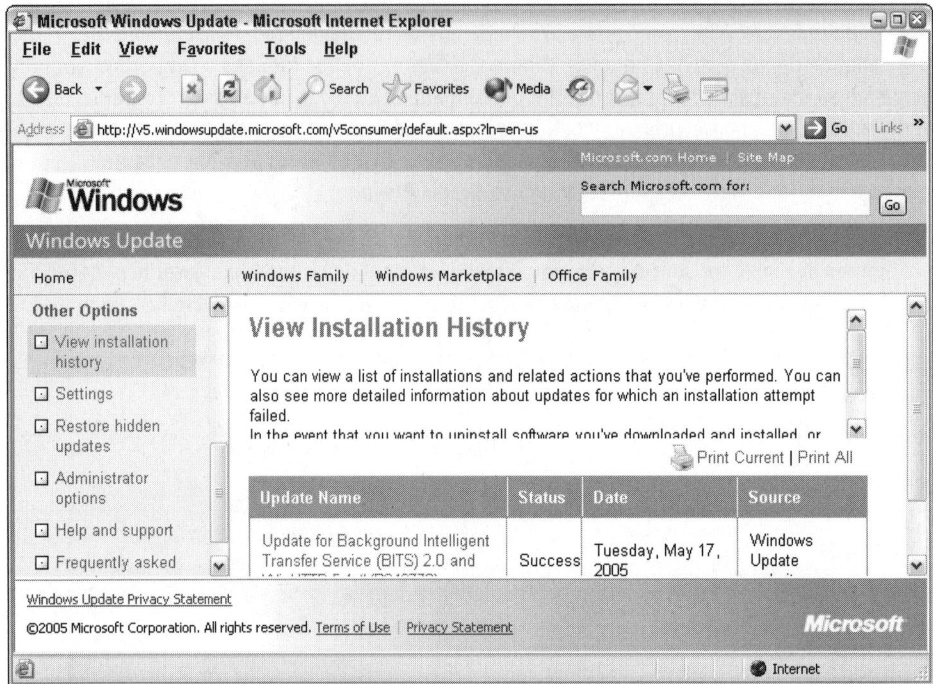

Reviewing the update installation history for a Windows XP system.

The View Installation History screen present list of all updates installed on your system is displayed, along with details of the method used to perform the update.

Using automatic updates

In many ways, Windows XP's Automatic Updates feature was born from both the strengths and weaknesses of the Windows Update Web site. Windows Update provides an easy way for users to keep abreast of the latest critical security updates and Service Packs, but it still presents one glaring weakness — only users who know enough (or remember) to visit the site regularly end up with critical security updates installed.

Automatic Updates was included with the original release of Windows XP to help address the issue, but even its capabilities were lacking. Specifically, in its original iteration Automatic Updates was capable of checking for and even downloading new updates from Windows Update servers on

the Internet, but didn't install these updates automatically. In other words, user systems might have had all critical updates downloaded, but if they ignored notification messages, these updates might never be installed.

With the release of Service Pack 2, Microsoft changed the default behavior of the Windows XP's Automatic Updates feature. Instead of relying on the user to configure Automatic Update settings and install updates as required, it added a new setting that would download and install all critical updates automatically. This recommended setting is enabled by default, and helps to ensure that users who might have previously ignored important updates now have them installed automatically.

Of course, putting the critical update process on "auto pilot" in this manner doesn't work for all users, which is the reason why Automatic Update settings can still be changed to meet different user needs or preferences.

Along with changing the way that Automatic Updates were configured, Service Pack 2 also added the Security Center tool to Windows XP's Control Panel. Security Center lets users know whether Automatic Updates are turned on, and whether the Windows XP system has firewall and anti-virus software installed and enabled.

Cross-Reference

Firewall software for Windows XP was explored in Chapter 6. Anti-virus software is looked at in more detail in Chapter 8.

Follow these steps to check the status of the Automatic Updates feature on your Windows XP system:

1. Click Start → Control Panel → Security Center. If the Security Center option is not shown in Control Panel, you need to install Service Pack 2.
2. Click the downwards pointing arrow in the Automatic Updates section to view your current settings, as shown in Figure 7-5.
3. If the Automatic Updates title includes a green icon, your system is already configured to download and install updates automatically. If the icon is red, Automatic Updates has been disabled. If the icon is yellow (Check Settings), your system has custom Automatic Update settings configured. To enable Automatic Updates in the recommended configuration, click Turn on Automatic Updates button.

Figure 7-5: The Windows Security Center tool.

The Automatic Updates tab on a Windows XP system with Service Pack 2 installed includes the following options:

- **Automatic (recommended).** When this option is selected, updates are downloaded automatically and then installed at the time specified. If your computer is turned off at the specified installation time, updates are installed the next time you restart your computer. In some cases it may still be necessary to accept an End-User Licensing Agreement before a particular update can be installed.
- **Download updates for me, but let me choose when to install them.** When this option is selected, updates are downloaded automatically. After the download process is complete, the Windows Update icon appears in the notification area for administrators, prompting them to install the updates.
- **Notify me, but don't automatically download or install them.** When this option is selected, the Windows Update icon appears in the notification area of the taskbar to alert administrators that new updates are available for download. After the update download process is complete, the Windows Update icon appears again, prompting for the updates to be installed.
- **Turn off automatic updates.** When this option is selected, Windows XP never checks for critical updates.

Note

On Windows XP systems prior to Service Pack 2, the Automatic Updates tab included similar configuration settings, but did not include the option to have updates both downloaded and installed automatically.

Follow these steps to configure Automatic Update settings on your Windows XP system:

1. Click Start → Control Panel → Security Center.
2. In the Manage security settings for section, click Automatic Updates.
3. On the Automatic Updates tab, select your preferred option, as shown in Figure 7-6. For most users, the Automatic (recommended) setting is the most appropriate choice.

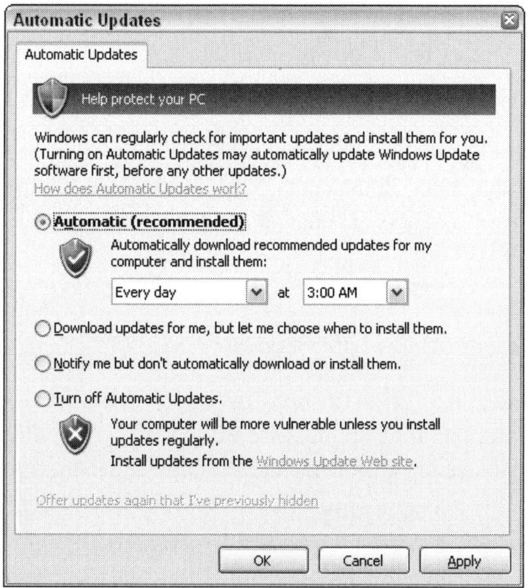

Figure 7-6: Configuring Automatic Update settings.

4. Click OK to close the System Properties window.

In cases where you select the option for updates to be downloaded but not installed, the Windows Update icon appears in the notification area of your taskbar when updates are ready to be installed (see Figure 7-7).

When you click this icon, the Automatic Updates installation window opens, prompting you to proceed with an Express or Custom installation. The Express option installs all downloaded updates; the custom option allows you to select which updates to install, as shown in Figure 7-8.

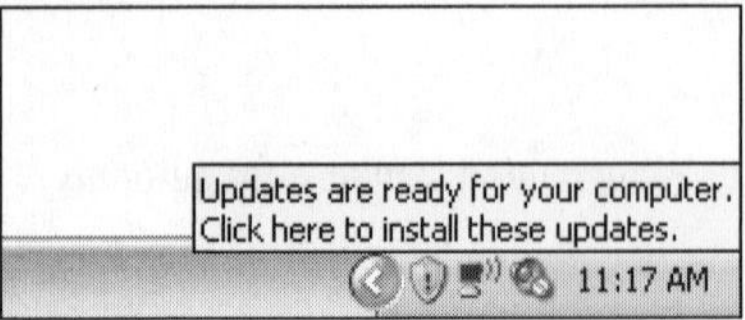

Figure 7-7: The Windows Update icon notifies you that updates are ready to be installed.

Figure 7-8: Installing downloaded updates manually.

If you ignore the Windows Update icon and then decide to shut down your Windows XP system, the Turn off computer window alerts you to the fact that updates are waiting to be installed (Figure 7-9). If you click the Turn Off button, the updates are installed, after which your computer is shut down automatically.

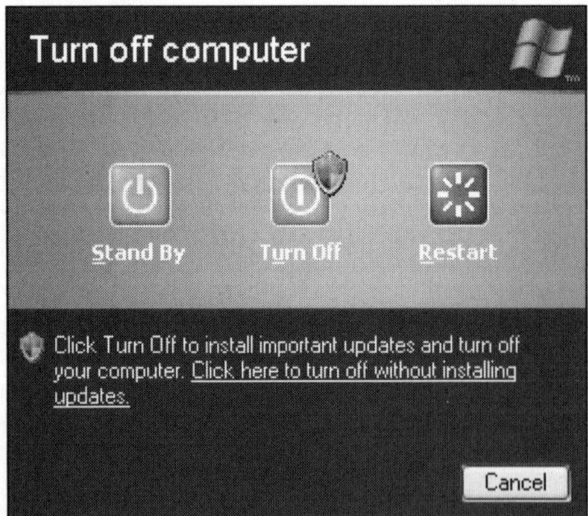

Figure 7-9: The Turn off computer dialog box when updates are waiting to be installed.

Tip

Unless you intend to be very diligent about checking for new Windows XP security updates and Service Packs regularly, configure the Automatic Updates tab to use the Automatic (recommended) setting.

Installing service packs and security updates manually

Methods such as Automatic Updates and the Windows Update Web site make the process of patching and protecting Windows XP systems easier than ever before, but downloading and installing these updates the old fashioned way is still a popular option. That's right — there are still plenty of users out there who would rather download and install updates manually, rather than rely on any automated process to do the job for them.

Note

Administrators of networks that include a Windows 2000 Server or Windows Server 2003 system can effectively create their very own Windows Update server in-house by installing Microsoft's free Windows Server Update Services (WSUS) software. After installed, this software acts as a local Windows Update server from which systems such as Windows XP can obtain critical security updates and service packs. Effectively, the WSUS system downloads updates once and then allows administrators to approve individual security updates and Service Packs for distribution on the network. For more details on WSUS, visit `www.microsoft.com/windowsserversystem/updateservices/default.mspx`.

In the vast majority of cases, this preference has nothing to do with the work involved in finding, downloading, and then installing individual updates. In a corporate or small office environment, the administrator's job is to ensure that all systems function correctly and are properly secured. As such, many administrators prefer to download and install updates on a test system first and then deploy the update after it has been proven to be stable and secure. This puts the administrator in control over how individual desktop systems are updated and minimizes the risk that an update could result in system downtime. In a nutshell, many administrators have learned that it's usually better to be safe than sorry.

Sometimes, the decision to go the manually update route has more to with practicality than control. A great example is the case of an administrator responsible for managing a network of Windows XP systems where only a slow dial-up Internet connection is available. If methods such as the Windows Update Web site or Automatic Updates were used in an attempt to update systems in this environment, the Internet connection would quickly come to a grinding halt, impacting other services like e-mail and Web browsing in the process. It's much more practical for the administrator to download each security update or Service Pack once and then use that download to update each computer on the network individually.

Note

Windows XP Service Packs commonly tip the scales as downloads of 200MB or more. Understanding that downloads of this size are impractical for users with very slow connections, Microsoft also makes all Service Packs available on CD. In the case of Windows XP Service Pack 2, Microsoft will send you the CD free of charge (note that delivery takes 4-6 weeks). To order the Service Pack 2 CD, visit `www.microsoft.com/windowsxp/downloads/updates/sp2/cdorder/en_us/default.mspx`.

Follow these steps to download and install Windows XP Service Pack 2 manually:

1. Click Start → Internet Explorer, or open your preferred Web browser.
2. In the Address bar, type **http://www.microsoft.com/technet/prodtechnol/winxppro/maintain/winxpsp2.mspx** and press Enter.
3. In the Get the Service Pack section, click the Download and Deploy Service Pack 2 to Multiple Computers link.
4. Click the Download button in the upper-right corner of the screen to begin the download.
5. When the File Download dialog box appears, click Save.
6. When the Save As dialog box appears, choose an appropriate folder location to save the Service Pack and then click Save.
7. Click Start → My Computer and browse to the folder where you saved the downloaded Service Pack file in Step 6.
8. Double-click on the file (named WindowsXP-KB835935-SP2-ENU.exe in the case of Service Pack 2) to begin the installation process.
9. At the Windows XP Service Pack 2 Setup Wizard Welcome screen, click Next.
10. At the License Agreement screen, click I Agree and then click Next.
11. At the Select Options screen, click Next.
12. At the Updating Your System screen (see Figure 7-10), the wizard checks to ensure you have enough disk space, backs up the files required to uninstall the Service Pack and then installs the new Service Pack. After the process is complete, click Finish to restart your system.

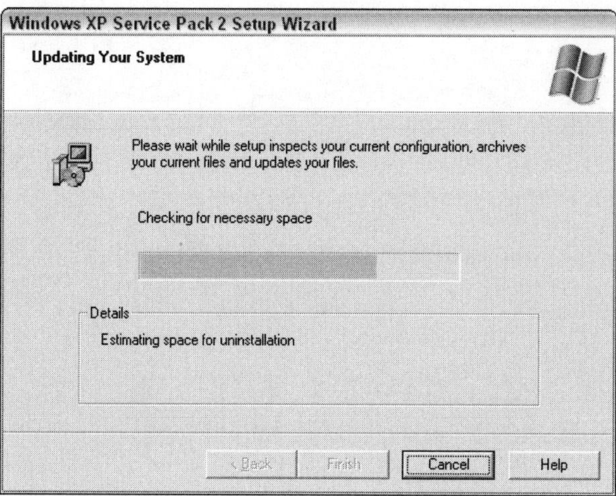

Figure 7-10: Installing Service Pack 2 manually.

Tip

When reinstalling Windows XP, you typically install the operating system using your original CD and then download and install the latest Service Pack version; however, it's possible to create a new Windows XP installation CD that already includes integrated versions of the latest Service Pack files, via a technique known as slipstreaming. After created, a slipstreamed CD can be used to install Windows XP — including the latest Service Pack — by doing nothing more than completing the normal operating system installation process. For details on creating a slipstreamed Windows XP CD that includes the latest Service Pack files, see the tutorial at `www.theeldergeek.com/slipstreamed_xpsp2_cd.htm`.

Follow these steps to download and install a security update for Windows XP manually:

1. Click Start → Internet Explorer, or open your preferred Web browser.
2. In the Address box, type **www.microsoft.com/technet/security/bulletin/summary.mspx** and then press Enter.
3. The Microsoft Security Bulletin Summaries and Webcasts page lists all security bulletins by their release date. Click the link for a particular release date and then click the Microsoft Security Bulletin Update link for that month.
4. In the Summary section, click Critical. A list of each individual critical security alert appears, as shown in Figure 7-11.

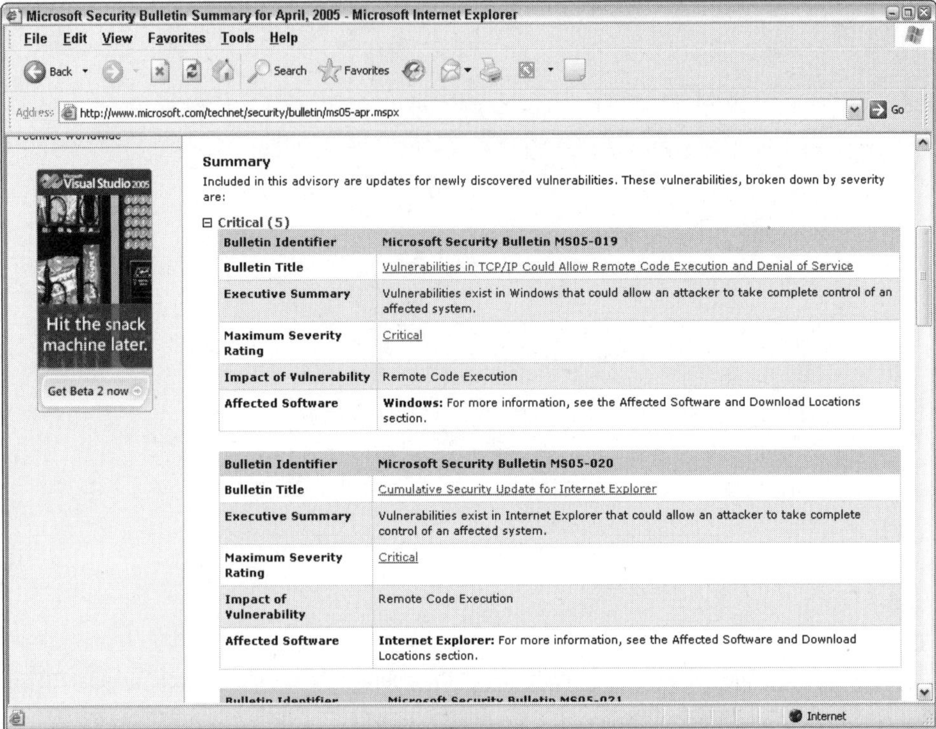

Figure 7-11: Reviewing all critical security updates in a particular bulletin.

5. Click the link in the Bulletin Title section of a particular alert. This opens the Knowledge Base (KB) page for the alert, as shown in Figure 7-12.
6. Click the Download the update link next to your Windows XP version in the Affected Software section.
7. Click the Download button in the upper-right corner of the screen to begin the download.
8. When the File Download dialog box appears, click Save.
9. When the Save As dialog box appears, choose an appropriate folder location to save the Service Pack and click Save.
10. Click Start → My Computer and browse to the folder where you saved the downloaded Service Pack file in Step 9.
11. Double-click on the file (named WindowsXP-KB893066-x86-ENU.exe in this example) to begin the installation process.
12. At the Software Update Installation Wizard screen, click Next.

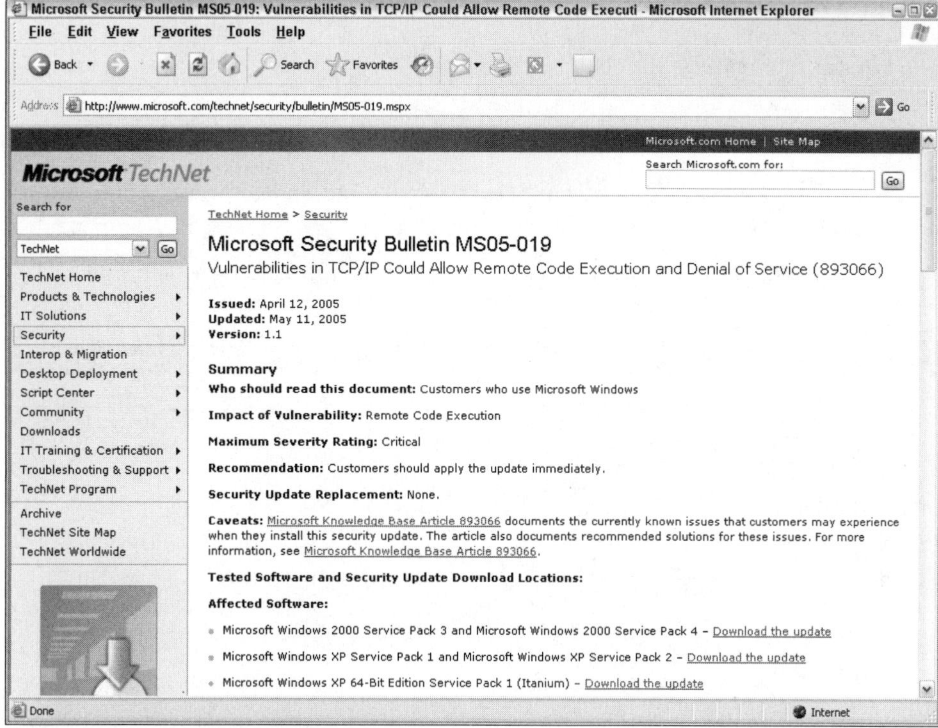

Figure 7-12: Reviewing the details of a security update.

13. At the License Agreement screen, click I Agree and then click Next.

14. When the installation process is complete, click Finish. Depending on which update you installed, you may be prompted to restart your computer.

Tip

If you prefer downloading and installing Windows XP updates manually, you can easily keep on top of things by subscribing to Microsoft Alerts, a free service that notifies you when new updates have been posted to the Microsoft Security Web site. These alerts can be sent to MSN Messenger, your e-mail program, or even a mobile device. To sign up for this service, visit `signup.alerts.msn.com/alerts/login.do?PINID=3274`.

Although most security updates and Service Packs install without issue, you may occasionally find that Windows XP experiences problems after patches are applied. Thankfully, in the same way that updates and Service Packs can be installed manually, they can also be uninstalled if necessary.

Follow these steps to remove an installed security update or Service Pack:

1. Click Start → Control Panel → Add or Remove Programs.
2. In the Add or Remove Programs window, check the Show updates checkbox at the top of the screen.
3. Scroll down in the Currently installed programs and updates window until you reach Windows XP - Software Updates.
4. Click the update you want to remove (see Figure 7-13) and then click Remove.

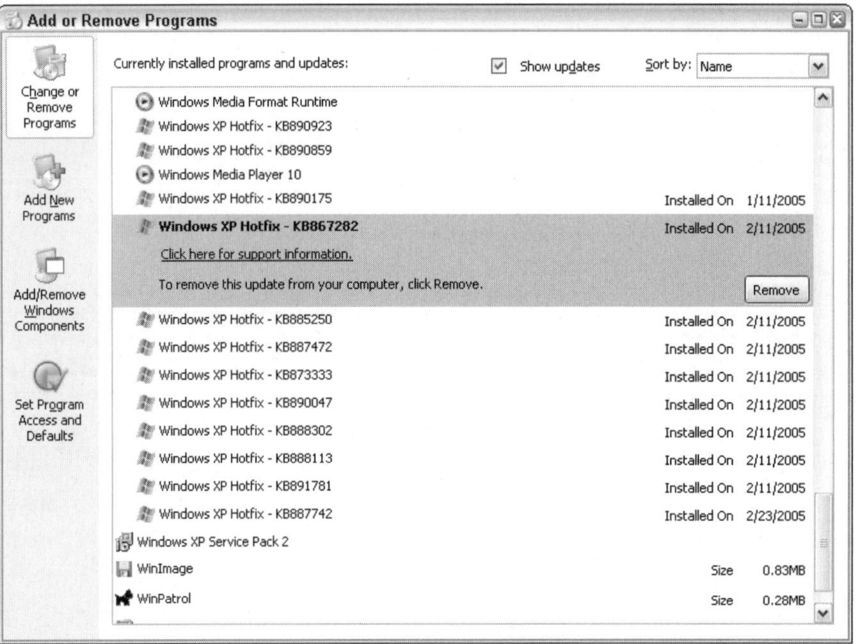

Figure 7-13: Manually removing a security update using Add or Remove Programs.

5. At the Software Update Removal Wizard screen, click Next.
6. When the warning window appears asking if you want to continue, click Yes.
7. Click Finish to complete the removal process. You may be prompted to restart your computer.

Tip

If you work in an office environment that includes many Windows XP systems, there's an easy way to determine which security updates and Service Packs have been applied to individual computers. Microsoft provides a tool known as the Microsoft Baseline Security Analyzer (MBSA) as a free download from its Web

site. After installed, this program is used to scan computers on a network in a bid to determine exactly which updates a system has installed, and which are still missing. To download MBSA, visit www.microsoft.com/technet/security/tools/mbsahome.mspx.

Patching Beyond XP

Securing Windows XP with the latest security updates and Service Packs is certainly important, but you also need to give some thought to the status of other installed software. It's less common for individual programs to be subject to the same types of security threats as an operating system, but it's not unheard of. From your personal firewall software to your preferred Web browser, it's possible that the version of a program you have installed could present a security risk.

The best way to stay abreast of the latest patches and updates for programs you have installed is to keep an eye on their developer's Web site. Most of these sites include a dedicated support section from which critical updates or patches can be downloaded as they're released. To check which version of a particular program you have installed for reference purposes, click Help→About Program as shown in Figure 7-14.

Figure 7-14: Checking the version of an installed program

Additionally, the following Web sites release security advisories related to specific programs, operating systems, and threats such as viruses as they're discovered:

- CERT Coordination Center — `www.cert.org`
- Bugtraq — `www.securityfocus.com/archive/1`
- Secunia — `www.secunia.com`
- CIAC — `www.ciac.org`

Summary

Updating Windows XP with the latest security updates and Service Packs is one of the most important steps that any user can take towards ensuring better system security. If left unpatched, a Windows XP system may be vulnerable to specific threats that are both well known and documented. The Automatic Updates feature provides the easiest way for users to keep a Windows XP system properly patched, since updates and downloaded and installed automatically. Windows XP can also be kept properly updated via the Windows Update Web site or by manually downloading and installing patches as they're released. If you do choose either of the latter options, however, it's entirely up to you to ensure that you're diligent about checking for updates regularly.

Chapter 8

Protecting Against Viruses

Nobody likes to be sick, and most people will do their best to steer clear of the latest bug — be it the flu, the common cold, or some other nasty virus. You don't have to be a doctor to recognize that prevention really is the best medicine, particularly when the alternative is acquiring and then trying to defeat the bug that's found you. Quite simply, you're almost always better off if you can avoid being infected in the first place.

When it comes to illnesses, computers and people share a common bond. Certainly, your PC is not susceptible to the common cold (although it is a very capable transmission vehicle!), but computers get sick too. In PC land, malicious programs and bits of code known as computer viruses cause the illnesses. From opening infected e-mail attachments to neglecting to apply the latest operating system security patches, there's no shortage of ways for your computer to be potentially infected by the latest bout of some particularly nasty virus.

Unfortunately, when your computer is infected with a virus, both its security and your privacy are very much at risk. Where computer viruses were once designed to be annoying or destructive, the viruses of today are of a much meaner and more malicious ilk. Some are designed to allow Internet users to remotely control your computer; others propagate themselves by using communications methods available on your PC such as e-mail or file sharing programs. There are even viruses designed with the explicit purposes of stealing credit card or online banking details from your PC.

The threats posed by viruses are very real, so both preventing and removing these pests need to be considered an absolute priority in the quest for a more secure Windows XP system. In this chapter you learn more about the different types of viruses that exist, what they're out to do, and methods that can be used to prevent them from infecting your system in the first place. You also learn about some of the tools that can be used to remove viruses from your PC if it is infected, even if you don't have anti-virus software installed. Most important, you learn how to ensure that your PC is properly geared up such that the threat of acquiring viruses in the future is as low as possible.

Understanding Viruses

In simple terms, a computer virus is a software program or a bit of scripted code designed to compromise the integrity of your PC or cause it harm. Many people wonder what would prompt someone to write a virus, but the potential reasons are almost as complex as human nature itself. Some people write viruses with financial gain in mind, looking to steal banking or credit card details from

your PC. Others are out to prove their programming prowess, or cause embarrassment to large corporations (such as Microsoft) by exploiting flaws in operating systems like Windows XP. Some are teenagers, university students, or just regular folks looking for a challenge or the notoriety associated with being the person who managed to unleash the latest virus to spread worldwide. Still others are looking to steal e-mail addresses for the purpose of sending spam, or even to use your PC as a "zombie" that can be remotely controlled to send junk e-mail messages or launch hacking attacks against different Web sites and corporations. There have even been cases where someone has claimed to write a virus with the intention of undoing the damage caused by a virus that preceded it.

Ultimately, there's little point in worrying about why viruses exist — they've been around since before the dawn of the PC age, and they're not going away anytime soon. Instead, you should focus your attention on understanding the risks that viruses pose, how to remove them if you are infected, and, most important, how to protect your computer against virus threats in the first place.

Types of viruses

The term "virus" has become a generic umbrella term used to describe almost all types of infectious and malicious code. Some people consider anything that they didn't explicitly install on their computer to be a virus; others categorize virus-like threats according to their infection techniques and goals. Broadly speaking, viruses can be divided into the following subcategories:

- Viruses
- Worms
- Trojan horses

Each of these virus categories is explored in more detail in the following sections.

Cross-Reference

Many people consider security threats such as spyware and adware to be viruses. Strictly speaking, these "malware" threats are different from viruses, even if their infectious aims and intentions are often similar. You learn more about dealing with malware threats in Chapter 9.

VIRUSES

Although the term is now used to generically describe a broad grouping of threats that also includes worms and Trojan horses, a *virus* is best described as malicious code with the capability to replicate itself. Viruses are typically attached to programs and files, infecting other programs and files as they're opened and executed. One of the key distinguishing traits of a virus is that it cannot replicate without direct user intervention of some sort, such as opening an infected file.

WORMS

Computer worms are fundamentally similar to viruses but with one key difference — a worm can replicate itself using different network communication methods without user intervention. For example, if a worm infects one computer as a result of that system missing a critical security patch, the worm might use the infected computer's Internet connection to scan for, detect, and infect other computers on the Internet that are unpatched and not properly secured. Some worms send out mass e-mail messages from an infected computer in an attempt to infect additional systems others copy themselves into folders used by P2P file sharing programs such as Kazaa as a means to replicate. The vast majority of dangerous viruses circulating on the Internet today are worms rather than traditional viruses. Because they don't require human intervention to spread, it's not unusual for a worm to infect thousands of PCs worldwide in just a few hours.

TROJAN HORSES

Named after the fabled wooden horse that helped Odysseus trick and defeat the Trojans at Troy, a Trojan horse is a type of virus that masquerades as a legitimate program, usually with the intent to install a "backdoor" program on your computer. In some cases, the Trojan horse program actually performs the legitimate task that it originally claimed to, such as functioning as an FTP client. In others, installing the Trojan simply installs the malicious backdoor program that allows remote users to connect to and control your PC via the Internet. Some Trojan horses are designed to turn your PC into a "zombie" for the purpose of sending spam e-mail messages or launching attacks against other computers. Others are designed with identity theft or spying in mind and represent a very serious risk to your personal privacy.

Virus risks

Viruses, worms, and Trojan horses always represent a risk to PC security and your personal privacy, but some are worse than others. In much the same way that a program can be designed to do just about anything, so too can a virus. The main difference between a regular program and a virus, however, is that a virus is usually designed with malicious intent in mind. Even a virus that does nothing inherently bad represents a real risk — after unleashed onto the Internet, it's not unusual for another user to take what was a relatively harmless virus to begin with, and then reprogram it to carry out more damaging tasks.

Some of the more common types of damage caused by viruses, worms, and Trojan horses include:

- Using your PC as a remotely controlled "zombie" for the purpose of sending spam e-mail or launching hacking (denial-of-service or DoS) attacks against other computers or Web sites.
- Theft of credit card information, banking details, or other personal information from your PC. This information can be used to purchase goods and services, potentially racking up thousands of dollars in charges to your accounts.
- Harvesting e-mail addresses to sell to spammers. In the world of spam, "known good" e-mail addresses are like money in the bank. Many viruses are design to infect your computer and then harvest all of the e-mail addresses present in your contact lists or address books, which are subsequently forwarded to a server on the Internet. Beyond simply harvesting addresses, many viruses attempt to forward themselves to users in your address book by sending these users infected e-mail attachments that appear to be coming from you personally.

- Shutting down security programs such as firewalls, anti-virus software, and anti-spyware tools. Knowing that security programs are the biggest barriers in their quest to infect or remotely control your computer, many virus writers have taken to disabling common security tools as part of their infection process.
- Installing backdoor programs that capture all of your PC activities in the background including screenshots, mouse clicks, keystrokes, and more. The information captured by these viruses can be forwarded to remote users on the Internet and then used for a variety of purposes ranging from identity theft to blackmail.
- Infecting individual files or program templates. Some viruses are designed to infect macros or templates in programs such as Microsoft Word, causing all documents you create to be infected as well. When an infected document is sent to another user and opened on their PC, the virus also infects that computer.
- Deleting files, formatting hard drives, or altering critical system settings. Some viruses are simply designed with destruction in mind, be it deleting your personal files, formatting or erasing disks, or even changing system configuration settings to the point that your PC no longer starts and needs to be completely reinstalled.

Ultimately, all viruses are dangerous and need to be taken seriously. Although some represent a bigger risk to your security and privacy than others, you should always assume that every virus is a danger to either you or your computer and take appropriate action immediately.

Implementing Virus Protection

The best way to keep your Windows XP system virus-free is by taking adequate preventative measures to reduce your risk of infection. Certainly installing anti-virus software is a good first step, but it's equally important to ensure that you keep this software properly updated with all of the latest virus definitions — if you install anti-virus software but neglect to update it regularly, your computer is still exposed to all of the newest viruses, which are usually the ones that pose the greatest risk.

Although running updated anti-virus software is probably the single best way to minimize the risk of a virus infection, using Windows XP and Internet tools (such as e-mail) wisely are arguably just as important. With this in mind, essential tasks and concepts toward keeping your Windows XP system virus-free include the following:

- Installing anti-virus software
- Keeping virus definition files updated
- Configuring virus scanning settings and options
- Scanning for viruses regularly
- Avoiding viruses using common sense and best practices

Each of these tasks is explored in more detail in the following sections.

Installing anti-virus software

The first step toward keeping your Windows XP system virus-free involves installing an anti-virus program. Many anti-virus programs available for Windows XP, but some of the most popular include:

- Norton AntiVirus, available from `www.symantec.com`
- McAfee VirusScan, available from `www.mcafee.com`
- Sophos Anti-Virus, available from `www.sophos.com`
- Panda Titanium Antivirus, available from `www.pandasoftware.com`
- AVG Anti Virus, available from `www.grisoft.com`

The anti-virus program that will work best for you is largely a matter of personal preference, as well as your budget. Many users seek out an anti-virus program that is packed with different features to address specific needs; some simply use the anti-virus program that shipped with their computer; others seek out "free" alternatives. Some of the more common features found in the popular anti-virus programs include:

- Real-time virus protection
- Scheduled virus scanning
- Automatic virus definition updates
- Inbound and outbound e-mail message scanning

Additionally, some anti-virus programs include extended capabilities to scan files sent and received over instant message chats in real-time, or detect and remove spyware. Some packages even go as far as to bundle multiple security tools together, as is the case with AVG Plus Firewall. This particular program groups anti-virus, anti-spyware, and firewall capabilities into a single security suite.

After Windows XP Service Pack 2 is installed, Windows Security Center can be used to determine the status of virus protection on your computer. Specifically, the Virus Protection section lets you know whether you have anti-virus software installed, and whether the virus definition files for this software are up to date. When anti-virus software is not installed (or your virus definition files are out of date), Windows Security Center also alerts you via an icon and notification balloon on your Windows taskbar.

Follow these steps to determine the current status of virus protection on your Windows XP system:

1. Click Start → Control Panel → Security Center.
2. In the Windows Security Center window, review the Virus Protection section as shown in Figure 8-1. If the status message displays anything other than ON, read the message provided to determine which steps you need to complete to protect your computer from viruses, such as installing anti-virus software, or updating an installed program's virus definition files.

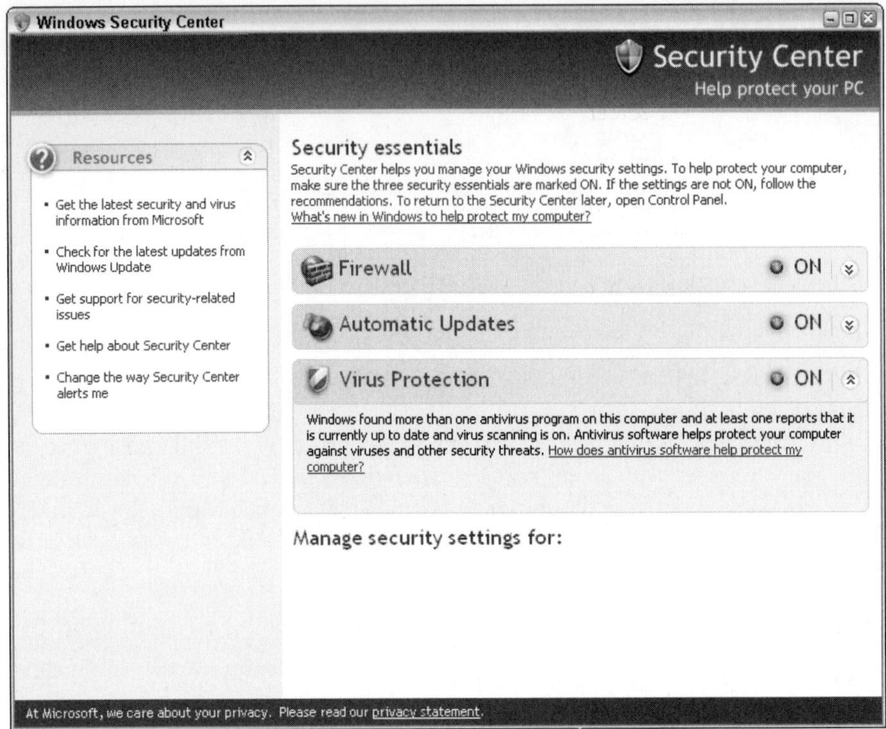

Figure 8-1: Reviewing the status of Virus Protection in Windows Security Center.

Note

The anti-virus software used for illustrative purposes in this chapter is AVG Free Edition, available from `free.grisoft.com`. AVG Free Edition is free for personal use (with no yearly subscription fees) and includes the common anti-virus program features outlined earlier in this section.

Follow these steps to install AVG Free Edition on your Windows XP system:

1. Click Start → Internet Explorer, or open your preferred Web browser. Head to free.grisoft.com and download the latest version of AVG Free Edition. After the download is complete, double-click the file to begin the installation process.
2. At the Welcome screen, click Next.
3. At the License Agreement screen, click Accept.
4. At the Acceptance Notice screen, click Accept.
5. At the Select Installation Type screen, click Next.

6. At the Confirmation screen, click Next.
7. At the Installation Summary screen, click Finish.
8. At the Installation Complete screen, click OK.
9. When the AVG First Run window appears, click Next.
10. At the AVG Free Update screen, click Next. (You will check for updated virus definition files in a later exercise.)
11. At the Create Rescue Disk screen, either select the option to create a rescue disk, or click Next.
12. At the Scan E-Mail Messages screen, click Next.
13. At the Computer Scan screen, click Next. (You will complete a full virus scan in a later exercise.)
14. At the AVG Free Registration screen, click Next, and click Continue. The AVG Free Edition Test Center screen appears, as shown in Figure 8-2. This is the primary working environment to initiate virus scans or check for updated virus definitions with AVG Free Edition.

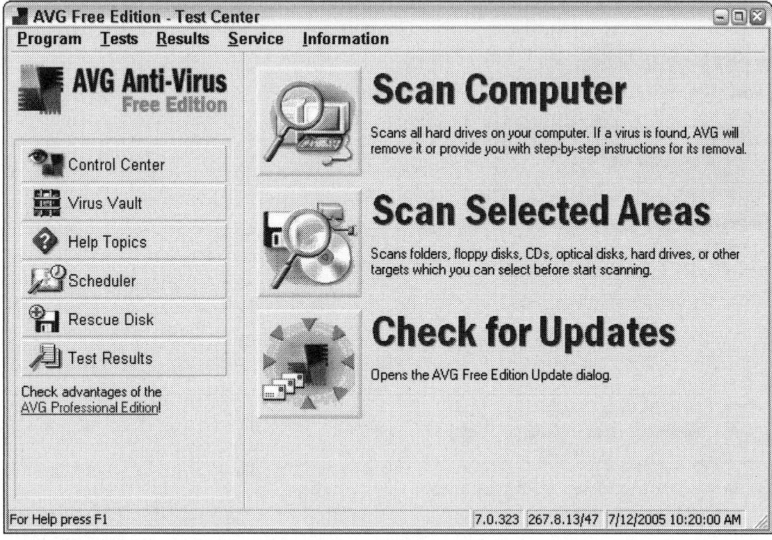

Figure 8-2: The AVG Free Edition Test Center window.

Updating virus definitions

After you install anti-virus software on your Windows XP system, it's critically important to keep it updated with the most recent virus definition files. If you neglect to download and install these updates as they're released (which is typically anywhere from once a day to once a week), your computer is susceptible to all of the newest viruses — the ones that typically present the greatest risk to all computers.

Thankfully, almost all anti-virus programs include a feature that allows you to check for (and then download and install) new updates automatically, according to a schedule that you define. Many anti-virus programs configure a virus definition update schedule automatically; others require you to enable the feature and configure a schedule manually.

Follow these steps to update virus definition for AVG Free Edition:

1. Right-click the AVG Free Edition icon on your taskbar and then click Check for Updates.
2. At the Update window check the Do not ask for the update source next time checkbox and then click Internet.
3. The AVG Update File Download window appears, followed by the Update selection screen (if new updates are available) as shown in Figure 8-3. Click the Update button. After the update process is complete, click OK.

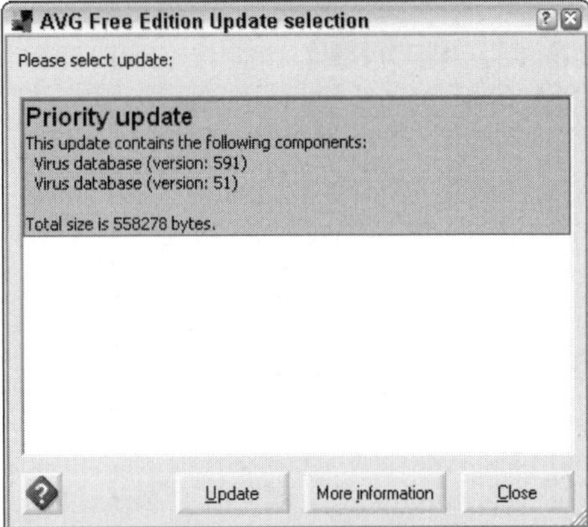

Figure 8-3: Downloading virus definition files with AVG Free Edition.

4. AVG Free Edition automatically checks for updates every day at 8:30 am. If you want to change this schedule, right-click the AVG Free Edition icon on your taskbar and click Launch AVG Control Center; then, right-click Scheduler and click Scheduled Tasks. To change the time at which updates are checked, click Update plan in Basic mode (as shown in Figure 8-4) and then click Edit Schedule to select a new update time.

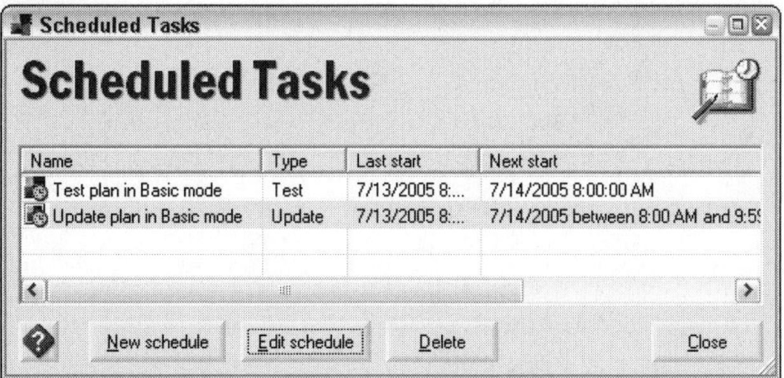

Figure 8-4: Reviewing scheduled tasks in AVG Free Edition.

Caution

Many people leave their Windows XP system at risk by letting the subscription to their anti-virus software lapse after its trial period ends. Unfortunately, you cannot rely on out-of-date virus definitions to protect you system from all the latest threats, which present the greatest risk. Either update your anti-virus software subscription or switch to a product such as AVG Free Edition to protect your Windows XP system and keep viruses at bay.

Configuring virus scanning options

Every anti-virus program implements slightly different default virus scanning settings, so it's important to ensure your Windows XP system is being protected to an appropriate degree. For example, some anti-virus programs scan every file that you attempt to open by default but do not scan e-mail messages unless you configure them to do so. Similarly, some anti-virus programs automatically scan the contents of any disk (floppy, CD, DVD, and so forth) that you insert into a drive; others only scan disks if you explicitly enable the option to do so. Never assume that your Windows XP system is being completely and thoroughly protected if you haven't taken the time to confirm its virus scanning settings and options.

Follow these steps to configure scanning options with AVG Free Edition:

1. Right-click the AVG Free Edition icon on the taskbar and then click Launch AVG Control Center.
2. Right-click AVG Resident Shield and then click Properties.
3. In the AVG Resident Shield window check the checkboxes in the Scan details and Advanced settings sections according to your scanning preferences. AVG Free Edition will scan floppy drives, program files, documents, e-mail files and use heuristic analysis by default, as shown in Figure 8-5.

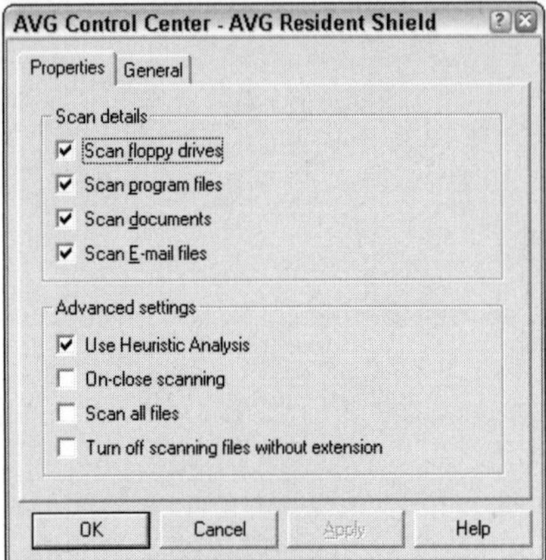

Figure 8-5: Configuring virus scanning options with AVG Free Edition.

Note

Heuristic analysis (often called heuristic scanning) is a technique by which anti-virus programs will attempt to detect virus-like activities, even when a file is not infected with any known virus. Heuristic scanning watches for suspicious behavior by files or programs, and when these are detected alerts you in a manner similar to any other virus. As a general rule, leave heuristic options in your anti-virus software enabled — they might just catch the latest viruses making the rounds on the Internet before your anti-virus vendor releases an update to address it.

4. Click OK to enable your new scanning options.

In addition to ensuring that scanning options are configured in a manner that addresses your needs, it's equally important to periodically test your anti-virus program to ensure that it's functioning correctly. You probably shouldn't download a virus-infected file from the Internet for the purpose of testing whether your anti-virus program will detect and quarantine it, but it's never a bad idea to ensure that features such as e-mail message scanning are enabled and functioning correctly. When an inbound or outbound e-mail message is scanned for viruses, a "certification" note to that effect (including details on the product used) is typically added to the footer of all e-mail messages.

Follow these steps to configure and test the inbound and outbound e-mail scanning capabilities of AVG Free Edition:

1. Right-click the AVG Free Edition icon on the taskbar and then click Launch AVG Control Center.

2. Right-click E-mail Scanner and then click Properties.
3. On the Plugins tab, click Configure. By default, AVG Free Edition scans all incoming and outgoing messages, as shown in Figure 8-6. Use the settings on this tab to configure additional e-mail scan settings, such as automatically removing certain types of e-mail attachments if necessary.

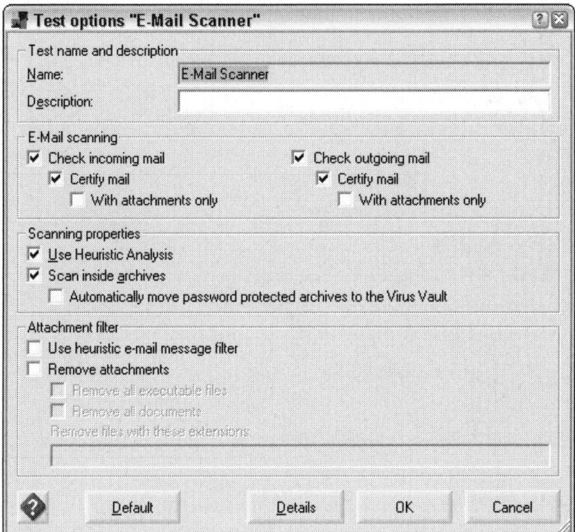

Figure 8-6: Reviewing e-mail message scanning options in AVG Free Edition.

4. Click the Details button. The E-mail scanning details window allows you to configure "certification" messages to be added to both incoming and outgoing messages. You can change the default message to your own custom message or leave the default messages intact. Click OK.
5. Open your preferred e-mail client program, for example Microsoft Outlook.
6. Compose a new message to yourself and then send the message. After this message is received, open it to view the message contents. The certification messages stating that the file was check for viruses when it was sent and received is displayed, as are details of the virus definition files used to scan the message, as shown in Figure 8-7.

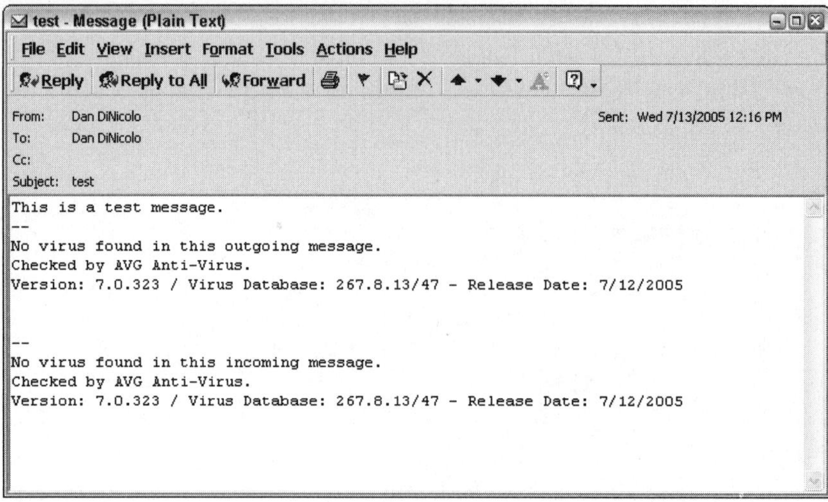

Figure 8-7: AVG Free Edition attaches a certification notices to all virus-scanned messages sent and received.

Scanning for viruses

After you have anti-virus software installed, its real-time protection feature typically scans all files that you attempt to access or open to ensure they're virus-free; however, it's possible that a virus found its way onto your system before the software was installed, and that other files that haven't been opened in a while may be infected. For this reason, it's important to perform complete virus scans of your hard drive and other disks frequently — at least per week.

In a manner similar to how anti-virus programs typically check for new virus definition file updates automatically, most also schedule a complete scan of your system for viruses either daily or once per week. As with all security-related tasks, it's never a bad idea to err on the side of caution when it comes to scanning for viruses. Running a full virus scan once per day may seem excessive, but the process generally takes under a half hour to complete (it depends on the size of your drives and the number of files to be scanned), and it's always better to be safe than sorry.

Of course, anti-virus programs also allow you to initiate virus scans manually if you'd rather have more control over how and when these scans occur. For example, you might choose to do a complete scan just before you head out to run errands, or scan certain drives only (such as C:) more frequently. All of the major anti-virus programs provide a high degree of flexibility when it comes to configuring virus scan settings, both via a schedule and manually.

Follow these steps to complete a full virus scan:

1. Right-click the AVG Free Edition icon on the taskbar and then click Launch AVG Test Center.

2. To complete a full scan of all drives on your computer, click the Scan Computer button. To scan only the drives you specify, click Scan Selected Areas instead. If you click Scan Selected Areas you are prompted to select the drives to scan, as shown in Figure 8-8.

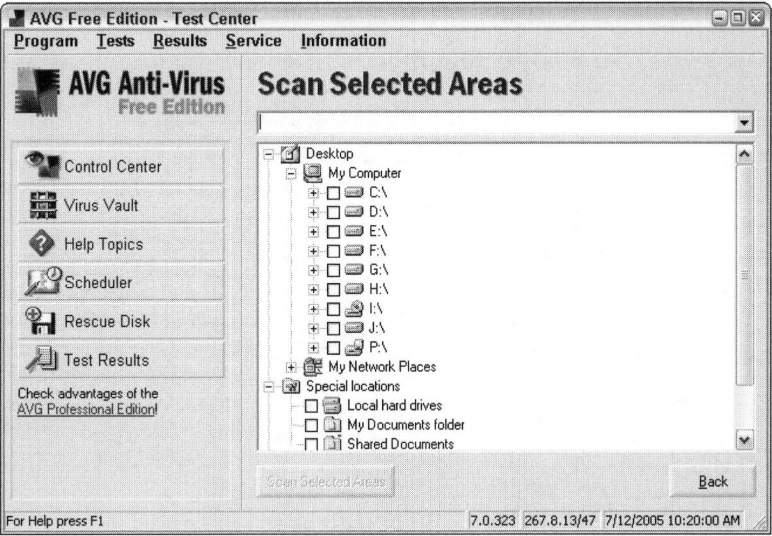

Figure 8-8: Anti-virus programs typically provide options to scan your entire computer or only selected areas.

3. Check the drives and locations that you want to scan for viruses and then click Scan Selected Areas.
4. After the scanning process is complete (this may take half an hour or more, depending on the number of drives and files to be scanned), the Finished window appears (as shown in Figure 8-9). Review and take action on any viruses that were found (if applicable) and then click Close.

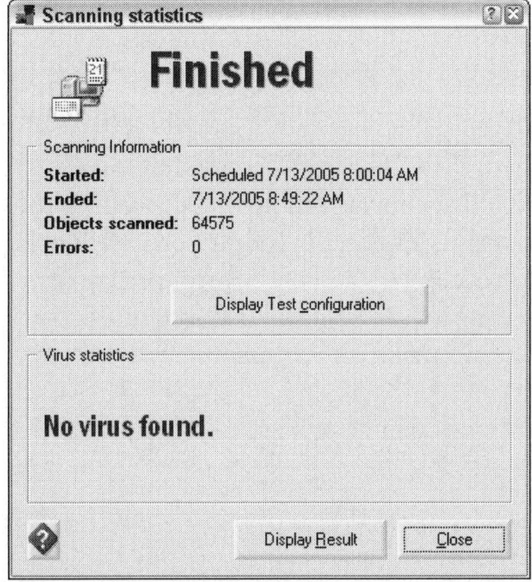

Figure 8-9: Results of a virus scan.

Beyond anti-virus software

Running anti-virus software with updated virus definition files and real-time protection features enabled is perhaps the best way to keep your system protected from virus threats; however, even the best-protected system can succumb to a new virus threat because there is usually a small lag between the time when a new virus (or a new variant of an existing virus) is discovered and a vendor's virus definition files are updated to address the threat. Some new viruses spread so rapidly that literally tens of thousands of systems are infected with hours, a situation that can typically be avoided by ensuring that you adhere to some basic guidelines and best practices to minimize your chances of acquiring an infection.

Use the following best practices to help ensure that your system remains free and clear of viruses to the greatest degree possible:

- Always run anti-virus software and keep it updated. Never disable it when connected to the Internet.
- Use anti-virus software that includes both inbound and outbound e-mail message filtering. Besides removing infected e-mail attachments, these programs typically warn you when you attempt to open file types commonly used to transmit viruses.
- Never assume that e-mail attachments received from friends, family, and colleagues are virus-free. Many worms are designed to infect one user's system and then use that user's e-mail address and contact list to send infectious e-mail attachments to others. If your anti-virus program doesn't scan e-mail messages as they're received, save attached files to disk and then scan them for viruses prior to opening them.
- Be very careful with files that you download from the Internet, and especially those found in Usenet newsgroups, on file sharing services, and FTP servers. Internet downloads are a notorious source for virus-infected files, so take the time to complete virus scans on every file that you download prior to opening it.
- Always keep your Windows XP system up to date with the latest security updates and patches. Many viruses, worms, and Trojan horse programs take advantage of operating system flaws to infect systems. The easiest way to keep your system protected from threats that try to exploit these flaws is to enable Windows XP's Automatic Updates feature. If you choose to download and install updates manually, do so regularly.
- Ensure that you have firewall software installed, and preferably one that offers both inbound and outbound packet-filtering capabilities. If all inbound ports are blocking connections, outside users cannot connect to your PC if a remote control program or Trojan horse infects it. Outbound filtering is also important, helping to stop viruses and other threats from connecting to the Internet to send off sensitive personal information or launch hacking attacks against other computers.
- Always think before you click, and never assume any file to be virus-free.

Removing Viruses

There may come a time where your Windows XP system (or one belonging to a friend) ends up being infected by a virus. It may be that you didn't have anti-virus software installed, enabled, or updated, which provided the opening that the virus needed to infect your system. Assuming that your PC is infected and you don't have anti-virus software install, it can be very difficult to tell. You may have noticed that your system is slower than usual, or that Windows XP is doing "weird things." When your computer is acting a little on the strange side, it's absolutely possible that it has acquired a virus infection, although other possibilities (such as a spyware infestation) do exist.

The obvious solution to removing a virus is to install anti-virus software, update it, and run a complete system scan is search of potential pests. Unfortunately, this isn't always possible—some viruses are now designed to disable (or prevent the installation of) anti-virus programs as part of doing their dirty work. Ultimately, this means that you need to look elsewhere for a way to get the virus off your system.

When push comes to shove in this way, you generally have three options. The first (and least attractive) would be to try and back up your personal files and e-mail and then reinstall Windows XP and all programs completely—a long and potentially arduous process. The second method that you could attempt would be to boot Windows XP into safe mode (by pressing F8 when your PC starts and selecting the appropriate option from the menu) and then attempt to scan for viruses or install an anti-virus program. This option sometimes does the trick, but it really depends on the virus you've managed to acquire, and the manner in which it has lodged itself on to your computer.

The third option is to explore the world of standalone virus removal tools. Almost all anti-virus vendors (as well as Microsoft) release free utilities for the purpose of helping you to remove a particular virus from your PC. Unfortunately, many of these tools are designed with removing a specific virus in mind, so if you're not sure what you've got, you'll have a tough go of things.

Thankfully, there are a few virus removal tools out there that are capable of detecting and removing all of the most common and dangerous viruses. One such tool is AVERT Stinger, a tool from McAfee that's capable of detecting and removing more than 50 pesky viruses including Sober, Sobig, Sasser, Netsky, MyDoom, and many others. Stinger is updated regularly to address the latest and greatest virus threats, so it's important to download the latest version from vil.nai.com/vil/stinger/ before you run your scan.

Caution

Never rely on virus removal tools such as McAfee AVERT Stinger as an alternative to using anti-virus software with real-time protection. These tools exist to help you remove dangerous viruses that might be infecting your PC, but they do nothing to stop your system from being infected (or re-infected) by viruses in the future.

Follow these steps to complete a virus scan with a third-party virus removal tool such as McAfee Stinger:

1. Click Start → Internet Explorer, or open your preferred Web browser. Browse to vil.nai.com/vil/stinger/ and then download Stinger. After the download is complete, double-click the file to open the program (no installation required).

2. When the Stinger window appears, click the Preferences button. This screen (shown in Figure 8-10) allows you to configure virus detection settings. Check additional options, if necessary, or simply click OK to leave the default settings intact.

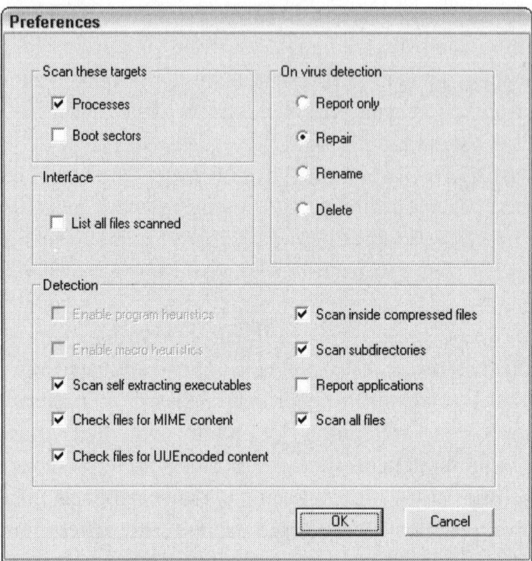

Figure 8-10: Configuring virus scanning and detection preferences with Stinger.

3. By default, Stinger only scans your C: drive in an attempt to detect viruses, as shown in Figure 8-11. If necessary, click the Add or Browse buttons to have the program scan other drives.

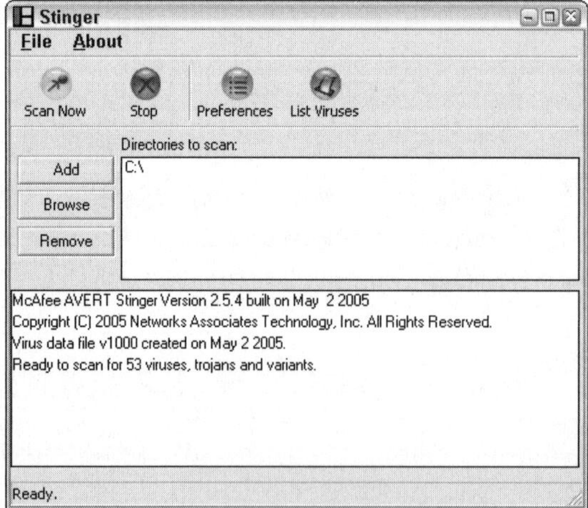

Figure 8-11: Stinger only scans drive C: by default, but it can be configured to scan the drives you specify.

4. After configured to scan the required drives, click Scan Now. Stinger scans the selected drives, a process that can take anywhere from a few minutes to much longer depending on the number of drives and files to be scanned.

5. After the scan is complete, the Stinger window displays the scan results, as shown in Figure 8-12.

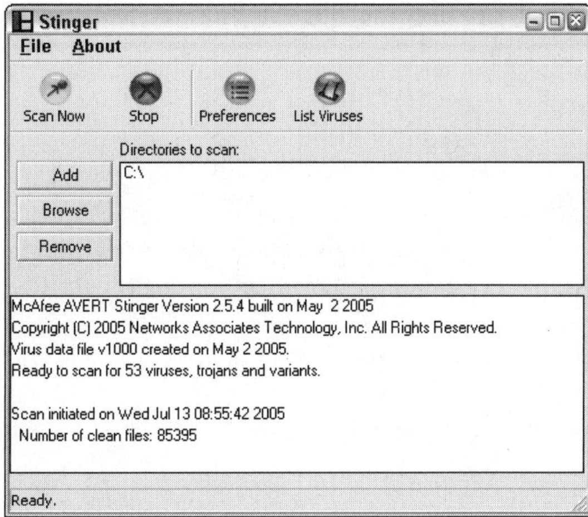

Figure 8-12: The results of a Stinger scan.

Danger, Read All About It!

There's no question that viruses present a very real danger to your Windows XP, but thankfully there's no shortage of great virus-related resources on the Internet. Whether you're trying to determine the risks that a particular virus poses, want to keep abreast of the latest virus threats, or are looking for a removal tool for a specific virus, the details you seek can always be found on a myriad of different Web sites.

Some of the more popular Web resources for finding details about viruses include:

- Microsoft Security Home Page (`www.microsoft.com/security/`)
- Symantec Security Response (`www.sarc.com`)
- CERT Coordination Center (`www.cert.org`)
- PC Magazine Security Watch (`www.pcmag.com/category2/0,4148,12,00.asp`)

Continued

Danger, Read All About It! (Continued)

In addition to providing detailed virus information, many of these Web sites also include a feature that alerts you to the latest virus threats by sending an e-mail, and some even include a dedicated Really Simple Syndication (RSS) feed for virus alerts. If you want to be informed of all the latest virus threats but not be deluged with related e-mail messages, RSS is often the least intrusive option. For details on accessing and subscribing to RSS feeds, see the PC Magazine article "RSS Rocks", available at `www.pcmag.com/article2/0,1759,1544705,00.asp`.

Summary

Infections from viruses, worms, and Trojan horses are amongst the most prevalent and constant threats to your PC's security and your personal privacy. New viruses are being developed and released onto the Internet almost daily, so it's critically important that you keep your PC properly protected and free of infection.

Keep the following points in mind when it comes to preventing and removing virus infections:

- Install anti-virus software, and keep it running and updated with the latest virus definitions at all times.
- Remember that running anti-virus software without updated virus definition files is almost the same as working without virus protection at all. At best, anti-virus software that hasn't been updated provides only a very small level of protection at leave your computer vulnerable to all of the latest and most dangerous virus threats.
- Use an anti-virus program that scans both inbound and outbound e-mail messages for viruses. This stops your computer from sending viruses to other users, and helps to ensure that your computer is properly protected when viruses are received in e-mail messages received from others.
- Always scan all programs and files downloaded from the Internet (or obtained from other users) for viruses prior to opening them.
- Update your virus definitions regularly. Use the scheduling capabilities of your anti-virus software to check for updates at least once per day.
- Run a complete virus scan for all drives on your computer at least once per week.
- Ensure that the latest security updates and Service Packs are applied to protect your Windows XP system. Many worms are designed to seek out and infect unpatched Windows XP systems.
- Install personal firewall software that supports both inbound and outbound packet filtering capabilities. A firewall won't actually remove or prevent a virus that finds its way onto your system, but it can help to minimize the damage that occurs as a result of a virus infection.
- Always think before you click. Never assume that any file is virus-free, regardless of its original source.

Chapter 9

Fighting Malware: Protecting Against Spyware, Adware, and Browser Hijackers

Imagine a world in which your every move is being watched — your comings and goings tracked, your telephone calls recorded, and all messages sent or received monitored by some nameless and faceless person or corporation. Sounds a little scary, doesn't it? The worst part is that this world already exists, and it's probably sitting right on your desk.

Malware — often referred to as spyware — is the latest in a breed of almost virus-like pests that have taken to infecting computers at an alarming rate. Unlike viruses, however, these new strains of infection are less concerned with spreading and more interested in keeping tabs on you. From tracking your online wanderings to collecting details of every key you press, there's literally an army of malware threats quietly infiltrating computers and stripping away the privacy of Windows users worldwide. Unfortunately, most people still have no idea what malware threats are, the dangers they pose, or the fact that their computer is (more than likely) already infected.

Thankfully, all is not lost. Although malware represents one of the largest and most wide-scale threats to PC security and personal privacy that the world has ever known, even a badly infected Windows XP system can be nursed backed to a clean bill of health with the right knowledge and tools. In this chapter you learn about what malware is, the different types of threats that exist, the real dangers that these threats pose, and finally the tools and techniques you can use to clean up your system and keep it protected from future threats.

Understanding Malware

Back in the good ol' days, viruses represented the most clear and present danger to a computer's security. As long as you were geared up with anti-virus software and the latest virus definition files, you could consider your PC to be adequately protected. Unfortunately, times have changed and a whole new breed of pests is now infecting computers at an alarming rate. The last few years have given to the rise of an entirely new set of threats broadly known as "malware," and it's been estimated that as many as 9 out of every 10 Windows computers are already infected by malware in one form or other.

Strictly speaking, malware and viruses are different beasts. Malware isn't nearly as concerned with propagating itself from computer to computer in the manner of a virus or worm. Instead, malware is most interested in infecting your computer for the purpose of spying on you, often tracking your Web surfing habits or logging all of your PC activities silently in the background. Other forms of malware are designed to mine your computer for useful bits of information or "hijack" your Web browser's configuration such that your home page and search settings are no longer under your control. Still others install "dialers" that can use your modem to call exotic locales and result in anywhere from hundreds to thousands of dollars of long distance charges being added to your monthly phone bill. Although originally seen as little more than an annoyance, malware is arguably the most prevalent and under-recognized threat in the PC world today.

Types of malware

In much the same way that the term "virus" is generically used to describe a group of threats that includes viruses, worms, and Trojan horses, "malware" is the umbrella terms used to describe different security and privacy risks that include spyware, adware, and browser hijackers. Each of these threats is technically a little different, but the line between what constitutes spyware and adware is blurry and subject to interpretation — quite simply, a given malware threat might be best described as "adware" based on how it behaves, but also include components that are more commonly associated with spyware. This lack of a clear definition means that many people generically refer to all malware threats as any one of malware, spyware, or adware. You can expect to see any of these terms used to describe the new breed of pests that have taken to infecting millions of PCs in a virtually silent assault.

SPYWARE

Objects deemed to be "spyware" include malicious programs or bits of code designed to spy on your and your PC-related activities. Some spyware objects silently track your Internet activities in the background, collecting details like the sites you've visited and then forwarding them along to a server on the Internet; others are more insidious, designed to steal personal information such as usernames and passwords, files, e-mail messages, and more. Unfortunately, the sky is the limit when it comes to what spyware is able to accomplish on a computer that hasn't been properly secured, and the problem of spyware infections is getting worse every day.

Most people have a fundamental problem understanding why anyone would want to spy on them specifically. The truth is that spyware developers are seldom after any specific person but rather aim to have their spyware component infect as many computers as possible — often with a profit motive. Some spyware developers use the information collected from your PC for Web marketing purposes; others are after usernames and passwords for your Internet banking account. It's a safe bet to assume that one day the information collected by spyware objects will be used for purposes such as blackmail, impersonation, and identity theft — if they're not being used for those purposes already.

Some of the more common types of spyware include:

- **Keyloggers.** A keylogger is a malware program designed to capture keystrokes, mouse clicks, and screenshots of your computer activities. After they collect this information and save it to a file, keyloggers typically forward it to a server on the Internet. In some cases this information is "mined" for details such as username and password combinations, but keyloggers can also be used to spy on correspondence such as e-mail, IM chats, and more.

- **Dialers.** A dialer is a particularly nasty breed of pest designed to use your modem for the purpose of calling long distance or "toll" calls to overseas locations for the purpose of racking up charges on your phone bill. For a dialer to function, your modem must be connected to a phone line, so dialup Internet users are particularly at risk. Don't expect to discover a dialer by those familiar modem sounds either — dialers typically work in the background, silently inflating the charges on your phone bill to astronomical levels.
- **Data miners.** A data miner is a pest designed to mine your PC for all sorts of useful information. The most common types of data miners are ones designed to track your Web surfing or PC usage habits and then use this information for marketing purposes such as displaying targeted advertisements as you browse the Web. Some data miners are designed to collect personal information about you (such as your name and address), or even lists of the programs installed on your PC. Although they may not represent a major security risk in the same manner as keyloggers or dialers, data miners are definitely a threat to your privacy — the ones used to collect information about your surfing habits today could easily be redesigned to harvest e-mail addresses or dig through the contents of your personal files tomorrow.
- **Tracking cookies.** Cookies are small text files used by Web sites and browsers to keep track of personalized user settings, customize content layout, and reduce the need to enter username and password information each time you visit sites that require you to log on. When used judiciously, cookies typically don't represent a security threat and do little to put your personal privacy at risk — in fact, many sites, such as those associated with online banking, require your browser to accept their cookies as part of the connection process. Although cookies are not dangerous in the same manner as viruses or other malware threats, they do represent a potential threat to your personal privacy. This is especially true with tracking cookies, where the cookie's reason for being it to keep tabs on all of the Web sites that you visit, and the ways in which you surf the Web. Ultimately, this information can be used to create a profile on your Internet activities or habits and then used to display targeted advertisements based on your personal interests.

ADWARE

Software is distributed over the Internet in a number of different ways. Some of the programs that you download and install are licensed commercial programs that must be paid for. Others known as shareware allow you to try the program for free but require you to purchase it if you intend to continue using it. Freeware is another popular type of software, where the developer grants you the right to use their program, free of charge.

Over the past few years, however, a new software distribution method has become increasingly popular. Adware, or advertising-supported software, provides a way for developers to release their software to the general public for free while still making money. The idea is that an advertiser's banner, message, or even another program is bundled together with the adware program for a fee, which keeps the developer in business. In effect, the money made from advertising is the developer's payment for creating the program.

Where once adware-style programs did little more than include the advertiser's banner somewhere within a program window, the adware of today is much more complex—and potentially dangerous. Many adware programs are designed to collect information about your PC or how you use the Internet, and then deliver targeted ads to you. Sometimes these ads are displayed with the main program window, and sometimes they're of the "pop-up" variety—those annoying browser windows that literally open out of nowhere to display an advertisement as you're trying to accomplish another task.

Perhaps the most common examples of adware in action are the "free" versions of popular file sharing programs like Kazaa and BearShare. These programs typically install an adware component (a separate program in the case of BearShare, as shown in Figure 9-1) during the program installation process, and most users "agree" to allow this—some adware programs let you know that an ad-related component is being installed on your PC, but others simply bury this detail in the licensing agreement. In effect, you agree to install adware on your PC (and have different types of information about you collected) by accepting the license agreement—it's up to you to read the fine print, after all.

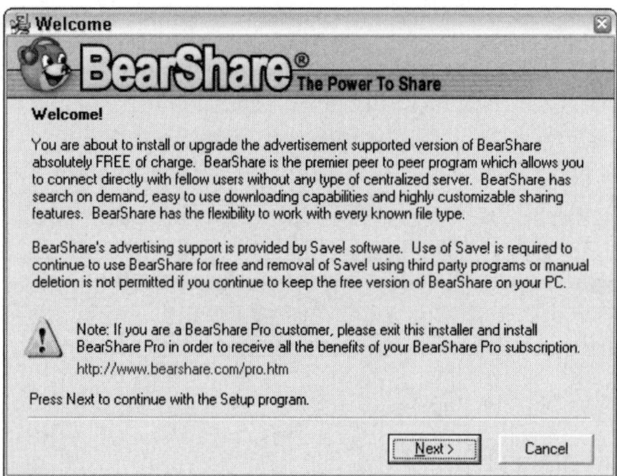

Figure 9-1: The free version of the popular BearShare file sharing program informs you that adware will also be installed.

There's little question that adware has the potential to put your privacy and security at risk, but the extent to which this is true varies largely from program to program. Some people think that giving away details of their usage or surfing habits by using adware is a better deal than paying for the "full" version of a program. Others find the deluge of pop-up windows or integrated banners often associated with adware programs to be annoying and beyond reproach. Certainly adware is a legitimate method for developers to be paid for their work, and not every adware program is dangerous. You should, however, always take the time to read the licensing agreement associated with an adware program before you install it. If the program doesn't include details about what information is being collected about you (if any) and how this information will be used, you're always better off seeking out an alternative program.

BROWSER HIJACKERS

As the name suggest, browser hijackers are all about taking control of your Web browser. Specifically, browser hijackers are a form of malware designed to replace your own Web browser settings with new values — ones that you typically cannot remove or change by traditional means. For example, a browser hijacker might change your browser's home page and search engine settings, or even add its own shortcut links to your Favorites or Bookmarks list. When you try to remove these entries and return to your original settings, a browser hijacker almost always undoes your changes and returns to its own preferred settings.

Browser hijackers are without a doubt one of the most annoying types of malware, but also have the potential to be both offensive and dangerous. For example, it's not uncommon for a browser hijacker to replace your preferred home page with a pornography or gambling site. Similarly, browser hijacks are seldom interested in changing browser settings alone — although this may be the "visual" part of the equation, most also infect your PC with various spyware and related objects that might be a threat to your security and privacy.

The most common and dangerous browser hijacker making the rounds on the Internet is known as CoolWebSearch. The particular pest is amongst the worst of the worst (and most prevalent) in the malware world, and can be next to impossible to remove even with the help of anti-spyware software. You'll learn more about detecting and removing browser hijackers (and specifically CoolWebSearch) later in this chapter.

How malware infects your PC

Malware typically infects PCs in a very different way than viruses and worms. Viruses typically rely on the user opening an infected file; worms can take advantage of operating system security "holes" that exists as a result of not applying patches and updates as they're released. Infecting a system with malware, on the other hand, often requires you to do nothing more than visit an infectious Web page or even click on a hyperlink.

Perhaps the primary reason why so many computers are infected by malware is a result of the sneaky nature of spyware developers. Some trick you into downloading malware objects by displaying misleading Web pages suggesting that your computer is already infected. Others use pop-up ads that appear to be normal Windows dialog boxes that coax you into clicking what is actually a link. There are even Web pages that download and install malware on your computer automatically when you do nothing more than visit a certain Web address.

Some of the most common ways in which malware infects PCs include via:

- **Program installations.** Malware is commonly bundled into seemingly legitimate programs, and installed on your system as part of the primary program's installation process. In some cases, the legitimate tool is designed with the purpose of distributing spyware. In others, a spyware developer has taking an existing program and recompiled it to include malware components.
- **Toolbar installations.** The capabilities of Internet Explorer and other Web browsers can be greatly extended through the use of legitimate third-party toolbars such as the ones offered by Google and Yahoo!. However, many third-party toolbars that appear to be loaded with useful features actually contain malware components. In some cases, toolbars

are installed into Web browsers such as Internet Explorer when you do nothing more than visit an infectious site or click a misleading links. Toolbars that extend the capabilities of browsers are commonly referred to as Browser Helper Objects, or BHOs.

- **Surfing the Web.** Some Web sites have been programmed by spyware developers to automatically download and install malware-related threats when you visit the site or a particular Web page. These sites typically take advantage of low security restrictions in Web browsers such as Internet Explorer to download and install malware components using technologies like ActiveX or Java. Malware threats that are downloaded and installed in this fashion are often referred to as "drive-by" downloads.
- **Pop-up ads.** Web browser pop-up windows are amongst the most notorious sources of malware infections. These smaller browser windows typically include an advertisement or warning message stating that your computer is already infected by spyware, or supposedly provide a link to a free spyware-removal tool. Others are designed to look like legitimate Windows dialog boxes, complete with Yes and No buttons. When used as a malware delivery vehicle, clicking these ads installs malware objects on your PC. It should be noted, however, that only a small percentage of pop-up ads relate to the installation of malware.
- **Cookies.** As you surf the Internet, chances are good that most of the Web sites you visit will place cookies on your PC, usually for legitimate purposes; however, many Web sites display banners provided by Web advertising services, which often track and collect visitor information via tracking cookies. Unless you've chosen to block all cookies or only allow ones from certain Web sites, chances are good that one or more tracking cookies are already present on your computer.

Cross-Reference

For details on managing browser security settings — including disabling pop-up windows, configuring cookie settings, and managing BHOs — refer to Chapter 5.

Signs of infection

The best way to determine whether your computer is infected by malware-related threats is to complete a scan with a dedicated spyware detection and removal tool; however, you should also keep an eye open for the following warning signs, which often indicate that your computer may be infected by any of a number of different malware threats:

- One or more pop-up windows appear each time that you log on to Windows XP or open your Web browser.
- Your computer is noticeably slower than in the past.
- You're experiencing system errors or crashes with greater frequency.

- Unfamiliar icons are present in your system tray.
- Your Web browser's home page has been changed to a new Web site.
- New and unfamiliar toolbars have been added to your Web browser.
- Your computer is behaving strangely or slightly different than it normally does.
- Your phone bill arrives and is loaded with charges for call made to toll numbers or overseas locations.

Note

If any of the warning signs outlined in the previous list describe your PC, it doesn't necessarily mean that your computer is infected by malware. It could be that your system infected by a virus, or in need of maintenance tasks such as removing unused programs and files or defragmenting your hard drive. Anytime that you notice behavior outside of expected parameters, however, it's not a bad idea to scan your system for possible malware threats.

Malware risks

There's simply no shortage of ways in which malware can cause you or your computer harm, with new and even more dangerous methods being developed all the time. Some of the security risks and common types of damage caused by malware include:

- Information and/or identity theft. Many malware threats are designed for the expressed purpose of stealing information from your PC. Items sought after can include virtually everything from username and password combinations to files to correspondence such as e-mail messages or IM chats.
- Internet tracking. A number of malware threats are aimed at tracking your Internet usage history and habits for the purpose of displaying targeted advertisements. Some of these objects track your Internet activities relatively anonymously, but others seek out personal details as well.
- System stability issues. Similar to any other piece of software, malware threats can be poorly programmed, and by extension lead to system stability issues or even crashes. Some malware objects are known to overwrite or replace important operating system files; others disable security programs such as anti-virus or firewall software.
- Inability to change Web browser settings. Almost all browser hijackers lodge themselves onto your computer such that it's virtually impossible to return to your original settings without using anti-spyware software or a dedicated threat removal program. In some cases, completely reinstalling your system is the only way to remove these pests for good.

- Inability to access certain Web sites. Many malware threats are designed to stop you from being able to access certain popular Web sites, or redirect you to other sites (typically carrying advertising) in cases where a page cannot be found.
- Inability to use your computer reliably. From relentless pop-up ads to disabled software, there's no shortage of ways in which malware can harm your computer such that you cannot use it reliably. For example, a number of malware threats continuously open pop-up windows with banner ads regardless of whether you close existing windows or even stop underlying processes such as Internet Explorer.
- Financial costs. Some of the more advanced and extreme malware threats are designed to hit you where it hurts — right in the pocketbook. Dialers almost always lead to massive charges on your phone bill, but malware that steals credit card or banking information can also lead to financial losses, not to mention identity theft issues.

Protecting Against Malware

Similar to viruses, the best ways to protect your system again the risks of malware is to stop these pests from finding their way onto your Windows XP system in the first place. Many users mistakenly rely on malware removal tools to keep their system protected, effectively allowing the "bad guys" in before periodically getting them out. Some of the key methods that can be used to protect your Windows XP system from being infected by malware include:

- Installing anti-spyware software
- Updating spyware definition files regularly
- Configuring real-time protection and advanced anti-spyware settings
- Scanning for malware regularly
- Thinking before you click

Each of these methods is explored in more detail in the following sections.

Installing anti-spyware software

It doesn't take much for malware objects to find their way onto your PC, even if you're being very careful about how you use your Windows XP system and the Internet. For this reason, it's imperative that you install anti-spyware software to ensure that your system remains properly protected, and preferable an anti-spyware program that offers real-time protection.

Some of the most popular anti-spyware software packages available for Windows XP include:

- Microsoft AntiSpyware (available from `www.microsoft.com`)
- Spybot Search & Destroy (available from `security.kolla.de`)
- McAfee AntiSpyware (available from `www.mcafee.com`)

- Webroot Spy Sweeper (available from `www.Webroot.com`)
- Ad-Aware (available from `www.lavasoftusa.com`)
- Trend Micro Anti-Spyware (available from `www.trendmicro.com`)
- eTrust PestPatrol Anti-Spyware (available from `www.pestpatrol.com`)
- Norton AntiVirus (which includes anti-spyware capabilities, available from `www.symantec.com`)

When researching different anti-spyware packages to find the one that works best for you, keep in mind that most of the free tools made available by different companies are reactive in nature and therefore do not provide real-time protection against malware threats. In most cases, the free versions of anti-spyware programs provide malware detection and removal capabilities, whereas the paid or full versions add real-time protection and other advanced features.

Note

The software used for illustrative purposes in this chapter is Microsoft AntiSpyware, available from www.microsoft.com/athome/security/spyware/software/. Many other anti-spyware software programs exist, but Microsoft AntiSpyware is free and one of top performing anti-spyware packages for Windows XP. For reviews of popular anti-spyware programs (including Microsoft AntiSpyware) visit the PC Magazine anti-spyware page at `www.pcmag.com/category2/0,1874,1639157,00.asp`.

Follow these steps to install Microsoft AntiSpyware:

1. Click Start → Internet Explorer, or open your preferred Web browser. Browse to `www.microsoft.com/athome/security/spyware/software/`.
2. At the Microsoft Windows AntiSpyware home page, click the TRY IT NOW link.
3. At the Validation Recommendation screen, click Continue.
4. At the Genuine Windows Download screen, click No, do not validate Windows at this time, but take me to the download; then click Continue.
5. Click Download. When prompted, save the installation file to a suitable folder. After the download is complete, double-click the file to begin the installation process.
6. At the Installation Wizard for Microsoft AntiSpyware Welcome screen, click Next.
7. At the Microsoft AntiSpyware License Agreement screen, click I accept the terms in the license agreement and then click Next.
8. At the Installation Folder screen, click Next.
9. At the Ready to Install Microsoft AntiSpyware screen, click Install.
10. At the Microsoft AntiSpyware Installation Complete screen, check Launch Microsoft AntiSpyware and then click Finish.

Updating spyware definition files

In much the same way that your anti-virus software is only truly useful if you've updated it to include the latest virus definition files, the same is true of anti-spyware programs. For these programs to effectively detect, remove, and protect against the latest malware threats, you need to update their definition files regularly. Some anti-spyware vendors offer updated definition files every day; others make updates available anywhere from a few time to once a week.

Follow these steps to check for updated spyware definition files manually with Microsoft AntiSpyware:

1. Click Start → All Programs → Microsoft AntiSpyware → Microsoft AntiSpyware Update.
2. The Microsoft AntiSpyware AutoUpdater window appears, as shown in Figure 9-2. Downloading new spyware definition files and updates may take anywhere from a few seconds to a few minutes. After complete, click Close.

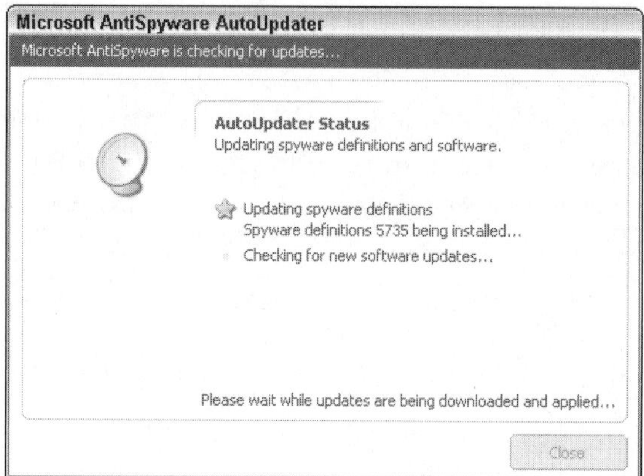

Figure 9-2: Updating spyware definition files in Microsoft AntiSpyware.

Note

By default, Microsoft AntiSpyware automatically updates its definition files once per day.

Configuring anti-spyware settings

Although the ability to detect, remove, and actively protect against malware threats are the primary goals of most anti-spyware packages, many of these programs include additional advanced features and settings worth exploring.

In the case of Microsoft AntiSpyware, detailed real-time protection settings and advanced tools showcase the different ways in which you can protect your system to a high degree, and also take advantage of the flexibility to selectively enable or disable different protection settings if necessary.

Microsoft AntiSpyware relies on three different security agents to keep tabs on over 50 different system checkpoint settings. These include:

- **Internet Agents.** Nine different Internet Agent Checkpoints are on the lookout for suspicious activities like unauthorized dial-up activity, changes to your Internet "safe sites" list, modifications to your TCP/IP settings, and more.
- **System Agents.** 25 different System Agent Checkpoints are included with Microsoft AntiSpyware for the purpose of detecting changes to your Hosts file, Windows Update settings, the list of programs configured to start automatically with Windows XP, and more.
- **Application Agents.** 25 different Application Agent Checkpoints stand guard to ensure that malware cannot infiltrate or make changes to your computer's program settings (particularly those associated with Internet Explorer). Examples of Application Agent Checkpoints integrated into Microsoft AntiSpyware include ones to detect changes to Internet Explorer URLs, your trusted sites list, script blocking and plug-in settings, and more.

Follow these steps to configure real-time protection settings with Microsoft AntiSpyware:

1. Double-click the Microsoft AntiSpyware icon on your taskbar to open the main program window, as shown in Figure 9-3.

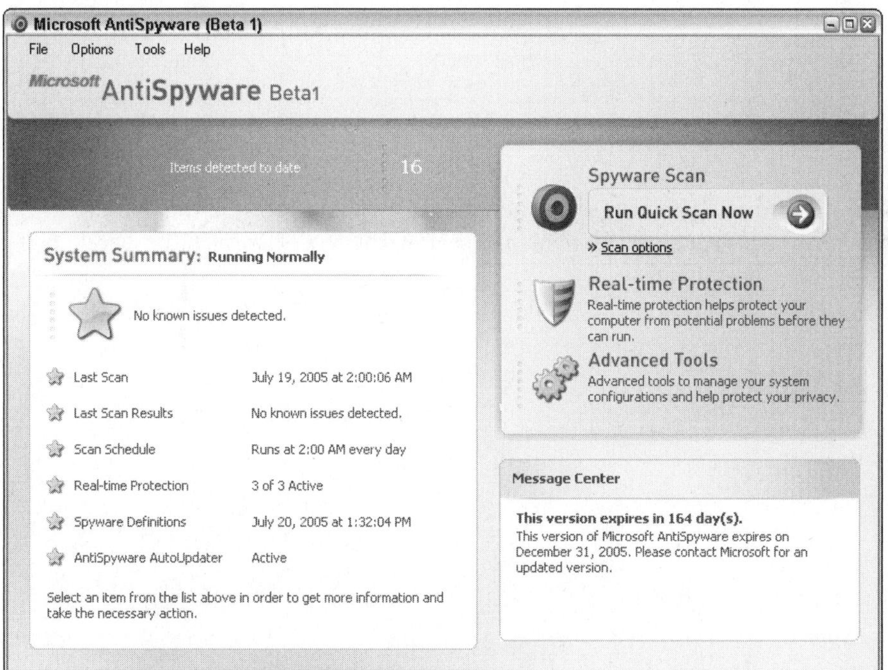

Figure 9-3: The Microsoft AntiSpyware main program window.

2. Click Real-time Protection. By default, all Security agents that offer real-time protection against spyware threats should be enabled, as shown in Figure 9-4.

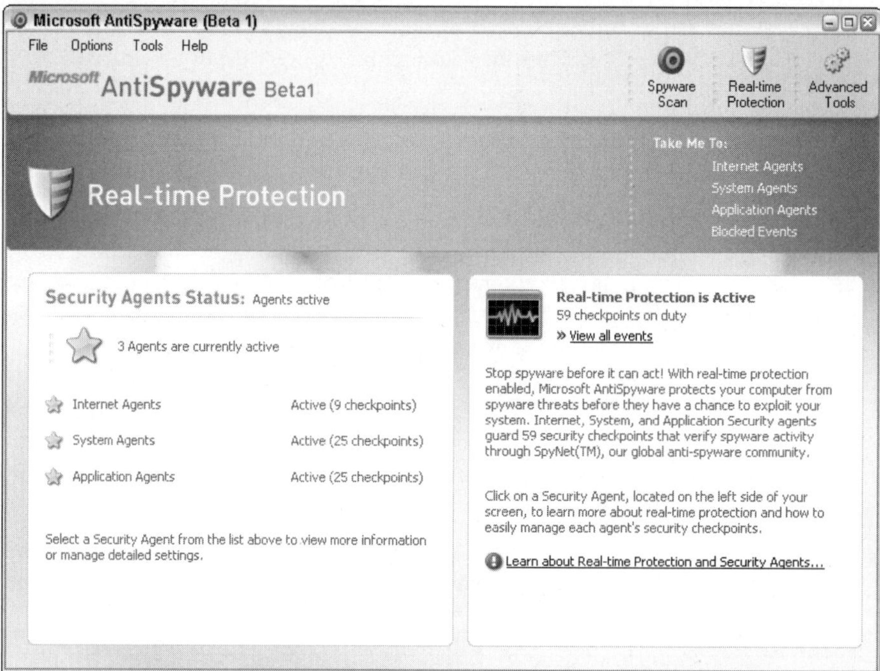

Figure 9-4: Three different security agents help to protect against malware threats in real-time.

3. Click Internet Agents to review the status of Internet Agent Checkpoints. When you click an individual agent, details about the checkpoint are displayed in the Checkpoint Details pane as shown in Figure 9-5.

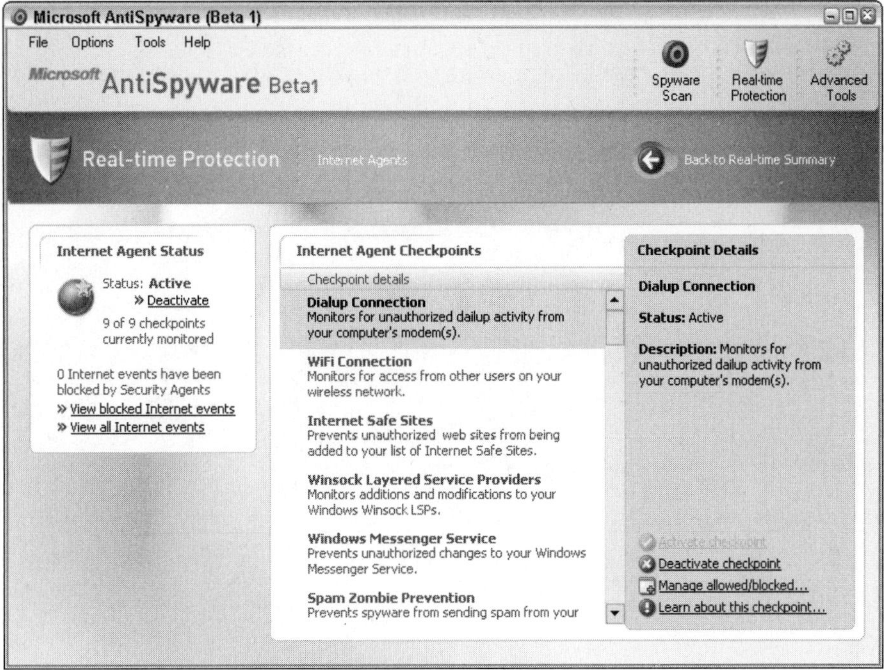

Figure 9-5: Each of Microsoft AntiSpyware's security agents consists of multiple checkpoints.

4. Click other Internet Agents to view their purpose and status and then click Back to Real-time Summary to view additional agent settings. As a general rule, you should leave all agent checkpoints enabled for the highest degree of protection against malware threats.

Beyond its real-time protection settings, Microsoft AntiSpyware also includes a number of advanced tools for the purpose of detecting and protecting against malware. The three advanced tools currently supplied with Microsoft AntiSpyware include:

- **System Explorers.** The System Explorers tool allows you to review, reconfigure, or delete different system settings that may have been altered by malware threats. For example, you can use this tool to remove items from your startup programs list, or managed installed toolbars in Internet Explorer.
- **Browser Restore.** The Browser Restore tool is included with Microsoft AntiSpyware to allow you to reset Internet Explorer settings that may have been changed as a result of a browser hijacker. It's important to note that simply resetting these settings doesn't necessarily mean that the browser hijacker that made the changes has been removed.
- **Tracks Eraser.** This privacy tool allows you to delete personal history settings that may be stored on your computer. For example, you can use this tool to delete lists of recently opened documents, your Internet Explorer URL history, temporary files, and more.

Follow these steps to use Advanced Tools in Microsoft AntiSpyware:

1. Double-click the Microsoft AntiSpyware icon on your taskbar to open the main program window

2. Click Advanced Tools to view the Advanced Tools screen, as shown in Figure 9-6.

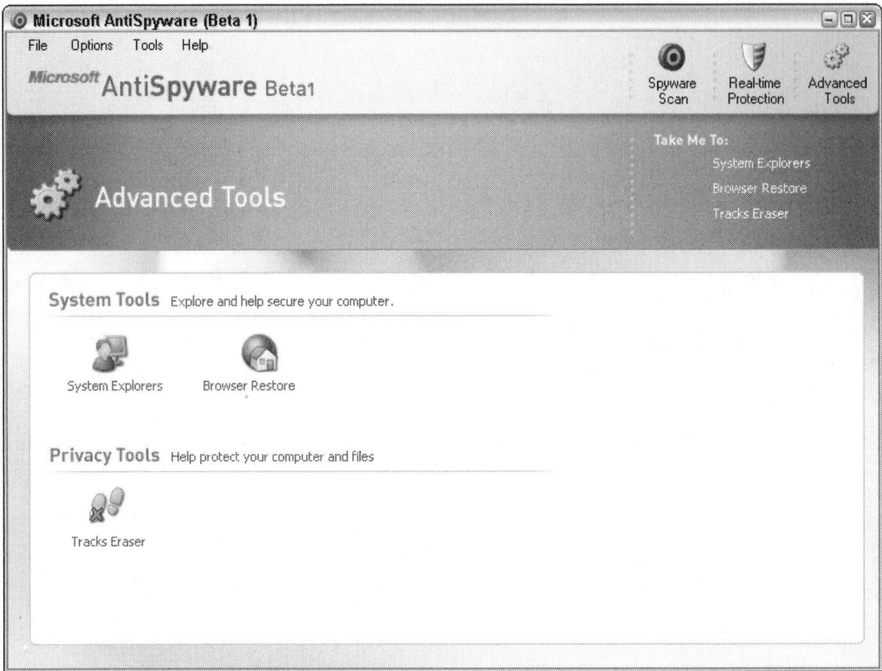

Figure 9-6: The Advanced Tools screen in Microsoft AntiSpyware.

3. Click System Explorers and then click individual items to view details on all system explorer objects installed on your computer. For example, to review all Internet Explorer browser helper objects installed on your PC, click IE BHOs, as shown in Figure 9-7. To learn more about an installed BHO, click its name. You can block or permanently remove any system explorer by using the shortcut links in the lower-right corner of the Microsoft AntiSpyware window, if necessary.

Figure 9-7: The System Explorers tool allows you to dig deeper into the configuration of programs like Internet Explorer.

4. Click Back to Advanced Tools to return to the Advanced Tools screen.
5. Click Browser Restore to open the Restore Internet Explorer Browser Settings screen, as shown in Figure 9-8. You can use this tool to return configurable IE settings to their default values, such as in cases where a browser hijacker has changed your customized settings. To view the current and default values for different settings, simply click a setting in the list and review the contents of the Details pane.

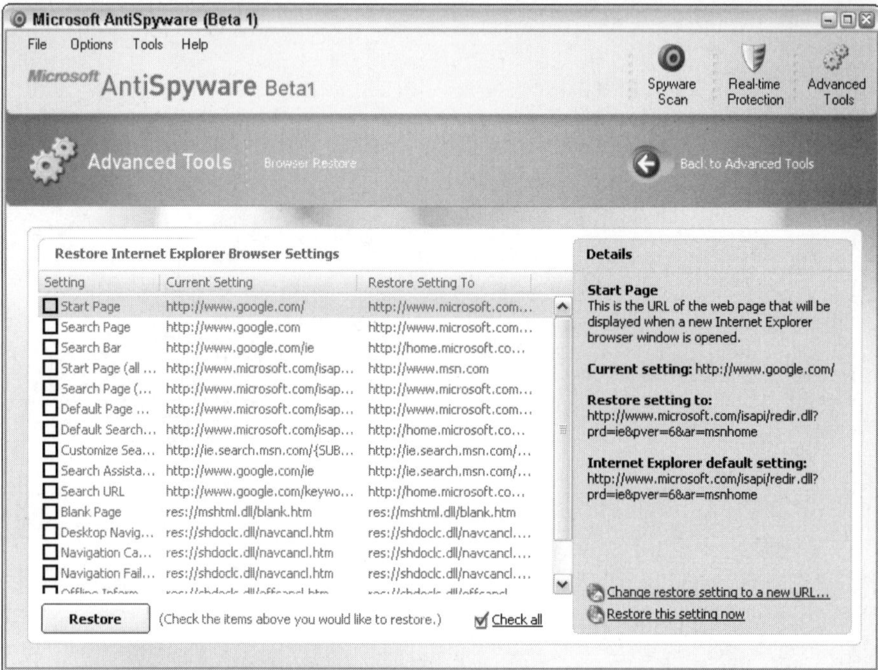

Figure 9-8: Use the Browser Restore tool to reset hijacked Web browser settings.

6. Click Back to Advanced Tools.
7. Click Tracks Eraser in the Privacy Tools section. This tool, shown in Figure 9-9, allows you to erase historical information stored in different programs or Windows components. To erase the contents of items such as your Recent Documents list, scroll to that item, check its checkbox, and click the Erase these tracks button.

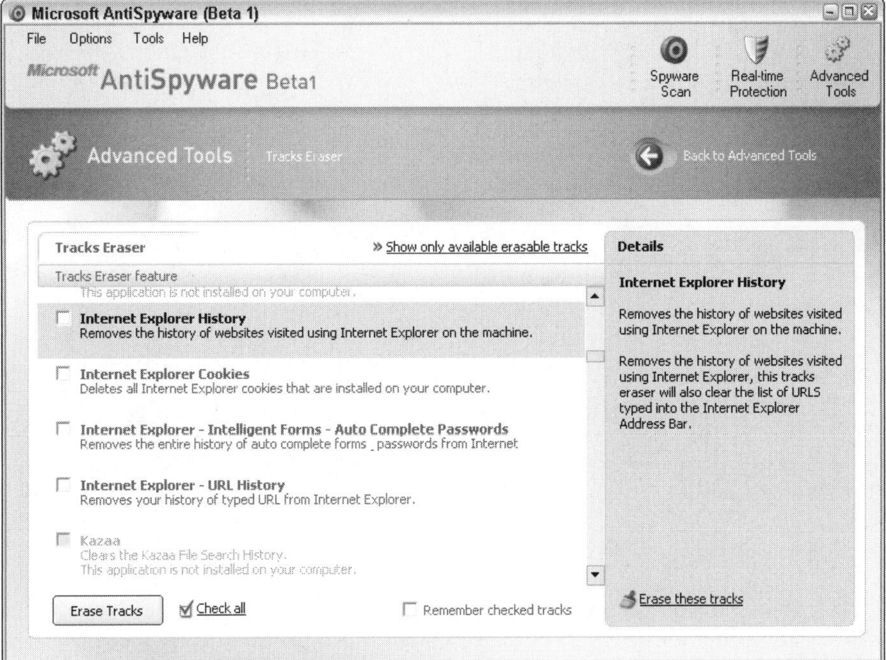

Figure 9-9: Use the Tracks Eraser tool to erase temporary files or details about the files and Web sites you've opened or accessed.

Scanning for malware

Although the real-time protection features of tools such as Microsoft AntiSpyware helps to ensure that your Windows XP system remains protected against new malware threats, it's still important to perform a complete system scan for spyware at least once per week at an absolute minimum. By default, Microsoft AntiSpyware scans for malware once per day, but this interval will be different depending on the anti-spyware program you decide to use. Along with the scan that Microsoft AntiSpyware performs automatically each day, you can also initiate more comprehensive scans manually.

Follow these steps to scan for malware with Microsoft AntiSpyware:

1. Double-click the Microsoft AntiSpyware icon on your taskbar to open the main program window.
2. In the Spyware Scan section, click Scan options.
3. At the Select your Scan Settings screen, click Run a full system scan (as shown in Figure 9-10) and then click Run Scan Now. The complete scan process may take anywhere from a few minutes to much longer depending on the speed of your computer and number of items to be scanned.

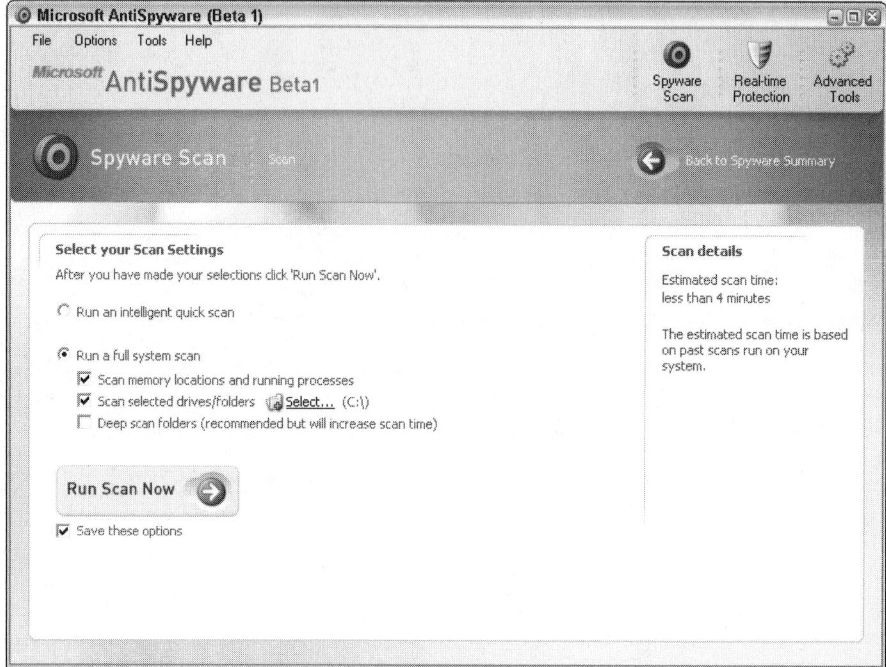

Figure 9-10: Configuring scan settings in Microsoft AntiSpyware.

4. After the scanning process is complete, the Scan Completed screen appears, as shown in Figure 9-11. If any spyware threats are detected on your PC, Microsoft AntiSpyware next gives you an opportunity to selectively remove or quarantine them as part of cleaning your system.

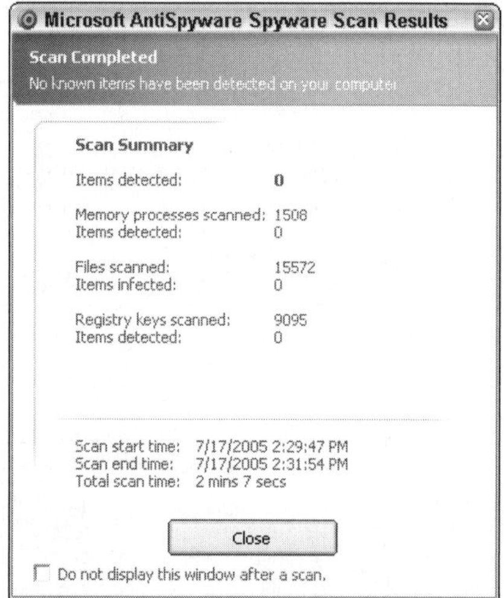

Figure 9-11: Results of a spyware scan.

Caution

If you complete a spyware scan and many different threats are detected, select the option to remove them, restart your computer, and complete another full scan. Some malware threats lodge themselves onto your system so forcefully that it can sometimes take two or even three scan passes to ensure that your system is clean and malware-free.

Beyond anti-spyware software

Installing anti-spyware software with real-time protection and keeping it properly updated is the single best way to ensure that your system remains free and clear of malware threats; however, it's also important to give some thought to how you use the Internet with an aim towards avoiding interactions with malware in the first place. Use the following best practices to help ensure that your system remains free and clear of malware threats to the greatest degree possible:

- Install anti-spyware software that includes real-time protection, and ensure that it's always updated with the latest spyware definition files. Scan for malware regularly.
- Install firewall software that includes both inbound and outbound filtering capabilities. If a malware threat that attempts to "phone home" is installed on your computer, a firewall capable of outbound filtering will likely alert you to the connection attempt.
- Install anti-virus software and keep it properly updated. Although typically not as comprehensive as anti-spyware tools, many anti-virus programs are capable of detecting malware threats and suspicious activities.
- Be careful about the Web sites that you visit, as less-reputable sites are common sources of malware infections. Visiting online casinos, pornography sites, and Web sites offering pirated materials (aka warez) may increase your malware exposure risk.
- Ensure that your Windows XP system is patched and protected with the latest security updates and Service Packs.
- If Internet Explorer is your preferred Web browser, ensure that you have its security settings configured appropriately (as originally outlined in Chapter 5). Switching to an alternative browser without ActiveX support can also help to reduce the risk of malware infections, so you may want to consider options beyond IE, such as Firefox, Opera, or Netscape. Regardless of the browser you choose, be sure to keep it updated with the latest security patches as they're released.
- If you're not using your modem to connect to the Internet or to send and receive faxes, disconnect it from your phone line.
- Use a Limited user account (rather than a Computer administrator account) to complete day-to-day tasks on a Windows XP system. Many malware threats (as well as viruses) rely on the current user having Computer administrator privileges to do their dirty work.

HOSTS with the Most

It's next to impossible to know which Web sites could be potential sources of malware infections via techniques like drive-by downloads. While you certainly wouldn't expect to be infected by a major site like Google or Yahoo!, the differences between legitimate and "fly by night" sites can sometimes be hard to distinguish. It's entirely possible that you could find yourself browsing to an infectious Web site by clicking the results provided by a search engine or a link supplied on another site.

Although it may be hard for the average user to determine which sites are safe and which are not, some people out there trying to create a roadmap of potentially dangerous sites. Specifically, some folks at the `MVPs.org` Web site have been busy creating a HOSTS file that includes entries for potentially dangerous sites.

When your Windows XP system tries to connect to a site like `www.pcmag.com`, it uses Domain Name System (DNS) servers to translate the name to the IP address associated with the site. Before it queries DNS for this information, however, it first checks its local HOSTS file, and if an entry for the site exists, using the IP address specified in the file instead.

The HOSTS file made available on the MVPs.org Web site lists hundreds of dangerous sites, and maps them all to a special IP address — 127.0.0.1. This is known as the "loopback" address, and when specified, contacts your local computer. So, in cases where you try to connect to a potentially dangerous site, the connection request is sent to your local computer, where the attempt is denied — leaving you safer in the process.

In addition to listing sites that include malware- and virus-related threats, the HOSTS file available from MVPs.org includes entries for online advertisers. This means that certain banner ads may be blocked if you download and use the file. If there are certain advertisements that you do want to view, however, you can always open the HOSTS file and place a # sign in front of any given entry. This tells the HOSTS file to ignore the line, allowing you to connect to the site (or see the ads) in question.

To obtain and install this HOSTS files, visit `www.mvps.org/winhelp2002/hosts.htm`. The site includes a regularly updated file that you can download, and details on installing correctly for Windows XP systems.

Removing Malware

As you now know, installing anti-spyware software and keeping it properly updated is the best way to keep your computer free of malware threats; however, there still may be times when you'll need to explore other tools to eliminate a specific malware threat, or you may just want to scan for malware with more than one tool, just to be on the safe side. In this section you learn more about using third-party malware removal tools, and how to deal with more advanced malware threats such as the CoolWebSearch browser hijacker.

Using spyware removal tools

As a general rule, you should never install and run more than one anti-virus program on your computer at the same time, lest the programs interfere with one another and leave your computer at risk. The same is generally true with anti-spyware programs, but as long as you're not trying to run two or more programs that offer real-time protection simultaneously, there's nothing wrong with installing multiple tools. In fact, you may just find that one tool detects (or can remove) a threat that another program had trouble with.

If you've already invested in one anti-spyware tool, there's no need to run out to purchase a second. Instead, consider downloading one of the many free spyware detection and removal tools from the Internet instead. The same vendors that produce the popular commercial tools typically make free versions of their programs available for download on their Web sites. So, you might opt to run Microsoft AntiSpyware as your primary anti-spyware tool and then periodically run scans with a tool such as Ad-Aware SE Personal for the sake of completeness.

If your computer is already infected by malware, you may have a tough time getting an anti-spyware tool installed to begin with. Many of the advanced threats are programmed to block popular anti-spyware tools from being installed, so it's possible that you may have to try installing two or three different programs before you find one that works. To increase your chances of success on an infected system, however, you may want to attempt the installation process from Windows XP's Safe Mode.

Caution

A wide variety of different tools exist for the purpose of removing malware threats, but don't assume that every scanning program is as "legitimate" as it looks or claims to be. Many of the supposed scanning tools that exist are of dubious origin, and some even produce "false positive" results as a way to entice you into purchasing the "full" version of the program. Before you purchase any anti-spyware program, check the "Rogue/Suspect Anti-Spyware Products and Web Sites list online at `www.spywarewarrior.com/rogue_anti-spyware.htm`.

Follow these steps to complete a malware scan with Ad-Aware SE Personal:

1. Click Start → Internet Explorer, or open your preferred Web browser. Browse to `www.lavasoftusa.com/software/adaware/` and then click the Download Ad-Aware here link. Choose a download link, and save the installation file to a suitable folder.
2. Double-click the Ad-Aware SE installation file to begin the installation process.
3. At the Ad-Aware SE Personal Welcome screen, click Next.
4. At the License Agreement screen, check I accept the license agreement and click Next.
5. At the Destination Location screen, click Next.

6. At the Install to All Users menu screen, click Next.
7. At the Start Installation screen, click Next. After the process is complete, click Finish to update the program's definition files and complete a full system scan. After the scanning process is complete, the Scan Complete screen appears, as shown in Figure 9-12. Click Next.

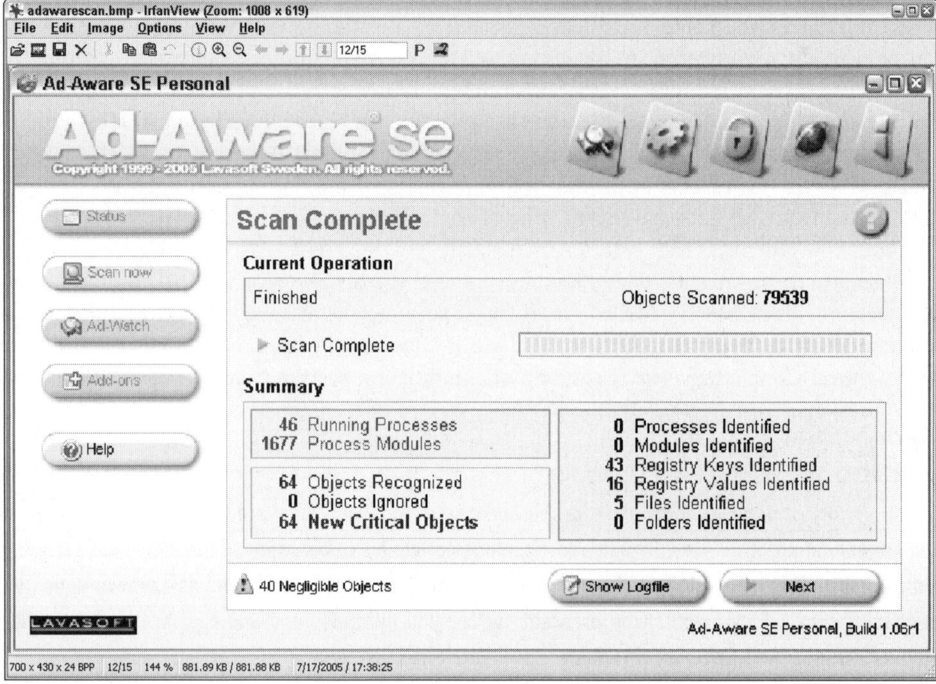

Figure 9-12: Results from a scan with Ad-Aware SE Personal.

8. At the Scanning Result screen, click the plus sign next to each "target family" detected. This displays the TAC rating for each group of objects, as shown in Figure 9-13. Objects with a higher TAC rating are considered to be more dangerous.

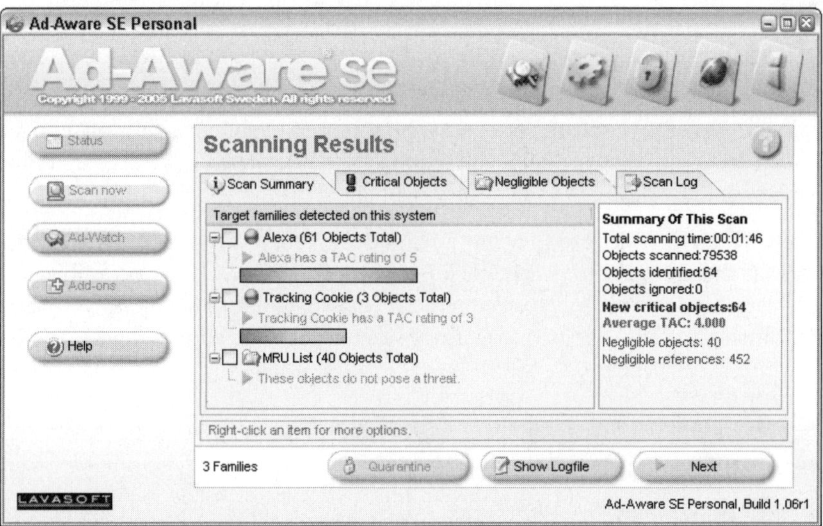

Figure 9-13: Viewing detailed scan results.

9. Check the checkboxes next to the items that you want Ad-Aware SE Personal to place into quarantine and then click Next. When the confirmation window appears, click OK.

Note

It's possible that you may run a scan with Ad-Aware SE Personal and then accidentally remove and quarantine legitimate items. If this happens you can always review quarantined items by clicking the Open quarantine list link on the Status screen and then select the option to restore items that were removed by accident. Additionally, you can opt to delete quarantined items such that they are unrecoverable.

Eliminating browser hijacks

Almost most anti-spyware tools are capable of detecting and removing almost all malware threats, a number of programs still have difficulty with some of the more complex (programmatically) pests, such as the CoolWebSearch browser hijacker. If you computer is infected with CoolWebSearch, your best bet is to try removing it with whichever anti-spyware tool you have installed first. Assuming that

your anti-spyware program doesn't get the job done, your next step should be to try a dedicated removal tool like Trend Micro's CWShredder.

CWShredder is a free tool designed to detect and remove only one specific threat, namely CoolWebSearch; however, a number of CoolWebSearch variants exist, and new ones are appearing all the time. CWShredder is updated regularly to deal with new variants as they're discovered, and truly represents your best chance of completely removing a CoolWebSearch infection once and for all.

Follow these steps to scan for and remove CoolWebsearch variants with CWShredder:

1. Click Start → Internet Explorer, or open your preferred Web browser. Browse to `www.trendmicro.com/cwshredder/` and then click the Remove CoolWebSearch link. Save the cwshredder.exe file to an appropriate folder.

2. Double-click cwshredder.exe to open CWShredder. When the main program window appears (as shown in Figure 9-14), click Fix to complete a scan for CoolWebSearch variants. If you choose Scan Only instead, CWShredder will not remove CoolWebSearch if it is found, but alerts you about any variants that are installed on your system.

Figure 9-14: CWShredder is the premier tool for removing the CoolWebSearch browser hijacker and its numerous variants.

3. When the CWShredder dialog box appears, click OK.

4. When the scanning process is complete, scroll through the result to determine whether any CoolWebSearch variants were found, and whether they were fixed. A sample results screen is shown in Figure 9-15.

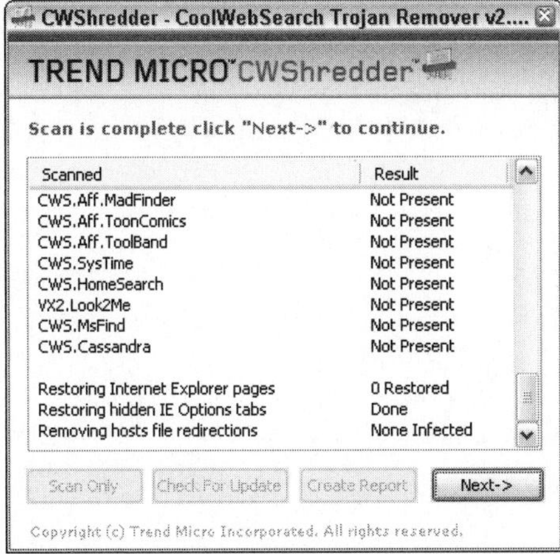

Figure 9-15: Results of a CWShredder scan.

CoolWebSearch may be the worst of a bad lot on the malware front, but it's certainly not the only malware threat that you may have trouble removing from your Windows XP system. Malware is constantly evolving, and although most of the popular anti-spyware tools are up to the task of detecting and defeating all of the latest threats, newer variants may sometimes slip through the cracks and remain undetected.

If you believe that your system is infected even after completing scans with multiple anti-spyware tools, your best bet probably lies in a tool such as HijackThis (available from `www.spywareinfo.com/~merijn/downloads.html`), a tool that scans for and detects all sorts of browser hijackers and browser-related malware issues. Effectively, HijackThis scans your system and creates a log of all browser-related settings (including BHOs) installed on your computer. The log includes details such as changed settings, suspect Registry entries, and the like. Ultimately, HijackThis is a tool for advanced users, but if you use it to scan your system, you can post it to Web sites like the support forums at SpywareInfo or CastleCops, and a forum user experienced with the tool should be able to help you determine whether a new malware threat or browser hijacker variant is present on your system.

All the Dirty Details

The world of malware is a shady place, and the Internet is loaded with hundreds of malware-related Web sites. Some are shrill sites hawking useless products that purport to detect and remove malware when it actual fact they do nothing useful at all. Others are lined with incorrect or misleading information in an attempt to trick you into a purchase, or worse, an infection. Thankfully, a number of excellent resources exist for the purpose of researching malware threats and getting help in cases where you find your PC infected.

Continued

All the Dirty Details (Continued)

Some of the best spyware-related resources on the Web include the following:

- **SpywareInfo** (www.spywareinfo.com)
- **CastleCops** (www.castlecops.com)
- **Microsoft AntiSpyware Home Page** (www.microsoft.com/athome/security/spyware/software/default.mspx)
- **SpywareWarrior** (www.spywarewarrior.com)
- **CA Spyware Encyclopedia** (www3.ca.com/securityadvisor/pest/search.aspx)
- **PC Magazine Antispyware Product Guides and Reviews** (www.pcmag.com/category2/0,1738,1639157,00.asp)

Summary

Malware is one of the biggest (yet least appreciated) threats to the security and privacy of Windows XP systems and users. With an estimated 9 out of 10 Windows systems infected by malware in some form or another, it's critically important for all users to scan for and remove any existing threats present on Windows XP systems and then take the necessary steps to avoid future infections.

Keep the following points in mind when it comes to keeping your Windows XP system free of malware-related threats:

- Install anti-spyware software that includes real-time protection. Keep it updated and then scan for malware threats regularly.
- Install a firewall that offers both inbound and outbound packet filtering capabilities to stop malware threats from "phoning home."
- Keep your system up to date by installing all of the latest security updates and patches.
- Don't underestimate the need to have both anti-virus and anti-spyware software installed on your PC simultaneously. These programs complement (rather than conflict with) one another.
- Consider installing more than one anti-spyware tool — a second opinion never hurts!
- Ensure that Internet Explorer is properly secured, or switch to an alternative Web browser such as Firefox, Opera, or Netscape.
- Be careful what you click, and stay away from shady Web sites — what appears to be a simple banner or dialog box may actually be the gateway to infecting your Windows XP system with another malware threat.

Part IV

Messaging Your Way to E-Mail Security

Chapter 10
The Dark Side of Spam

Chapter 11
Securing E-mail Messages Using Encryption and Digital Signatures

Chapter 10

The Dark Side of Spam

Invent a new method of communication and someone will eventually come up with a way to manipulate it for monetary gain. First came traditional junk mail in the form of those unsolicited flyers, pamphlets, and letters that have no doubt found there way into your postal mailbox. Next came the telemarketers, taking advantage of your personal phone number to pitch you carpet cleaning and lawn care service — as you've just sat down to dinner, of course. The rise of the fax machine brought with it printouts for everything under the sun; then along came e-mail — is it really any surprise that your Inbox is overloaded with so many "spectacular" offers?

Hate it as everyone might, junk e-mail — commonly referred to as ***spam***, but also called unsolicited commercial e-mail (UCE) — isn't going away any time soon. Quite simply, it costs next to nothing to send a spam e-mail message to millions of users, and if all those messages result in even one or two sales, its mission accomplished in the eyes of the sender (lovingly referred to as the "spammer"). You may have a hard time believing that anyone would consider purchasing something advertised in a spam message, but it happens all the time. One spammer that was recently convicted in the U.S. is purported to have made in excess of $24 million hawking various products over a six-year period. In other words, as long as there's money to be made from spam, it will continue to find its way into your e-mail Inbox.

Traditional spam messages that try to sell a product or service are really little more than an annoyance — certainly a big annoyance if you receive hundreds of these messages per day but still relatively harmless. Unfortunately, the very nature of spam has undergone a marked shift in the past couple of years, to the point where junk mail can represent a very real and serious threat to you and your computer. At the more harmless end of the spectrum, opening a spam e-mail message can alert the sender that your address is valid, thus resulting in even more spam. On the more dangerous end are messages that include viruses, those that try to fool you into giving away sensitive personal details, and even ones that attempt to scam you out of money. Ultimately, even a seemingly harmless e-mail message from someone you know can be very bad news.

In this chapter you learn more about how spam finds its way into your e-mail Inbox and different techniques that can be used to minimize your exposure to these pesky messages. Let the (uphill) battle begin!

Understanding Spam

It's a very lucky person who uses an e-mail account for more than a few weeks without receiving their first spam e-mail message. It all starts innocently enough, usually with a single message hawking some silly product or service. It doesn't take long, however, for that one message to be quickly followed by another two, then four, and then perhaps 10 or more per day. Within a few months, your Inbox can literally be overwhelmed by junk e-mail messages, to the point where you don't even want to check your e-mail.

To understand (and ultimately fight) spam, it's important to be familiar with the following concepts:

- How spam finds you
- Why spam can be a security threat

You learn more about these important concepts in the following sections.

How spam finds you

If junk e-mail messages are finding their way into your Inbox, it's happening for one of two reasons. The first (and most common) is that someone has managed to obtain your e-mail address. The second is that the spammer has actually "guessed" your address, adding your name or a popular term to common domain names such as @hotmail.com.

Spammers typically acquire your e-mail address by one of the following methods:

- Harvesting
- Web site registrations
- Viruses

Each of these techniques is explored in more detail in the following sections.

HARVESTING

Harvesting is the process by which most e-mail addresses are acquired by spammers. In a nutshell, any time that you post your e-mail address online — be it to a public Web site or Usenet newsgroup — it becomes susceptible to programs (known as e-mail address harvesters) designed to traverse the Internet, collecting addresses along the way.

To avoid having your e-mail address harvested and used as a destination for spam, never post your address online. For cases where you do need to post an address for others to contact you, never use your primary address. Instead, set up a secondary account (with a free Web mail service, for example) to use as your "public" e-mail address, and submit this address as required.

Unfortunately, you can expect your secondary address to be a major target for spam, along with legitimate messages; however, this is still better than dealing with large numbers of junk mail messages in the account used to correspond with friends, family, and business associates.

Caution

Many people recommend alternate techniques of posting your e-mail address online to avoid spam. Common examples include replacing the @ symbol with (at), or including the term "nospam" within your address and reminding senders to remove this term to send you a message. Although these techniques may fool very primitive harvesting programs, don't expect them to keep you spam-free. Any harvesting program that can recognize an e-mail address can also be programmed to detect and collect addresses that are masked using these primitive techniques.

WEB SITE REGISTRATIONS

Another popular way for spammers to obtain your e-mail address is by getting you to supply it via a Web site registration form of some sort. Most reputable Web sites never resell or give away your e-mail address under any circumstances, but there's really nothing stopping other sites from doing with your address as they please. As such, spammers commonly purchase lists of addresses from various sources online, including companies that "buy" valid lists of addresses from other sites.

As with posting your e-mail address online, avoid submitting your primary e-mail address when completing Web-based registration forms. Instead, set up a secondary address for this purpose.

Note

Not every Web site to which you submit your e-mail address is unscrupulous enough to sell your address and other personal information, but many do. Most sites spell out exactly what they will or will not do with your information as part of their "terms of service" disclaimer, making it well worth at least a quick glance—especially for phrases like "third parties." In addition to disclaimers, many sites also include a dedicated privacy policy page that outlines who they use the information you submit, how it is stored, and so on. The World Wide Web Consortium has even developed a standard that deals with the use of personal information by Web sites. For more information on the standard known as the Platform for Privacy Preferences Project (P3P), visit `www.w3.org/P3P/`.

VIRUSES

Over the past few years, viruses have become an exceedingly popular way for spammers to obtain e-mail addresses. Although the methodology varies from virus to virus, the general idea is that a virus infects a computer and then scans that system for e-mail addresses. In most cases, the virus immediately begins searching through users' address books and contact lists, harvests all addresses into a file, and sends the file on to an Internet server.

Ultimately, this means that your e-mail address can end up in the hands of spammers through no fault of your own. All it takes is for a harvesting virus to infect a computer where your e-mail address is in the user's address book or contact list. You obviously can't control what other people do with their own computers, but it doesn't hurt to remind friends and family members about the importance

of running anti-virus software, keeping it up to date, and scanning for viruses frequently. Of course, in the same way that a virus on a friend's computer can lead to more spam for you, the reverse is also true — when a harvesting virus infects your PC, it may be people in your address book who end up on the wrong end of the spam town.

Why spam can be a security threat

Normally seen as little more than an annoyance, spam messages are becoming more of a threat to security and privacy every day. Where once their objectives were relatively limited to profit motives, the spam messages of today not only try to "sell" but also infect, steal from, and even scam the recipient. Some of the primary security and privacy threats associated with spam include:

- Viruses
- Beacons
- Phishing
- Scams

Each of these threats is looked at in more detail in the following sections.

VIRUSES

Many viruses are designed to harvest e-mail addresses, but it's also not uncommon for spam e-mail messages to contain virus-laden attachments as well. In some cases, this is the result of a virus infecting one PC and then mailing itself out to all the addresses in the infected computer's contact list. In others, a spammer knowingly sends out an infected e-mail attachment to a list of users, hoping that at least a few users will open the attachment, become infected, and in turn propagate the virus even further.

Your best protection against e-mail-based viruses is to install anti-virus software that includes real-time scanning of all incoming and outgoing e-mail messages. These programs typically quarantine infected attachments automatically, but for them to be truly effective you must be diligent about keeping your virus definition files up to date.

BEACONS

One of the most common problems faced by spammers is trying to determine whether e-mail addresses on their lists are valid. In the eyes of the spammer, a "known good" e-mail address is much more valuable than addresses where the validity of the address is suspect. Spammers rely on their messages being able to reach functioning and in-use mailboxes and as such have taken steps to confirm whether or not a given address is in use.

One of the most popular methods that spammers use to confirm an address is through the use of "beacons" (see Figure 10-1). In the world of e-mail, a beacon is a signal to the spammer that your address is in good, and that their message has at least been opened. Although different beaconing methods exist, the most popular is to send e-mail messages in HTML format (messages that include different fonts, colors, images, and so forth). When these messages are opened, a request is sent from your computer to download any images it includes from a Web server. This Web server then tracks that the request came from the message sent to you via a unique code included in the specific message you received. Ultimately, this beacon tells the spammer not only that your address is valid but also that you read (or at least briefly opened) the message.

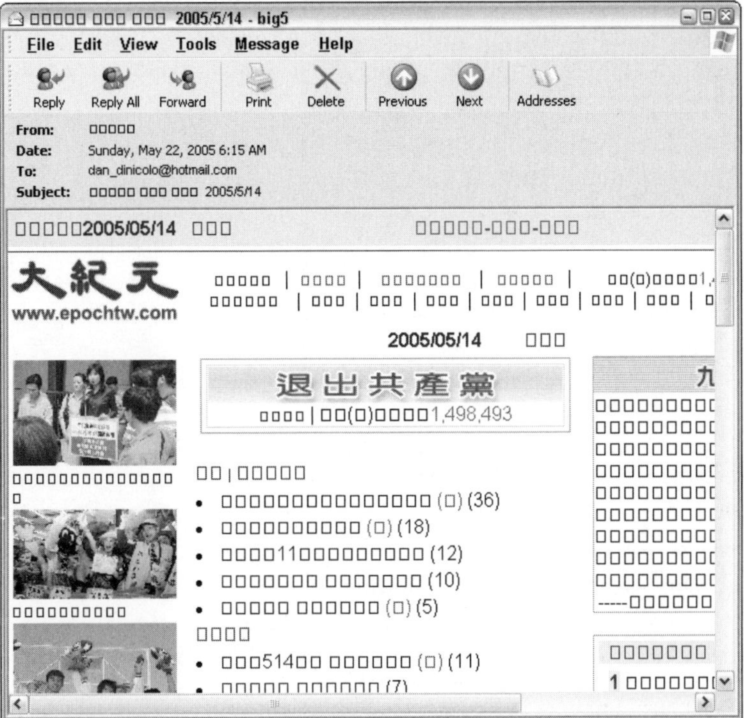

Figure 10-1: Images and other Web elements in HTML-formatted e-mail messages can act as "beacons" for spammers.

Caution

If a spam e-mail message that you receive includes a link that you can click to be removed from the spammers list, never click it. Although a small percentage of spammers might actually remove you from their list, the vast majority will simply use your click as yet another type of beacon signaling that your e-mail address is valid. In most cases, clicking these links and submitting your e-mail address for removal will actually result in you receiving even more spam.

After Windows XP Service Pack 2 is installed, Outlook Express automatically prevents beacons from functioning by not allowing any requests to Web sources to be processed when an e-mail message is opened. When messages that need to download items from the Internet are opened, Outlook Express displays a message stating, "Some pictures have been blocked to help prevent the sender from identifying your computer. Click here to download pictures," as shown in Figure 10-2. Click this message only if you're sure that the message is from a known and trusted source, such as an e-mail-based newsletter to which you subscribe.

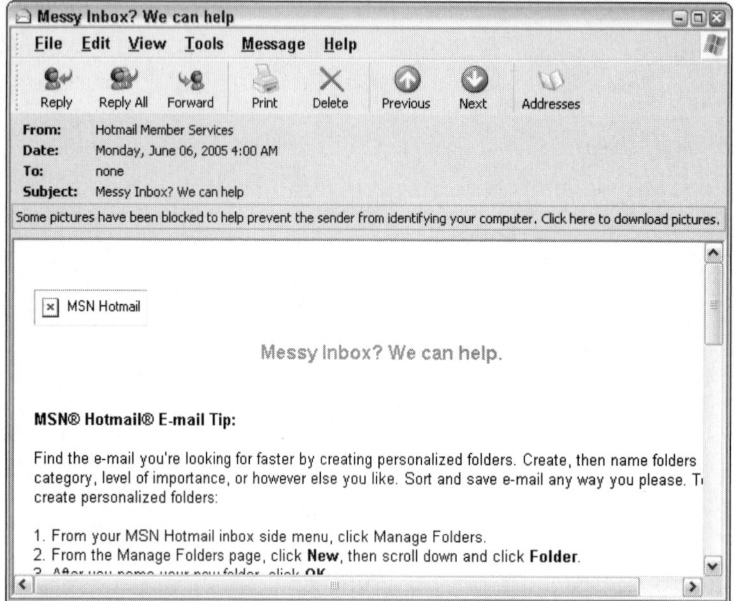

Figure 10-2: After Windows XP Service Pack 2 is installed, Outlook Express automatically stops images and code embedded in HTML e-mail messages from being displayed.

If you're using an e-mail client program other than Outlook Express, it may or may not include a specific feature for dealing with beacons; however, almost every e-mail client program includes an option to view all messages as plain text, which eliminates the possibility of the message attempting to contact the Internet. To determine how to view all e-mail messages you receive as plain text in your e-mail client, consult the program's Help file. In Outlook Express, open Tools → Options → Read and check the Read all messages in plain text checkbox.

Caution

Opening a spam e-mail message can signal that your e-mail address is valid, but spammers also rely on another technique in their quest to find valid addresses — the seemingly harmless "out of office" reply. Also referred to as an Autoresponder, these are messages that you typically configure when you're going to be away from e-mail for a few days. After enabled, every e-mail message that you receive from another user results in an automatic reply being sent back to the sender. Although legitimate senders usually appreciate out of office replies (because they know you're away and not ignoring them), they're also a boon to spammers who use the replies to determine that your address is valid. If you do plan on using out of office replies, create a rule that only sends these messages to people already in your address book or contact list. You learn more about creating e-mail message rules later in this chapter.

PHISHING

The spelling may be different, but persons engaging in "phishing" are definitely looking to hook something — usually sensitive personal information such as username and password information for online banking or auction Web sites.

In its most common form, phishing involves a spammer sending you an e-mail message that looks as if it was sent from a bank/payment service or a popular online auction Web site. The message usually states that the Web site needs you to log on to confirm your username and password and provides you with a link to submit your information. When you click the link (which may appear 100 percent legitimate), your Web browser opens and displays a page that may look identical to the site suggested in the message. In reality, however, the site is a fake. If you submit your information, it's actually sent to the spammer/scammer who originally sent the message, giving them full and unrestricted access to your account. It's not uncommon for phishing "victims" to find that funds have been transferred from their accounts, or that high-priced auctions have been set up under their username. In the case of the auction, the scammer sets up the auction using your username, sells the item to the highest bidder, and then collects the winner's money. After the scam is complete, the scammer and the money are long gone, and you're left on the hook to deal with the aftermath.

Ultimately, the best way to ensure that you're never a phishing victim is to ignore and delete any e-mail messages stating that you need to supply information about your account. If you do receive such a message and believe it to be legitimate, contact the company who sent the message by phone, or by visiting their Web site directly. Most legitimate companies (and especially those involved in financial transactions) will never ask for your personal account details in an e-mail message. If you believe that you have been tricked into supplying your username and password as a result of a phishing scam, contact the company in question, or log on to your account and change your password immediately.

Note

For more details on phishing and phishing-related scams, visit `www.antiphishing.org`.

SCAMS

While they've received a fair amount of press coverage over the past few years, many e-mail users continue to fall for a variety of "scam" messages received by e-mail. The most popular of these are the so-called "419" messages, named after a related section of the Nigerian criminal code (the country where the scam is purported to have originated). These particular messages ask you to help someone transfer money out of the sender's country for a portion of the proceeds, but a number of related scams exist — for example, some inform you that you've won the lottery or a certain prize. In all cases, you must pay a transfer fee or supply your banking details in to claim your bounty, which is effectively the scam. As unbelievable as it sounds, some individuals have be duped out of tens of thousands of dollars (and more) after falling for this trickery.

Although you might be tempted to reply to the sender of these messages, don't. If you do want to take action, visit the Spam Reporting Addresses Web site at `banspam.javawoman.com/report3/scam1.html` for details on contacting the appropriate authorities in your home locale.

Note

For some good reading on 419 and related Internet scams, visit the 419 Coalition Web site at `home.rica.net/alphae/419coal/index.htm`.

Fighting Spam

After the spammers find you, it won't be long before your Inbox is completely overwhelmed by junk e-mail. The fight against spam is definitely an uphill (and arguably impossible to win) battle, but there are a number of different ways that you can work towards reducing your junk e-mail intake. Some of the primary methods and techniques that can be used to fight spam include the following:

- Using the filtering and security capabilities of e-mail client software such as Outlook Express
- Installing anti-spam software
- Using plain old common sense

Each of these concepts is explored in more detail in the following sections.

Fighting spam with Outlook Express

As the e-mail client software included with Windows XP, this section focuses on fighting spam via the built-in capabilities of Outlook Express. Although many of the anti-spam features of Outlook Express are enabled by default and require no further configuration on your part, a number of additional features — not necessarily designed for dealing with spam alone — can also be used to help cut back on your spam intake. Some of the primary methods that can be used to deal with spam in Outlook Express include:

- Creating message rules
- Blocking senders
- Configuring message security settings
- Changing the way you view e-mail messages

These concepts and their configurations are looked at in more detail in the following sections.

CREATING MESSAGE RULES

One of the most powerful features in Outlook Express is the capability to configure "rules" that can be applied to incoming and outgoing messages. Rules are triggered when the criteria you specify are met, after which the actions you specify are taken. For example, you could create a rule that looks for all messages that include the words "university diploma" and then specify that when a message includes this phrase, it should automatically be moved to your Deleted Items folder. In other words, messages that meet the criteria specified in the rule will never end up in your Inbox, having been dealt with by the configured rule, automatically.

Caution

If you opt to create message rules in an e-mail client program such as Outlook Express, keep in mind all messages that meet the criteria you specify — possibly including legitimate messages — are subject to the rule. Before you delete the contents of a folder such as Deleted Items, always take a moment to ensure that it does not contain any "real" e-mail messages.

Outlook Express allows you to create as many of these types of rules as possible, but it's important to recognize that rules aren't only used to fight spam. For example, you could create a rule called "mail from Mom" and then specify that every time a message is received from your mother's e-mail address, it is automatically moved to a folder that you've created named "Mom." This would help to keep all messages from your mother neatly organized in one folder, rather than scattered amongst all the other messages in your Inbox.

Although using Outlook Express message rules to fight spam can be somewhat effective, it also represents an uphill battle. Spammers employ different techniques and trickery in an attempt to get past your rules and ensure their messages reach your Inbox. For a closer look at some of these techniques, see the "How Spammers Beat The "Rules"" sidebar.

The only realistic way to slow spam through the use of message rules would literally be to create hundreds of rules to account for all manner of spammer messages and tactics. That's not terribly realistic for most users, but creating a few key rules can be helpful if you tend to receive many of the same types of spam on a regular basis. For example, if you receive more than a few "university diploma" spam messages per week, setting up a rule for these messages can at least cut down on the number of spam e-mail messages that you need to deal with.

Follow these steps to create a new message rule in Outlook Express:

1. Click Start → Outlook Express.
2. Click Tools → Message Rules → Mail.
3. In the New Mail Rule window, check one or more conditions and actions for your rule, as shown in Figure 10-3. Note that a message must meet all of the conditions you specify in order for the configured action(s) to be taken.

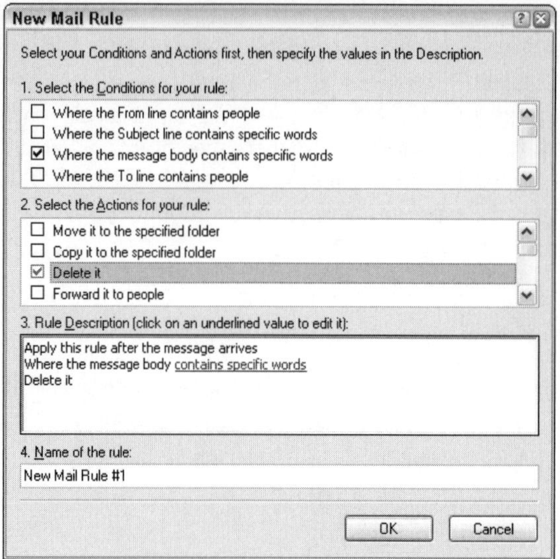

Figure 10-3: Creating a new message rule in Outlook Express.

4. Click the hyperlink in the Rule description section to configure settings for your condition. For example, if your condition is "Where the message body contains specific words," click the link that reads "contains specific words."

5. At the Type Specific Words window, enter the words that you want to use as your filter, as shown in Figure 10-4. Click the Add button to add these words or phrases to the list, and click OK once complete.

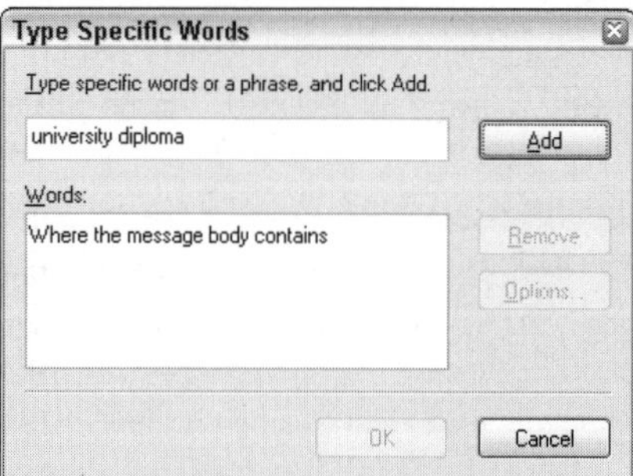

Figure 10-4: Adding words and phrases to a message rule.

6. Enter a name for your new rule in the Name of the rule section and then click OK to add the rule. This opens the Message Rules window, which displays a list of all configured rules, as shown in Figure 10-5. Use this window to add, modify, or delete rules as necessary. Click OK to close the Message Rules window.

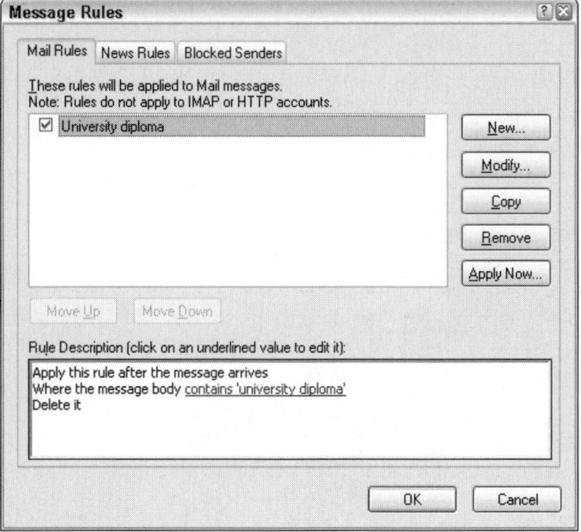

Figure 10-5: Use the Message Rules window to add, modify, and delete rules.

BLOCKING SENDERS

Another Outlook Express feature that can be used to combat spam is the program's Blocked Senders List. In effect, this is a list of all e-mail addresses (or even domain names like hotmail.com) from which you do not want to receive messages. Individual e-mail addresses can be added to this list manually or by clicking a spam e-mail message and selecting Message → Block Sender. Unfortunately, the Blocked Senders List feature only works with POP3 e-mail accounts, and cannot be used with HTTP or IMAP e-mail services.

How Spammers Beat the "Rules"

The unfortunate thing about e-mail rules is that they have to be specific by their very nature. If you specify that messages with the term "university diploma" should be moved to your Deleted Items folder, only messages that include this exact term will be moved. To get past a rule such as this one, spammers employ a very simple technique — they just never use that exact term and phrase. So, even after configuring your rule you would still receive messages with subject lines like "un1veristy diploma," "university dip!oma," and so on. Neither of these subjects is an exact match to the rule and as such would not be moved to your Deleted Items folder when received.

Creating individual rules for all possible iterations of the term "university diploma" is obviously unrealistic. For this reason, many e-mail users opt to install anti-spam software, which uses a variety of techniques to identify spam based on common phrases, patterns, and more. You learn more about anti-spam software later in this chapter.

Follow these steps to manually add e-mail addresses to your blocked senders list:

1. Click Start → Outlook Express.
2. Click Tools → Message Rules → Blocked Senders List. The Message Rules window opens to the Blocked Senders tab, as shown in Figure 10-6.

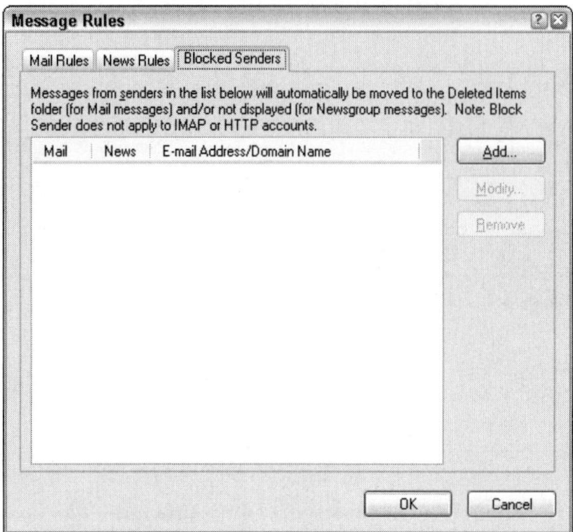

Figure 10-6: The Blocked Senders tab in Outlook Express.

3. Click the Add button. In the Add Sender window, type the name of the e-mail sender address that you want to block, as shown in Figure 10-7. Click OK.

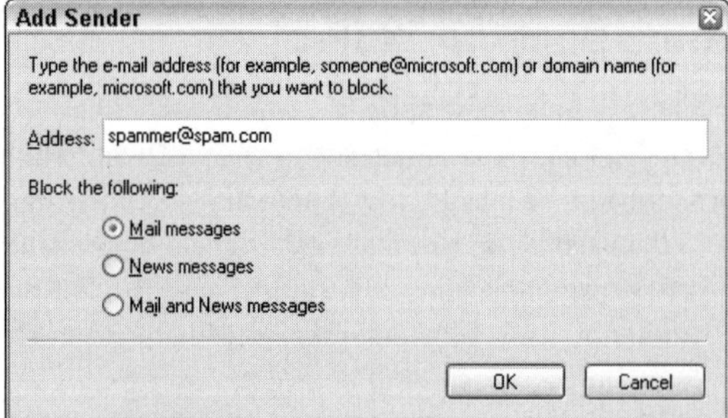

Figure 10-7: Adding an e-mail address to your Blocked Senders list.

4. Add additional addresses to this list as necessary and then click OK once complete.

Although blocking spammers' e-mail addresses might seem like an effective way to combat spam, it's not always an appropriate solution. The main issue is that spammers seldom use the same address to send you messages, and rarely use a valid e-mail address. In other words, blocking an address that a spammer has already used to send you a message is generally futile as it's unlikely to be used again. This technique, however, is helpful in cases where you've somehow managed to end up on an e-mail newsletter list and are receiving repeated messages from the same source. If you can't dig up the details of how to remove yourself from these (typically) opt-in lists, adding the sender's e-mail address to your Outlook Express Blocked Senders List can prove an appropriate solution.

CONFIGURING MESSAGE SECURITY SETTINGS

Along with its message rules and blocked senders' features, Outlook Express also includes additional configurable security settings accessible via Tools → Options → Security, as shown in Figure 10-8.

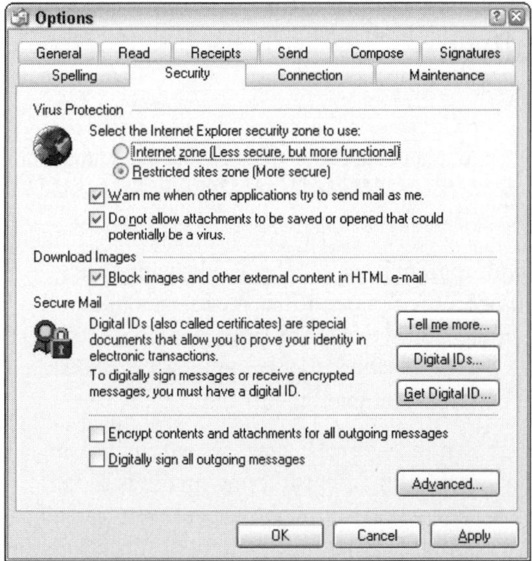

Figure 10-8: Outlook Express security options.

The name of the Virus Protection section on this tab is somewhat misleading — it doesn't offer any virus protection in the traditional anti-virus sense, but does offer a degree of protection against common virus and spyware tactics.

The IE Security Zone settings allow you to configure how Outlook Express deals with HTML-based e-mail messages, using restrictions similar to those originally looked at in Chapter 4. The remaining settings in this section are enabled (checked) by default. The first checkbox alerts you when other programs (such as viruses) try to send out messages via Outlook Express; the second blocks dangerous virus attachments from being saved and opened. As a best practice, you should leave both of these boxes checked.

Note

When the Do not allow attachments to be saved or opened that could potentially be a virus option is checked in Outlook Express, potentially dangerous attachments are removed from messages by default. Files types that are automatically removed from messages include those ending in .asp, .bas, .bat, .chm, .cmd, .com, .exe, .hlp, .hta, .inf, .isp, .js, .jse, .lnk, .msi, .mst, .pcd, .pif, .reg, .scr, .url, .vbe, .vbs, .ws, and .wsh.

The Security tab also includes a section called Download Images. When the Block images and other external content in HTML e-mail checkbox is checked (as it is by default), Outlook Express protects you from the possibility that these elements are being used as a beacon by spammers. As with the previous settings, keep this setting enabled as a security precaution and to help reduce the possibility that you'll receive more spam as a result of viewing a junk e-mail message.

Filtering spam with antispam software

Some of the more popular anti-spam software packages include:

- **K9.** This free program works in conjunction with your regular e-mail client to automatically classify incoming messages as legitimate or spam. K9 works only with POP3 e-mail accounts and can be downloaded from www.keir.net/k9.html.
- **McAfee SpamKiller.** This popular anti-spam program from McAfee works with POP3, IMAP, and even HTTP e-mail accounts such as Hotmail. SpamKiller downloads updated lists of new spam filters automatically, helping to keep your Inbox protected from the latest known spam messages. This comprehensive and powerful anti-spam program is available from www.mcafee.com/myapps/msk/, and costs approximately $40.
- **MailWasher Pro.** This anti-spam program, shown in Figure 10-9, works with POP3, IMAP, and HTTP e-mail accounts and uses a variety of different filtering methods to help reduce your spam intake. It even includes a feature whereby you can delete spam e-mail messages from your mail server before downloading them to your computer. A trial version of MailWasher Pro can be downloaded from www.mailwasher.net. After 30 days, the product can be registered for $37.
- **POPFile.** This free e-mail classification program can be "trained" to detect spam and automatically organize other incoming e-mail messages into different folders according to your preferences. POPFile can be downloaded from popfile.sourceforge.net.
- **SpamPal.** This free e-mail classification program uses filtering techniques and Realtime Blackhole Lists (RBLs) in an attempt to keep your Inbox spam-free. SpamPal works with both POP3 and IMAP e-mail accounts, and can be downloaded from `www.spampal.org`.

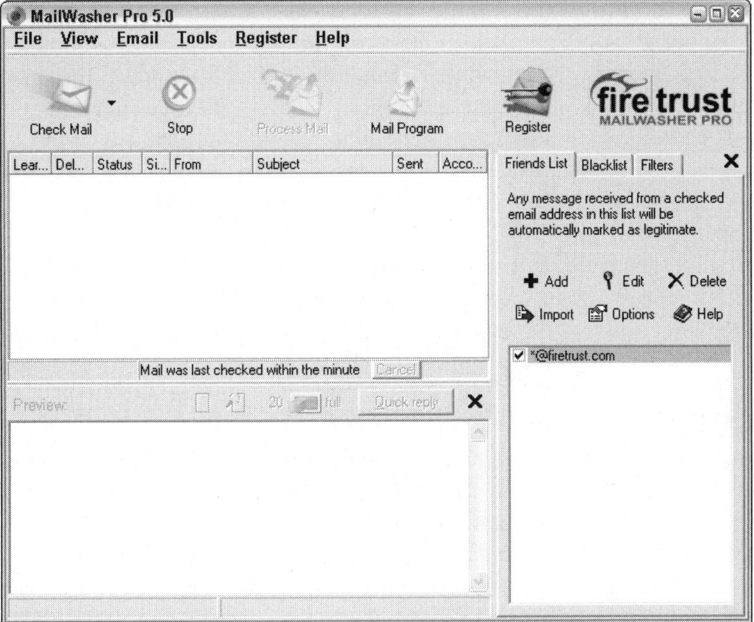

Figure 10-9: MailWasher Pro is a popular commercial anti-spam program.

Note

The preceding list of anti-spam programs is only a small collection of some of the more popular products available. For a more comprehensive list of anti-spam programs and other spam-related resources, visit the Coalition Against Unsolicited Commercial E-mail Website's resource page at `www.cauce.org/about/resources.shtml`.

The primary security and anti-spam features of these software packages include the following:

- Bayesian filtering
- Whitelists and blacklists
- Realtime blackhole lists (RBLs)
- Keyword filtering

Each of these security and anti-spam features is explored in more detail in the following sections.

BAYESIAN FILTERING

Using message rules to filter out spam is difficult, as spammers use variations in spelling and punctuation to avoiding matching the keywords or phrases you configure. With this weakness in mind, most anti-spam programs employ a technique known as Bayesian filtering. Bayesian filtering is a technique that uses statistical methods in an attempt to determine whether an e-mail is or is not spam, based on its subject and message contents. Over time, the anti-spam program's Bayesian filters "learn" which message are spam and which are not (based on which messages you flag as spam) and then use this information in its spam "calculations."

Ultimately, Bayesian filtering is a great feature, but it can take a while to gather enough information to determine whether incoming messages are spam with a fair degree of accuracy. Additionally, this method suffers from a problem known as "false positives," as outlined in the "Positively False?" sidebar.

WHITELISTS AND BLACKLISTS

In addition to Bayesian filtering, most anti-spam programs also include the capability to define what are known as blacklists and whitelists. A blacklist is effectively the same as a blocked senders list, meaning that you will never receive messages from addresses (or domain names) on this list.

In contrast, a whitelist (sometimes called a "friends" list) is a list of e-mail addresses from whom messages should always be received and never discarded. For example, you could add all e-mail addresses belonging to friends, family members, and business associates to your whitelist to ensure that messages from these senders are never blocked as potential sources of spam. In some cases, an anti-spam program will even allow you to block all e-mail messages except those from users on your whitelist. If you communicate only with a small number of people via e-mail, whitelists provide a very effective way to keep your Inbox spam-free.

Positively False?

One reason why using anti-spam software can often be just as frustrating as not using it has to do with a situation known as "false positives." A false positive is an occurrence where your anti-spam software deems that a legitimate e-mail message (such as one from a friend, family member, or business associated) is actually spam. This can happen for a variety of reasons, such as the message's subject or body including spam-like terms or phrases, or simply matching some pattern or set of characteristics commonly identified with spam.

If you do choose to go the anti-spam software route, be sure to take a quick peek into the folder where junk mail messages are stored every week or so (and especially before you empty the folder to delete messages). You'll likely find that at least a few legitimate messages have been mistakenly flagged as spam, so take the opportunity to move these messages to your Inbox.

As a guard against false positives, most anti-spam programs include a feature whereby addresses that appear on your "whitelist" will never be marked as spam, regardless of their contents. Whitelists are looked at in more detail in the following section.

Caution

Blacklists and whitelists are both great ideas in principle, but use them with care. For example, if you choose to receive messages from addresses on your whitelist only, you'll miss all legitimate messages from people whose addresses do not appear on this list. Similarly, if you use blacklists to block entire domain names (such as hotmail.com), any message from a recipient at a hotmail address is automatically blocked.

REALTIME BLACKHOLE LISTS (RBLs)

It is very rare for a spammer to set up their own e-mail server for the purpose of sender their messages. Instead, spammers search the Internet looking for misconfigured servers that allow any user to send e-mail messages and then use these servers as their spam-sending gateway. When messages are sent through these misconfigured servers, the owner of the server is usually contacted to alert them to the situation — often via a barrage of angry messages from those who have received the spam. If the owner takes the steps necessary to properly secure their server, all is generally well. If they ignore the messages and continue to allow their server to be used as a gateway for spam, however, any one of a number of organizations may add the server's name and IP address to what is known as a Realtime Blackhole List (RBL).

In the world of e-mail, RBLs serve as a regularly updated source of information about e-mail servers that act as a gateway to spammers. Many anti-spam programs enable you to take advantage of the information provided by RBLs by allowing you to "subscribe" to the RBL and check all incoming messages against it. When the anti-spam software determines that a message was sent via a server that appears on an RBL list, the message (assumed to be spam) is automatically deleted.

Overall, enabling the RBL-checking feature of your anti-spam software is a good idea. A number of different RBL services exist, with the ORDB (`www.ordb.org`) and Spamhaus (`www.spamhaus.org`) amongst the most popular. Although subscribing to an RBL won't cease the spam tide completely, it can help to significantly reduce your intake.

KEYWORD FILTERING

In much the same way that e-mail client programs such as Microsoft Outlook and Outlook Express include the capability to block e-mail messages that include certain keywords or phrases (using message rules), this feature is also often included in anti-spam software packages. It generally doesn't matter whether you use your e-mail or anti-spam program's version, but it's a good idea to pick one or the other for the sake of keeping settings organized and consistent.

Defeating spam with good ol' common sense

Sometimes the best defenses are also the most simple, and this is especially true when it comes to dealing with spam. Two of the key non-software solutions to defeating spam include the following:

- Protecting your e-mail address
- Knowing when to accept defeat

Each of these concepts is looked at in more detail in the following sections.

PROTECTING YOUR E-MAIL ADDRESS

The easiest way to protect your e-mail Inbox against the scourge and security threats of spam is to always protect your primary e-mail address. Although the idea of keeping any and all of your e-mail addresses spam free is a noble one, it's simply not practical. Over time, any address that you post online or submit in Web registration forms is going to be hit by spam, one way or another.

Understanding that receiving spam e-mail messages is more or less a guaranteed eventuality, keep the following points in mind when it comes to minimizing your spam exposure:

- Create a secondary e-mail address and use this address in all cases where submitting an e-mail address is required.
- Never post your primary e-mail address on Web pages or when registered for access to password-protected Web sites.
- Never use your primary e-mail address in Usenet newsgroup postings.
- Never submit your primary e-mail address as the address to which online newsletters should be sent, if possible.

Although none of these methods guarantees that your primary e-mail account will never receive spam messages, it will help to significantly minimize your intake. When managed correct and not posted online, it's absolutely possible for your protected e-mail address to take in next to no spam at all.

KNOWING WHEN TO ACCEPT DEFEAT

Kenny Rogers probably never imagined that the lyrics to his song "The Gambler" would be used in a analogy in the fight against spam; however, you truly do need to understand the value of the line "you've got to know when to hold 'em, know when to fold 'em" when it comes to dealing with spam.

In a nutshell, any e-mail account that already receives tens (if not hundreds) of spam messages per day is in all likelihood a lost cause. You could invest a great deal of time and money into trying to fend off spam, but things really can and do get to a point where the fight just isn't worth fighting any more. Whichever way you cut it, battling spam just isn't a good investment if things are already out of hand.

With that in mind, it may be best to cut your present "spamtastic" account goodbye, once and for all. A new e-mail address is literally a fresh (and spam-free) start, a chance to take what you now know about how spam finds you and not make the same mistakes again. Although there certainly isn't any such thing as an e-mail account that will remain 100 percent spam-free over time, it is possible to have one that can be close. Along with being much less annoying, your new account also ensures that you're less susceptible to the security threats that are increasingly creeping into Windows XP by way of spam — if you're serious about your online security and privacy, that alone is reason to consider making the switch.

New Address = Fresh Start

Switching to a new e-mail address may seem like a drastic and unrealistic step in fighting the war on spam, but it must be considered as an option if your spam intake becomes overwhelming. Quite simply, you can't undo mistakes, and if your e-mail address has found its way into spammer circles, there's nothing that you can really do to stem the tide. Certainly you can invest time and money into the battle, but at the end of the day, it's you versus hundreds — if not thousands — of spammers. In other words, the odds of you winning are just not very good.

Most people look at changing their e-mail address as a bad idea — what will happen to all those people who already have their e-mail current address, after all? Although the risk of someone (especially a business contact) not being able to get in touch may seem high, the risk is quite easy to mitigate with the right approach.

Let's say that you create a new e-mail address (more on that shortly). Start by sending a message to all of your friends, family members, and contacts from your current e-mail address, letting them know that you're switching to a new address. Outline the reason (too much spam!), and let them know your new e-mail address; then, send them a second message from the new address, asking them to add the new address to their contact list or address book, and to use it for all future correspondence. While you're at it, let them know that you're going to keep an eye on your "old" address for a month or two. Every time that you receive a message at your old address, send back a reply and a "reminder" that your address has changed.

Of course, there may also be people who you cannot contact, and who will still try to e-mail you at your old address. For this purpose, consider setting up an "out of office" reply on your old address that informs people that the address they have sent the message to no longer valid. In this message, specify an alternate way to contact you, perhaps via a business phone number or alternate e-mail address (like a new and temporary free Web mail address). Just don't provide your "new" official address in this automatic reply, lest it become a new target for spammers.

As far as obtaining a new address is concerned, just sign up for a new Web mail address if that's the route you prefer, or contact your ISP about creating a new e-mail address on their service. Many ISPs provide you with up to five free e-mail addresses as part of using their service, so this shouldn't be a problem. If it is, contact their customer support line, explain the situation, and they should be more than willing to help — less spam sent to you means less useless work for their mail servers. If your ISP refuses to help, tell them that you're consider another switch — to a different service provider. You'd be amazed as how persuasive an argument that can be!

Summary

Although new and innovative ways of fighting spam are being developed all the time, spammers have a vested interest in keeping up with (and working to circumvent) these techniques as well. Unfortunately, this cat-and-mouse game is more than just an annoyance—spam e-mail messages can (and often do) represent a real risk to system security and your personal privacy. Keep the following points in mind when it comes to minimizing your exposure to spam e-mail messages:

- Never post your primary e-mail address online. When you must submit e-mail addresses on the Internet, dedicate a secondary address to this purpose.
- Never open e-mail messages or attachments from unknown senders. These messages often include beacons and viruses.
- If you must continue to use an e-mail account that is being overwhelmed by spam, take advantage of security features in your e-mail client program, or consider installing an anti-spam program.
- If your current e-mail account is being deluged by spam, consider switching to a new primary e-mail address.

Chapter 11

Securing E-mail Messages Using Encryption and Digital Signatures

Over the course of the last decade or so, no single technology has had as much of an impact on the way people communicate as e-mail. Where once corresponding meant writing or typing letters to be sent via the postal system, today electronic messages can be exchanged almost instantly—quite literally at the click of a button.

E-mail makes it amazingly simple to keep in touch with friends, family, and business contacts worldwide; however, this convenience comes with a price; e-mail is not a secure communication mechanism by default and offers nothing in the way of true privacy or confidentiality. Every e-mail message that you send can potentially be intercepted, read, and modified by other users on its journey from the sender to the recipient. Compounding the issue, e-mail offers absolutely no guarantees that a message originated from the person listed as the sender. Others can send e-mail messages pretending to be you, or anyone you correspond with.

Although the idea that someone else is reading or intercepting their e-mail is a little too "1984" for some people, the reality is that every single unsecured message you send or receive is potentially at risk. Think of every "normal" e-mail message that you've ever sent or received. Then, ask yourself how comfortable you would feel if a third party was reading or collecting those messages, sending messages in your name, or pretending to be the person you're corresponding with. In the world of unsecured e-mail, each of these scenarios is not only possible, but also very easy to accomplish.

If you've ever used an e-mail client program such as Microsoft Outlook Express, you've probably noticed a couple of buttons designed to Encrypt and Digitally Sign messages. In this chapter you learn about how secure e-mail systems work, how to configure your Windows XP system to support secure e-mail, and ultimately how to make use of methods such as encryption and digital signatures to secure the contents of e-mail messages and validate the identities of people with whom you correspond.

The Need for E-mail Security

E-mail has existed as a communication mechanism for a very long time. In fact, the first e-mail message sent between users over a network happened on the ARPANET — the predecessor of today's Internet — back in 1971. Although much has changed since then, the majority of e-mail messages sent today still share one very important trait with those from more than 30 years ago — they're not in any way secured by default.

Some of the key security issues associated with normal, unsecured e-mail communications includes the following:

- **Eavesdropping.** E-mail messages are sent over the Internet and other networks in plain text format by default. Any user on a network over which the message is traveling can potentially capture the message stream and read its contents. Similarly, any user with administrative privileges on both the sending and receiving mail servers (and desktop computers for that matter) can open and view the entire contents of any user's mailbox folders, and read through their messages. Unfortunately, there is no easy way to tell whether other people are reading messages that you send or receive. If you send any e-mail message without securing it, understand that its contents are never truly confidential.
- **Spoofing.** Spoofing is a technique whereby messages are sent in a manner that makes them appear to be from a different user. For example, a malicious person could send e-mail messages to other users that appear to be coming from you, using your e-mail address. This technique is commonly used to propagate viruses and spam e-mail messages. Without implementing e-mail security techniques that prove a sender's identity, it is virtually impossible to prove that a message came from the sender listed in its From field.
- **Modification.** In the same way that unsecured e-mail messages can be eavesdropped upon, their contents can also be modified in transit between a sender and recipient. Any user who can gain access to an e-mail message (whether by capturing it or accessing it on a mail server or desktop computer) can modify its contents to display a different message, or even delete it completely. When e-mail security techniques are not implemented, messages can be modified at any point between the sender and recipient, without either party's knowledge.
- **Repudiation.** Based on the various ways in which unsecured e-mail messages can be forged or manipulated, it is never truly possible to prove who sent a message. This can have serious repercussions in both legal and business matters.

Although using unsecured e-mail to communicate with friends and family might not appear to have any inherent security risks, most people send e-mail messages without giving privacy as much as a second thought. This is especially dangerous in cases where messages contain sensitive information, such as health, business, financial, and personal details.

This isn't to say that you must secure every e-mail message you send. Although that certainly wouldn't be a bad idea, properly securing e-mail is sometimes beyond the capabilities of less experienced users. With that in mind, using unsecured e-mail is typically fine if the security and privacy of a particular message is not a concern; however, in cases where sensitive information must be sent (or where verifying the identities of the sender and receiver is important), making use of encryption and sender identification techniques is not only suggested but highly recommended.

Tip

An easy way to determine whether the e-mail message you're sending needs to be secured is to ask yourself whether you would announce its details to a room full of strangers. If the answer is yes, an unsecured message will probably do. If the answer is no, you should take the necessary steps to ensure the message is properly secured.

Secure E-mail Components

E-mail communications can be secured using a number of different methods and techniques. The most popular and widely used of these methods, however, are ones based on a scheme known as public key cryptography. In a public key cryptographic system, users are assigned a personal digital certificate that is used to both validate their identity and enable the secure exchange of information through the use of encryption.

Public key cryptography systems are typically composed of the following primary elements:

- Certificates
- Certificate Authorities (CAs)
- Public and private keys

Each of these elements is explored in more detail in the following sections.

Certificates

Certificates form one half of the foundation upon which public key cryptography systems are built. Although a certificate is technically nothing more than a file that can be stored on your computer, it acts as your personal digital identification — in fact, personal digital certificates are often referred to as "digital IDs."

You've probably already come into contact with certificates in some form, perhaps without even knowing it. When you visit a secured Web site (those starting with an https:// address), the server "presents" it's identification in the form of a Web site certificate. This certificate allows both you and your Web browser to validate the site's true identity, and ultimately enables all traffic passed between your computer and the Web site to be securely encrypted. In cases where a Web site does not have a certificate installed, secure HTTP communications cannot occur.

In the world of e-mail, personal certificates are usually issued by entities known as Certificate Authorities (CAs). You complete a certificate request process with a CA as part of registering for a certificate, and ultimately obtain your personal certificate from the CA if the request is approved. A number of different public certificate authorities exist, including companies such as Thawte and VeriSign. Some CAs deal with the general public; others issue certificates for larger corporations only.

After you have a personal certificate installed, you can digitally sign e-mail messages you send, as well as decrypt messages that other users send to you.

Note

Some public key cryptographic systems, such as PGP, do not rely on CAs to issue certificates. PGP is explored in more detail later in this chapter.

Certificate Authorities (CAs)

Certificate Authorities (CAs) are the entities responsible for issuing digital certificates, and represent the other half of the foundation upon which public key cryptographic systems are built. Public CAs not only generate certificate files (in a format known as X.509), but also digitally sign the certificates they issue. In this way, a CA acts a kind of trusted third party responsible for identifying the organizations or individuals to whom they issue certificates. When a CA signs your certificate, they're effectively saying that they vouch for your identity.

Note

The certificates issued by CAs work with e-mail programs that support the Secure/Multipurpose Internet Mail Extensions (S/MIME) protocol. Both Microsoft Outlook and Outlook Express support S/MIME, as do most third-party e-mail client software packages.

Consider again the Web site example and specifically completing a credit card purchase online. When you reach the payment portion of the process (where you submit your personal details and credit card number), an encrypted connection is used. Your Web browser typically notifies you of this by displaying a lock icon towards the lower-right corner of its window; however, your browser does more than just ensure a secure connection alone — it also verifies that a trusted CA has signed the Web site's certificate, thus verifying its identity. In cases where a trusted CA's signature is not found on the certificate, your Web browser typically displays a warning message alerting you to the fact that this site may not actually be who it's claiming to be.

CAs exist to help create a hierarchy of trust upon which a secure identification and encryption infrastructure can be built. Windows XP systems (more specifically, programs such as Internet Explorer and Outlook Express) implicitly trust certificates issued by public CAs like Thawte and VeriSign. These CAs sign every certificate they issue, creating a hierarchy of trust. In other words, if you send your personal certificate to another user, their e-mail program verifies that a trusted CA (in this case, Thawte) signed it. Because the other user's e-mail program "trusts" certificates signed by Thawte, it inherently trusts you. CAs are trusted by way of having their "root" or "top-level" certificates included with Windows XP by default. In cases where a user attempts to communicate with you using a certificate that wasn't issued by a trusted CA, a warning message is typically displayed to alert you to the fact.

Public and private keys

In a public key cryptographic system, every person issued a certificate is also issued a pair of keys. One key in this pair is known as the public key and the other as the private key. The idea is that only the private key can decrypt a message encrypted by its associated public key, and vice versa.

This two-key methodology is also referred to as asymmetric encryption. The fundamental idea behind this scheme is that you can freely distribute your public key to anyone, but your private key is for your use only.

Many people find this idea confusing, but it's actually quite simple. Your public key has only two real purposes: it allows others to verify your digital signature, as well as encrypt messages they're sending to you. In other words, if another user encrypts a message with your public key, only your private key can decrypt and open that message. As long as nobody else has access to your private key, messages encrypted by your public key remain for your eyes only. Similarly, when you sign a message with your private key, only your public key can verify your signature. As such, when users receive a signed message from you, they know that only your private key could have been used to sign the message, and that it is indeed from you.

As you might expect, this scheme requires that your private key remain properly secured. Operating systems such as Windows XP store your private key is a protected storage area inaccessible to other users.

Caution

If you ever suspect that your private key has been stolen or compromised by a hacker or another user, you should cease using it immediately. If another user does have access to your private key, they can read your encrypted e-mail messages and sign messages with your digital signature. The process of invalidating a key pair is known as certificate revocation, and is explained in a sidebar later in this chapter.

How Secure E-mail Works

The following sections explain how digital signatures and encryption work in the context of verifying a sender's identity and securing the contents of e-mail messages. A step-by-step example of the processes involved is also provided for illustrative purposes.

Digital signatures

Digital signatures exist to verify the identity of the person who sends an e-mail message. In basic terms, a user with a personal certificate installed composes an e-mail as they normally would and then selects an option (in their e-mail client program, for example Outlook Express) to digitally sign the message. When the recipient receives the message, he verifies this digital signature, proving that the message came from the sender and was not in any way modified in transit.

Note

In cryptographic terms, proving that a message came from the actual sender is commonly referred to as "non-repudiation" or "authentication." An e-mail not modified in transit is said to have "message integrity."

Digital signatures do nothing to encrypt the contents of a message — the process of signing a message is designed to prove the sender's identity, and to ensure that the contents of the message haven't been altered since the message was sent.

In a public key cryptographic system, messages are signed via a process whereby the contents of a message are run through an algorithm that always produces a fixed-length output known as a hash value. This hash value is signed with the sender's private key and sent along with the message.

When the signed message reaches its destination, the recipient uses the sender's public key to decrypt this signed hash value (in actual fact, the client e-mail program does this on the user's behalf). This process only succeeds if the real sender's private key was used to sign the hash. If the process fails and the hash value cannot be decrypted, the recipient knows that the message is not from the sender specified.

Assuming that the public key can decrypt the hash value, the sender's system runs the message through the same algorithm to produce its own hash of the message. If the results are the same as those included with the original message, the recipient knows that the message has not been altered in any way since it was originally signed. If so much as a single character in the message was changed in transit, the hash value calculated by the recipient's computer would produce a different result, and the recipient would know that the message had been tampered with.

Note

Public key cryptography is both slow and computationally taxing due to the long key lengths used by the RSA encryption scheme (typically 1024 bits in length). For this reason, most public key systems make use of what is known as a "session" key to encrypt or digitally sign messages. In the case of digitally signing a message, a one-time session key (usually 128 bits long) is used to sign the hash value attached to the message; then, the session key is encrypted by the sender's private key and included with the message as well. When the recipient receives the message, they use the sender's public key to decrypt the session key and then use the session key to decrypt the hash value. This method makes public key cryptography more efficient, as its takes much less time to encrypt or decrypt a session key than it would to perform the process on an entire e-mail message, attachments, and so forth. For the sake of clarity, use of session keys is assumed throughout this chapter when not explicitly mentioned.

Encryption

In the context of e-mail security, encryption exists for the purpose of protecting the contents of messages, including attachments. When an e-mail message is encrypted, its contents are scrambled such that they cannot be read until the correct decryption key is applied.

To send an encrypted e-mail message, the sender must have a copy of the recipient's public key on their computer. If the recipient's public key is present, the sender simply composes the e-mail message as they normally would and then selects an option in their e-mail client program to encrypt the message. The message (including any attachments) is then securely encrypted and forwarded to the intended recipient.

When the recipient receives the message and tries to open it, her own private key is applied to the message in an attempt to decrypt it. Assuming that the correct private key is present on her computer, the message is decrypted and displayed in the same manner as any other unsecured e-mail message.

It's important to remember that you can only send an encrypted message to another user if you have a copy of their public key. On Windows XP e-mail client software packages such as Outlook Express, your personal e-mail certificate is automatically attached to all e-mail messages that you digitally sign, and your public key is included in the certificate. So, if you want another user to be able to send encrypted messages to you, send them a digitally signed message — this effectively provides them with the required copy of your public key. If you want to send other users encrypted messages, have them send a digitally signed message to you.

Tip

If you're interested in the finer details of how different cryptographic systems work, check out the excellent multi-part Cryptography FAQ at `www.faqs.org/faqs/cryptography-faq/`.

Digital signatures and encryption in action

The processes by which e-mail messages are digitally signed and encrypted is best illustrated with an example. The following steps outline a situation where two users — Dan and Jessica — want to engage in secure e-mail exchanges using encryption and digital signatures:

1. Both Dan and Jessica register for and install personal e-mail certificates from the CA of their choice.
2. Dan wants Jessica to encrypt all e-mail messages that she sends him. Dan knows that Jessica needs his public key to do this, so he sends her a digitally signed e-mail message.
3. Jessica receives the digitally signed e-mail message, which includes an attached copy of Dan's personal certificate and public key. Her e-mail program uses Dan's public key to decrypt the hashed signature included with the message, and verify that the message was not altered in transit.
4. Jessica then composes a new e-mail message to Dan and attaches pictures from her last vacation. Before sending the message, she selects the option to encrypt it. Her e-mail program uses Dan's public key to encrypt the message (including attachments) and then sends it off.

5. Dan receives the encrypted e-mail message from Jessica. His e-mail program applies his private key to the message to decrypt its contents. The message is decrypted, and Dan can now read its contents and open the pictures attached to the message.

In this example, Jessica can send Dan encrypted e-mail messages because she has a copy of his public key. If Dan wanted to send encrypted e-mail messages back to Jessica, he would need a copy of her public key first. The easiest way for Jessica to provide Dan with her public key would be for her to send him a digitally signed e-mail message.

Tip

For secure e-mail to be truly effective, both parties engaged in a communication process should have their own personal e-mail certificates installed. Although you can't force anyone into obtaining a certificate, you can get the ball rolling by installing one of your own. If you begin digitally signing your e-mail messages and asking others to encrypt all messages they send to you, there's a better chance that they'll take an interest and obtain a personal e-mail certificate also.

Obtaining, Installing, and Managing Digital Certificates

Before you can take advantage of e-mail security features, you need to obtain and install a personal e-mail certificate. In this section you learn more about the registration process associated with requesting a certificate, how certificates are installed, and how certificate-related management tasks are accomplished with Windows XP's Certificates MMC snap-in.

Obtaining a personal digital certificate

The first step in obtaining your own personal e-mail certificate is to register for one with a CA. Although some CAs charge a yearly fee for this service, you can obtain a certificate for free from a number of different sources.

Thawte is an example of a CA that offers free personal e-mail certificates. These free certificates identify you as a Thawte Free-mail Member (rather than by your real name), and include your e-mail address as identification. In other words, no real process is undertaken to verify your true identity. Thawte simply verifies that your e-mail address is valid and then lists this address in the certificate's Subject field.

Although a free personal certificate will not include your actual name, it does provide the same digital signing and encryption capabilities as paid certificates. In other words, you won't find functionality lacking as a result of going the "free" route.

Note

Thawte's free personal e-mail certificates are used for illustrative purposes throughout this chapter. You can register for personal e-mail certificates from a number of different CAs, but the registration process steps and certificate installation processes will differ from the steps listed here.

Follow these steps to register for a free personal e-mail certificate from Thawte:

1. Click Start → Internet Explorer or open your preferred Web browser.
2. In the Address box, type `https://www.thawte.com/e-mail/` and press then Enter.
3. At the overview screen, click the Join button.
4. When the Terms and Conditions window opens, review the agreement and then click Next.
5. At the New Registration screen (Figure 11-1), type in your Surname and First Name and then specify your Date of Birth and Nationality. After complete, click Next.

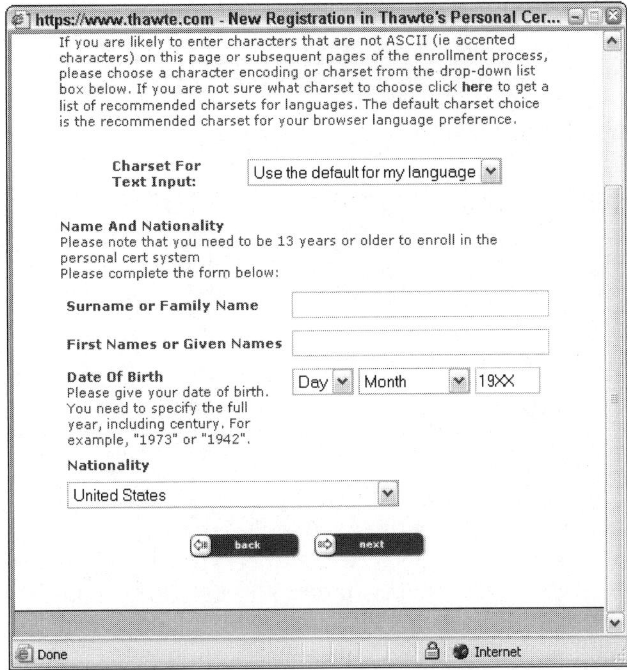

Figure 11-1: The new certificate registration process.

6. At the Requesting ID Information screen, type your national identification number and select an identification type from the list.

7. Type in the e-mail address that will be associated with your certificate with the understanding that the certificate can only be used in conjunction with the e-mail address you supply. Click Next.
8. At the Personal Preferences screen, click Next.
9. At the Password Setup screen, type and then confirm the password that will be used to protect your certificate and act as the logon password for your Thawte account. Select a strong password to protect your certificate, as you would with any important user account. Click Next.
10. At the Password Questions screen, enter you telephone number and then configure five password questions that can be used to retrieve your password in the event you forget it. After complete, click Next.
11. At the Please Confirm Enrollment Information screen, review all of your configured settings and then click Next if the information is correct. At this point, phase 1 of the certificate enrollment process is complete. An e-mail is sent from the Thawte system with additional instructions to complete the process. In general, you should receive this e-mail within 15 minutes of completing these steps.
12. Open your e-mail client and look for a new e-mail message with the Subject "Thawte Mail Ping." This message includes a link to continue the registration process, as well as two important values marked Probe and Ping (Figure 11-2).

Figure 11-2: E-mail message received during the certificate registration process.

13. Click the Web link included in the message to open the Enter Your Probe and Ping page in your Web browser. Enter the Probe and Ping values from the message in the spaces provided and then click Next.
14. If the Probe and Ping values entered are correct, your Thawte username is verified. Click Next. If a dialog box appears prompted you to log on, enter your Thawte username and password.
15. At the Thawte Personal Certification home page, click the Certificates link in the left menu.
16. Click the request a certificate link.
17. At the Request a Certificate page, click the Request button under X.509 Format Certificates, as shown in Figure 11-3.

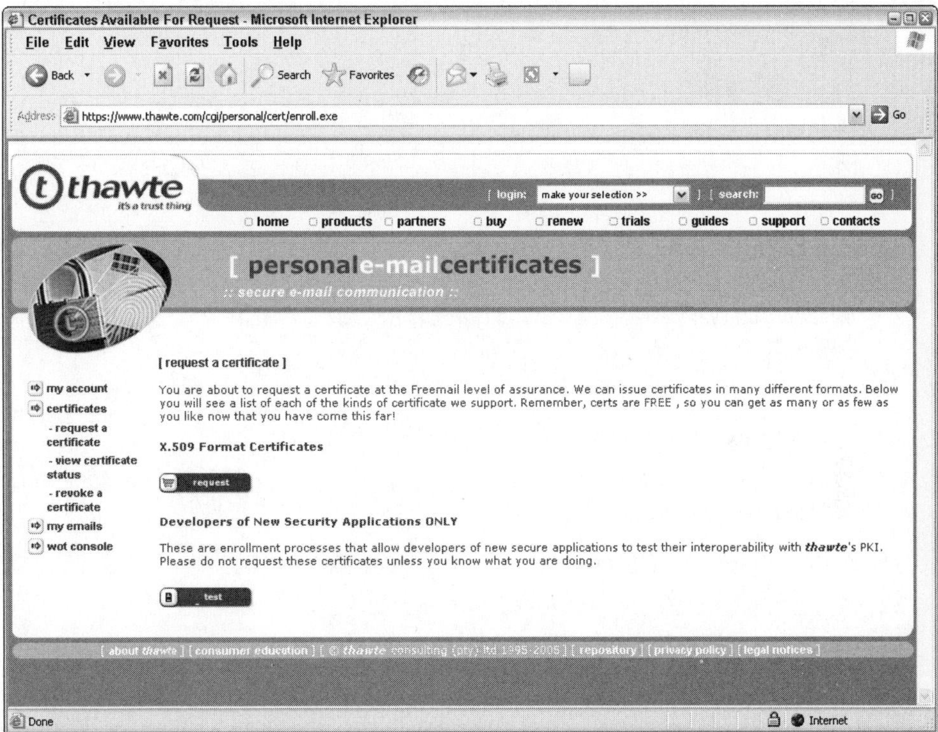

Figure 11-3: Requesting a certificate.

18. When the Certificates Available for Request window appears, select the option that corresponds to your preferred e-mail client and Web browser as shown in Figure 11-4 and then click Request.

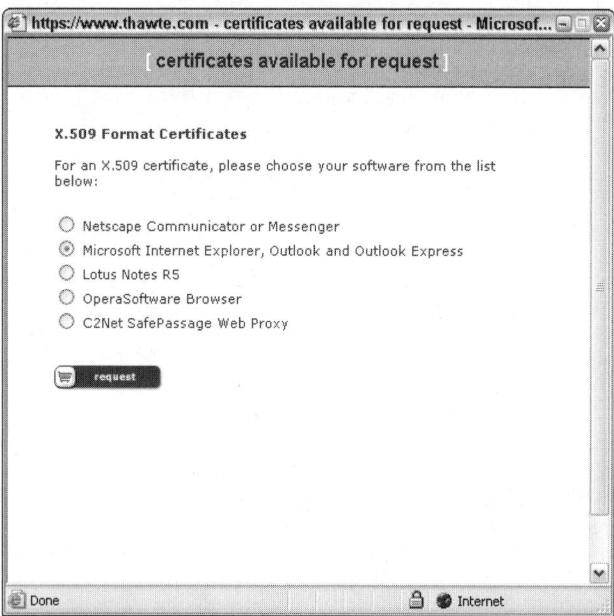

Figure 11-4: Choosing a certificate format.

19. At the Configure Certificate Name screen, click Next.
20. At the Configure E-mail Address for Certificate screen, check the box next to your address and then click Next.
21. At the Configure Extranet Capabilities for Certificate screen, click Next.
22. At the Configure X.509v3 Certificate Extensions screen, click Accept.
23. At the Generate Certificate Public Key screen (shown in Figure 11-5), click Next.

Figure 11-5: Generating a public key.

24. When the Potential Scripting Violation dialog box appears asking whether you want to request a certificate now, click Yes.
25. When the Creating a new RSA exchange key window appears, click OK.
26. At the Confirm Certificate Request screen, click Finish. The certificate request process is now completed, but it may take anywhere from a few hours and a few days for your certificate to be issued. An e-mail message is sent to you to confirm your certificate request and another when the certificate has been issued and is ready to download.

Tip

It is possible to have your name added to the free personal certificate issued by Thawte by way of a program known as the Web of Trust (WOT). The WOT consists of people worldwide who are designated as notaries for the purpose of confirming your identity. Depending on their level of experience, WOT notaries can assign you points towards earning your "trusted" designation. After you earn 50 of these points, your name can be added to your free personal certificate. For more details on the Thawte WOT program visit `www.thawte.com/wot/`.

Installing a personal digital certificate

After you've completed the certificate registration process, it can take anywhere from a few minutes to a few days before your certificate is issued and ready to install. This time period depends upon how busy the CA is (obviously issuing free certificates is a somewhat lower priority for a commercial organization), but also relates the CA's processes for verifying your identity. In the case of free personal certificates, the validation process is usually completed quite quickly. In the case of paid certificates being issued to military or bank personnel, for example, the validation process might take considerably longer.

Follow these steps to install your free personal e-mail certificate:

1. Open your e-mail client and look for a new e-mail message with the Subject "Thawte Personal Cert Issued."
2. Click the Web link included in the message. When prompted, enter the username and password configured during the certificate request process.
3. At the Install Your MSIE Certificate page (Figure 11-6), click the Install Your Cert button.

Figure 11-6: Installing a certificate.

4. When the Potential Scripting Violation dialog box appears and asks whether you want to install the certificate, click Yes.

5. When the Certificate Installation Complete dialog box appears (Figure 11-7), click OK.

Figure 11-7: Confirmation message for a successfully installed certificate.

Managing a personal digital certificate

On a Windows XP system, certificates are managed using the Certificates MMC. This snap-in allows you to import, export, view, and delete certificates as necessary.

Follow these steps to review your new personal e-mail certificate in the Certificates MMC:

1. Click Start → Run.
2. In the Open textbox, type mmc and then click OK.
3. Click File → Add/Remove Snap-in and then click the Add button.
4. At the Add Standalone Snap-in window, click Certificates and then click Add.
5. At the Certificates snap-in window, click Finish. Click the Close button on the Add Standalone Snap-in window and then click OK at the Add/Remove Snap-in window.
6. In the MMC window, expand Certificates → Personal → Certificates, as shown in Figure 11-8.

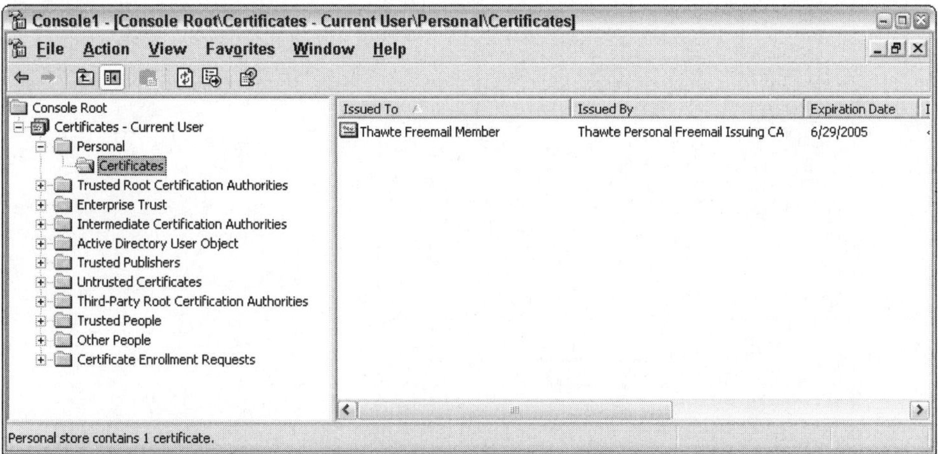

Figure 11-8: Viewing the contents of your personal certificate store.

7. Double-click on the Thawte Free-mail Member certificate to view it, as shown in Figure 11-9.

Figure 11-9: Viewing your personal e-mail certificate.

8. Click the Details tab to view the settings associated with the certificate (Figure 11-10).

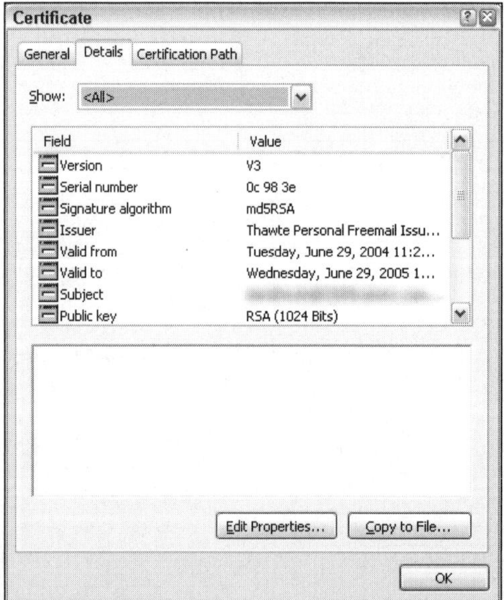

Figure 11-10: The Details tab for a personal e-mail certificate.

9. Click OK to close the certificate.

Most users will have very limited interaction with the Certificates MMC; however, this tool is the primary interface via which existing certificates can be imported and exported. If you plan on sending and receiving secured e-mail messages from multiple computers, or if you're planning to upgrade to a new PC, your personal e-mail certificate should come for the ride. If this certificate (and especially its private key) is not moved to your new system, you will not be able to open existing encrypted files nor digitally sign new messages.

Even in cases where you do not need to move your personal certificate to a different computer, you should still take the time to export it (along with your private key) for backup purposes.

Follow these steps to export your personal certificate, including your private key:

1. If necessary, open the Certificates MMC snap-in as outlined in the previous activity.
2. Expand Certificates → Personal → Certificates.
3. Right-click the Thawte Free-mail Member certificate, and select All Tasks → Export.
4. When the Certificate Export Wizard welcome screen appears, click Next.
5. At the Export Private Key screen, click Yes, export the private key and then click Next.
6. At the Export File Format screen, ensure that the Enable strong protection option is selected as shown in Figure 11-11. Click Next.

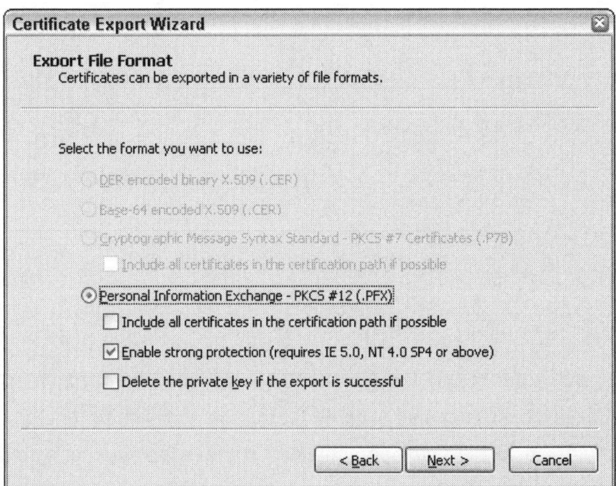

Figure 11-11: Exporting your certificate, including your private key.

7. At the Password screen, enter and confirm a strong password that will be used to protect your private key. Click Next.
8. At the File to export screen, enter an appropriate and recognizable name and folder location to store your certificate, as shown in Figure 11-12. Click Next.

Figure 11-12: Select a storage location and file name for your exported certificate.

9. Click Finish. When the Exporting private exchange key window appears, click OK.
10. At the Certificate Export Wizard dialog box, click OK.
11. As a final step, burn your exported certificate to a CD or removable disk, and store it in a safe place.

Note

To import your certificate on another computer, open the Certificates MMC on that system, expand Certificates → Personal, right-click the Certificates folder, and click All Tasks → Import. The Certificate Import Wizard walks you through the process of adding your existing personal certificate to the new computer.

Revoking Certificates

Understanding that it is possible for certificates and their private keys to be compromised, lost, or stolen, public key systems include a process to "revoke" certificates. When an e-mail certificate is revoked, it is no longer considered to be valid for the purpose of digitally signing or encrypting messages.

To revoke a certificate, you typically need to contact the issuing CA to have it added to what is known as a certificate revocation list (CRL). All CAs maintain a list of revoked certificates that can be checked by client e-mail programs to determine a certificate's validity.

To revoke your Thawte Free-mail certificate, log on to the Thawte Web site using the account you created during the original certificate request process. The Certificates menu includes an option called Revoke a Certificate, as shown in the following figure.

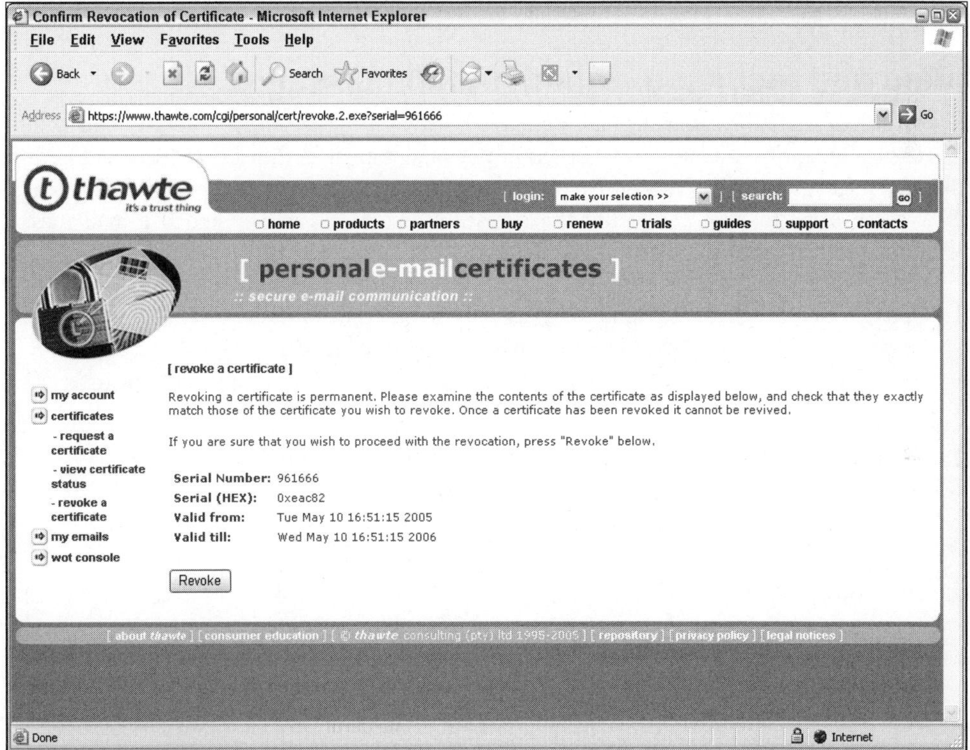

Revoking a certificate.

It's important to note that once a certificate is revoked, it is no longer valid and can be "revived." As such, you would need to request and install a replacement certificate and then send a copy of this new certificate to all users with whom you engage in secure e-mail correspondence.

Signing and Encrypting E-mail Messages

After your personal certificate is installed, it's time to get down to the business of securing your e-mail messages by using encryption and digital signatures. In this section you learn more about sending and receiving digital signed and encrypted e-mail message using Windows XP's native e-mail software, Outlook Express.

Note

The steps to digitally sign and encrypt e-mail messages outlined in this section assume that you're using Outlook Express as your e-mail client. For details on completing these tasks with Microsoft Outlook or other e-mail clients, consult that program's Help file.

Sending and receiving signed e-mail messages

As you now know, digitally signing e-mail messages both verifies the sender's identity and helps to ensure message integrity. Thankfully, after your personal e-mail certificate is installed, sending signed e-mail messages and verifying the signatures on messages you receive is exceptionally simple.

Follow these steps to read and verify the signature associated with a signed e-mail message received from another user:

1. Open Outlook Express and look for a digitally signed e-mail message. The icon for signed messages in Outlook Express looks similar to an envelope with a red seal attached. If you don't have a digitally signed message in your Inbox at present, complete the next set of activity steps first and then return to these steps.

2. Open the signed e-mail message. The Security Help screen appears by default when you open a signed message, as shown in Figure 11-13.

Figure 11-13: The Security Help screen appears when you open a digitally signed message in Outlook Express.

3. Click the Continue button. The contents of the message now appear like any unsigned e-mail message.

4. Click the red seal icon in the upper-right corner of the message. This opens the Security tab for the message, as shown in Figure 11-14. Notice that the e-mail address associated with the signature is displayed, along with messages stating that the contents of the message are unaltered, and that the signature is trusted.

Figure 11-14: The Security tab displays details associated with a digitally signed message.

5. Click View Certificates.
6. In the View Certificates window (Figure 11-15), you can view the certificate used to sign this message (the sender's certificate), as well as add the sender's certificate to their entry in your address book. Click Add to Address Book.

Figure 11-15: Use the View Certificates window to view the certificate used to digitally sign a message or add the user's certificate to your address book.

7. When the Outlook Express dialog box appears, confirming that the certificate was added to the user's address book entry, click OK.
8. Click OK to close the View Certificates and message detail windows.
9. In the main Outlook Express program window, click Tools→Address Book.
10. Double-click the entry for the user whose certificate you added in Step 6.
11. Click the Digital IDs tab, as shown in Figure 11-16. With the recipient's digital certificate stored on your system, you can now send this user encrypted e-mail messages.

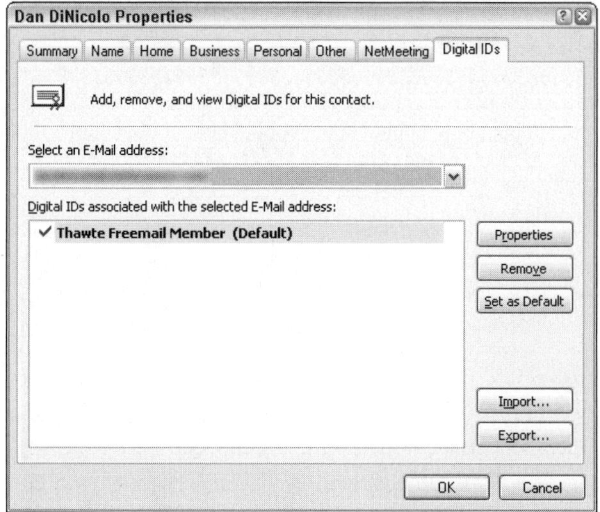

Figure 11-16: The Digital IDs tab in a user's address book entry displays certificates associated with that user.

Caution

Most Web-based e-mail services (such as those offered by MSN Hotmail, Yahoo! Mail, and Google's Gmail) are not capable of sending and receiving digitally signed and encrypted e-mail messages due to a lack of support for the S/MIME protocol. As such, you shouldn't expect Webmail users to be able to read signed or encrypted messages you send them. When in doubt, send them a digitally signed test message, and have them respond if they can open and read the message correctly. Alternatively, ask them to use an S/MIME-compliant e-mail client such as Outlook Express for the purpose of engaging in secure message exchanges.

Follow these steps to digitally sign an e-mail message you are sending to another user:

1. Open Outlook Express and then click Create Mail.

2. Compose the e-mail message as you normally would, complete with the recipient's e-mail address and a suitable subject line.
3. In the message window, click Tools → Digitally Sign, as shown in Figure 11-17. The read seal icon is added to the upper-right corner of the message window.

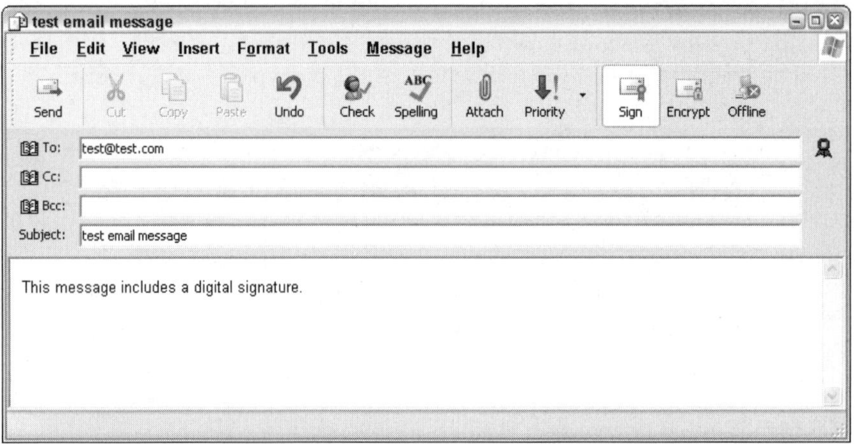

Figure 11-17: A digitally signed message.

4. Click the Send button.
5. When the Signing data with your private exchange key window appears (Figure 11-18), click OK. The signed message is sent to the recipient, including a copy of your certificate and public key.

Figure 11-18: This dialog box is displayed when your public key is being accessed.

Sending and receiving encrypted e-mail messages

In a manner similar to working with digital signatures, it's easy to decrypt encrypted messages that you receive, or send encrypted messages to other users. Remember that to send encrypted messages to others, you need to have a copy of their public key (included in their personal certificate) available on the computer from which you're sending the message.

Follow these steps to read an encrypted message received from another user:

1. Open Outlook Express and look for an encrypted e-mail message. The icon for encrypted messages in Outlook Express looks similar to an envelope with a blue lock attached.
2. Open the encrypted e-mail message. The Security Help screen appears by default when you open an encrypted message, as shown in Figure 11-19.

Figure 11-19: This Security Help message appears when you open an encrypted message.

3. Click the Continue button. The contents of the message now appear similar to any unencrypted e-mail message.
4. Click the blue lock icon in the upper-right corner of the message. This opens the Security tab for the message, as shown in Figure 11-20. Notice that the Encryption section lists the message as having been encrypted.

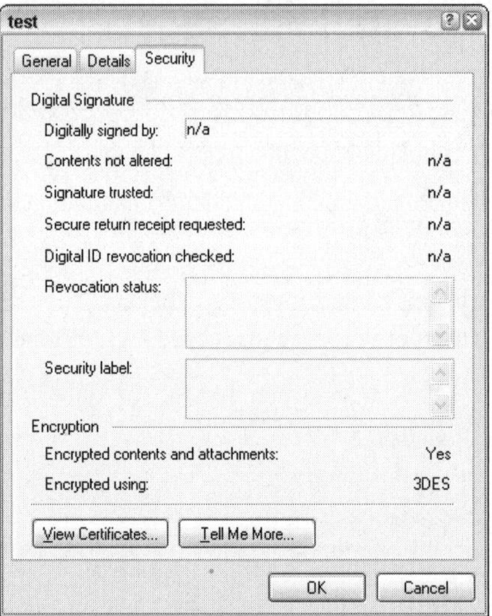

Figure 11-20: The Security tab for an encrypted message.

5. Click the View Certificates button.
6. In the View Certificates window, click the Encryption Certificate button.
7. At the bottom of the General tab, you find a message stating that you have a private key that corresponds to this message (Figure 11-21). Ultimately, this means that your public key was used to encrypt the message.

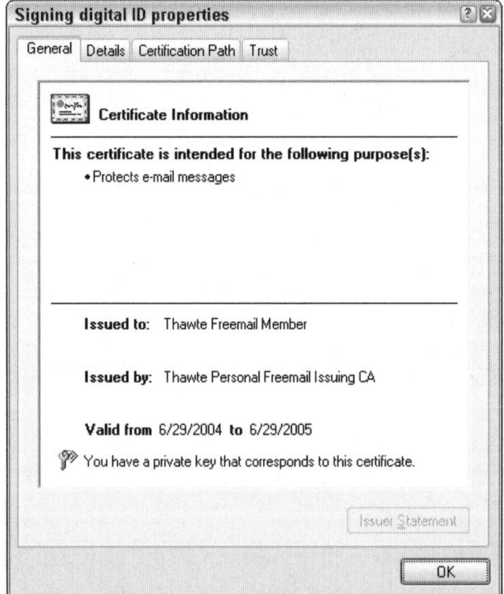

Figure 11-21: Viewing the certificate that was used to encrypt a message.

Outlook Express Security Options

If you don't want to go through the hassles of manually encrypting and signing every e-mail message that you send, Outlook Express makes it possible to have all messages digitally signed and/or encrypted by default.

To enable these settings, open Outlook Express and select Tools → Options → Security. At the bottom of the Security tab you'll find checkboxes marked Encrypt contents and attachments for all outgoing messages and Digitally sign all outgoing messages, as shown in the following figure.

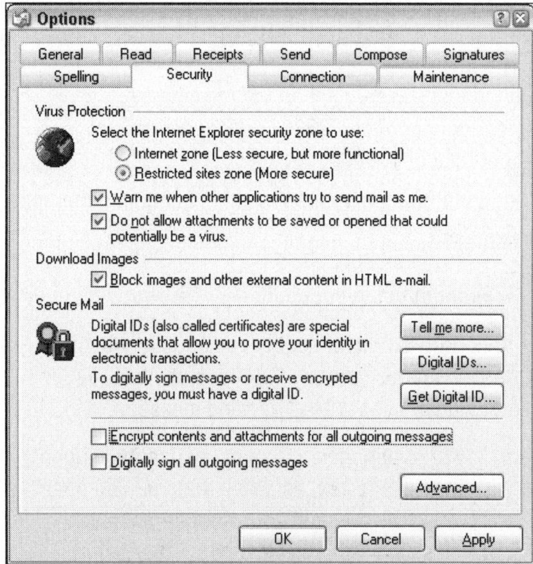

Configuring Outlook Express Security Options.

As a general rule, select the option to Digitally sign all outgoing messages only. If you select the option to encrypt all messages, you receive errors messages every time you attempt to send a message to a user whose public key is not present on your system. Based on this, it's better to encrypt e-mail messages on a case-by-case basis.

In addition to these settings, the Security tab in Outlook Express includes a button marked Advanced. If you click this button, the Advanced Security Settings window opens, as shown in the following figure.

Continued

Outlook Express Security Options (Continued)

Configuring Advanced Security Settings in Outlook Express.

Options found on the Advanced Security Screen include the following:

- Warn on messages less than this strength. This drop-down menu lets you specify the minimum strength level associated with encrypted messages you send. When a sender's public key specifies a less strength, Outlook Express prompts you with a warning message.
- Always encrypt to myself when sending e-mail. When this option is selected, the messages that you send to others are also encrypted with your public key, ensuring that you can open and read your stored copies of the message, for example those in your Sent Items folder. If deselect, you are not able to read encrypted messages that you've sent to other users because only their public key was used to encrypt the message.
- Include my digital ID when sending messages. As its name suggests, this options automatically adds your certificate (and public key) to all signed messages you send.
- Encode message before signing (opaque signing). If this option is selected, a recipient is only able to read your message if they're using an S/MIME-compliant e-mail system that can verify your signature. If you select this option and the user is using a non-S/MIME e-mail client, they are not able to read the message, even though it is not encrypted.
- Add senders' certificates to my address book. When this option is selected, Outlook Express automatically adds the certificates associated with signed messages you receive to your address book.
- Check for revoked Digital IDs. When this option is set to Only when online, Outlook Express automatically checks to ensure that all certificates being used are valid, and have not been revoked.

For users working with Microsoft Outlook, similar advanced message security settings can be found under Tools → Options → Security → Settings.

Follow these steps to encrypt an e-mail message you are sending to another user:

1. Open Outlook Express and then click Create Mail.
2. Compose the e-mail message as you normally would, complete with the recipient's e-mail address and a suitable subject line.
3. In the message window, click Tools > Encrypt, as shown in Figure 11-22. The blue lock icon is added to the upper-right corner of the message window.

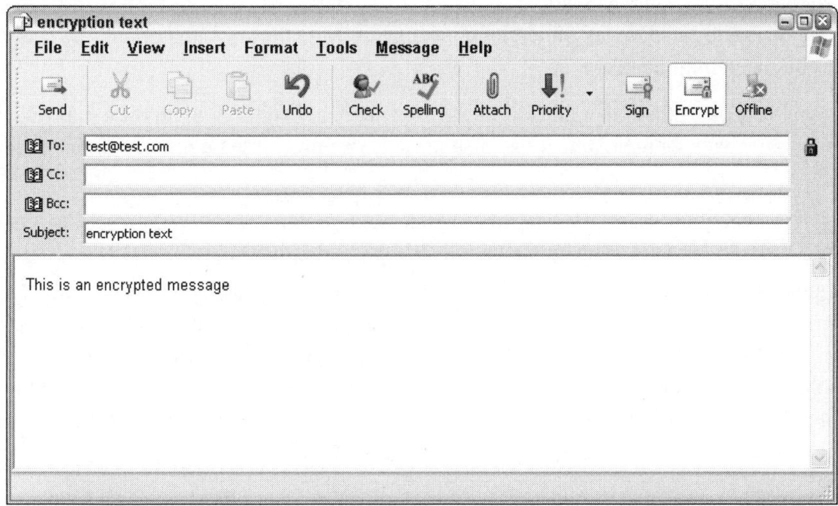

Figure 11-22: An encrypted e-mail message.

4. Click the Send button. The message is encrypted with the recipient's public key and then sent like any other e-mail message.

Digitally signing and encrypting messages are separate and distinct processes that use different keys; however, there's nothing stopping you from digitally signing and encrypting the same message — in fact, it's a great idea. By encrypting a message with the recipient's public key, you ensure that its contents are securely protected and inaccessible by everyone besides the recipient. By digitally signing the same message with your private key, the recipient can verify that the message actually came from you, and was not altered in transit.

Secure E-mail Alternatives

As noted at the beginning of the chapter, a number of different e-mail techniques exist for the purpose of purpose of securing e-mail messages. Most of the popular methods rely on public key cryptography, which has proven to be a very secure and effective method when used correctly. Unfortunately, public key systems also suffer from two fundamental problems. A user needs to have at least a basic understanding of the purpose of certificates and public/private keys, as well as why encryption and digital signatures are important. Also, the same user needs to figure out how to get the whole system up and running correctly, including the processes by which certificates are obtained, installed, and ultimately used. In a nutshell, using public key cryptography to secure e-mail communications is a great idea, but understanding its underlying theories and processes is often too much to ask of inexperienced users.

With the complexity of traditional public key systems in mind, a number of different e-mail security products and services have been developed as alternatives. Some of the more popular methods include:

- Pretty Good Privacy (PGP), a public key system that functions in a manner similar to S/MIME, but relies on user-created certificates and key pairs rather than those created by a CA. PGP is a popular secure e-mail alternative that uses a Web-of-trust model to verify user identities — in effect, users sign each other's keys as a way to promote and generate trust in the system. The ideas behind PGP have spawned work on a proposed Internet standard known as OpenPGP. Unfortunately, although both S/MIME- and PGP-based public key systems offer fundamentally similar levels of e-mail security, the two methods are not interoperable. For more information on PGP, visit `www.pgp.com`. For details on OpenPGP, visit `www.openpgp.org`.
- Secure e-mail services, a broad group of e-mail providers that offer secure messaging services. Some secure e-mail providers offer a Webmail-style product; others protect messages using different security plug-ins for e-mail clients such as Outlook and Outlook Express. The encryption and authentication techniques used by these providers vary widely, ranging from certificate-based systems to password-based encryption and signing. Some of the more popular secure e-mail service providers include Hushmail (`www.hushmail.com`), S-Mail (`www.s-mail.com`), and Stealth Message (`www.stealthmessage.com`).
- Secure e-mail programs, another broad group of dedicated security programs designed to help users easily secure their e-mail messages. An example of one such program is Steganos E-mail Encryption, part of the Steganos Security Suite. This tool creates encrypted e-mail messages that can be added to normal e-mail messages as a password-protected ZIP or CAB file. In this case, the recipient must know the password used to decrypt the message and read it's contents. To learn more about Steganos Security Suite, visit `www.steganos.com`.

Summary

E-mail-based communications are not secure by default. When not properly secured by way of techniques such as public key cryptography, messages can potentially be read, deleted, and modified by other users, and the identity of senders can easily be falsified. As such, e-mail security techniques such as encryption and digital signatures should always be used to protect message contents and verify the identities of message senders. Keep the following points in mind when it comes to e-mail security:

- Obtain and install a personal e-mail certificate
- Encrypt all sensitive messages using the recipient's public key
- Digitally sign all e-mail messages you send to prove your identity (and distribute your certificate and public key) to users with whom you correspond
- Always ensure that your private key is suitable protected
- Create and securely store a backup of your personal certificate and private key
- In cases where using a CA-based public key cryptographic system isn't viable, consider using alternative methods (such as PGP) to protect your e-mail correspondence

Part V

Protecting Your Files

Chapter 12

Controlling Access to Your Personal Files

Windows XP is absolutely loaded with features, but its capability to function as a true multi-user operating system is amongst the most useful. As the Windows XP system's owner, you have the ability to configure critical security settings in a centralized manner, and individual users are allowed to customize their working environment in a manner not unlike having their own PCs. Perhaps the best part is that resources such as files, printers, and even Internet access can be shared amongst all users.

For all the benefits that sharing resources provides, however, individual users still value their privacy, especially when it comes to their personal files. Nobody likes the idea of having others root through their belongings, be they the contents of a closet or their My Documents folder. Unfortunately, Windows XP does little to secure individual user's files by default, leaving the business of ensuring that your personal files remain private firmly in your hands.

Thankfully, implementing some much-needed privacy for your personal files and folders isn't terribly difficult. Windows XP includes support for a file system that's all about privacy, allowing you to control whether certain users and groups can open, edit, and even delete your files and folders. Its name is NTFS, and if you're serious about security and privacy, it's the file system that you want to use. Quite simply, if you opt to use any other file system, you're opting for no file system security at all.

In this chapter you learn more about the NTFS file system, including how to configure permission settings to control access to your personal files and folders. Two different permission configuration techniques are explored — the first is better suited to less experienced users; the second puts more power into the hands of those with a need for greater flexibility and control over the security of their Windows XP system. Regardless of the method you choose to work with, configuring NTFS permissions is all about ensuring that you're in control of your personal files and that you call the shots when it comes to how (or even if) other users are allowed to interact with your files.

Understanding File System Security

To store files on a computer's hard disk, the disk must first be divided into one or more formatted drives (often referred to as volumes or partitions), such as the familiar Drive C. As part of formatting a drive to store data, you need to choose a file system, and Windows XP supports three different file system options — FAT, FAT32, and NTFS.

Both FAT and FAT32 are considered "legacy" file systems, born in the days of older operating systems such as DOS and Windows 95. With the release of their Windows NT operating system many years ago, Microsoft introduced a new file system into the mix—NTFS. The NTFS file system brought with it many advancements, including support for larger drive sizes and more efficient use of disk space. The most important feature included with NTFS, however, was its support for configuring files and folders with different security permissions, giving users a greater degree of control over who could access their files, and to what extent. For example, you could use NTFS permissions to allow all users to read your personal files, but not change them. Alternatively, you could grant some users full control over the files within a certain folder while denying all other users the ability to access the folder completely.

Note

Neither the FAT nor FAT32 file systems support the configuration of local security permissions. These file systems are primarily included with Windows XP for the purpose of backwards compatibility with older Windows versions that do not support NTFS. For example, if your computer were configured in a multi-boot arrangement that included Windows XP and an older Windows version such as Windows 98, drives that both operating systems need to access must be formatted with a file system that the two share in common, such as FAT or FAT32. For details on dual-booting Windows XP with other operating systems, see the Microsoft TechNet article available at `support.microsoft.com/default.aspx?scid=kb;en-us;306559&sd=tech`.

Ultimately, if you want to ensure that your Windows XP system is secured to the greatest extent possible you would be well advised to ensure that any and all drives on your hard disk are formatted with the NTFS file system. The good news is that NTFS is the primary option for formatting drives on a Windows XP system and is selected by default (unless otherwise specified) during the operating system installation process. In other words, your Windows XP system's drives are likely already formatted with the NTFS file system.

Follow these steps to determine which file systems are in use by drives your Windows XP system:

1. Click Start → My Computer.
2. Right-click a drive letter (such as C:) and then click Properties. The General tab in the Properties window displays the file system used by the drive, as shown in Figure 12-1.

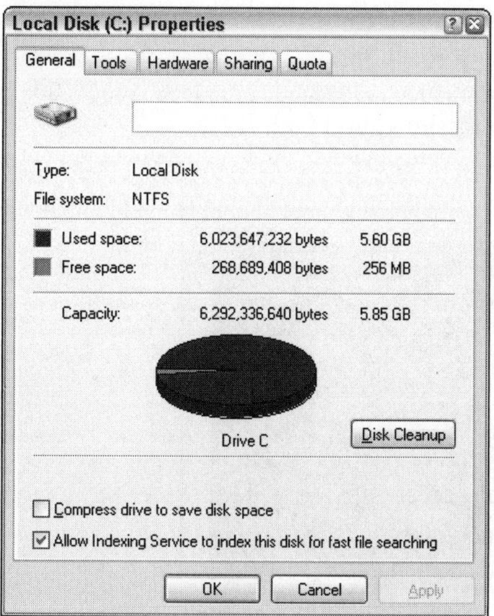

Figure 12-1: Reviewing a drive's file system.

If your Windows XP system's drives are already using the NTFS file system, you're good to go on the file system front. If you've found drives formatted with the FAT or FAT32 file systems, however, it's important to understand that these drives offer nothing in the way of file security capabilities.

Thankfully, Windows XP offers a way to convert existing drives from the FAT or FAT32 file systems to NTFS without the need to format (and thus delete all files stored on) the drives. A command line utility known as CONVERT.EXE can be used to change a FAT or FAT32 drive to NTFS, thus allowing you to take advantage of the ability to implement security permissions on existing files and folders as per your needs.

Note

Converting a drive from the FAT or FAT32 file system to NTFS is a one-way process. You cannot convert an NTFS-formatted drive to the FAT or FAT32 file systems for security reasons (as any previously-configured permissions would be unsupported and thus lost). The only way to switch an NTFS drive to FAT or FAT32 is to reformat the drive, in which case all files stored on the drive would be deleted.

Follow these steps to convert drive using the FAT or FAT32 file system to NTFS:

1. Click Start → All Programs → Accessories → Command Prompt.
2. At the command line, type **convert j: /fs:ntfs**. In this example, drive J: would be converted from the FAT or FAT32 file system to NTFS. Specify the correct letter for the drive you want to convert and then press Enter. When prompted, enter the volume label for the drive (typically NEW VOLUME or Local Disk by default) and then press Enter.

3. The conversion process may take anywhere from a few seconds to a few minutes to complete, depending upon the size of the drive and number of files it contains. In some cases, you'll be prompted to restart Windows XP to complete the conversion process. When finished, the Conversion Complete message appears, as shown in Figure 12-2.

```
Command Prompt

C:\Documents and Settings\Dan>convert j: /fs:ntfs
The type of the file system is FAT32.
Enter current volume label for drive J: NEW VOLUME
Volume NEW VOLUME created 7/24/2005 9:20 PM
Volume Serial Number is C80B-8DC0
Windows is verifying files and folders...
File and folder verification is complete.
Windows has checked the file system and found no problems.

1,042,522,112 bytes total disk space.
1,042,518,016 bytes available on disk.

        4,096 bytes in each allocation unit.
      254,522 total allocation units on disk.
      254,521 allocation units available on disk.

Determining disk space required for file system conversion...
Total disk space:                    1020096 KB
Free space on volume:                1018084 KB
Space required for conversion:          8395 KB
Converting file system
Conversion complete

C:\Documents and Settings\Dan>_
```

Figure 12-2: Converting a drive to NTFS.

Caution

As a precaution, you should always back up any and all critical personal files prior to attempting to convert a drive from FAT or FAT32 to NTFS. If something goes awry during the conversion process, there is a slim possibility that you could lose access to portions (or all) of the drive being converted.

After your Windows XP system includes one or more drives formatted with the NTFS file system, you can get down to the business of securing individual files and folders with NTFS security permissions. On Windows XP Home systems, NTFS security permissions are implemented via a feature known as Simple File Sharing. On Windows XP Professional systems, however, permissions can also be configured manually to provide a greater (and more granular) level of control over which users can access files and folders, and to what extent. Both methods of securing files and folders with NTFS permissions are explored in the following sections.

Using Simple File Sharing

In the interest of making the implementation of NTFS security permissions as easy as possible for most users, Windows XP introduced a new feature known as Simple File Sharing. In a nutshell, Simple File Sharing was designed to make it easier for users to implement NTFS security or shared folder permissions, often by doing no more then checking a checkbox.

To account for the fact that different users will have different file security needs, Windows XP's Simple File Sharing feature allows users to configure permissions settings to any of five different "levels." Each level provides a different degree of security protection for a folder and its contents, so it's important to ensure that you configured security levels correctly. If you don't get your levels right, other users may be granted complete access to your personal files, allowing them to change (and even delete) them at will. Similarly, other users may not have been granted enough access to a particular folder, which in turn impacts their ability to complete required tasks.

You learn more about the five configurable security levels available via the Simple File Sharing feature in the following sections.

Level 1: my documents (private)

One of the easiest ways to keep your personal files more secure is to configure your My Documents folder to Level 1. Configuring Level 1 security on this folder prevents all other users from being able to access files and sub-folders stored within it, effectively making the contents of the folder private and for your eyes only — even Computer administrators are not granted any permissions to access the contents of the folder.

Tip

For an added degree of security and privacy, configure the Level 1 option on the folder bearing your username under C:\Documents and Settings. This enforces Level 1 security settings on your entire user profile (rather than your My Documents folder only), including stored e-mail messages, documents, desktop settings, and more.

Who Owns What?

Although Computer administrators are not granted any permissions to a folder configured to Level 1 security, all Computer administrators have the ability to "take ownership" of files and folders stored on a Windows XP system. If a Computer administrator did opt to take ownership of your My Documents folder, they could then (as the folder's new owner) apply new permissions to the folder that would grant them access to its contents.

Although Computer administrators can take ownership of any file or folder stored on a NTFS drive, what they cannot do if "give" ownership back. In other words, if an administrator has taken ownership of a folder you've configured with Level 1 security, they cannot easily change the ownership of the folder back to you after they're done rummaging around. In fact, the only way that they could pull off this feat would be to log on with your user account and take ownership back in your name. If you have a good password, this shouldn't be easy and would require them to change your password first— another tip that something may be up.

Continued

Who Owns What? (Continued)

Unfortunately, if a Computer administrator were to take ownership of one of your folders and configure permissions that granted them access to its contents, you would probably never know. The only real way to determine if something along these lines has occurred is to check the ownership and permission information associated with folder. You learn more about reviewing file and folder permission later in this chapter, but you can follow these steps to determine the owner of a file or folder on a Windows XP system with Simple File Sharing disabled:

1. Click Start→My Computer.
2. Browse to the file or folder for which you want to check ownership information. Right-click this folder and then click Properties.
3. Click Security→Advanced→Owner. The Owner tab displays information about the current owner of the file or folder, as shown in the following figure.

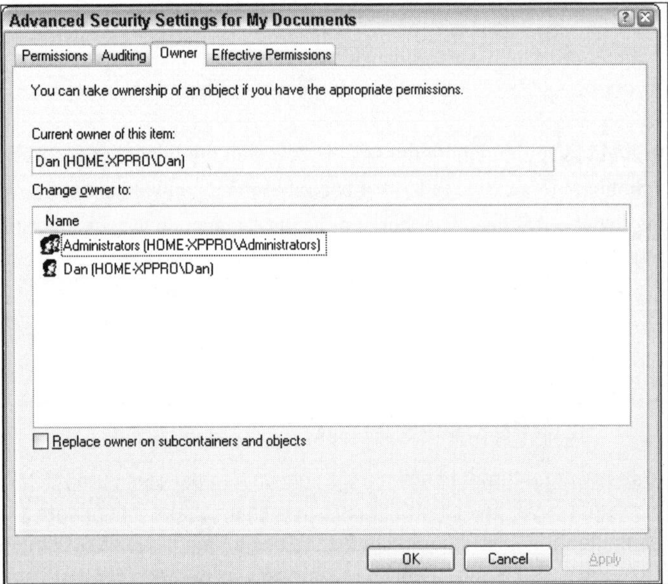

Reviewing ownership information for a folder.

Ultimately, the only way to ensure that a Computer administrator cannot access the contents of your files and folders is through the use of file encryption techniques. You learn more about implementing file encryption security in Chapter 13.

When a folder such as My Documents is configured to Level 1, the following permissions are applied:

- Owner (the use who owns the folder) is allowed Full Control.
- System (the Windows XP operating system) is allowed Full Control.
- The folder is not shared over the network.

Follow these steps to enable Level 1 security on a folder:

1. Click Start → My Computer.
2. Right-click the folder bearing your username (for example, Dan's Documents) and then click Sharing and Security. In the Local sharing and security section, check the Make this folder private checkbox, as shown in Figure 12-3. Click OK.

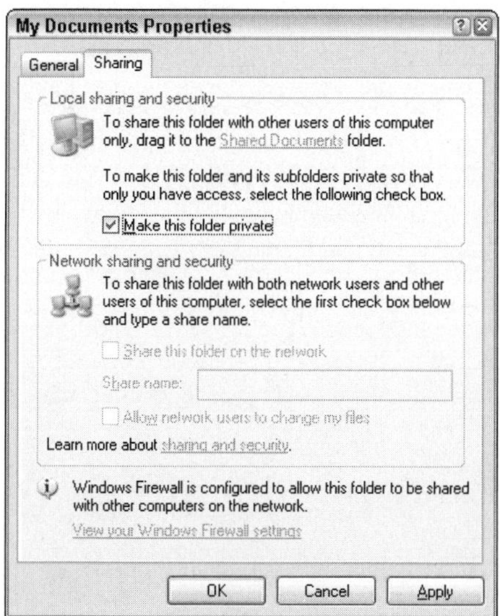

Figure 12-3: Configuring a folder to use Level 1 security.

Level 2: my documents (default)

Level 2 is the Simple File Sharing permission applied to your My Documents folder by default. When this option is configured, your folder is not private in the same manner as with Level 1. Instead, all Computer administrators are also granted Full Control over the contents of the folder.

When a folder is configured to Level 2, the following permissions apply to users:

- Owner is allowed Full Control.
- Administrators are allowed Full Control.

- System is allowed Full Control.
- The folder is not shared over the network.

Follow these steps to enable Level 2 file security:

1. Click Start→My Computer.
2. Right-click the folder bearing your username (for example, Dan's Documents) and then click Sharing and Security. Uncheck the Make this folder private and Share this folder on the network checkboxes, as shown in Figure 12-4. Click OK.

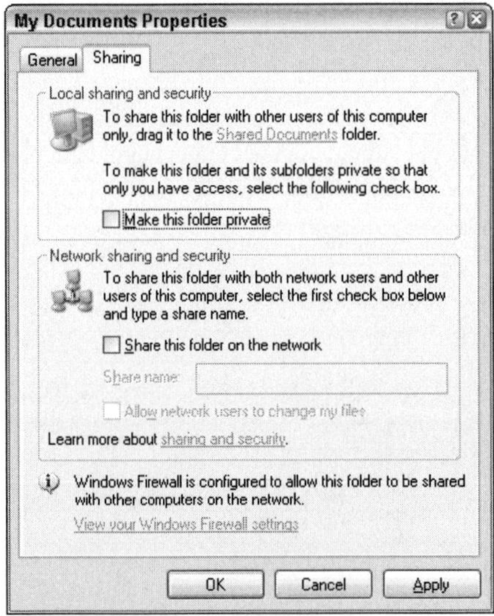

Figure 12-4: Configuring a folder to use Level 2 security.

Level 3: files in shared documents available to local users

One of the benefits of using a multi-user operating system such as Windows XP is that it gives you the ability to share files with other users. In cases where you need to share a file with another user who is not a Computer administrator, however, you cannot store the file anywhere in your My Documents folder—when configured to both Level 1 and Level 2, other users cannot gain access to the contents of this personal folder.

Understanding that local users often need to share files with one another, Windows XP's Simple File Sharing feature offers Level 3 security. Level 3 security provides a folder named Shared Documents to act as a location via which users can exchange files. When files are saved to this folder, all other local users have at least some level of access to the files within the folder.

When a folder is configured to Level 3, the following permissions apply to users:

- Owner is allowed Full Control.
- System is allowed Full Control.
- Administrators are allowed Full Control.
- Power Users (a group available on Windows XP Professional systems) are allowed Change.
- Restricted Users (effectively, Limited Users), are allowed Read.
- The folder is not shared over the network.

Note

You learn more about the specific actions permitted by permissions such as Read, Change, and Full Control later in this chapter.

Follow these steps to enable Level 3 security:

1. Click Start→My Computer.
2. Double-click the Shared Documents folder (shown in Figure 12-5). Any files that you save or copy into this folder will be accessible to all other local users of the Windows XP system.

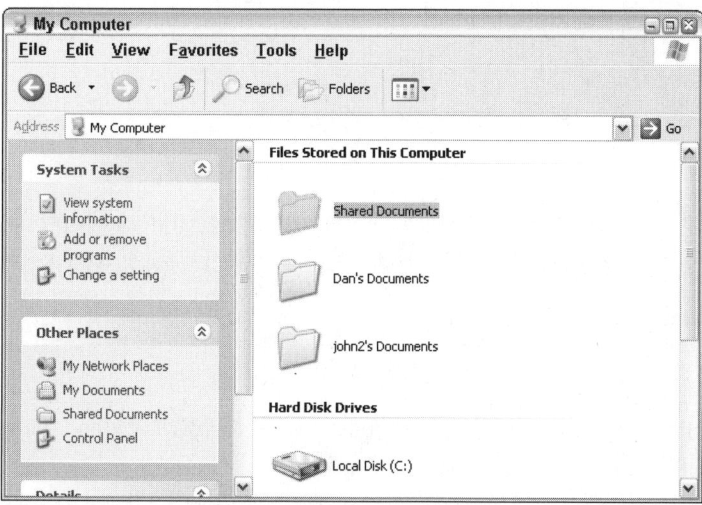

Figure 12-5: Configuring a folder to use Level 3 security.

Note

In the context of system security, "local" users are those who log on and interact with a Windows XP system's desktop directly; "network" users are those accessing shared resources (such as shared folders or printers) from another computer on the network.

Level 4: shared on the network (read only)

Simple File Sharing's Levels 1 through 3 apply to local users only — in other words, users working from other PCs connected to your network have no access to these folders. In some cases, however, you may want to grant network users the ability to access folders stored on your Windows XP system, and Level 4 security makes this type of sharing possible — albeit to a limited degree.

When a folder is configured to Level 4, the following permissions apply to users:

- Owner is allowed Full Control.
- Administrators are allowed Full Control.
- System is allowed Full Control.
- Everyone is allowed Read. The Everyone group is a special group included with Windows XP that literally includes everyone — both people with dedicated user accounts, and those without accounts (Guests).
- The folder is shared over the network, and the Everyone group is allowed the shared folder Read permission. This effectively allowed any user who connects to the folder from another computer on the network to open and read files but not change their contents or delete them.

Cross-Reference

You learn more about shared folders and related security permissions for network users in Chapter 15.

Follow these steps to enable Level 4 file security:

1. Click Start → My Computer.
2. Browse to the folder that you want share over the network. Right-click it and then click Sharing and Security.
3. On the Sharing tab, check the Share this folder over the network checkbox, and ensure that the Allow network users to change my files checkbox is unchecked, as shown in Figure 12-6. Click OK.

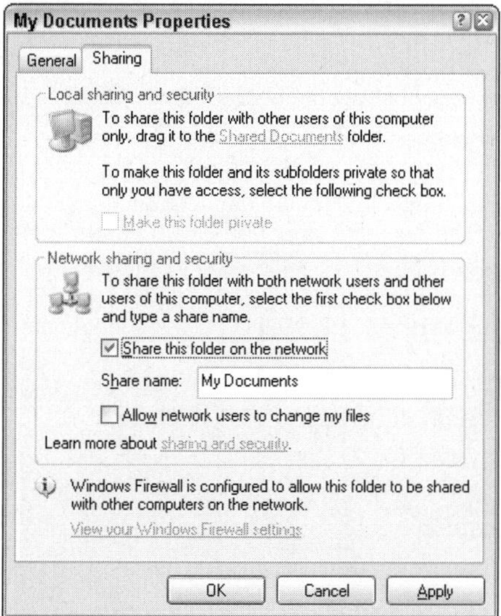

Figure 12-6: Configuring a folder to use Level 4 security.

Note

You cannot configure a private folder (Level 1) for sharing (Level 4 or Level 5) until the option to "Make this folder private" option on the folder's Sharing tab is disabled.

Level 5: shared on the network (read and write)

Level 5 security is fundamentally similar to Level 4, with the major difference being that Level 5 allows local users to modify files within a folder, and network users to do the same. From a security standpoint, Level 5 is the least restrictive permission level that you can apply with Simple File Sharing.

When a folder is configured to Level 5, the following permissions apply to users:

- Owner is allowed Full Control.
- Administrators are allowed Full Control.
- System is allowed Full Control.
- Everyone is allowed Change.
- The folder is shared over the network, and the Everyone group is allowed the shared folder Change permission. This effectively allowed any user who connects to the folder from another computer on the network to open, read, modify, and even delete existing files, as well as save new files to this folder.

Follow these steps to enable Level 5 file security:

1. Click Start→My Computer.
2. Browse to the folder that you want share over the network. Right-click it and then click Sharing and Security.
3. On the Sharing tab, check the Share this folder over the network checkbox, and ensure that the Allow network users to change my files checkbox is checked, as shown in Figure 12-7. Click OK.

Figure 12-7: Configuring a folder to use Level 5 security.

Note

If you configure folder security settings using Simple File Sharing and then disable the Simple File Sharing feature (on a Windows XP Professional system), any permission levels that you've configured for folders still apply.

Configuring File and Folder Security Settings Manually

Although Simple File Sharing's concept of security "levels" may seem somewhat confusing at first, the security capabilities defined by each level address all of the most common user file security needs. Even so, Simple File Sharing's way of implementing NTFS permissions is far from flexible — you really don't get much in the way of options as to whom security permissions apply. In other words, you can't use Simple File Sharing to configure a folder such that another user named Charlie is allowed Full Control, Maria is Allowed Read, and all other users are denied access to the folder completely.

When you need or want more flexibility in how NTFS security permissions are applied, it's time to disabled Windows XP's Simple File Sharing feature. Unfortunately, this is only possible on Windows XP Professional systems, which allow you to configure NTFS permissions in a more granular and manual fashion — literally by specifying exactly which users or groups should have access to a particular folder, and to what degree. Windows XP Home doesn't let you disable Simple File Sharing, but don't let that stop you — see the " Getting Beyond Simple with Safe Mode" sidebar for a trick on getting past Simple File Sharing on Windows XP Home systems.

Follow these steps to disable Simple File Sharing on a Windows XP Professional system:

1. Click Start → My Computer → Tools → Folder Options → View.
2. In the Advanced settings section, uncheck Use simple file sharing (Recommended), as shown in Figure 12-8. Click OK.

Figure 12-8: Disabling Simple File Sharing on a Windows XP Professional system.

After Simple File Sharing is disabled, you have the ability to configure standard NTFS permissions for all files (and folders) stored on NTFS drives. In basic terms, two broad categories of NTFS permissions exist — one that are allowed, and ones that are denied. When a particular permission is allowed, a user or group can perform the actions associated with the permission. When a permission is denied, the user or group cannot perform its associated actions. So, if the Administrators group is

allowed Full Control over a file, and one specific user (who is also a Computer administrator) is explicitly denied access to the same file, all Computer administrators would have full control over the file, with the exception of the one user who was denied — denied permissions always "trump" allowed permissions.

When you open the Security tab in the properties of a file stored on an NTFS drive, a number of different permissions can be allowed or denied. The following list outlines (and explains capabilities associated with) the NTFS permissions that can be assigned to users and groups for a file.

- **Read.** The Read permission allows users to open and view files, as well as the permissions, attributes, and ownership information associated with a file.
- **Write.** The Write permission allows a user to change the contents of a file and its attributes.
- **Read & Execute.** The Read & Execute permission allows users to run executable file (such as programs) and perform actions allowed by the Read permission.
- **Modify.** The Modify permission allows user to modify the contents of a file or even delete it, as well as perform the actions allowed by the Read, Read & Execute, and Write permissions.
- **Full Control.** The Full Control permission gives users complete control over a file including the ability to change its attributes, permissions, and even ownership details.

Note

In addition to the "standard" NTFS file permissions in the previous list, a number of "special" NTFS permissions can also be applied that provide for an even more granular level of control over what users can and cannot do to a file stored on an NTFS drive. For example, the Read Permissions special permission can be used to allow a user to view the permissions configured for a file or folder, but nothing more. As a general rule, you'll seldom (if ever) need to configure special NTFS permissions. If you're curious about these permissions, however, you can view them by clicking the Advanced button on the Security tab, clicking a permission entry on the list, and clicking Edit.

Follow these steps to configure permission settings on a file with Simple File Sharing disabled:

1. Click Start → My Computer.
2. Browse to the file for which you want to configure NTFS security permissions. Right-click the file and then click Properties.
3. Click the Security tab. A list of the permissions currently assigned to different users and groups is displayed, as shown in Figure 12-9.

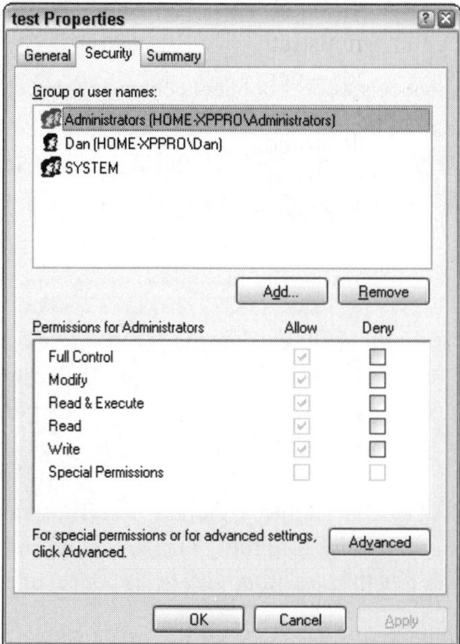

Figure 12-9: Reviewing the NTFS permissions associated with a file.

Note

When the permission entries associated with a file or folder are grayed out and cannot be changed, it means that they have been inherited from a parent object. For example, if you find the permission entries grayed out on the Security tab in the properties of a file, it means that permissions have actually been configured at a higher folder level.

4. Click the Add button. In the Select Users or Groups window, type the name of the user or group for which you want to configure NTFS security permissions for the file and then click OK.
5. On the Security tab ensure that the user or group added in the previous step is selected and then check the checkbox next to the NTFS security permission that you want to grant. The following example shows the Allow Full Control permission being granted for a user named Dan.
6. Click OK to apply the new permissions.

Caution

Never change the NTFS permissions associated with system-related files or folders because doing so many render your system unstable or unable to boot. Never make changes to include the root of drives (for example changing permissions on the Security tab for your C: drive), or the Windows, Documents and Settings, and Program Files folders. As a general rule, you should only change NTFS permissions on files or folders that you create.

The ability to configure NTFS permissions on individual files is handy, but if you ever need to change the permissions assigned to more than a few files, the process can be cumbersome. Thankfully, a quicker method of assigning permissions exists — when you assign NTFS permissions on the Security tab of a folder, those same permissions are applied to any files and sub-folders it contains by default.

The NTFS permissions that can be applied to folders are slightly different than those associated with files, simply because files and folders are fundamentally different. The following list outlines (and explains capabilities associated with) the NTFS permissions that can be assigned to users and groups for a folder.

- **Read.** The Read permission allows users to view files and subfolders stored within a folder, as well as details such as the folder's attributes, permissions, and ownership information.
- **Write.** The Write permission allows users to add files or subfolders to a folder, change folder attributes, and view permission and ownership information.
- **List Folder Contents.** The List Folder Contents permission allows users to view the contents of folders and subfolders.
- **Read & Execute.** The Read & Execute permission allows users to browse through a folder, even if they don't have other permissions for the folder. Additionally, it allows users to perform actions allowed by the Read and List Folder Contents permissions.
- **Modify.** The Modify permission allows users to delete a folder, as well as perform actions allowed by the Read, Write, and Read & Execute permissions.
- **Full Control.** The Full Control permission gives users complete control over a folder including the ability to change its attributes, permissions, and even ownership details.

Follow these steps to configure permission settings on a folder with Simple File Sharing disabled:

1. Click Start → My Computer.
2. Browse to the folder for which you want to configure NTFS security permissions. Right-click the folder and then click Properties.
3. Click the Security tab. A list of the permissions currently assigned to different users and groups is displayed, as shown in Figure 12-10.

Figure 12-10: Reviewing the NTFS permissions associated with a folder.

4. Click the Add button. In the Select Users or Groups window, type the name of the user or group for which you wish to configure NTFS security permissions for the folder and then click OK.
5. On the Security tab ensure that the user or group added in the previous step is selected and then check the checkbox next to the NTFS security permission that you want to grant. The following example shows the Allow Full Control permission being granted to the folder for a user named Dan.
6. Click OK to apply the new permissions.

As a general rule, you should always follow the "principle of least privilege" when assigning users or groups NTFS permissions on files or folders. This principle dictates that you only grant users the absolute minimum level of access that they require, and nothing more. So, if a user should only be able to view but not change a file, grant them the NTFS Allow Read permission, rather than something less restrictive such as Modify or Full Control. From a security perspective, less is always more when assigning NTFS permissions.

Note

When you configure NTFS security permissions on a folder, all files within that folder (and any subfolders) inherit the new permission settings automatically. You can change the behavior of permission inheritance by clicking the Advanced button on the Security tab in the properties of a folder, double-clicking a permission entry, and selecting a different option from the "Apply onto" drop-down menu.

Getting Beyond Simple with Safe Mode

The Simple File Sharing feature cannot be disabled on Windows XP Home systems as it can with the Professional version; however, for Windows XP Home users who want the ability to configure NTFS security permissions in a more granular fashion, all is not lost. Standard-style NTFS permissions can be configured on a Windows XP Home system, albeit with a little trickery involved.

It's not immediately apparent (or terribly well documented for that matter), but the Simple File Sharing feature is not enabled if you boot Windows XP into Safe Mode. As such, you can access all of the standard NTFS permissions on a Windows XP Home system by restarting in Safe Mode, configuring your required file and folder permissions, and restarting normally. Although the permissions that you configure from Safe Mode won't be visible via the Simple File Sharing interface, they still apply to all users who attempt to access a file or folder. If you ever need to change these permissions, simply restart in Safe Mode, make the necessary changes, and restart normally once again.

To boot Windows XP into Safe Mode, press the F8 key when you first start your computer to display the boot options menu. From here, select the Safe Mode option and then log on with a Computer administrator account. When you open the Properties of a file or folder to the Security tab, notice that standard NTFS permissions can now be applied — even on a Windows XP Home system.

This method may not be the most convenient, but using Safe Mode is the most practical way to bypass the limitations of Simple File Sharing when you want the ability to configure Windows XP Professional-style NTFS security permissions on a Windows XP Home system.

Summary

Selecting the right file system and then configuring the drives on your Windows XP system with the necessary permission settings is an important part of keeping your personal files safe, secure, and private. Keep the following points in mind when configuring security settings to control access to your personal files and folders:

- NTFS is the most secure file system choice for Windows XP systems. If your system's drives are formatted with the FAT or FAT32 file systems, consider converting them to NTFS.
- NTFS permissions can be configured using Windows XP's Simple File Sharing feature. Configure your My Documents folder to Level 1 protection to stop other users from being able to view or open your personal files.
- For an added degree of protection, configure the Level 1 option on the folder bearing your username under C:\Documents and Settings. This enforces Level 1 security settings on your entire user profile, including stored e-mail messages, documents, desktop settings, and more.

- For more control over how NTFS permissions are applied to files and folders, disable Simple File Sharing and then configure permission settings manually. On Windows XP Home systems, you can bypass Simple File Sharing by booting into Safe Mode.
- Always follow the principle of least privilege when assigning NTFS permissions — never grant any user or group a greater degree of control over files and folders than they require.
- NTFS permissions are not infallible — although they can help to secure and protect your personal files, a Computer administrator can always take ownership of folders and change their NTFS permissions to grant themselves access. For complete file and folder protection, encryption is always the best option.

Chapter 13

Improving File Security Using Encryption

Dealing with the aftermath of a lost or stolen computer is never a pleasant experience. Although the initial sting might relate to the financial costs associated with losing your expensive hardware, the real pain sets in when you consider the loss of your personal files. Even if you've been diligent about doing backups, it's now possible that somebody else has access to everything stored on your computer, from customer lists to sensitive personal correspondence.

It would be nice to think that your strong user account password and clever use of NTFS permissions can keep your data safe, but that's only the case if your computer is now in the hands of someone interested only in the hardware. These people typically format the computer's hard drive and couldn't care less about your files. When it comes to dealing with a stolen or lost computer, this is the best-case scenario. Unfortunately, if an unscrupulous person now has access to your PC, there's a good chance that they're going to at least try "mining" through your data, looking for information of interest. From credit card details to business information, most computers are a veritable treasure trove of useful information.

A good password and correctly applied NTFS permissions helps in the event that your computer falls into the wrong hands, but only a little. If the person in possession of your computer knows even a little about Windows XP, they could easily remove its hard drive, install it in a computer on which they have a Computer administrator account, and "take ownership" of all of your files—effectively giving themselves access to everything stored on the disk.

Whether you're looking for a way to securely protect your files in the event your computer is stolen, or just looking for a way to keep other users (including Computer administrators on the computer you use) away from your files, encryption is the answer. In this chapter you learn more about Windows XP's native encryption facilities, as well as third-party encryption programs.

Encryption Options

As you learned in Chapter 11, encryption is a security feature whereby a file or e-mail message are effectively scrambled to prevent others from opening or viewing its contents. Standards such as the Data Encryption Standard (DES), Triple DES (3DES), and the Advanced Encryption Standard (AES) are examples of some of the popular algorithms used to securely encrypt data. Users who do not have the correct password or "key" are denied the ability to decrypt these protected items, helping to ensure that they remain for your eyes only.

When it comes to encrypting sensitive or important files on a Windows XP system, two primary options exist. These include the following:

- Windows XP's native Encrypting File System (EFS)
- Third-party encryption programs

The following sections and the remainder of this chapter explore these methods and techniques in more detail.

Encrypting File System (EFS)

A feature known as the Encrypting File System (EFS) acts as Windows XP's native file encryption facility. Although its name makes it sound like a traditional file system in the manner of FAT, FAT32, or NTFS, EFS is not a file system used to format drives and disk partitions. Instead, it's a feature available to protect files stored on drives that use the NTFS file system, with encryption settings configured as file and folder attributes.

Available on computers running Windows XP Professional only, EFS encryption provides a higher level of file protection than techniques such as NTFS security permissions. When a file is encrypted with EFS, only the user who encrypted the file has the ability to decrypt and view its contents by default; however, EFS in Windows XP does provide the capability to share encrypted files with other users if necessary, and designate what is known as a Data Recovery Agent for cases where the user who encrypted a file cannot decrypt it but needs to restore it.

Along with offering the highest levels of native file security on a Windows XP Professional system, EFS also makes the process of encrypting and decrypting files almost completely seamless. After a file is protected with EFS, encrypting and decrypting it is as simple as opening or saving any other Windows file.

Third-party encryption programs

Windows XP Home doesn't include the ability to securely encrypt files using EFS, but all is not lost. A variety of third-party encryption programs exist for the purpose of securing files, folders, and drives on any Windows XP system. If you are running Windows XP Home Edition and want to take advantage of the high levels of file security provided by encryption, see the section on third-party encryption solutions later in this chapter.

Traveling Lightly

Using file encryption techniques to protect files is especially useful in cases where you're worried about the possibility of your computer (especially a laptop) being lost or stolen. If the sensitive information stored on your computer is encrypted, at least your sensitive files remain protected, even if the hardware itself is lost.

Although file encryption might seem like the ultimate file security answer, it's actually trumped by an even simpler method — not storing sensitive files on your computer at all. In cases where you don't require regular access to your important files, or can do without them on a business trip, it's much

safer to simply remove them from your PC. Use external hard drives, writeable CD/DVDs, or other "offline" methods to store critical files rather than tote them with you when they're not required. When it comes to protecting your data, it's always better to be safe than sorry.

Protecting Files with EFS

There's no denying that strong file encryption offers some of the highest levels of file security possible. However, using different encryption techniques without understanding how they work (and the precaution you need to take) can be dangerous. Begin randomly encrypting data without understanding the risks, and you can easily find yourself unable to access your own files. Encryption techniques may be designed with an eye towards keeping others from opening and viewing your files, but if used incorrectly (or flippantly), it's just as easy to lock yourself out — for good.

To use Windows XP's EFS encryption capabilities effectively (and safely), it's important to be familiar with the following:

- How EFS works
- How to designate a Data Recovery Agent (DRA)
- How to encrypt files and folders
- How to manage EFS encryption keys

Each of these concepts and tasks is explored in more detail in the following sections.

How EFS works

EFS works in a way that is fundamentally similar to any public key cryptographic system. When a user encrypts a file or folder for the first time, an EFS certificate is automatically created (and stored) for their user account, along with a public/private key pair. Although the encryption and decryption processes associated with EFS are completely transparent to users, a number of functions take place in the background.

Imagine that you create a folder under My Documents called My Encrypted Files. If you save a file to this location and then select the option to encrypt it, the following processes take place:

1. Windows XP generates a unique key to encrypt the file, known as a File Encryption Key (FEK). The FEK is fundamentally similar to the unique session key used to encrypt an e-mail message or the transfer or information between your Web browser and a secure Web site.
2. After creating the unique FEK and using it to encrypt the file, Windows XP encrypts the FEK with your public key. After the FEK is encrypted, it is stored in the headers of the encrypted file.

When you attempt to open (decrypt) a file that was encrypted with your EFS public key, the following processes take place:

1. Windows XP notes that the file you trying to open is encrypted. As such, it attempts to use your private key to decrypt the FEK.
2. If the FEK is successfully decrypted, it is then used to decrypt and open the file.

In cases where another user has encrypted a file that you attempt to open, your private key will not be able to decrypt the FEK, which in turn cannot be used to decrypt the file. Only the user who encrypted a file is able to decrypt and view it by default.

Caution

The encryption capabilities provided by EFS stops other users from opening and reading your protected files, but don't overlook the importance of configuring correct NTFS permissions on encrypted files or the folders that store them. For example, if you place an EFS encrypted file in a folder where all users have the NTFS Allow Full Control permission, other users will not be able to decrypt and read the contents of the file, but that won't prevent them from deleting it. In cases where you need your encrypted files to be accessible to you alone, save them to a folder location that only you have access to, such as within the hierarchy of your My Documents. For more details on making your My Documents folder private, refer to Chapter 12.

Designating a data recovery agent

When you encrypt a file using EFS, only your user account's private key can be used to decrypt the FEK stored with the file by default. If you private key is ever lost or changed, you will not be able to decrypt the FEK and therefore will not be able to decrypt and open the file.

Backing up your EFS certificate and private key is a great way to help ensure that you will be able to access EFS encrypted files should a problem occur, but you should also consider assigning at least one user the role of Data Recovery Agent (DRA).

In simple terms, a DRA is a user account (usually a Computer administrator) who has the ability to decrypt and restore EFS encrypted files, should the need arise. When a DRA exists, this user account's private key is also used to encrypt a copy of each file's FEK. Ultimately, this means that both the user who encrypts a file and the DRA can decrypt the file if necessary. For example, if you encrypt a file and your private key is subsequently lost or destroyed, the user designated as the DRA will always be able to log on and decrypt the file, ensuring that access to it is not lost for good.

Designating a user account as the DRA for your Windows XP system is always a good idea and considered a best practice. Although the chances of your private key being lost or destroyed may be small, other problems can occur when EFS encryption is being used. For example, if a Computer administrator were to reset or change your password, you would automatically lose access to all of your EFS encrypted files. This is a security feature that helps to ensure that a Computer administrator cannot change your password and log on with your account to open and view your encrypted files. If this was to happen and a DRA were not designated, access to your encrypted files would be lost. If a DRA were designated, however, this user account would be able to log on and restore your encrypted files.

Windows XP does not designate a DRA by default, so it's up to you to select a user account for this purpose. Instead of using an existing user account as a DRA, you may want to consider creating a Computer administrator account dedicated to the task and then log on with this account only when an EFS encrypted file needs to be decrypted and restored. As always, the DRA user account should be assigned a strong password.

Designating a DRA is a two-step process. You need to log on with the user account that will act as the DRA and generate a recovery certificate. After complete, you use the Local Security Policy MMC to add the DRA's certificate to your Windows XP system's public key policy.

Follow these steps to create an EFS certificate for the user account to be designated as the Data Recovery Agent:

1. Log on to Windows XP using the user account that will act as your EFS Data Recovery Agent.
2. Click Start → All Programs → Accessories → Command Prompt.
3. Type **cipher /R:recoverycert** and then press Enter.
4. When prompted, type a strong password that will be used to protect the Data Recovery Agent's private key and then press Enter.
5. Type the password again to confirm it, and press Enter. The certificate for the Data Recovery Agent is generated, as shown in Figure 13-1. Close the Command Prompt window.

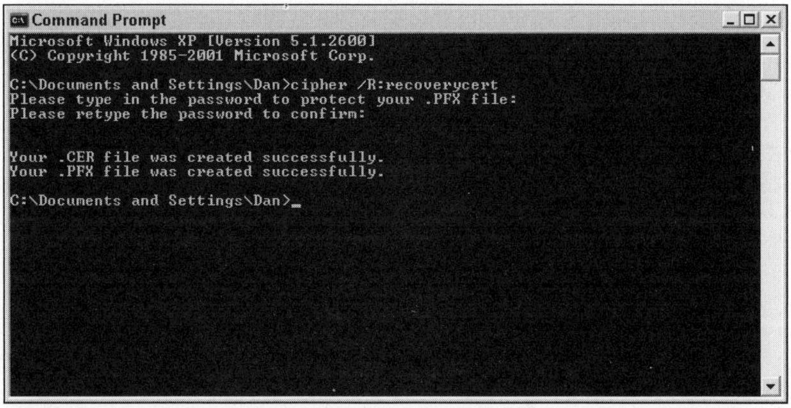

```
Command Prompt
Microsoft Windows XP [Version 5.1.2600]
(C) Copyright 1985-2001 Microsoft Corp.

C:\Documents and Settings\Dan>cipher /R:recoverycert
Please type in the password to protect your .PFX file:
Please retype the password to confirm:


Your .CER file was created successfully.
Your .PFX file was created successfully.

C:\Documents and Settings\Dan>_
```

Figure 13-1: Creating a certificate for a Data Recovery Agent with the Cipher command.

Follow these steps to add the DRA's certificate to your Windows XP system's public key policy:

1. Click Start → Control Panel → Administrative Tools → Local Security Policy.
2. Expand Public Key Policies.

3. Right-click the Encrypting File System folder and then click Add Data Recovery Agent.
4. At the Add Recovery Agent Wizard Welcome screen, click Next.
5. At the Select Recovery Agents screen, click Browse Folders. Browse to the recoverycert.pfx file created in the previous exercise and then click Open. Your Data Recovery Agent user account is now listed as shown in Figure 13-2. Click Next.

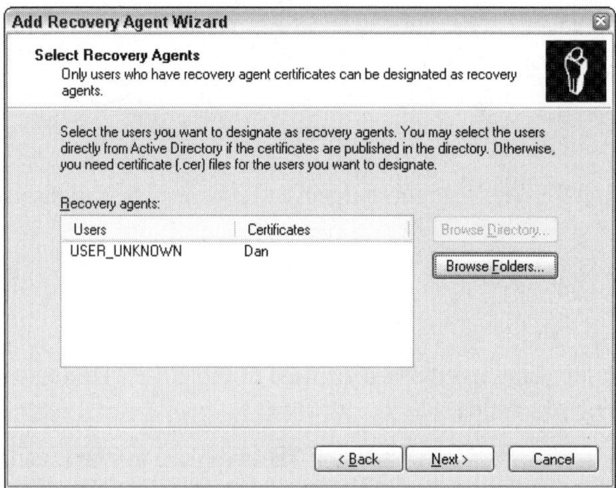

Figure 13-2: Selecting a Data Recovery Agent.

6. Click Finish to complete the process. The certificate of this user account is now listed in the Encrypting File System folder, as shown in Figure 13-3. This user is now able to open and recover all EFS encrypted files, including those encrypted by other users.

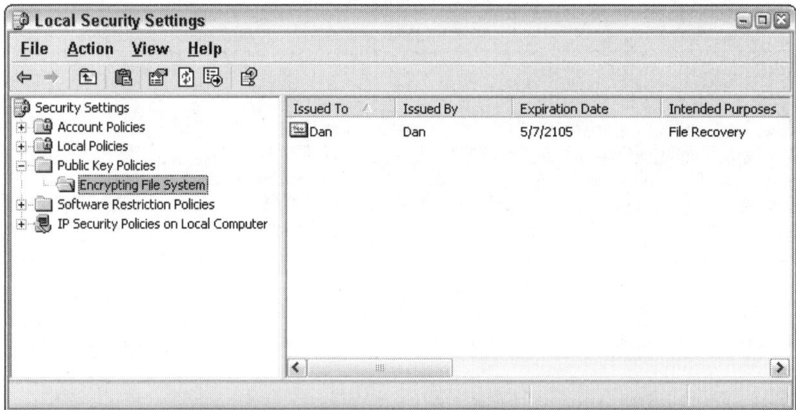

Figure 13-3: Viewing Data Recovery Agents in EFS Public Key Policy.

Encrypting files and folders

EFS encrypts and decrypts files in a completely transparent manner. After a file is encrypted by your user account, decrypting it is as simple as opening the file. Similarly, re-encrypting an open file that you've changed is accomplished by saving it as you would any file.

Windows XP allows you to encrypt files stored on drives that use the NTFS file system, with the exception of operating system files. Although you can encrypt files individually, an easier way to work with EFS is to set the encryption attribute on a folder instead. When you set the encryption attribute on a folder, the folder itself is not encrypted; however, every file that you save to that folder is automatically encrypted without the need to make changes to the attributes of each individual file.

Note

Windows Explorer makes encrypted files and folders easier to spot by displaying their names in green text.

Follow these steps to encrypt a folder using Windows Explorer:

1. Log on to Windows XP with your everyday user account.
2. Click Start → My Computer.
3. Browse to drive C and then create a new folder named Encrypted Files.
4. Right-click the Encrypted Files folder and then click Properties.
5. In the Attributes section of the General tab, click the Advanced button.
6. In the Compress or Encrypt attributes section, check Encrypt contents to secure data, as shown in Figure 13-4. Click OK.

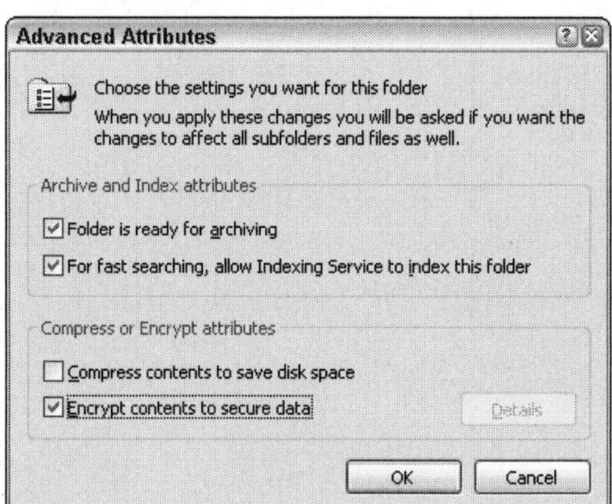

Figure 13-4: Encrypting a folder.

7. Click OK to close the properties of the Encrypted Files folder. The name of this folder now appears in Windows Explorer in green text, alerting you to the fact that the encryption attribute is configured.
8. Click Start → All Programs → Accessories → Notepad.
9. In the Notepad window, type **This is my encrypted file** and then click File → Save As.
10. Browse to the Encrypted Files folder, name the file Test.txt and then click Save. Because the file has been saved to a folder with its encryption attribute set, this new file is encrypted automatically.
11. Right-click the Test.txt file and then click Properties.
12. Click the Advanced button in the Attributes section. The file is encrypted, as shown by the fact that the Encrypt contents to secure data box is checked.
13. Click the Details button to open the Encryption Details window, as shown in Figure 13-5. Notice that your user account name is listed in the Users Who Can Transparently Access This File section, and that the Data Recovery Agent user account configured earlier is listed in the Data Recovery Agents For This File As Defined By Recovery Policy.

Figure 13-5: Reviewing the details associated with an encrypted file.

Note

Although the Advanced Attributes window makes it appear possible, you cannot enable both the compression and encryption attributes on a file or folder simultaneously.

After you've encrypted a file, it is accessible only to your user account and the DRA, assuming that one has been designated. When another user attempts to access a file that you've encrypted, they cannot decrypt the file, and therefore cannot view its contents.

Follow these steps to test the security of an encrypted file:

1. Log on to Windows XP with a user account other than the one used to encrypt the folder in the previous exercise and your defined Data Recovery Agent.
2. Click Start→My Computer, and browse to the Encrypted Files folder on your C drive.
3. Double-click the encrypted Test.txt file. Because this user account does not have access to the encrypted file, the Notepad window opens but an Access Denied message appears, as shown in Figure 13-6.

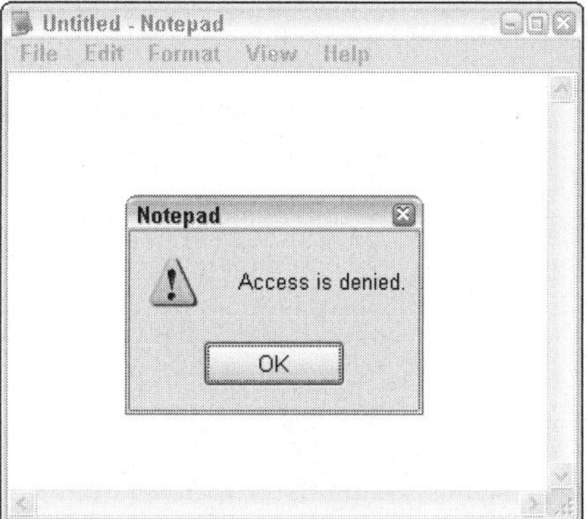

Figure 13-6: Message displayed when you try to open an encrypted file belonging to another user.

In most cases, you encrypt files to keep them secure and inaccessible to other users; however, there may be times when you want the security benefits that encryption provides, but also want one or more other users to be able to access these protected files. Windows XP's EFS feature makes it possible to share encrypted files, if necessary.

When you encrypt a file for multi-user access, you need not only to encrypt the file but also to specify the other user accounts that should be able to decrypt it. When other user accounts are granted access to an encrypted file, their private keys are also used to encrypt the file's FEK, thus allowing them to decrypt the FEK and the file it protects. EFS encrypted files can only be shared on a file-by-file basis—you cannot configure EFS encryption on a folder for multi-user access.

Tip

If you plan to share encrypted files with another user, make sure that these files are stored in a folder location to which the other user has access. For example, if you've stored the encrypted file in your My Documents folder and have made the folder private (as outlined in Chapter 12), other users will not be able to gain access to the file due to NTFS permission restrictions.

Follow these steps to share an EFS encrypted file with another user:

1. Log on to Windows XP with your everyday user account.
2. Click Start → My Computer, and browse to the Encrypted Files folder on your C drive.
3. Right-click the Test.txt file and then click Properties.
4. In the Attributes section, click the Advanced button and then click the Details button in the Compress or Encrypt attributes section.
5. Click the Add button and then select the user with whom you want to share access to the file, as shown in Figure 13-7. Click OK three times. This user now has access to the encrypted file.

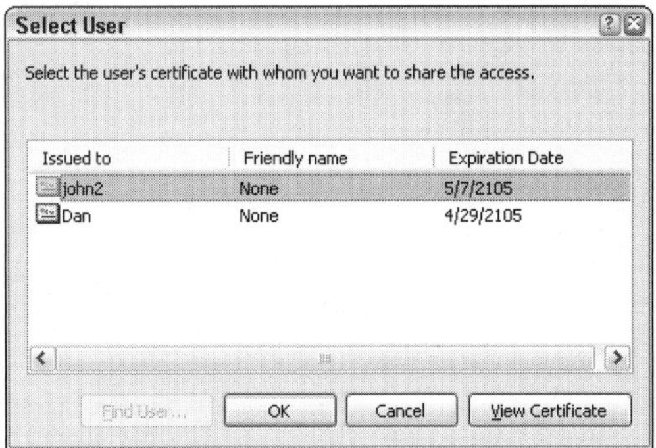

Figure 13-7: EFS allows you to share access to encrypted files with other users.

Note

If you want to share an encrypted file with another user but cannot find their username listed when you click the Add button on the Encryption Details window for the file, the user probably does not yet have an EFS certificate. To generate a certificate for the user, have them log on and encrypt a file. Windows XP then automatically creates and assigns the necessary EFS encryption certificate for their account.

Managing EFS encryption keys

If you do decide to use EFS to securely encrypt important files, it's absolutely essential to ensure that your EFS certificate (including your private key) is properly backed up. If you do not back up your certificate and lose access to your private key for any reason (as a result of a system crash, for example), you will not be able to decrypt and restore your files. Designating a DRA helps you to gain access to these files in the event of a problem specific to your user account, but a system crash could also mean that the DRA's certificate and private key will be inaccessible. For this reason, you should immediately export and securely store a copy of your EFS certificate and private key once you begin using EFS to encrypt files.

Follow these steps to export your EFS certificate and private key:

1. Click Start → Run.
2. In the Open textbox, type mmc.exe and then click OK.
3. Click File → Add/Remove Snap-in.
4. Click Add.
5. At the Add Standalone Snap-in window, click Certificates and then click Add.
6. At the Certificates snap-in window, click Finish.
7. Click Close and then click OK.
8. Expand Certificates - Current User → Personal → Certificates. Your EFS certificate will be listed, as shown in Figure 13-8.

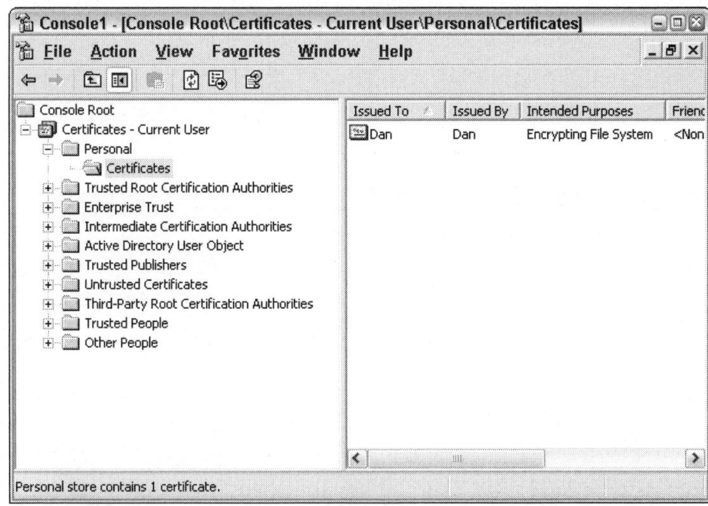

Figure 13-8: Use the Certificates MMC to manage your EFS certificate.

9. Right-click your EFS certificate, and click All Tasks → Export.
10. At the Certificate Export Wizard Welcome screen, click Next.
11. At the Export Private Key screen, click Yes, export the private key, and click Next.
12. At the Export File Format screen, click Next.
13. At the Password screen, enter and then confirm a strong password to protect your certificate and private key; then click Next.

14. At the File to Export screen, click the Browse button and then browse to the folder in which you want to store the exported certificate. Enter a name for the certificate in the File name textbox and then click Save.
15. Click Next and then click Finish.
16. Save the exported certificate to a floppy disk or CD and then save it in a safe place in case you ever need to import it in the future to gain access to an EFS encrypted file.

Tip

In addition to your own EFS certificate, you should also export and safely store a copy of your designated Data Recovery Agent's certificate and private key. This ensures that files encrypted by all users can also be recovered in the future, if necessary.

If you do lose access to your EFS certificate and private key, you can restore it from your backed up version by opening the Certificates MMC, expanding Certificates — Current User → Personal → Certificates, right-clicking on the Certificates folder, and selecting All Tasks → Import. Follow the steps of the Certificate Import Wizard to restore the backed up copy of your certificate and regain access to your EFS encrypted files.

Using a Third-Party Encryption Solution

Although EFS is a great encryption solution for Windows XP Professional users, this feature is not included with Windows XP Home Edition. Thankfully, a number of third-party programs can be used to fill this void, making the security benefits of file encryption accessible to users whose systems lack EFS capabilities.

Every third-party file encryption program uses slightly different techniques to securely encrypt files, folders, and even entire disks. Some rely on public key cryptographic systems to encrypt and decrypt files; others make use of password protection schemes. In most cases, these programs use the Advanced Encryption Standard (AES) algorithm to offer anywhere from 128- to 256-bit encryption protection. As an encryption standard, AES is robust enough to meet the needs of just about any user — even the US government uses AES to protect files deemed classified to "top secret" levels.

Although there's no shortage of personal encryption programs available for Windows XP, this section focuses on two in particular — Dekart Private Disk and Dekart Private Disk Lite. Both of these products are explored in more detail in the following sections.

Dekart Private Disk Light

Dekart Private Disk Lite is the free (for personal use) version of Dekart's Private Disk program. Although not as feature-rich as the "full" version, this program offers excellent file security that easily meets the needs of most users. It can be downloaded from `www.dekart.com/free_download/?prod_name=private_disk_light`.

Dekart Private Disk Light allows you to define one or more "private disks" on your system. These private disks are actually individual files (stored on drives such as C:) that act as encrypted storage locations for other files. For example, you might opt to create one private disk with a storage capacity of 100 MB to securely protect important documents. As part of creating this private disk, the program asks you to assign it a drive letter and password; then, when you need to open your encrypted files or save new files to your private disk, all you need to do is open Dekart Private Disk Light, select the option to connect to your private disk, and enter the correct password. After complete, your private disk is "mounted," and accessible like any other drive letter in Windows Explorer. When disconnected, all files stored on the disk remain securely encrypted, and your private disk drive letter is not accessible.

Caution

If you forget the password used to encrypt a private disk, you effectively lose access to all files stored on the encrypted drive for good.

Follow these steps to create a new private disk with Dekart Private Disk Light:

1. Click Start → All Programs → Dekart → Private Disk Light → Private Disk Light.
2. When the Dekart Private Disk Light window opens (Figure 13-9), click Create.

Figure 13-9: Dekart Private Disk Light allows you to create virtual encrypted drives.

3. At the New Private Disk window, click Browse. Browse to the folder location where you want to save your private disk file, enter a filename, and click Open.
4. Use the Disk letter drop-down box to specify a drive letter for your private disk (such as Z:) and then specify a size for the disk, as shown in Figure 13-10. Click Create.

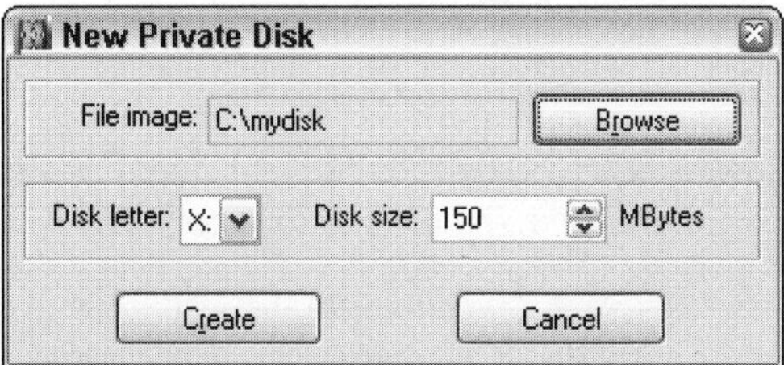

Figure 13-10: Creating a new private disk.

5. At the Encryption Password window, enter and confirm a strong password to protect your private disk; then click OK.
6. After the new private disk is successfully created, the Dekart Private Disk Light window prompts you to format the disk. Click OK.
7. When the Format window appears, configure settings for your drive including its file system and volume label and then click Start.
8. When the Format dialog box appears, click OK.
9. When the format process is complete, click OK and then close the Format setting window.
10. After created and formatted, you new private disk is connected automatically. If you open My Computer, the drive letter assigned to your private disk should now be visible and accessible in the Devices with Removal Storage section, as shown in Figure 13-11.

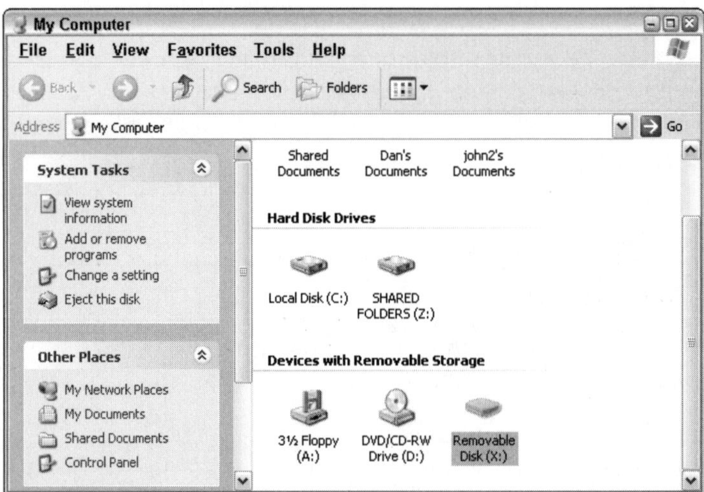

Figure 13-11: A connected private disk is displayed as a removable disk in Windows Explorer.

11. Click the Disconnect button to disconnect your private disk.

Follow these steps to connect to and save files to your private disk.

1. Click Start → All Programs → Dekart → Private Disk Lite → Private Disk Lite.
2. Click Connect.
3. When the Connect Private Disk window appears, browse to the file that you originally specified as your private disk storage location. Click the file and then click Open.
4. When the Password dialog box appears, type your password and then click OK.
5. Click Start → All Programs → Accessories → Notepad.

6. In the Notepad window, type **Testing Dekart Private Disk Light**.
7. Click File → Save As. Browse to your private disk's drive letter, enter a filename, and click Save. The file is encrypted automatically and stored on your private disk.

After your private disk has been created, cut existing sensitive files from folders such as My Documents, and paste them into a folder on your private disk to ensure they're securely encrypted.

Cross-Reference

After moving sensitive files to your encrypted private disk, you should erase all remnants of the original unencrypted versions. You learn more about securely erasing files from drives in Chapter 14.

Dekart Private Disk

Private Disk Light will meet the file encryption needs of most users, but the full version of the program — Dekart Private Disk — offers a number of additional features and capabilities that may represent a worthwhile investment for some users.

In addition to the capabilities offered by Dekart Private Disk Light, Dekart Private Disk includes the capability to:

- Connect to private disks from Windows Explorer
- Hide a private disk's storage file
- Connect to private disks in read-only mode
- Restore NTFS permissions and shared folder settings upon connecting
- Create password-protected backup disks
- Backup disk encryption keys
- Disconnect private disks automatically after a timeout period
- Encrypt files stored on USB, CD, DVD, and other removable drives

For a complete overview of the differences between Dekart Private Disk and Dekart Private Disk Light, see the product comparison table at `www.dekart.com/products/file&disk_encryption/private_disk_light/`. To download a trial version of Dekart Private Disk, visit `www.dekart.com/free_download/?prod_name=private_disk`.

Summary

Encryption offers the highest possible levels of protection for your personal files. Although its security benefits are great, it's vital that encryption be treated with respect — in the same way that encryption serves its purpose in keeping others from accessing your personal files, it also has the potential to lock you out of your own files if you're not careful. Keep the following points in mind when it comes to securely encrypting files:

- Always designate a DRA if you plan to encrypt files using EFS.
- Always export and securely store a copy of your EFS certificate and private key, along with those belonging to the DRA. Have other users do the same for their user accounts.
- Set the EFS encryption attribute on folders rather than individual files when possible.
- If you choose to share EFS encrypted files, ensure that they're stored in a folder location that is accessible to other users.
- If you are using EFS to encrypt files for personal access only, store them in a folder to which other users do not have access.
- If you're running Windows XP Home Edition, use a third-party file encryption program such as Dekart Private Disk Light to protect your files.
- When using a third-party encryption program to protect your files, take steps to ensure that you do not forget the password(s) used to decrypt and access your files.

Chapter 14

Erasing Files and Hard Drives Securely

When is a deleted file not a deleted file? When you use Windows XP to delete the file, of course! Although it may seem strange, the built-in processes by which Windows XP normally deletes files and folders don't actually remove the items from your hard drive in a permanent manner. In fact, many of the files that you might believe to have been deleted for all eternity can actually be recovered quite easily with the right software tools in hand. That's good news if you've accidentally deleted a file and now want to attempt to recover it, but very bad news is you have some expectation that deleted items are actually permanently erased for good.

From a security perspective, the ability to erase files permanently such that they cannot be recovered is a necessary feature. Unfortunately, Windows XP does not include any built-in tools or utilities that are capable of deleting files in such a manner. In fact, if you rely on features such as the Recycle Bin to delete files, you need to be aware that there's always the potential for a user with the right tools and expertise to reclaim all or some portion of every file you've deleted. In a nutshell, Windows XP's offers nothing in the way of tools capable of securely erasing data.

Thankfully, a number of third-party tools help to bridge this security lapse. In this chapter you learn how to use Eraser, a free tool designed to securely erase files, folders, and even free disk space to levels that meet or exceed even US government standards. Furthermore, you learn how to cover your Internet and program activity trails, stopping others from learning which files you've been working with or which Web site you've been visiting. Finally, for cases where you've purchased a new PC and are getting ready to donate or "hand down" your old one, you learn how to securely erase your old hard drive to ensure that your personal data is erased, once and for all.

Traditional Ways of Deleting Files

In the world of Windows XP, files and folders are typically deleted by sending them to (and then emptying) the Recycle Bin. On a larger scale, entire disks can be deleted by using techniques such as formatting drives, or even deleting them completely. In the following sections you learn more about these methods, including why they cannot be considered secure alternatives in cases where you need to erase files, folders, or even the contents of a hard drive permanently.

Using the Recycle Bin

Windows XP is an operating system rife with second chances, and perhaps no "feature" illustrates this as clearly as the aptly named Recycle Bin. When you select the option to delete a file or folder in Windows Explorer, Windows XP automatically "moves" the item to the Recycle Bin, where it sits until you make the decision to get rid of it for good. In other words, files that you delete aren't actually deleted until you give the word that the Recycle Bin should be "emptied."

Note

Although Windows XP moves most files deleted with Windows Explorer to the Recycle Bin, not all deleted files are dealt with in this manner. In cases where a very large file or folder is being deleted, it may be deemed too large for the Recycle Bin and Windows XP lets you know that it intends to bypass this step and delete the file for good. Additionally, when files are deleted from the command line using the DEL command, they are deleted immediately rather than sent to the Recycle Bin.

In many ways, this is a good thing. If you accidentally choose the option to delete a file and then realize that you've made a mistake, you can open the Recycle Bin, click on the file in question, and select Restore to undo the error and return the file to its original location (see Figure 14-1). When you empty the Recycle Bin, however, Windows XP considers the file to be gone for good.

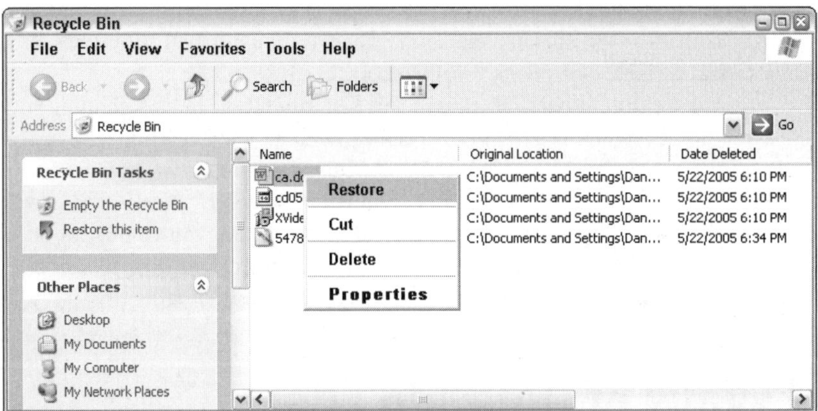

Figure 14-1: Files sent to the Recycle Bin can be restored if you've deleted a file in error.

Although a file emptied from the Recycle Bin might appear to be deleted for good, it may still exist because of the way that Windows XP deletes files. Instead of physically deleting or erasing the areas of disk space in which the files resided, the space is marked as being "available" or not currently in use. Other programs (and Windows XP) now look at this space as they would any other area of uninhabited disk space and can use it for storage if necessary.

This methodology is the primary reason why deleted files often can be recovered with specialized "undelete" software. Instead of relying on the information provided by Windows XP, these tools scan parts of the hard disk marked as "available," looking for accessible files. In cases where the disk space once occupied by a file has not been used to store other data, these programs can typically access the deleted file for recovery purposes.

Formatting and deleting partitions

In much the same way that Windows XP doesn't go to the trouble of ensuring that files emptied from the Recycle Bin are actually permanently deleted for good, formatting or deleting a partition offers no guarantees that the files stored on a drive will be permanently inaccessible. In the case of formatting an existing drive (see Figure 14-2) Windows XP simply deletes the contents of the drive's partition table, marking all areas of the drive as empty and accessible. As with deleting a file, the contents of the drive are still present, and potentially recoverable with "undelete" tools.

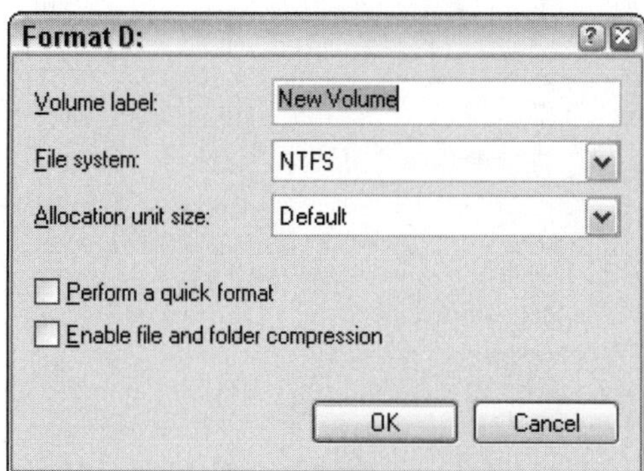

Figure 14-2: Formatting a disk makes it appear to be empty, but files might still be recoverable even after the fact.

The same is true when a partition is actually deleted using a tool like Disk Management or FDISK. Here again, Windows XP doesn't erase or destroy the contents of the partition. Instead, it fools programs (and even itself) into believing that the partition no longer exists, allowing the newly freed space to be used for the purpose of creating new partitions or extended existing ones.

Recovering Deleted Files

Whether you see the way that Windows XP deletes files as a good thing or a bad thing is largely a function of where you're standing. If you've accidentally deleted a file and want the greatest chance of recovery, the method offers promise. If you want files you delete to be permanently erased, Windows XP's methodology isn't a suitable solution.

Assuming that you have deleted files (using the Recycle Bin or other methods outlined in the previous sections) that you now want to restore, your best chance of recovery is through the use of specialized "undelete" software. These programs scan your hard disk looking for deleted files, providing lists of those that can potentially be recovered. An example of one such program is File Scavenger (`http://www.quetek.com`), as shown in the following figure.

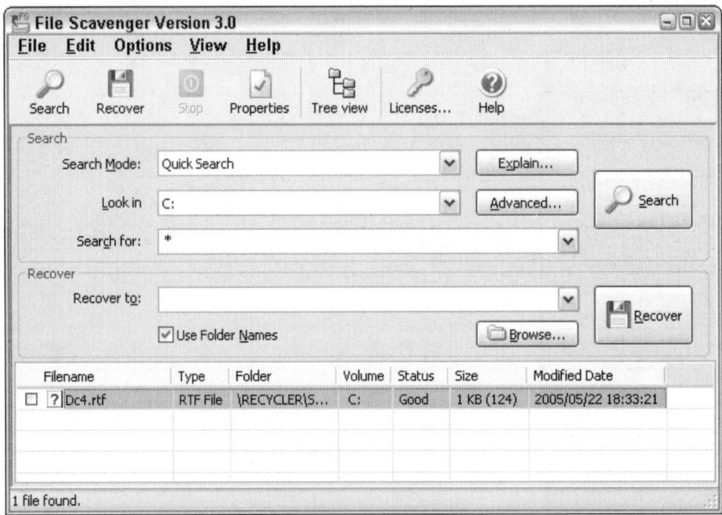

Using File Scavenger to search for deleted files.

As part of its scanning process, File Scavenger lists all deleted files that it finds, and assigns each a "status" that outlines the relatively probability that the file can be recovered. For example, the chances of recovering a file marked "good" are high; however, there's little chance that a file marked "poor" can actually be restored.

Whether a file can actually be restored is largely a function of whether any portion of the disk space it inhabited is now being used to store another file. If the disk space has been reused, the chances of a successful recovery are quite low. This is one of the reasons why you need to be careful to keep disk activity to a minimum after you accidentally delete a file. If you don't, the likelihood that the disk space will have been reused is much higher.

For this reason, you should make a point of installing "undelete" programs such as File Scavenger before you need them. If you try and install these programs after accidentally deleting a file, it's possible that the disk space used to install the program might end up being the same disk space inhabited by your deleted file, making recovery next to impossible.

Erasing Files Securely

When security and privacy are not concerns, there's really nothing wrong with using Windows XP's built-in methods to delete files and folders. However, there's also a good chance that your computer stores all sorts of sensitive information that you would rather have erased permanently. From old business records to personal financial statements, there's no question that some files are just more sensitive than others. Any time that you want to securely erase data once and for all, you need to move beyond the native capabilities offered by Windows XP.

Thankfully, a number of programs exist for the purpose of securely erasing files. One of the most popular options on this front also happens to be free — Eraser, available from `www.heidi.ie`. When you install Eraser and select the option to erase a file or folder, this tool doesn't just delete the item's partition table entry. Instead, it overwrites the physical disk space occupied by the file a number of times, to the point where recovering the original data is extremely difficult, if not impossible.

In its default configuration, Eraser offers four different methods that can be used to overwrite disk space and, thus, erase files:

- **Gutmann.** This default file erasing method overwrites the disk space used by a file a whopping 35 times.
- **US DoD 5220.22-M (8-306. / E, C and E).** This method, named after a U.S. Department of Defense standard, overwrites the disk space used by a file seven times.
- **US DoD 5220.22-M (8-306. / E).** This method, also named after a US DoD standard, overwrites the disk space used by a file three times.
- **Pseudorandom Data.** This method overwrites the disk space used by a file once.

In addition to Eraser's default options, you can also define custom erasing settings to meet your own personal needs or preferences.

Tip

If you're interested in the deep, dark, and very technical details behind securely deleting data from disk drives, visit `www.cs.auckland.ac.nz/~pgut001/pubs/secure_del.html` to read Peter Gutmann's Secure Deletion of Data from Magnetic and Solid-State Memory paper.

Follow these steps to configure erasing preferences with Eraser:

1. Click Start → All Programs → Eraser → Eraser.
2. Click Edit → Preferences → Erasing. The Preferences: Erasing window opens, as shown in Figure 14-3.

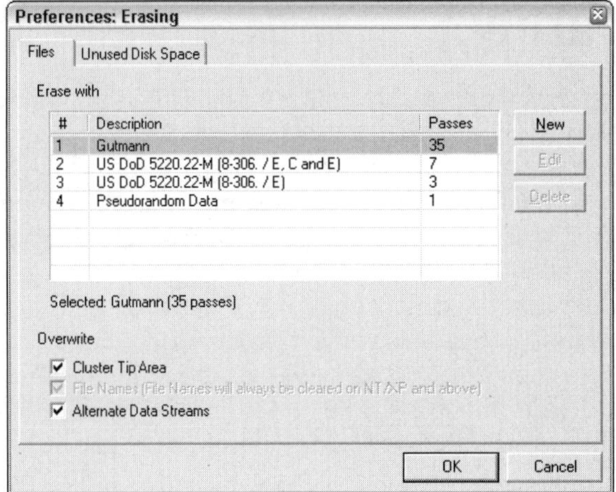

Figure 14-3: Eraser includes four predefined erasing methods, but you can also define your own.

3. On the Files tab, click the erasing method you want to use, such as the US-DoD 5220.22-M method that overwrites data using seven passes.
4. Click the Unused Disk Space tab.
5. Click the erasing method that should be used to overwrite free disk space, as shown in Figure 14-4.

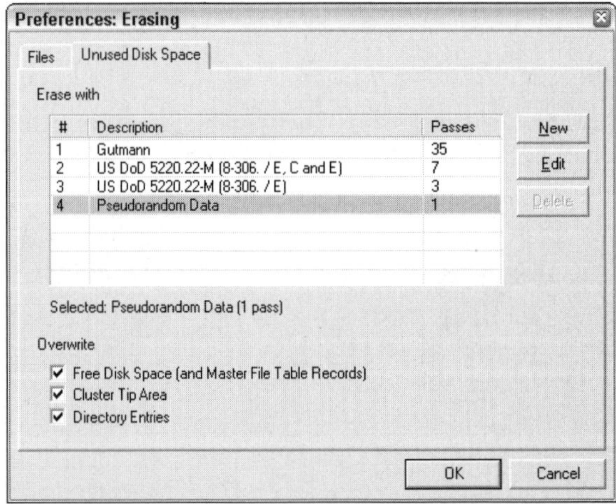

Figure 14-4: Eraser overwrites unused disk space in a single pass by default.

6. Click OK to save your changes.

Follow these steps to securely erase a file with Eraser:

1. Click Start → My Computer.
2. Browse the folder that contains the file you want to securely erase.
3. Right-click the file, and select the Erase option, as shown in Figure 14-5.

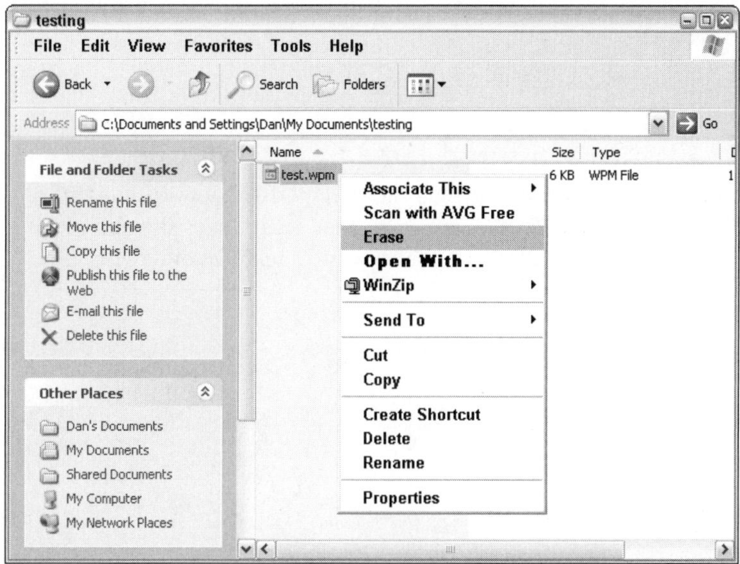

Figure 14-5: To erase a file permanently, select Erase from the shortcut menu in Windows Explorer.

4. When the Confirm Erasing dialog box appears (see Figure 14-6), click Options. This opens the Preferences: Erasing window, allowing you to configure (if necessary) specific erase settings for the file currently being erased.

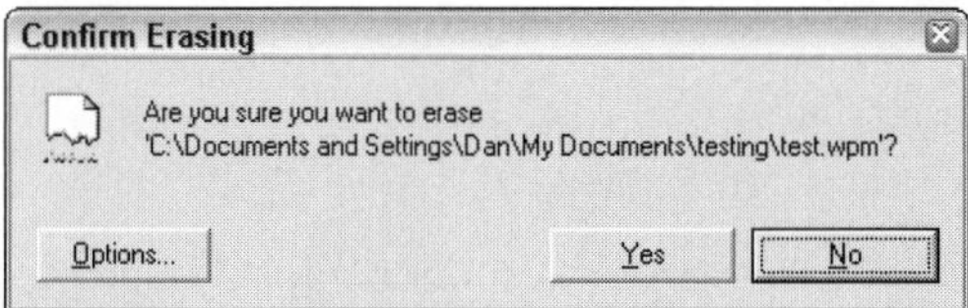

Figure 14-6: The Confirm Erasing dialog box allows you to configure specific erasing settings and confirm that you want a file permanently erased.

5. Select your preferred erasing method for this file, and click OK.
6. At the Confirm Erasing dialog box, click Yes. The Eraser dialog box shows the progress of the overwriting process, as shown in Figure 14-7.

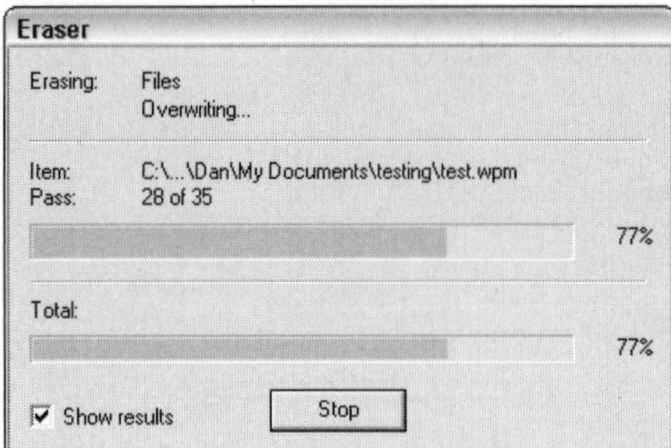

Figure 14-7: Eraser overwrites files with 35 passes by default.

7. When the erasing process is complete, the Erasing Report window outlines information about the process, as well as details of any errors that occurred, as shown in Figure 14-8. If necessary, click Save As to save details of the report to a text file; otherwise, click Close.

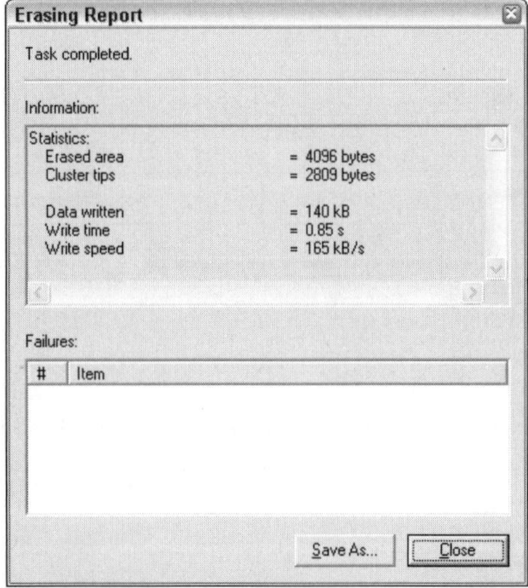

Figure 14-8: The Erasing Report window lets you know whether the erasing process was successful.

If you want to continue to use Windows XP's Recycle Bin as a temporary storage location for deleted files, by all means do. With Eraser installed, you can right-click the Recycle Bin icon on your desktop at any time and then click Erase Recycle Bin (rather than Empty Recycle Bin) to securely delete its contents, once and for all.

Erasing Unused Disk Space?

It may not seem necessary, but allowing Eraser to overwrite your system's unused disk space is a good idea from a security perspective. Even though a particular area of "free" space on a partition may not currently hold any data, that doesn't mean that it never did. In fact, areas of the disk that are currently considered to be empty by Windows XP more than likely hold at least portions of the files that were once stored there.

To help ensure that all of these bits and pieces of old files are completely removed, Eraser is configured to overwrite free disk space in a single pass. Although using a single pass is not the most secure option, it is used by default in the interest of speed; however, any of Eraser's built-in erasing methods can be selected as alternatives. In fact, you can even specify your own custom settings (such as overwriting data nine times using a particular set of patterns) if that's what you prefer.

After installed, Eraser automatically creates and schedules a new job that erases free space on Drive C every day at 12 a.m.. To view or change the details of this job, click the Scheduler button in the Eraser window, right-click the job, and select Properties, which brings up the Task Properties window shown in the following figure.

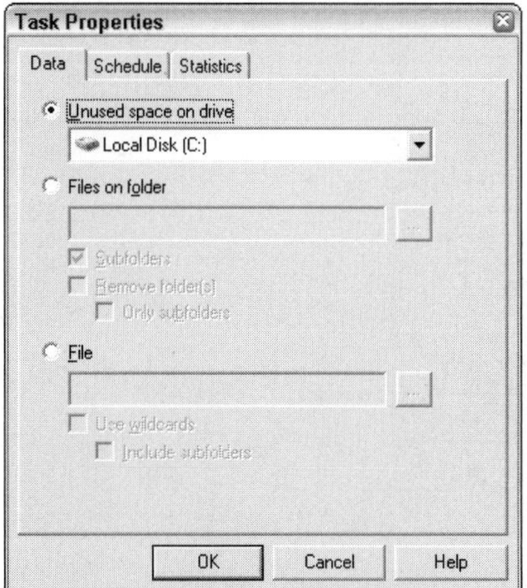

Configuring scheduled task settings.

From the Task Properties window, you can change what gets erased on the Data tab, the time and frequency of the job on the Schedule tab, and review details pertaining to each time the job has run on the Statistics tab.

If your hard disk includes more than one partition on which you would like to erase free space from all drives as part of this scheduled job, select the Local Disks option from the Unused disk space on drive menu on the Data tab. When the Local Disks option is selected, the unused disk space on all partitions is overwritten, instead of free space on Drive C alone.

Alternatively, you can create new scheduled tasks for Eraser by clicking File → New Task and then configuring settings to meet your needs. A scheduled task can be run at any time by right clicking its entry on the Scheduler tab and then selecting the Run option.

Covering Your Tracks

As part of trying to make your computing experience as fast and painless as possible, Windows XP automatically stores all sorts of information relating to how you're using your PC. For example, when you visit a Web page, Internet Explorer automatically adds its address (URL) to your browsing history list, making it easier to reach the same site in the future. Similarly, parts of sites (such as images) are temporarily stored on your hard drive to eliminate the need to download them again on subsequent visits.

Windows XP uses similar techniques to store lists of files you've recently used, allowing these lists to act as shortcuts the next time you need to open a file. If you launch a program like Microsoft Word and select File → Open, clicking the History shortcut displays shortcuts to files that you've recently opened, as shown in Figure 14-9.

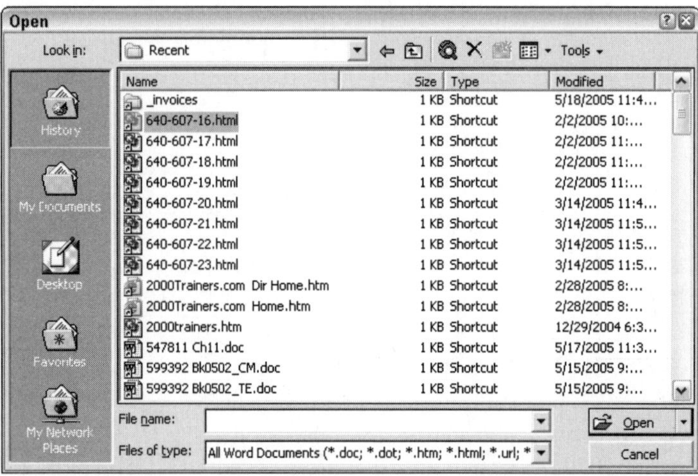

Figure 14-9: Most Windows programs include a built-in history feature to make finding recently used files easier.

Benefits aside, allowing Windows XP and other programs to store historical information about files you've opened or sites you've visited also has an impact on your personal privacy. For example, say that you decide to let a friend use your computer (perhaps to check their e-mail) while logged on with your user account. After opening a Web browser such as Internet Explorer, your friend can easily view a complete list of all the Web sites you've recently visited, and even review the keywords you've been searching for. In other words, your "tracks" are left in plain view. Even if each person has their own personal user account, Computer administrators still have the ability to dig through other users' file access and Web surfing histories.

Ultimately, it's up to you to decide whether you're comfortable with other users potentially knowing which files you've opened, and which Web sites you've been visiting. If you're fine with the idea of leaving your tracks in plain view, there's nothing left to do; however, if you'd rather a little more privacy, you should clear the information that Windows XP and other programs track, at least periodically.

Some of the personal history items that are commonly stored on Windows XP systems include:

- **Temporary Internet files.** This folder contains cached copies of Web pages, images, and other files downloaded as part of surfing the Internet with Internet Explorer.
- **Cookies.** Web browsers store cookie files set by Web sites that you visit for future reference
- **URL history.** By default, most Web browser store lists of the addresses of Web sites that you visit in their Address bar, allowing you to use the drop-down menu feature to quickly select the site's address for subsequent visits.
- **Chat history.** Instant messaging programs (such as ICQ) save the details of your online chats for future reference.
- **Recently used files.** Windows XP and many third-party programs save lists of recently used files which act as shortcuts to open those files more quickly the next time you use a program.
- **Temporary files.** Almost all programs store temporary working copies of files that you have opened. Some programs delete these files automatically after a file has been saved; others leave the temporary version intact and stored on your hard disk for longer periods.

Both Windows XP and individual programs typically include ways to delete tracks such as history lists or temporary files. For example, if you open Internet Explorer and click Tools→Internet Options, the Temporary Internet files section on the General tab includes buttons to delete both cookies and files, as shown in Figure 14-10.

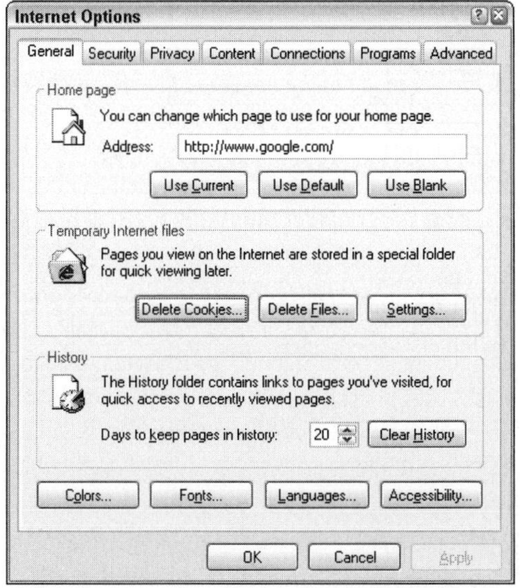

Figure 14-10: Internet Explorer gives you the ability to delete Temporary Internet files and cookies.

Unfortunately, different programs and tools store history items in different ways, meaning that deleting your tracks manually can be a time-consuming and frustrating undertaking. Many different third-party tools exist for the purpose of deleting Internet and file tracks with a single click, but this capability is also built into Microsoft's AntiSpyware program. To get at this capability, open Microsoft AntiSpyware and then click Advanced Tools. The Tracks Eraser feature is designed to improve privacy by clearing over 50 different activity trails from your computer, as shown in Figure 14-11.

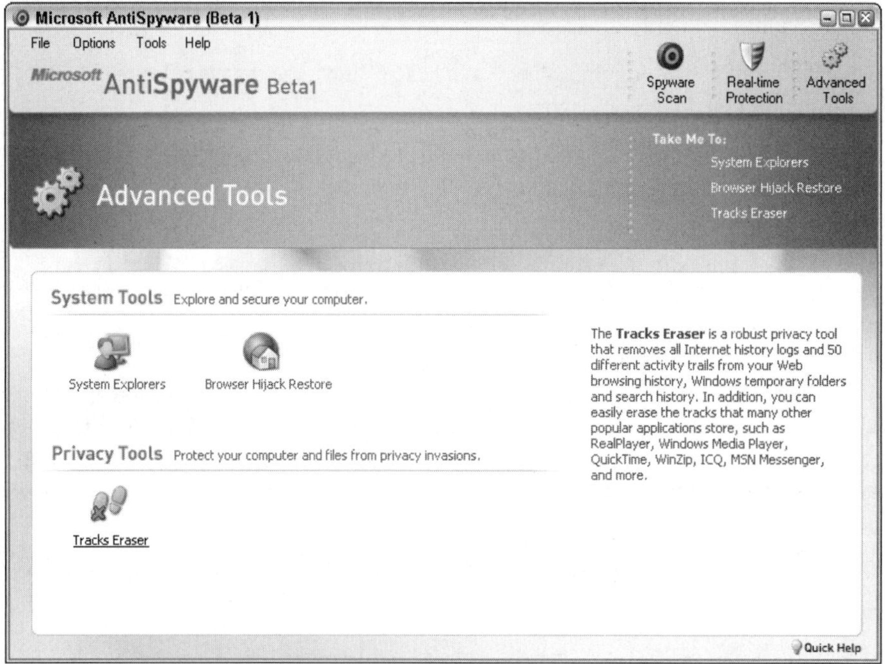

Figure 14-11: Microsoft AntiSpyware includes privacy tools such as Tracks Eraser.

Follow these steps to erase your Internet history logs and/or program activity trails with Microsoft AntiSpyware:

1. Click Start → All Programs → Microsoft AntiSpyware → Microsoft AntiSpyware.
2. Click Tools → Advanced Tools → Tracks Eraser.
3. At the Tracks Eraser screen, check the checkbox next to each program or element for which you want your activity trail erased (see Figure 14-12).

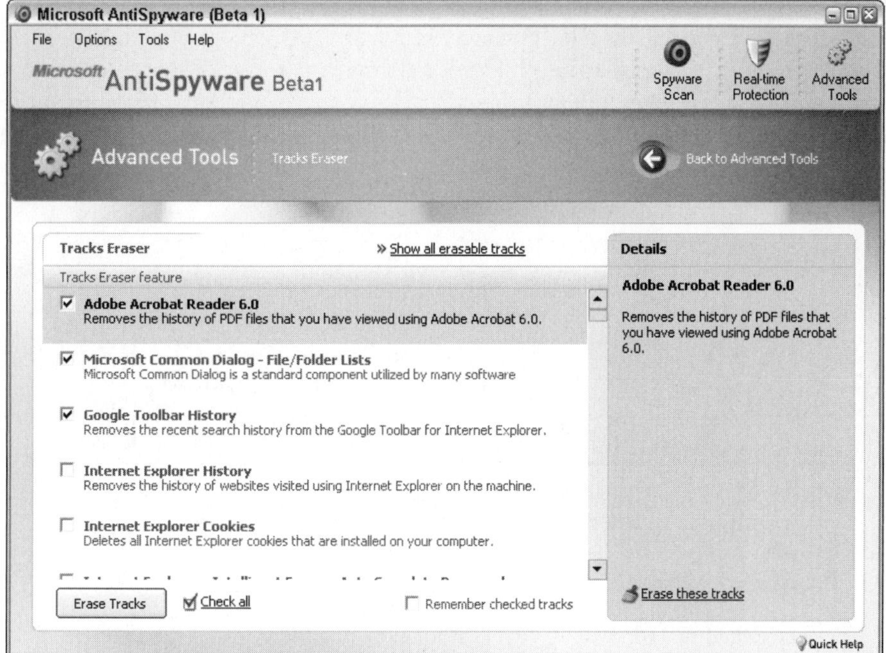

Figure 14-12: Erasing your Internet and file tracks with Microsoft AntiSpyware.

4. When complete, click the Erase Tracks button.
5. When the Clean Privacy Settings? dialog box appears, click Yes. When the Tracks Erased dialog box appears, click OK.

Although Microsoft AntiSpyware erases your program activity trails and other temporary files, it does so in a manner similar to deleting any file. In other words, because the disk space occupied by items such as Temporary Internet files isn't overwritten and securely erased, it's conceivably possible that another user could recover these items. For cases where you want to ensure that these files cannot be "restored," use a program such as Eraser to overwrite and securely delete them.

Follow these steps to configure Eraser to securely erase the contents of your Temporary Internet files folder automatically, according to a defined schedule:

1. Click Start → All Programs → Eraser → Eraser.
2. Click the Scheduler button.
3. Click File → New Task.
4. Click Files on folder and then browse to C:\Documents and Settings\username\Local Settings\Temporary Internet Files, where username is your Windows XP logon name. Check the Subfolders checkbox to include files stored in subfolders, as shown in Figure 14-13.

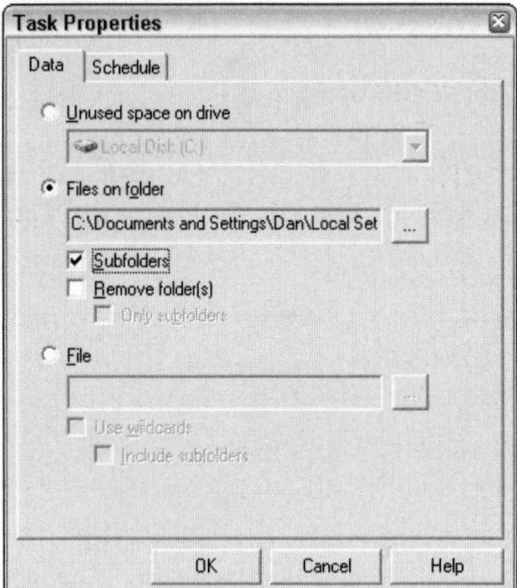

Figure 14-13: Configuring Eraser to securely erase the contents of your Temporary Internet files folder.

5. Click the Schedule tab.
6. Pick a day and time for the task to be run, as shown in Figure 14-14.

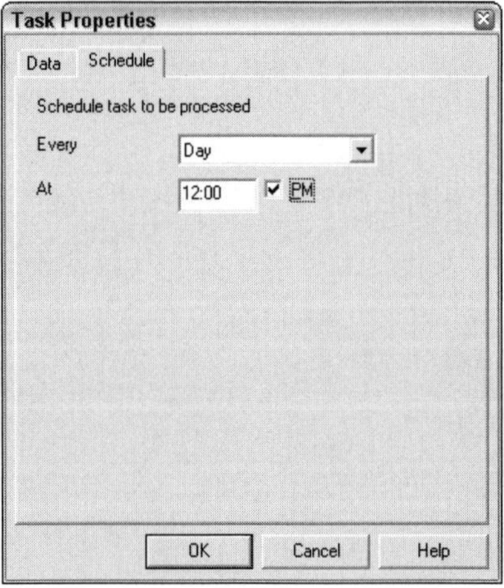

Figure 14-14: Configuring the schedule associated with an Eraser task.

7. Click OK to save the new task. Optionally, repeat these steps to erase the contents of other folders according to a schedule you specify.

Clearing Virtual Memory

To avoid those dreaded "out of memory" errors that occur when you have too many programs running simultaneously, Windows XP uses a feature known as virtual memory. In this setup, Windows XP allocates a portion of your computer's hard disk space as a virtual extension to memory, effectively tricking programs into believing that more RAM is available for use than the actual physical amount installed.

RAM works at much faster speeds than a hard drive, so Windows XP always uses RAM as its primary working memory area; however, as RAM fills up, the oldest items in memory are "swapped" to your computer's hard disk to make room for newer items. The process by which Windows XP moves files back and forth between RAM and a hard disk is known as "paging"; the file on your hard drive that acts as the virtual extension to RAM goes by the name pagefile.sys.

When Windows XP shuts down, the contents of the paging file are not cleared by default, making it possible for its contents (including files you may have been working on) to be read by user with the right tools and access to your computer. As such, you should consider configuring XP such that it automatically clears the contents of pagefile.sys as part of its shutdown process.

Clearing Windows XP's paging file at shutdown is easy accomplished if you have Eraser installed. Just open the program, head to Edit → Preferences → General, and check Enable clearing of paging file (swap) at shutdown, as shown in the following figure.

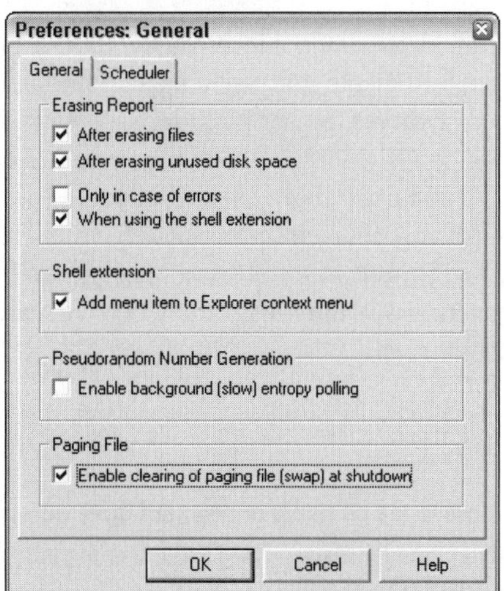

Configuring Eraser to clear Windows XP's paging file at shutdown.

Alternatively, you can enable this setting by editing the Registry. Just open the Registry Editor (regedit.exe), browse to HKEY_LOCAL_MACHINE\SYSTEM\CurrentControlSet\Control\Session Manager\Memory Management, and change the value of ClearPageFileAtShutdown from 0 to 1. After you reboot, Windows XP automatically clears your system's paging file as part of every shutdown process. This makes the shutdown process take a little longer but helps to increase the overall security of your Windows XP system.

Erasing Hard Drives Securely

Purchasing a newer and faster computer is always exciting but always raises the issue of what you should do with your old PC. Many people hand their old system down to a friend or family member, but donating or recycling these machines has become an increasingly popular option.

Although there's no denying that donating and recycling old systems are both more socially responsible options that throwing a computer away, it's critically important to ensure that you completely and securely erase the system's hard drive prior to going this route. In fact, you should securely erase the hard drive of any PC that you don't plan to use any more, regardless of where it ends up. Quite simply, it's not worth taking the risk that someone will find or purchase the computer and then have the ability to sift through your old personal files and settings. Even if you format the drive and delete its partitions, chances are good that any user could restore at least some of your old file by using an "undelete" utility.

Note

If you're looking for some insight into the types of information that are commonly recovered from old hard disks and discarded PCs, visit `www.pcmag.com/article2/0,1759,919827,00.asp` **and** `www.computing.co.uk/news/1161309`.

For both security and practical reasons, you cannot securely delete the contents of any hard drive while Windows XP is running. To get this job done, you need to create and use a special bootable floppy disk or CD that includes a tool designed to securely erase drives. Eraser includes just the tool, known as Darik's Boot and Nuke.

In a nutshell, Darik's Boot and Nuke creates a bootable CD or floppy disk that allows you to boot into a command line environment and specify settings for erasing your computer's hard disk. This program allows you to specify how many times the disk should be overwritten, using settings similar to those used by Eraser. After the process is complete, recovering any data from the CD is virtually next to impossible.

Caution

Darik's Boot and Nuke is an exceptionally dangerous tool that can erase the contents of any hard drive permanently. After you create this disk, be sure to label it appropriately and never leave it lying around or in your computer's disk drive. Because the disk does not require Windows XP to be running to function, ensure that your computer is not configured to boot from a floppy disk or CD drive in your BIOS settings (as originally outlined in Chapter 2). If you computer can boot from these devices, any user could insert a "nuke" disk on your system and use it to securely erase the entire contents of your drive.

Follow these steps to create a bootable floppy disk containing Darik's Boot and Nuke:

1. Click Start → All Programs → Eraser → Create Nuke Boot Disk.
2. When the WinImage Self Extractor window opens, select the drive letter for your floppy drive from the Floppy drop-down menu. Insert a blank floppy disk into the drive and then click OK.

Follow these steps to securely erase the entire contents of your computer's hard drive using Darik's Boot and Nuke:

1. Insert the boot floppy disk created in the previous activity in your floppy disk drive.
2. Restart your computer to boot from the floppy disk. You may need to change the drive boot order in your BIOS settings first in order for this step to work.
3. At the Darik's Boot and Nuke Warning Screen (Figure 14-15), type **autonuke** and then press Enter. Alternatively, press the Enter key to walk through the process step-by-step.

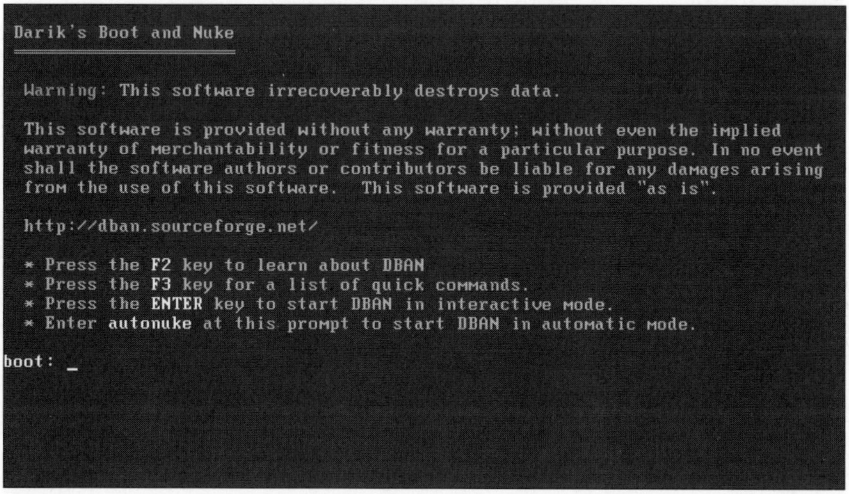

```
Darik's Boot and Nuke

 Warning: This software irrecoverably destroys data.

 This software is provided without any warranty; without even the implied
 warranty of merchantability or fitness for a particular purpose. In no event
 shall the software authors or contributors be liable for any damages arising
 from the use of this software.  This software is provided "as is".

 http://dban.sourceforge.net/

 * Press the F2 key to learn about DBAN
 * Press the F3 key for a list of quick commands.
 * Press the ENTER key to start DBAN in interactive mode.
 * Enter autonuke at this prompt to start DBAN in automatic mode.

boot: _
```

Figure 14-15: Darik's Boot and Nuke can be used to securely delete the contents of entire hard drives.

Note

In cases where you need the entire contents of a hard drive to be 100% unrecoverable, the only effective option is to first securely erase the drive and then literally destroy it via methods like incinerating or pulverizing the physical drive. It may sound extreme, but physical destruction is still the method used by governments to "sanitize" disks that contain classified information deemed "Top Secret."

Summary

When you delete files, folders, or even entire disk partitions using Windows XP's native tools, the methods used make it possible for items to be recovered using a variety of tools. For cases where the data you delete must be erased and unrecoverable, you need to turn to third-party tools such as Eraser and Darik's Boot and Nuke. Keep the following points in mind when it comes to deleting files, folders, settings, and drives:

- Erase sensitive files using a program such as Eraser to ensure they cannot be recovered.
- Use the highest number of passes possible when choosing a secure file deletion method. At 35 passes, the Gutmann method offers excellent protection.
- Periodically erase your Internet and file activity trails using a program such as Microsoft AntiSpyware to improve personal privacy.
- Schedule secure erase operations on folders such as Temporary Internet files, and even unused disk space.
- Prior to donating or giving away an old PC, take the time to securely erase its hard drive using a tool such as Darik's Boot and Nuke.

Part VI

Securing Your Home Network

Chapter 15

Securing Shared Folders and Printers

One of the first human interaction skills that we're all taught is the importance of sharing. Children are encouraged to share toys during playtime, and adults borrow things from neighbors all the time. Although there's little question that sharing has benefits, it can also have a downside — remember the hedge trimmer that you leant out six months ago and haven't seen heads or tails of since? How about the corner of your garage stacked full of items borrowed from your neighbor? When not managed properly, the whole business of sharing things can turn into one big ugly mess (often quite literally!).

Although slightly different from the world of tools, household items, or even the proverbial cup of sugar, sharing resources is perhaps the most important concept behind setting up a computer network. When you have a network at home or at the office, users can share resources such as printers and files almost seamlessly. A user sitting at one PC can send documents to a printer connected to another computer, or share a certain folder on their PC such that all other users can view, store, and manage the files it contains from across the network. From making better use of resources to making access to information more convenient, networks and sharing go hand in hand.

Unfortunately, in much the same way that your neighbor may not have gotten around to returning your extension ladder, sharing on a computer network doesn't always run as smoothly as it should. For example, if you grant all users on your network access to an expensive colour laser printer, you might find an employee using it to print off a dozen sets of their summer vacation photos. Or, you may have shared a folder on your computer to enable your spouse to access open an important document, only to learn that he or she deleted all of the files in the folder by accident. Anytime you share anything, you're taking at least a small risk.

When you want to take advantage of the benefits of sharing resources on a computer network but reduce your risk exposure at the same time, you need to explore ways in which you can secure things to an appropriate degree. For example, you might choose not to allow some users to access a certain printer, or deny a user the ability to do anything more than open and read the files in a shared folder. In this chapter you learn about the File and Printer sharing features of Windows XP, and specifically how to implement restrictions on how other network users can make use of shared resources.

Sharing Network Resources

The ability to share network resources is a core feature of both the Windows XP Home and Professional operating systems. A Windows XP system is capable of acting as a network client for the purpose of connecting to resources shared from other computers, or as a basic network server that hosts the shared resources that other client computers connect to.

The specific feature that allows a Windows XP system to share resources over a network is called File and Printer Sharing. After enabled, File and Printer Sharing allows other computers to connect to a Windows XP system for the purpose of accessing:

- **Shared Folders.** A shared folder is much like any other folder stored on the hard drive of a Windows XP system. The primary difference between a regular folder and one that has been shared is that the contents of a shared folder are accessible to other computers on the same network. For example, you might decide to create a new folder called SharedFiles and then share this folder. When shared, other computers on the network can connect to the folder using tools such as My Network Places, or by mapping a drive letter to the folder, making it accessible like any other drive in My Computer.
- **Shared Printers.** A shared printer is similar to any other printer installed on a Windows XP system. The major difference between a regular printer and a shared printer is that a shared printer is accessible to other client computers on the same network. When a printer is installed but not shared, only the people using the computer it is connected to can print to it. When shared, other users can connect to the printer over the network and then send print jobs to it in the same manner as they would with a locally attached printer.

You learn more about how to share and secure both folders and printers in the following sections.

Sharing Folders

Windows XP makes it easy to share the contents of folder with other network users. By default, both Windows XP Home and Professional systems use a feature known as Simple File Sharing to make the process of configuring shared folders easy for the average user. On Windows XP Home systems, Simple File Sharing is primary method used to share folders, and cannot be disabled. Simple File Sharing can be disabled on Windows XP Professional systems, allowing more advanced users to achieve a greater degree of control over how folders are shared and to what degree. You learn more about how Simple File Sharing is disabled (and why you might want to go this route) later in the chapter.

Note

For security reasons, users with Limited user accounts are not allowed to share folders or printers.

Follow these steps to enable file sharing on a Windows XP system using the Network Setup Wizard:

1. Click Start → My Computer.
2. Browse to the folder that you want to share with other users on your network. Right-click that folder, and then click Sharing and Security, as shown in Figure 15-1.

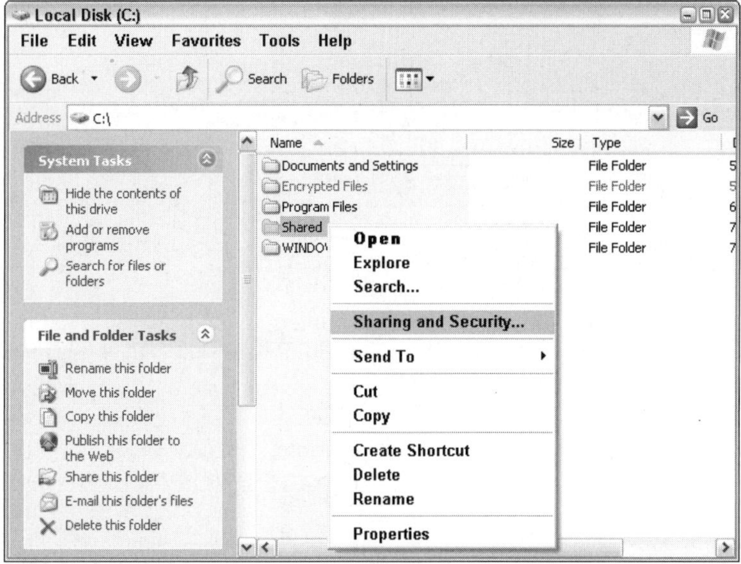

Figure 15-1: Right-click a folder and then click Sharing and Security to configure shared folder settings.

3. In the Network sharing and security section of the Sharing tab, click the Network Setup Wizard link. If you have already shared a folder on your Windows XP system, this link is not present. To share a folder when this link is not present, move on to the steps in the next activity.
4. At the Network Setup Wizard Welcome screen, click Next.
5. At the Before you continue screen, click Next.
6. At the Do you want to use the shared connection screen, click Next.
7. At the Give this computer a description and name screen type a description for the computer, and (optionally) give the computer a new name as shown in Figure 15-2. Click Next.

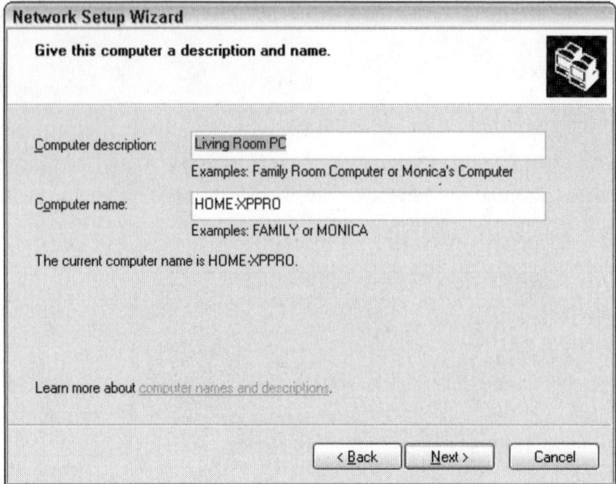

Figure 15-2: Use the Network Setup Wizard to get Windows XP ready for sharing and other networking tasks.

8. At the Name your network screen, enter the name for your workgroup, as shown in Figure 15-3. Click Next.

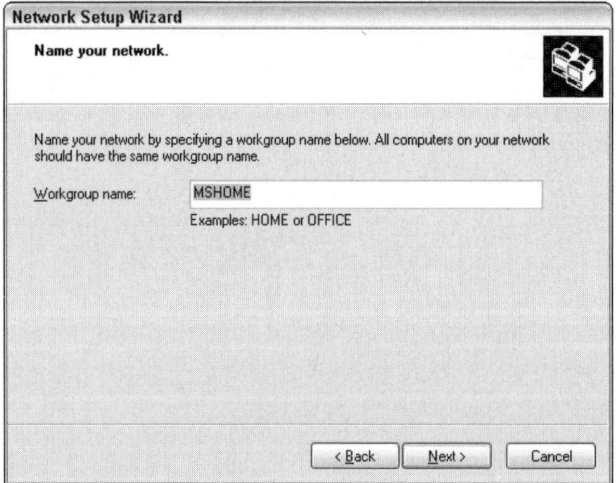

Figure 15-3: All computers on the same network should use the same workgroup name.

9. Review your configuration changes at the Ready to apply network settings screen and then click Next.
10. At the You're almost done screen, click Just finish the wizard, click Next, and click Finish.
11. Restart Windows XP when prompted.

After you complete the Network Setup Wizard and restart Windows XP, follow these steps to share a folder:

1. Click Start → My Computer.
2. Browse to the folder that you want to share with other users on your network. Right-click that folder and then click Sharing and Security.
3. Check Share this folder on the network. In the Share name box, type a network name that will be used to identify this shared folder to other computers on the network (as shown in Figure 15-4). This name does not have to be the same as the folder's current name. If you want to share the folder but have it remain hidden from users browsing the network using tools such as My Network Places, append the dollar ($) sign to the end of the share name. For example, a shared folder named sharedfiles$ will not appear when other users browse for shared folders on the network.

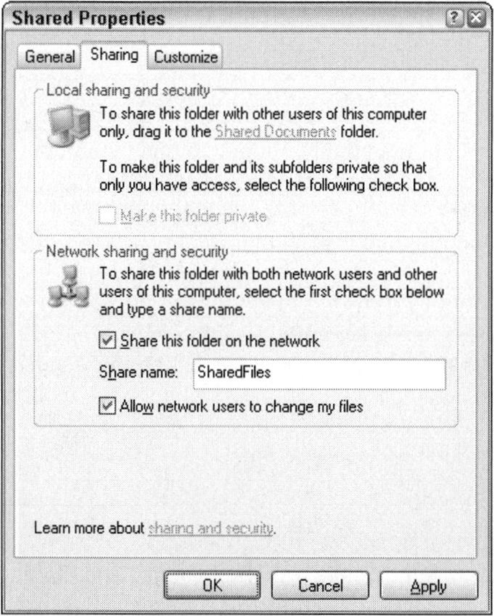

Figure 15-4: Configuring shared folder settings.

Note

To access a shared folder that has been hidden, click Start → Run and then type `\\computername\sharefoldername` where computername and sharedfolder names are the names of the computer where the shared folder resides, and the name of the shared folder respectively. After the correct path has been entered, click OK to connect to the shared folder. This method can actually be used to connect to any shared folder — not just those that have been hidden with the $ symbol.

4. Optionally, check (or uncheck) the Allow network users to change my files checkbox. When this option is checked, network users are able to make changes to files stored within the shared folder.

5. Click OK to implement and save your changes. When shared, a folder's icon changes to include a small hand graphic as shown in Figure 15-5.

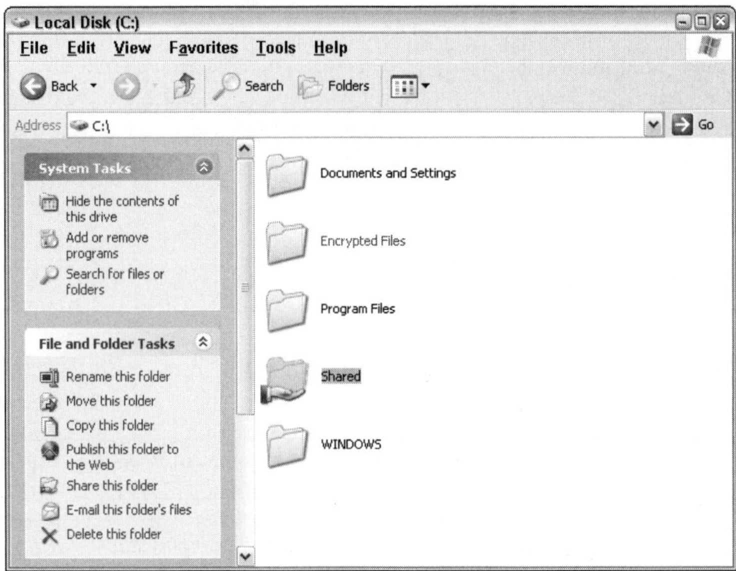

Figure 15-5: Shared folders are identified by an icon that includes a small "serving" hand.

Note

You cannot share all folders on a Windows XP system. Specifically, the Documents and Settings, All Programs, and WINDOWS folders cannot be shared, nor can folders in other user's profiles—for example, another user's My Documents folder.

When Simple File Sharing is enabled, you only have limited control over the security of a shared folder. Specifically, if you check the Allow network users to change my files checkbox on the Sharing and Security tab, all users effectively have complete control over the shared folder, including the ability to add, modify, or delete files. If this option is unchecked, network users can open and read files stored in the shared folder, but not change or delete these files.

Connecting to Shared Folders

After a folder is shared, other users can connect to it from their computers, over the network. While a variety of different methods can be used to connect to a shared folder, two of the most common are by browsing for the folder using My Network Places, or by what is known as "mapping a network drive." When a user opts to connect to a shared folder by mapping a network drive, they assign the shared folder a drive letter (such as X:) and then can connect to the folder by browsing to Drive X: in My Computer.

For a user sitting at another computer to be able to connect to a shared folder successfully, some additional configuration is almost always necessary. The first option is to enable the Guest user account on the computer hosting the shared folder. This allows all network users to connect to the shared folder as Guest, and access its contents without issue. For a security standpoint, however, enabling the Guest account is never a good idea.

A better way to ensure that network users can gain access to a shared folder is to set up Limited user accounts for them on the computer where the shared folder resides. For example, if you want a user named Mark to be able to access the shared folder over the network, create a user account named Mark on the computer where the shared folder resides, and assign the account a password; then, when Mark attempts to access the shared folder, he can provide his username and password when prompted. Alternatively, create a user account for Mark that uses the same username and password combination that he uses on his local computer. If you go this route, Mark is never prompted for additional information when connecting to the shared folder — Windows XP notes that the username and password combination are consistent, and allows the connection.

To connect to a shared folder using My Network Places, complete the following steps:

1. Click Start → My Network Places.
2. Under Network Tasks, click View Workgroup Computers.
3. Double-click your Workgroup's name.
4. Double-click the name of the computer on which the shared folder resides. A list of all folders shared from that computer appears, as shown in the following figure.

Continued

Connecting to Shared Folders (Continued)

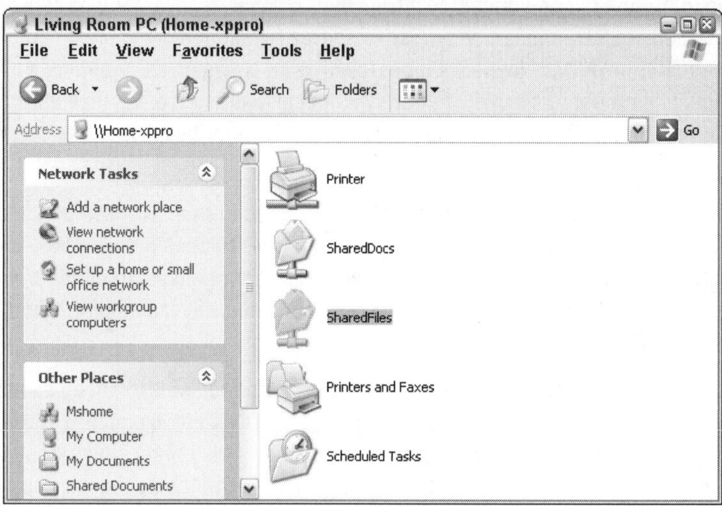

Reviewing shared folders on a computer named Home-xppro.

5. Double-click the shared folder you want to access to view its contents and then interact with files as you would with other tools like My Computer.

To map a drive letter to a shared folder and then access this drive using My Computer, complete the following steps:

1. Click Start → My Computer → Tools → Map Network Drive.
2. In the Map Network Drive window (as shown in the following figure), select a drive letter from the Drive drop-down list and then click the Browse button. Browse to the shared folder you want to map the drive letter to and then click OK. If you want the mapped drive to be accessible every time you log on to Windows XP, ensure that the Reconnect at logon box is checked and then click Finish.

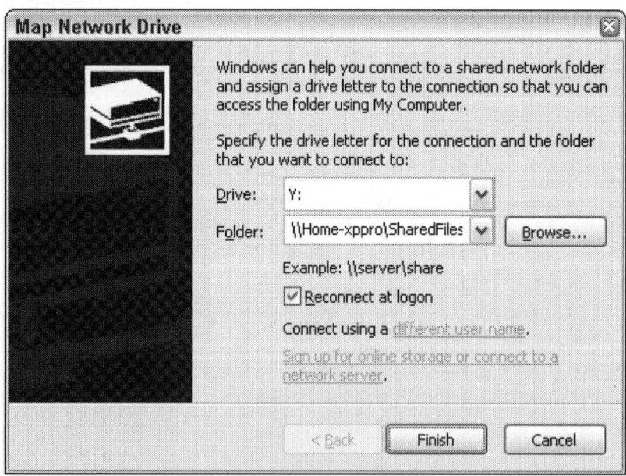

Mapping a drive letter to a shared folder.

3. The mapped drive now appears in the My Computer window, as shown in the following figure. You can now interact with the shared folder as you would any other local drive.

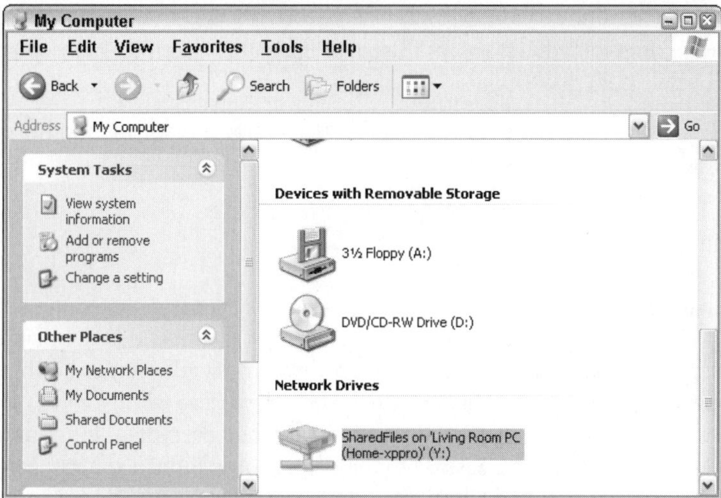

Accessing a mapped network drive in My Computer.

Securing Shared Folders

When you share a folder on a Windows XP system without any Service Packs installed, the shared folder permissions that are assigned to the folder couldn't be less restrictive—everyone who connects to the folder over the network is literally granted full control over the entire folder contents. Although this setting provides the greatest degree of flexibility for all network users (who can then add, modify, and delete items within the folder at will), it also presents a substantial security risk—all users (including guests) can connect to the folder and do with its contents as they please. Microsoft addressed this potential issue when Service Pack 1 was released, changing the default shared folder setting to only allow network users to open and read files stored in shared folders.

Unfortunately, when Simple File Sharing is enabled, you really have only two configurable security options for shared folders—either you grant all network users the ability to do as they please within the folder, or limit them to opening and reading files only. Simple File Sharing was literally designed with simplicity in mind, rather than customizable security.

On a Windows XP Professional system, Simple File Sharing can be disabled in favor of using what are sometimes referred to as standard shared folder permissions. The standard shared folder permissions available on a Windows XP system when Simple File Sharing is disabled include:

- **Read.** The Read permission allows network users to open and read files, but not modify their contents or delete them outright.
- **Change.** The Change permission allows network users to open, read, and modify existing files, as well as add or delete files within the folder.
- **Full Control.** The Full Control permission allows network users to perform any function on items within the shared folder.

When Simple File Sharing is disabled, the default permission assigned to a shared folder is Allow Read to the Everyone group. The permissions that you should assign to a shared folder depend upon how you want that folder to be used. For example, if you only want network users to be able to open and read (but not change) the contents of a folder, assign the Allow Read permission to the Users group (which includes only users with valid user accounts, rather than everyone). If users should be allowed to change files, grant the Change permission to the Users group. From a security perspective, you're better off granting permissions to the Users group rather than Everyone. Everyone is literally anyone that may be able to connect to the shared folder, including hackers, other wireless users within range, and so forth.

Note

Shared folder permissions apply only to users who connect to the folder over the network.

Follow these steps to disable Simple File Sharing and configure shared folder security settings on a Windows XP Professional system:

1. Click Start → My Computer → Tools → Folder Options → View.
2. In the Advanced settings section, uncheck Use Simple File Sharing (Recommended), as shown in Figure 15-6. When Simple File Sharing is disabled, you can configure additional shared folder security settings via the Sharing tab in the properties of a folder. Click OK.

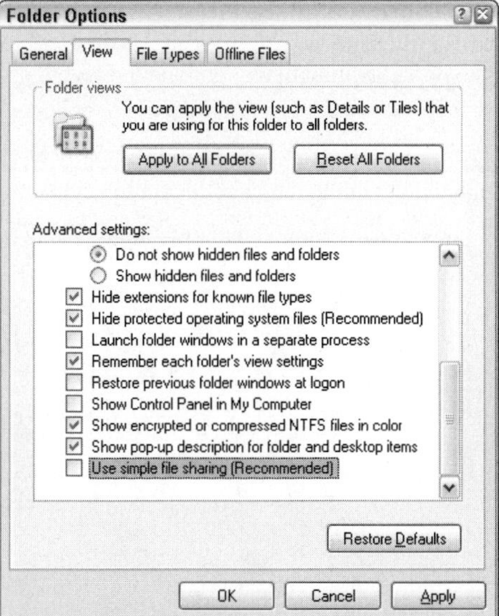

Figure 15-6: Disable Simple File Sharing on Windows XP Professional systems to configure standard permissions.

3. Browse to the shared folder for which you want to configure security settings. Right-click this folder, and then click Sharing and Security. This opens the folder's Properties window to the Sharing tab, as shown in Figure 15-7.

Figure 15-7: The Sharing tab when Simple File Sharing is disabled.

4. Click the Permissions button. This opens the shared folder's Permissions window, as shown in Figure 15-8. By default, the Everyone group is granted the Allow Read shared folder permission (assuming that SP1 or higher is installed).

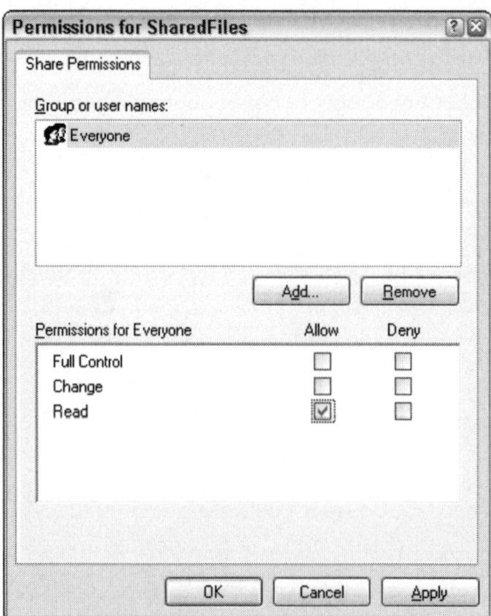

Figure 15-8: The Everyone group is granted Allow Read access to a shared folder by default when SP1 or higher is installed.

5. If necessary, add or remove users or groups on this list using the Add and Remove buttons. To configure shared folder security settings, click the name of the user or group and then check or uncheck the required permissions in the Allow or Deny columns. Click OK to close the folder's Permissions window and then click OK again to implement your shared folder permissions.

In most cases the default shared folder permission (Allow Read to the Everyone group) works just fine, but only if user don't need to change files stored in the shared folder. (If they do, Allow Change is a better option.) In cases where a folder is configured with both shared folder and NTFS permissions (as explored in Chapter 14), the more restrictive of the permissions apply to network users. In other words, if the NTFS permissions on a folder are set to Allow Read for a user, and the shared folder permissions that apply to the same user is Allow Full Control, the user's effective permission when accessing the folder over the network would be the more restriction option — Allow Read.

Tip

You cannot disable Simple File Sharing on Windows XP Home systems, as you originally learned in Chapter 14. However, if you're running Windows XP Home and want to access shared folder (or even printer) permissions, restart your system in Safe Mode. Simple File Sharing is not enabled in Safe Mode, giving you access to all of Windows XP's "standard" permission features. After you restart normally, Simple File Sharing is again enabled, but the permissions assigned from Safe Mode still apply.

Additionally, shared folder permissions "combine" in a manner similar to NTFS permissions. For example, if a user account is granted the Allow Read shared folder permission, and that user is also a member of the Administrators group that has been granted the Allow Full Control permission, the user's effective shared folder permission would be Allow Full Control. The only exception to this rule is when permissions are explicitly denied—a denied permission always takes precedence over an allowed permission.

Cross-Reference

Ensuring that shared folders are properly secured is especially important on wireless networks. If your wireless network isn't properly secured, other wireless users within range of your network can connect to it, and potentially gain access to your shared folders and printers. You learn more about wireless networks and some of their associated security risks in Chapter 16.

Through the Firewall

If your Windows XP system is protected by Windows Firewall, users on your network should be able to connect to shared folders and printers without issue. Windows Firewall automatically enables an exception (as shown in the following figure) for File and Printer Sharing connections coming from users on the local network, but blocks these same types of connections from Internet users.

Continued

Through the Firewall (Continued)

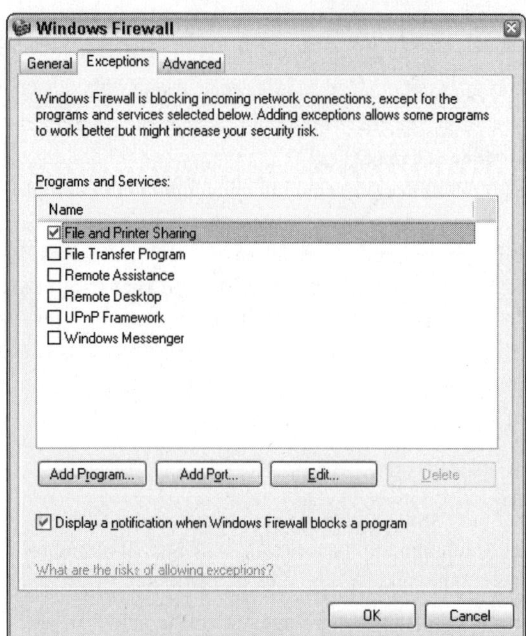

Enabling an exception for File and Printer Sharing in Windows Firewall.

If you're running a third-party firewall program and find that other users on your network cannot connect to your shared folders and printers, the firewall's configuration is almost always the issue. To configure these firewalls to allow incoming File and Printer Sharing connections, ensure that the service is configured to allow incoming connections in the Trusted zone, as illustrated for Kerio Personal Firewall in the following figure.

Configuring Kerio Personal Firewall to allow incoming File and Printer Sharing connections from computers in the trusted zone.

In some cases, it may be necessary for you to manually open the ports used by File and Printer Sharing for other users on your network to connect to shared folders and printers correctly. The ports that need to be opened for this purpose include TCP 139, TCP 445, UDP 137, and UDP 138. For more details on configuring firewall settings, refer to Chapter 6.

Sharing Printers

Similar to folders, printers can also be shared over a network. When shared, other users on the network can connect to the printer and send their print job to it, in much the same way they would with a printer directly connected to their local PC. Sharing printers makes a great deal of sense on networks that have many client computers. Rather than installing a dedicated printer on each and every PC (or moving files to a computer with a printer using a floppy disk or CD), a single shared printer can be used by all network users, helping to reduce costs significantly. Any printer connected to a Windows XP system (or directly to the network, as is the case with printers that include their own network adapter card) can be shared to allow multi-user network access.

Follow these steps to share an existing installed printer:

1. Click Start → Control Panel.
2. Double-click Printers and Faxes. A list of all installed printers and fax devices appears, as shown in Figure 15-9.

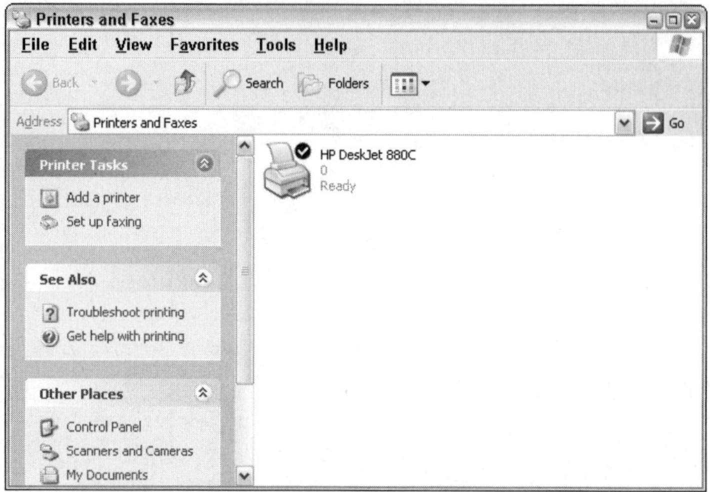

Figure 15-9: The Printers and Faxes applet in Control Panel.

3. Right-click the printer you want to share, and click Sharing.
4. On the Sharing tab, click Share this printer. Enter a name that will be used to identify this printer on your network, as shown in Figure 15-10. Click OK.

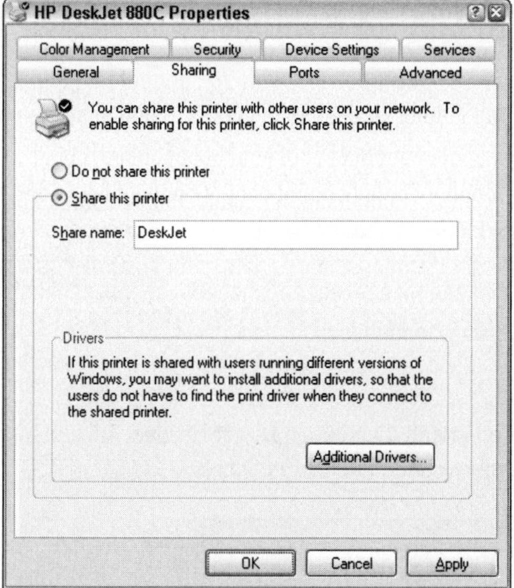

Figure 15-10: Sharing a printer.

5. When shared, the icon for the printer changes to include a small hand as shown in Figure 15-11.

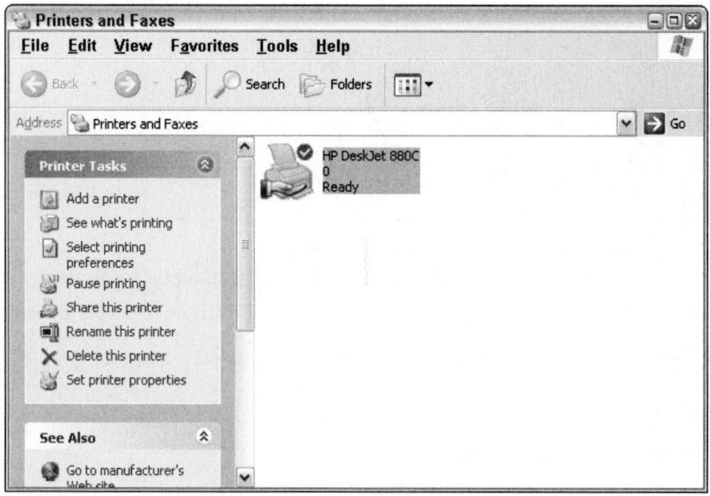

Figure 15-11: The "serving" hand icon designates a shared printer.

Connecting to Shared Printers

Once a printer is shared, network users who want to print to it first need to connect to it to properly install the device's drivers. Windows XP provides a number of different ways to find and connect to shared printers, but two of the most common methods used are browsing for the printer in My Network Places or using the Add Printer Wizard.

To connect to a shared printer using My Network Places, complete the following steps:

1. Click Start→My Network Places.
2. Under Network Tasks, click View Workgroup Computers.
3. Double-click your Workgroup's name.
4. Double-click the name of the computer on which the shared printer resides. A list of all printers shared from that computer appears, as shown in the following figure.

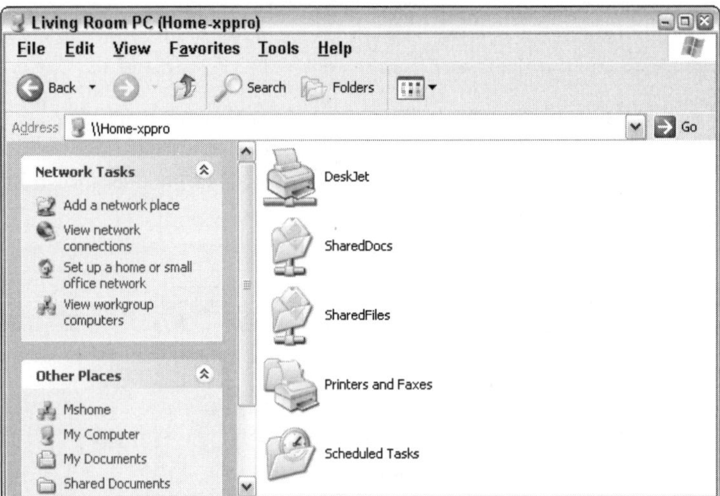

5. Right-click the shared printer you want to install and then click Connect. The shared printer now appears in Printers and Faxes, similar to all other installed printers.

To install a shared printer using the Add Printer Wizard, complete the following steps:

1. Click Start→Printers and Faxes.
2. In the Printer Tasks section, click Add a printer.
3. At the Add Printer Wizard Welcome screen, click Next.
4. At the Local or Network Printer screen, click A network printer or a printer attached to another computer. Click Next.
5. At the Specify a printer screen, click Connect to this printer (as shown in the following figure) and then click Next.

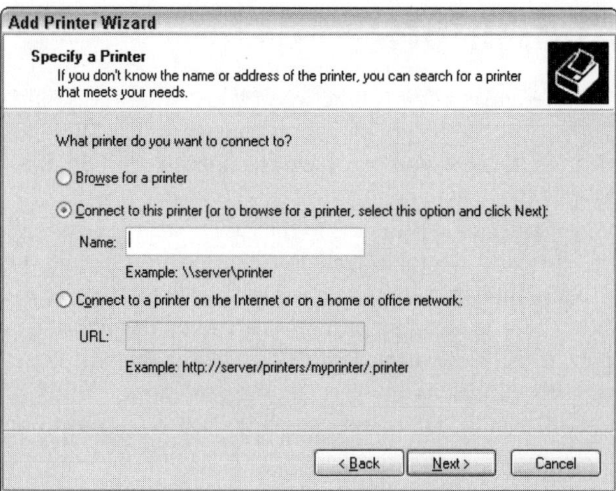

6. At the Browse for printers screen, browse to the shared printer on your network, click on it, and click Next.
7. At the Default Printer screen, specify whether this printer should be the default printer for your computer, click Next, and click Finish.

After the shared printer is installed, you can send a print job to it from the Print dialog box in any program, as shown in the following figure.

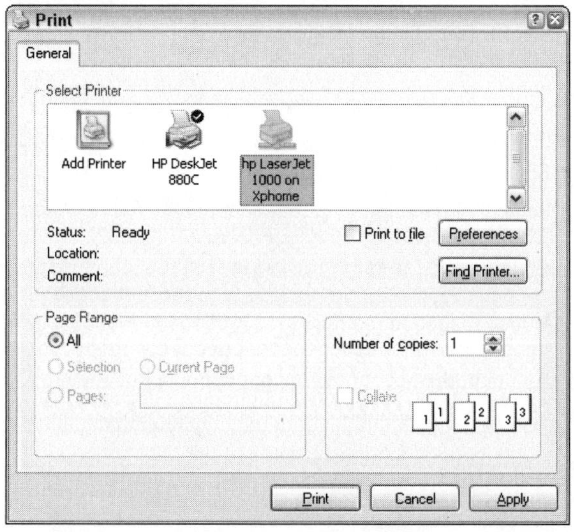

Securing Shared Printers

It may not really seem necessary, but there may come a time when you'll want the ability to better secure a shared printer. By default, any user can print to any printer shared from a Windows XP system. Although this option is suitable in most cases, you may have an expensive printer that you want to control access to for some or all network users.

Perhaps the best example of needing to secure a printer is in the case of an expensive colour laser or ink jet model. The "consumables" (ink or toner cartridges) for these printers can be very expensive, and it often only takes printing a few large or color-intensive jobs before refills or new cartridges are required. You probably don't want someone bleeding your new cartridges dry printing their vacation photos if they're not supposed to be using the printer for that purpose. Similarly, some printers are installed for dedicated purposes such as printing invoices, reports, or checks. If this is the case, shared printer permissions can be used to stop others from sending their own jobs to the printer completely.

Beyond simply allowing or denying the ability to print to a given device, printer permissions also allow you to define the level of control that a user should have over a give printer. For example, you could allow some users to print, but not delete or change the order of other users' jobs that may already be in the print queue. Or, you may want a particular user to be able to manage all users' documents, or even change a printer's configuration settings if necessary. Printer permissions make all of these scenarios possible.

Windows XP includes the ability to configure three primary printer permissions. These include:

- **Print.** The Print permission allows users to send print jobs to a printer, and manage their own jobs. For example, a user with the Print permission has the ability to delete a print job that they've sent to the printer in error, if necessary. By default, the Print permission is assigned to the Everyone group.
- **Manage Printers.** The Manage Printers permission gives a user complete control over a given printer. This includes the ability to print to the printer and manage both their own and other user's print jobs. For example, a user with the Manage Printers permission could delete or pause another user's print job, if necessary. Additionally, users with the Manage Printers permission can change any and all of a printer's configuration settings. By default, Computer administrator users have the Manage Printers permission for all installed printers.
- **Manage Documents.** The Manage Documents permission gives a user the ability to print to a printer, as well as manage print jobs belonging to other users. Effectively, this permission gives the user more power than the Print permission, but does not grant the ability to change printer settings.

Note

The default printer permission (Allow Print for the Everyone group) makes it possible for literally anyone who can connect to a shared printer to send print jobs to it. This includes hackers and (if applicable) wireless

users within range of your network. Although not terribly common, it's not unheard of for an outside user to connect to a printer and send huge print jobs to the device, only because they can. For a better degree of security over your printers, consider assigning the Allow Print permission to individual user accounts on your network and granting the Allow Manage Printers permission to the Administrators group only.

Follow these steps to configure printer security settings on a Windows XP Professional system:

1. Click Start → My Computer → Tools → Folder Options → View.
2. In the Advanced settings section, uncheck Use Simple File Sharing (Recommended). When Simple File Sharing is disabled, you can configure printer security settings via the Security tab in the properties of a printer. This tab is not available with Simple File Sharing enabled. Click OK.
3. Click Start → Control Panel → Printers and Faxes.
4. Right-click a printer and then click Properties.
5. Click the Security tab.
6. Click Administrators in the Groups or user names list to view the printer permissions assigned to members of the Administrators group, as shown in Figure 15-12.

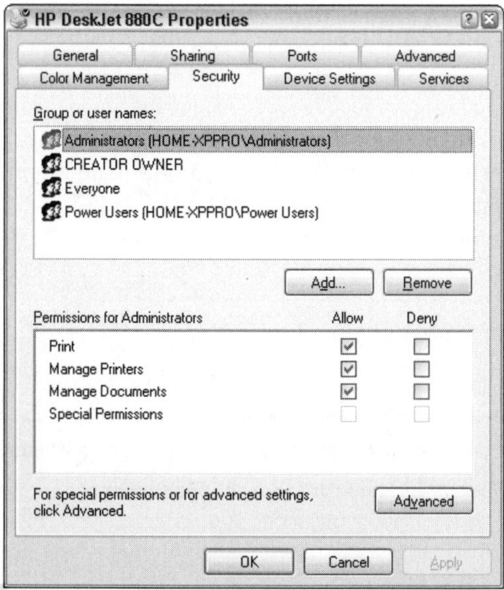

Figure 15-12: You have greater control over printer security settings when Simple File Sharing is disabled.

7. Click Everyone in the Groups or user names list to view the printer permissions assigned to all other users (including Guests) as shown in Figure 15-13. The Everyone group has only the Allow Print permission assigned by default.

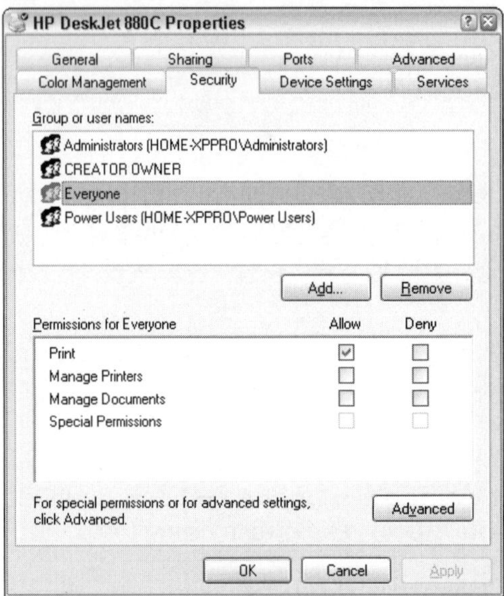

Figure 15-13: Printer permissions assigned to the Everyone group.

8. If necessary, add or remove users or groups on this list using the Add and Remove buttons. To configure printer security settings, click the name of the user or group and then check or uncheck the required permissions in the Allow or Deny columns. Click OK to close the printer's Properties window and implement your new permissions.

Tip

The Security tab is not accessible in the properties of a printer on a Windows XP Home system due to the mandatory use of Simple File Sharing. If necessary, you can configure printer permissions on a Windows XP Home system by restarting your computer in Safe Mode, where Simple File Sharing is disabled.

Printer permissions "combine" in much the same way as shared folder permissions. For example, if a user is granted the Allow Print permission, but is also a member of a group granted the Allow Manage Printers permission, that user's effective permission would be Allow Manage Printers. Similarly, denied printer permissions always take precedence over any allowed permissions.

Summary

Sharing resources such as folders and printers on a network is one of the primary reasons for implementing a network in the first place; however, it's important to ensure that shared resources are properly secured in a manner that meets your needs and requirements. Failing to properly implement security settings puts your shared resources at risk, and may lead to them being accidentally deleted, modified, or otherwise misused. Keep the following points in mind when securing shared folders and printers:

- Share folders and printers that you want other network users to be able to access.
- Configure shared folder and printer security settings such that users only have the level of access to the resource that they actually require.
- Never give any user a greater degree of access to a shared resource than they require. For example, if users should only be able to open and read files in a shared folder, grant them the Allow Read permission, rather than Allow Full Control.
- If you want to stop all users from accessing a particular resource that is currently shared, disable it sharing setting.

Chapter 16

Securing Windows XP on Wireless Networks

The wireless network was a blessing bestowed upon home and small office users thinking about installing a network. Gone are the days where running unsightly blue cables across floors, through walls, and into an overflowing closet was the only option for computer users with a penchant for sharing. Today, wireless networking makes it possible to share everything from printers to Internet access over nothing more than thin air.

The latest and greatest wireless technologies make setting up a network easier than ever before, but this path is fraught with peril and security risks. Where wired network users seldom worried about anything more than having a good firewall in place to protect their Internet connection, wireless networks face threats from anyone within range of their signals. Compounding the issue is the fact that in their default configuration, wireless network devices offer no real security — any suitably equipped user within range can connect to the network and effectively do as they please.

With this in mind, taking the time to properly secure a wireless network and the Windows XP systems connecting to it is absolutely critical. In this chapter you learn about wireless networking support in Windows XP, along with the risks associated with leaving a wireless network unsecured. Most importantly, you learn about the specific methods and wireless networking features that can be used to secure wireless devices, up to and including using strong encryption to protect all wireless communications on your network.

Windows XP and Wireless Networking

Windows XP is the first Microsoft operating system to include built-in support for wireless networking. When equipped with a wireless network adapter card, a Windows XP system typically needs no additional client software installed to connect to wireless networks. As long as the wireless network cards supports it, a Windows XP feature known as Wireless Zero Configuration handles all the details of discovering and connecting to available wireless networks within range.

The name associated with this feature is somewhat misleading. Windows XP automatically detects and prompts you to connect to unsecured wireless networks within range; however, in cases where a wireless network is protected by advanced security features such as encryption, at least a small amount of configuration is always required.

Wireless A-B-G's

Wireless devices come in three main "flavors"—802.11a, 802.11b, and 802.11g. Based on standards developed by the Institute of Electronics and Electrical Engineers (IEEE) and equipment manufactured by a variety of different companies, all wireless networking devices are not created equal. The letter that trails the 802.11 designation serves an important role in describing how a given wireless device communicates and interoperates with other wireless equipment:

- 802.11a. These devices use the 5GHz frequency range to communicate at speeds up to 54Mbps but cannot interoperate with 802.11b or 802.11g equipment.
- 802.11b. The original wireless networking standard, these devices use the 2.4GHz frequency range to communicate at speeds up to 11Mbps and can interoperate with newer 802.11g equipment.
- 802.11g. These devices also use the 2.4GHz frequency range to communicate at speeds up to 54Mbps and can interoperate with older 802.11b equipment.

802.11b and 802.11g wireless networking devices are much more popular than their 802.11a counterparts and often considerably less expensive; however, these devices work in the same frequency range as a number of other wireless consumer electronics products (including cordless phones and speakers), making them more prone to interference issues.

Some manufacturers produce multimode wireless networking equipment that adheres to all three 802.11 wireless standards, a great option for users who move between different wireless networks frequently. For most home and small office users, however, choosing 802.11g devices represents the best long-term value in terms of speed, interoperability, and price.

Although Wireless Zero Configuration makes it easier to detect and connect to wireless networks, it's almost equal parts friend and foe. If you're configuring your own wireless network, you'll be happy when Windows XP automatically discovers it. You probably won't be quite as thrilled, however, when your neighbor's Windows XP system detects your wireless access point, allowing him to connect to your network, root through your shared files, and "borrow" on your high-speed Internet connection.

Although wireless networks implement little in the way of security or privacy features by default, all is not lost. A wireless network that includes Windows XP systems can be fully secured to a level that rivals a traditional wired network. To properly secure a wireless network, however, you need to be familiar with the following:

- How Windows XP discovers and attempts to connect to wireless networks
- Windows XP's wireless tools and configuration settings
- The security risks associated with leaving wireless networks unsecured
- How security settings are configured on wireless access points and Windows XP wireless clients

The follow sections outline Windows XP's wireless networking processes and tools (as well as the security risks associated with unsecured wireless networks) in more detail. The techniques and steps necessary to secure wireless access points and their communications with Windows XP systems are explored later in this chapter.

Windows XP wireless settings

Windows XP's wireless tools and configuration settings are effectively hidden from view until you install a wireless network adapter card in your computer. After your wireless network card is detected and installed, an icon for it is added to Network Connections in Control Panel, and the Wireless Zero Configuration service gets down to the business of scanning for wireless networks.

NOTIFICATIONS

Assuming that your wireless network card is installed correctly and that your wireless access point is powered on, Windows XP almost instantly displays a notification balloon in your system tray stating that one or more wireless network have been detected (see Figure 16-1).

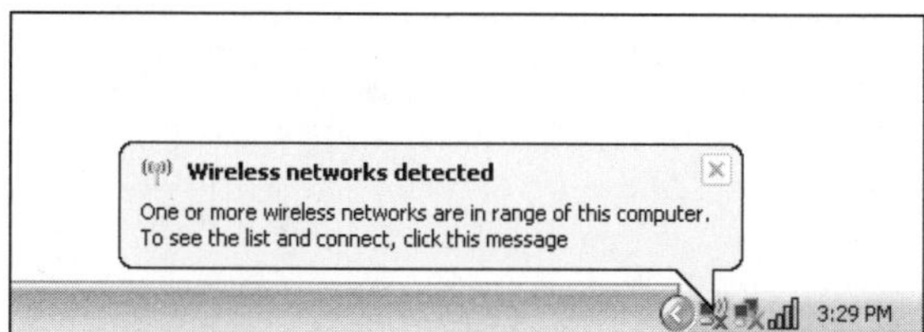

Figure 16-1: Notification about detected wireless networks.

When you click this message, all available wireless networks within range are displayed. Depending on your proximity to other wireless networks, it's possible that more than one wireless network will appear in the window shown in Figure 16-2.

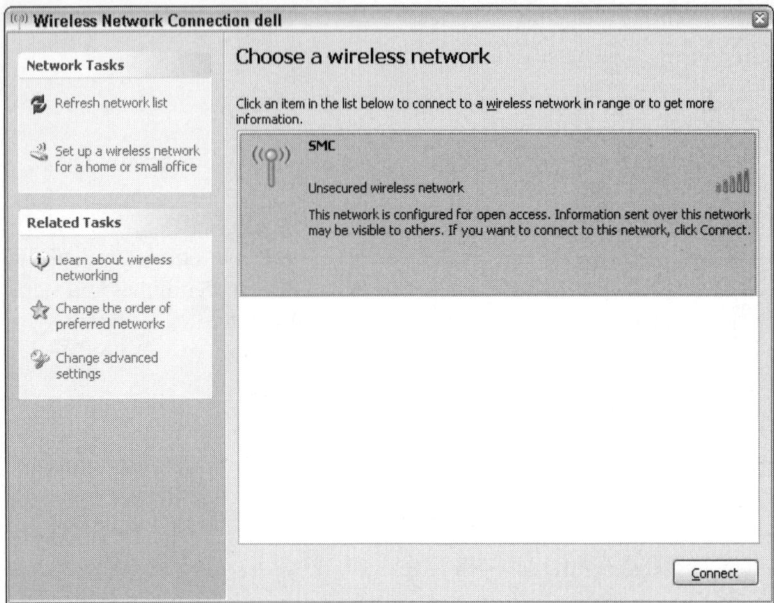

Figure 16-2: The Choose a wireless network window.

To connect to your wireless network, select the appropriate network name from this screen and then click Connect. When prompted with the message stating that this in an unsecured network, click Connect Anyway. If you're unsure of the default name of your wireless network, check the documentation supplied with your access point.

As part of the default connection process, Windows XP acquires an IP address from your access point and then displays the Connected status message, as shown in Figure 16-3.

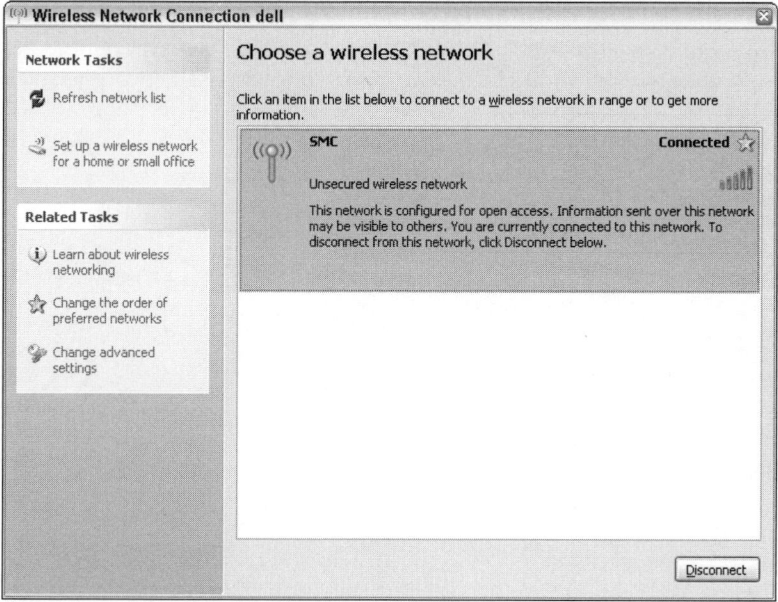

Figure 16-3: A connected wireless network.

After you connect to this first wireless network successfully, Windows XP adds it to the top of its "preferred networks" list and attempts to connect to it automatically anytime you're within range.

Tip

Windows XP systems with a wireless network card installed include a wireless network status icon in the system tray. If you hover your mouse over this icon, details about your network connection (or lack thereof) are displayed. If you right-click the icon, a menu appears that includes handy shortcuts to tools such as Network Connections and the Choose a wireless network window.

WIRELESS NETWORK CONNECTION PROPERTIES

The majority of Windows XP's wireless network settings are configured using Network Connections in the Control Panel. To view these setting, right-click the icon for your wireless network adapter card and then select Properties→Wireless Networks, as shown in Figure 16-4.

Figure 16-4: The Wireless Networks tab in the Properties of a wireless network card.

The Wireless Network tab includes the following settings:

- Use Windows to configure my wireless network settings. When this box is checked, Wireless Zero Configuration is being used to configure your wireless network card. When unchecked, you must use the wireless client utility provided with your wireless network card to configure its settings.
- Available networks. Clicking the View Wireless Networks button opens the Choose a wireless network window.
- Preferred networks. This section lists your preferred wireless networks, in order. Every wireless network that you connect to is automatically added to this list. The Add and Remove buttons allow you to manually specify which networks should be included in this list; the Move Up and Move Down button are used to configure the order in which connections should be attempted. Clicking the Properties button allows you to configure additional settings for a network, such as wireless encryption methods and key values.

The Preferred networks section also includes the Advanced button. Click this button to open the Advanced window, as shown in Figure 16-5.

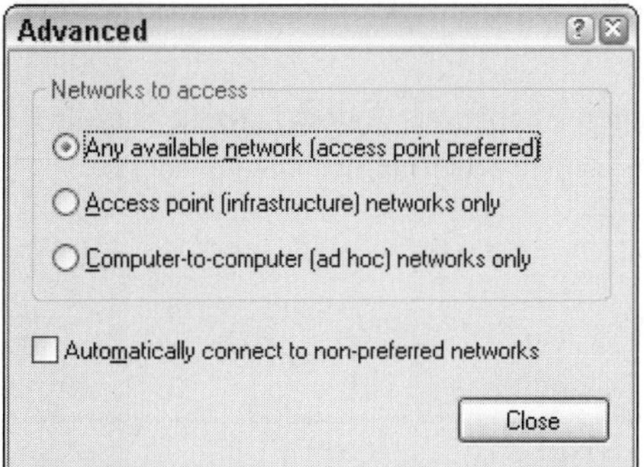

Figure 16-5: Configuring advanced network settings.

The Networks to access section of this window offers three choices:

- Any available network (access point preferred). When this option is selected, Windows XP will attempt to connect to any available network on your Preferred networks list, giving precedence to wireless networks that include an access point.
- Access point (infrastructure) networks only. When this option is selected, Windows XP attempts to connect only to available networks on your Preferred network list that include an access point.
- Computer-to-computer (ad-hoc) networks only. When this option is selected, Windows XP attempts to connect only to wireless networks on your Preferred network list that do not include an access point.

Note

A wireless network that does not include an access point is known as a "computer-to-computer" or "ad-hoc" network. Ad-hoc networks make wireless networking more flexible, in that they allow you to create a network between two or more computers without the need for an access point acting as an intermediary. If your wireless network includes an access point and is not moved between networks regularly, consider configuring the Access point (infrastructure) networks only option from the Preferred networks Advanced settings window. This option stops your computer from forming or attempting to connect to ad-hoc networks.

The Advanced window also includes a setting called Automatically connect to non-preferred networks. If you select this option, Windows XP automatically attempts to connect to any wireless network within range, even if it is not on your list of preferred networks. As a wireless security best practice, do not enable this setting. If you do, there's a good chance that you could find yourself connected to another user's wireless network without their permission.

Configuration settings associated with specific wireless networks are explored later in this chapter.

Tip

If you want to stop Windows XP from automatically connecting to a particular wireless network, click its name in the Preferred networks list and then click Properties. On the Connection tab, uncheck Connect when this network is in range.

Which Wireless Tool?

Although it's rare with newer equipment, it is possible that your wireless network card will not support Wireless Zero Configuration. In such a case, Windows XP will not be able to detect and configure your wireless network card automatically, so you need to install the client software provided by the card's manufacturer.

Even if Windows XP supports your wireless network card, installing the manufacturer's client software program is not a bad idea. These programs are more than just basic wireless network configuration tools, often including advanced settings and features for your particular make and model. For example, the Dell Wireless WLAN Card Utility shown in the following figure includes card diagnostic programs, a wireless monitoring tool, detailed signal strength information, and more.

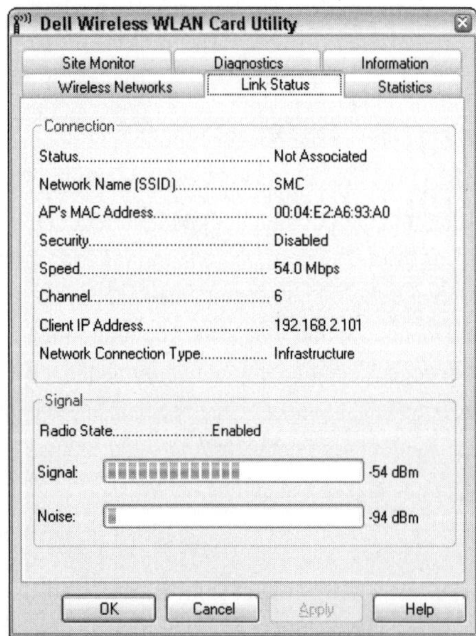

The Dell Wireless WLAN Card Utility included with Dell wireless network cards.

Windows XP allows the Wireless Zero Configuration service and dedicated wireless client programs to peacefully co-exist in most cases; however, you can only configure your wireless network settings using one service or the other. For example, if the Use Windows to configure my wireless network settings option is enabled, the Wireless Networks tab in the properties of your wireless network connection is the active configuration tool. If you uncheck this option, control over wireless network settings is passed on to the network card's client software program.

If you haven't installed the software included with your wireless network card, consider doing so. Even if you don't use it to configure your wireless network settings, you'll likely gain access to a whole slew of useful wireless tools and utilities.

Tip

If your Windows XP system has a wireless network card installed that you're not using, disable it as a security precaution. To do this, open Control Panel→Network Connections, right-click your wireless network card, and click Disable.

Security risks on wireless networks

In the same way that you should never leave any computer or network connected to the Internet without the protection of a firewall, you should never any wireless network improperly secured. Although there's no question that the Internet—and its millions of users who can potentially connect to any computer anywhere worldwide—presents a bigger security risk overall, it's equally important to think "locally." When a wireless user within range connects to your unsecured network, the firewall protecting your network has no say in the matter; the front door may be locked, but the back door is wide open.

Of course, you won't have an entire Internet's worth of users within physical range of your wireless network. In fact, there may only be one or two other wireless users close enough to connect. However, the fact that these users can potentially gain access to your private network by doing nothing more than clicking a button marked Connect presents a very real risk.

Tip

In reality, experienced users and hackers do not typically rely on the built-in wireless networking capabilities of Windows XP to discover wireless networks within range. More commonly, they employ dedicated wireless network discovery tools that can track, map, and save details about networks as they're encountered. One great example of such a tool is Network Stumbler, available from `www.netstumbler.com`. In addition to being the network discovery tool of choice for those seeking out wireless networks, Network Stumbler is an excellent auditing tool that can help you to determine what information your wireless network exposes under different security configurations.

Users within range who can connect to your unsecured wireless network can potentially:

- Use or hijack your high-speed Internet connection
- Gain access to your personal files and other resources your private network
- Make changes to the configuration of your wireless access point and its security settings
- Capture all of your wireless network traffic and track your communications

Not all users within range of your network are unscrupulous enough to connect to it without your permission, but temptation and curiosity get the best of a many people. So, rather than gamble that others aren't using your wireless network, take the time to be sure they're not. After implementing the necessary security settings on your access point and wireless clients, other users within range should never be able to connect to your network.

War Driving

It may sound very much like spy-versus-spy, but in well-populated areas a pastime known as "war driving" has become popular amongst those with a passion for wireless networking. With a name derived from an old-school hacking technique known as "war dialing" — where hackers would use software and modems to automatically dial phone numbers in the hope that a computer would answer on the other end — war driving (or walking for that matter) is only becoming more popular.

A war driver is a wireless user who roams around, looking for wireless networks to which to connect. In some cases, the user is looking for a high-speed Internet connection to temporarily "borrow"; in others, their motives are more malicious, aimed at accessing files and information stored on the network's computers. It's been estimated that more than half of all wireless networks are improperly secured, so there's no shortage of networks for these users to stumble upon and through.

Unfortunately, the potential security issues associated with techniques such as war driving don't end with the user who just happens upon your network. Quite to the contrary, many of the people engaged in this "hobby" are well equipped, using laptops, external antennas, and even portable GPS (Global Positioning System) devices to map the precise locations of unsecured wireless networks — information that often ends up being posted (complete with detailed maps) on the Internet.

This isn't to say that everyone engaged in war driving has bad intentions; however, leaving any wireless network improperly secured poses real risks, of which access by war drivers is just another to consider. For more information on the wacky world of war driving, check out `www.wardriving.com`.

Securing Wireless Access Points

Similar to most computing devices, wireless access points are pre-configured with factory default settings. Designed in a plug-and-play fashion, you can usually take a brand new access point out of its box, plug everything in, and have your wireless network up and running in minutes.

Although this makes it exceptionally easy for any user to set up a wireless network, leaving default access point settings intact represents a serious security risk. At issue is the fact that wireless access points broadcast their network name automatically, making themselves visible to all wireless users within range. Unfortunately, these default network names are almost always the same and identify the access point's manufacturer. Armed with this information, any user can easily obtain the device's default configuration settings online, including its administrative password.

As a best practice, always change the following settings on a wireless access point:

- The password used to access the administrative interface
- The wireless network name

The configuration of these settings is explained in more detail in the following sections.

Note

Wireless access points are manufactured by a variety of companies, each with their own lineup of different makes and models. Most of these devices include similar features and capabilities, but the steps used to configure them can vary from one model to another. For precise details on configuring the security settings outlined in this chapter on your wireless access point, consult its user manual, Help file, or manufacturer's Web site.

Changing the default administrator access password

Almost all wireless access points include an integrated Web-based administrative interface for the purpose of making configuration changes. You gain access to this interface by opening your preferred Web browser and entering the access point's management IP address, usually 192.168.1.1 or similar. Assuming that you've entered the address specified for your model, the access point's login screen appears, similar to the one shown in Figure 16-6.

Figure 16-6: The login screen for an access point's administrative interface.

To log in to the access point for the first time, you need to supply the default administrative password assigned to your model and then click the Login button.

Unfortunately, the passwords assigned to access points by default are inherently insecure due to the fact that they're so well documented. For example, the default password associated with some access points is the manufacturer's name; in other cases, it's blank or literally "password." Just about anyone can find the default password associated with an access point in minutes — if not seconds — on the Internet.

Because wireless networks are not secure by default, changing your access point's administrative password is imperative. If you don't change this value, other wireless users within range can connect to and use your wireless network at will, not to mention exercise complete control over the configuration of your access point.

Follow these steps to change the password used to access the administrative interface of your wireless access point:

1. Click Start → Internet Explorer, or open your preferred Web browser.
2. In the Address box, type **192.168.1.1**, or the correct address for your access point make and model. Press Enter.

3. At the logon screen, type the default password specified in your access point's user manual. Click the Login button.

4. After logged in, look for a section marked System or Passwords. On the SMC access point used in this example, passwords are changed from System → Password Settings, as shown in Figure 16-7.

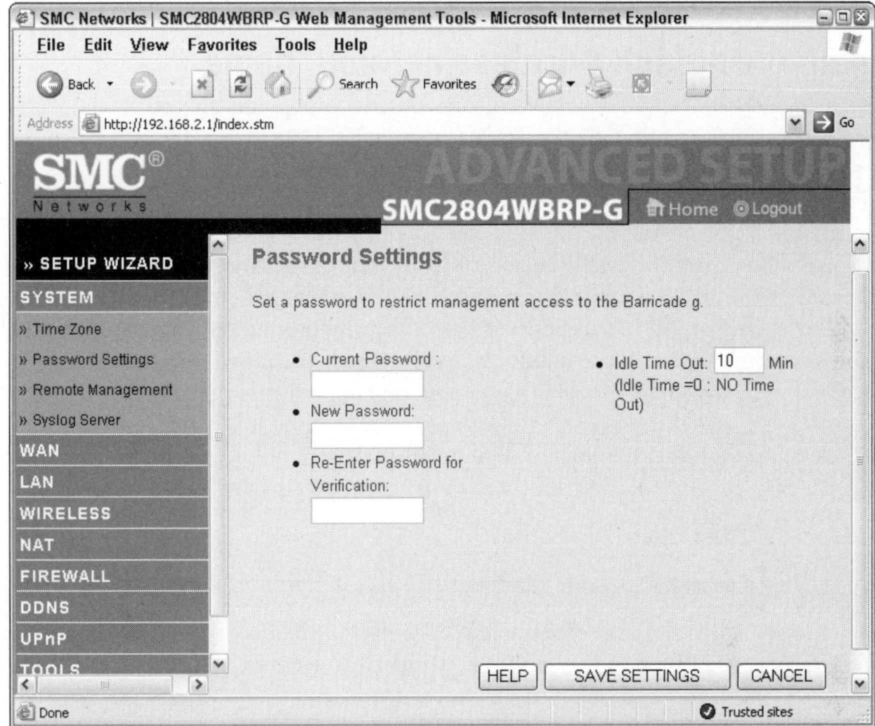

Figure 16-7: The Password Settings configuration screen.

5. Type the access point's current password; then type your new password and confirm it. Be sure to protect the device with a strong password, according to the password best practices outlined in Chapter 2.

6. Some access points include the capability to configure a setting called Idle Time Out. This setting controls how long a logged in user session can remain idle before it is logged off automatically. Configure an appropriate setting (shorter time periods offer better security) and then click Save Settings.

Tip

Although all wireless access points include the capability to change the default administrative password to a new value, some also allow you to change the username used to log on. If your access point includes this capability, change both the username and password to unique values for added security.

Changing the default wireless network name

Along with a default administrative password, all wireless access points are configured with a default wireless network name. Known as a Service Set Identifier (SSID), this name is used to distinguish between wireless networks, and is typically configured with the access point manufacturer's name by default. For example, the default SSID name on a Linksys access point is typically "linksys;" SMC access points uses the SSID "smc."

Access points broadcast their SSID name to allow wireless clients to discover them; however, using the default SSID makes it easy for other users within range to identify the access point's manufacturer, and by extension, its default password. As a security precaution, you should always change the SSID of your wireless network to a unique (and less easily identified) value.

Follow these steps to change the SSID name used on your wireless network:

1. Click Start → Internet Explorer, or open your preferred Web browser.
2. In the Address box, type **192.168.1.1**, or the correct address for your access point make and model. Press Enter.
3. At the logon screen, type your administrative access password. Click the Login button.
4. After logged in, look for a section marked Wireless, Wireless Settings, or similar. On the SMC access point used in this example, the wireless network SSID is changed from Wireless → Channel and SSID, as shown in Figure 16-8.

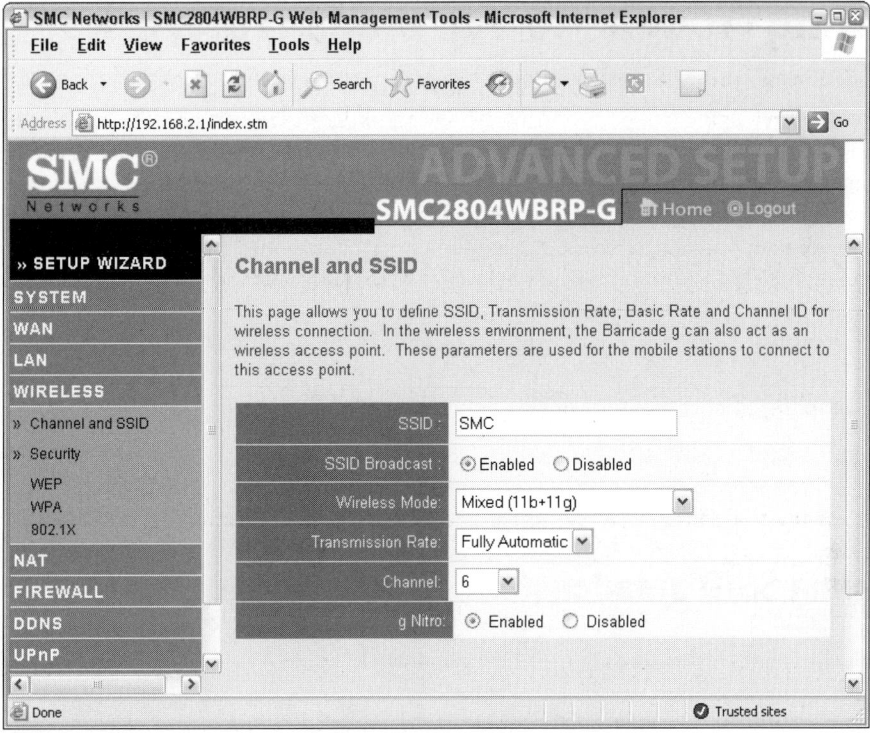

Figure 16-8: Configuring an SSID name for a wireless network.

5. In the box marked SSID (ESSID on some access points), type a unique name to identify your wireless network. As a general rule, don't choose a name that makes it easy to identify you personally, but do choose a word or name that you'll remember. After complete, click Save Settings.

Tip

Many wireless access points include built-in Ethernet switch ports for the purpose of connecting wired computers and other non-wireless components to your network. These models often include the capability to deny administrative interface access to wireless computers. If enabled, this setting provides an additional layer of security by restricting configuration of the access point only to wired computers. If your wireless access point includes this feature, enable it. It requires you to make configuration changes from a wired computer, but it prevents other wireless users from tampering with your access point's settings.

Limiting Access to Wireless Networks

Changing the default SSID name and administrative password for your wireless access point are both important steps in helping to secure your wireless network; however, neither does anything to prevent other wireless users within range from forming an association with your access point, and effectively connecting to your network at will.

In this section, you learn more about two techniques that can be used to limit the exposure and accessibility of your wireless network. Although neither offers complete protection from an experienced hacker, both are an important part of the defense-in-depth approach to network security, and should be implemented on all wireless networks.

These wireless security techniques explored in this section include:

- Disabling broadcast of the wireless network name (SSID)
- Implementing MAC address security

The following sections explore both of these wireless security procedures in more detail.

Disabling SSID broadcast

By default, access points broadcast their SSID name as a way to announce their presence to wireless client systems. These broadcasts are heard by Windows XP and used to display its list of "available" wireless networks within range.

Changing the SSID name is important insomuch as it stops the access point model (and its associated default password) from being easily discovered; however, this does nothing to stop the existence and availability of the network from being broadcast to all wireless clients within its range. If you want to stop your wireless network from being announced in this way, you need to make it disappear.

To complete this magical act, you need to disable the SSID broadcast "feature" on your wireless access point. When SSID broadcast is disabled, Windows XP and other wireless clients systems will not discover your network automatically, nor display it as an "available" wireless network for their users to connect to.

Follow these steps to disable SSID broadcast on your wireless router:

1. Click Start→Internet Explorer, or open your preferred Web browser.
2. In the Address box, type **192.168.1.1**, or the correct address for your access point make and model. Press Enter.
3. At the logon screen, type your administrative access password. Click the Login button.
4. In the administrative interface, look for a section marked Wireless, Wireless Settings, or similar. On the SMC access point used in this example, the SSID broadcast setting is changed from Wireless→Channel and SSID.
5. Select the option to disable SSID broadcast (see Figure 16-9) and then click Save Settings.

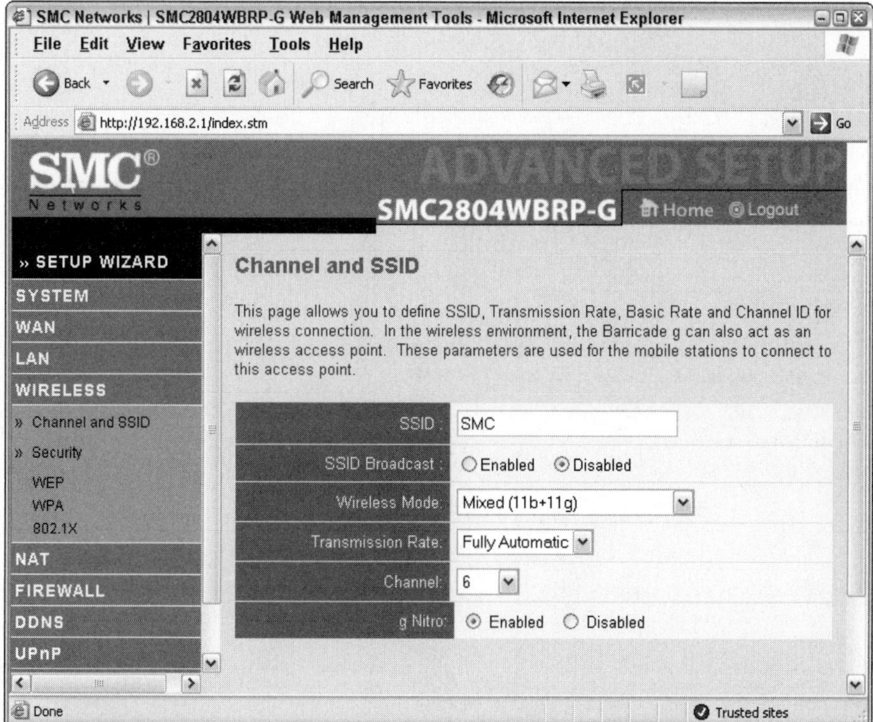

Figure 16-9: Disable SSID broadcast to improve wireless network security.

Disabling SSID broadcast stops your wireless network from being announced as "available" to Windows XP systems and other wireless clients in range of your access point; however, without additional layers of security (such as encryption), users within range can still use a range of wireless network discovery tools to find your network. These tools do not rely on these SSID announcements to find wireless networks. Instead, they listen for wireless network traffic, extracting captured information to determine the details associated with networks within range. Disabling SSID broadcast offers a great way "hide" your network from casual and less experienced wireless users, but it does not make your wireless network completely invisible. Nonetheless, you should always disable SSID broadcast as a wireless security precaution and best practice.

There is a small downside to disabling SSID broadcast, namely that your own wireless client systems no longer discovers your wireless network automatically. Thankfully, it's easy to help your Windows XP systems "find" these hidden wireless networks — all you need to do is manually configure them with the same SSID name used by your network.

Follow these steps to configure Windows XP to connect to a wireless network that has SSID broadcast disabled:

1. Click Start → Control Panel.
2. Double-click Network Connections.

3. Right-click the icon for your wireless network card and then click Properties.
4. Click the Wireless Networks tab.
5. Click the Add button.
6. In the Network name (SSID) box, type the SSID name for your network (see Figure 16-10). Assuming that you aren't configuring any wireless encryption settings for your network at this point, select Disabled from the Data encryption drop-down menu and then click OK.

Figure 16-10: Manually configuring the SSID name for a wireless network with SSID broadcast disabled.

7. Click OK to close the properties window for your wireless network connection.

Implementing MAC address security

Hiding your wireless network is one way to limit its accessibility to outside users within range, but it won't stop more advanced users who *can* find the network from forming an association with your access point. Thankfully, almost all wireless access points include a feature to control exactly which systems can connect, in the form of Media Access Control (MAC) address security settings.

In the world of networking, MAC addresses (also known as physical or hardware addresses) are the individually unique identifiers assigned to each and every network card by its manufacturer. Although other addresses assigned to a network card may change (as is the case with IP addresses), a network card's MAC address belongs to it and it alone.

Knowing this, almost all access point manufacturers include a security feature in their products that enables you to configure a list of MAC addresses with which the access point is allowed to communicate. In other words, you configure the access point with a list of the MAC addresses assigned to wireless network cards in use on your network, and the access point will deny communication attempts coming from network cards with MAC addresses that are not on this list.

MAC address security is not enabled on wireless access points by default, so it's up to you to find and then configure the correct addresses for the wireless computers on your network. MAC addresses are made up of 12 hexadecimal digits (a numbering system that includes the numbers 0 through 9 and letters A through F), usually displayed in a format similar to `00-90-4B-24-B9-10`.

Follow these steps to determine the MAC address associated with your wireless network cards:

1. Click Start → All Programs → Accessories → Command Prompt.
2. At the command line, type **ipconfig/all** and then press Enter.
3. In the Windows IP Configuration results, look for the section pertaining to your wireless network adapter card, as shown in Figure 16-11. Note the Physical Address value, which is the MAC address of your wireless network adapter card.

```
Command Prompt
C:\Documents and Settings\Dan>ipconfig /all

Windows IP Configuration

        Host Name . . . . . . . . . . . . : xphome
        Primary Dns Suffix  . . . . . . . :
        Node Type . . . . . . . . . . . . : Unknown
        IP Routing Enabled. . . . . . . . : Yes
        WINS Proxy Enabled. . . . . . . . : No

Ethernet adapter Wireless Network Connection dell:

        Connection-specific DNS Suffix  . :
        Description . . . . . . . . . . . : Dell TrueMobile 1300 WLAN Mini-PCI Card
        Physical Address. . . . . . . . . : 00-90-4B-24-B9-10
        Dhcp Enabled. . . . . . . . . . . : No
        IP Address. . . . . . . . . . . . : 192.168.2.101
        Subnet Mask . . . . . . . . . . . : 255.255.255.0
        Default Gateway . . . . . . . . . : 192.168.2.1
        DNS Servers . . . . . . . . . . . : 192.168.2.1

Ethernet adapter Local Area Connection:

        Media State . . . . . . . . . . . : Media disconnected
        Description . . . . . . . . . . . : Broadcom 440x 10/100 Integrated Controller
        Physical Address. . . . . . . . . : 00-0B-DB-18-0A-54

C:\Documents and Settings\Dan>_
```

Figure 16-11: Use the ipconfig /all command to find the MAC address associated with your wireless network card.

After you've acquired the MAC addresses for all of your wireless network cards, it's time to enable MAC address security settings on your access point.

Follow these steps to implement MAC address security on your wireless access point:

1. Click Start → Internet Explorer, or open your preferred Web browser.
2. In the Address box, type **192.168.1.1**, or the correct address for your access point make and model. Press Enter.

3. At the logon screen, type your administrative access password. Click the Login button.
4. In the administrative interface, look for a section marked MAC Address Security, Wireless MAC Filter, or similar. On the SMC access point used in this example, MAC address security settings are enabled and configured from Firewall → MAC Filter, as shown in Figure 16-12.

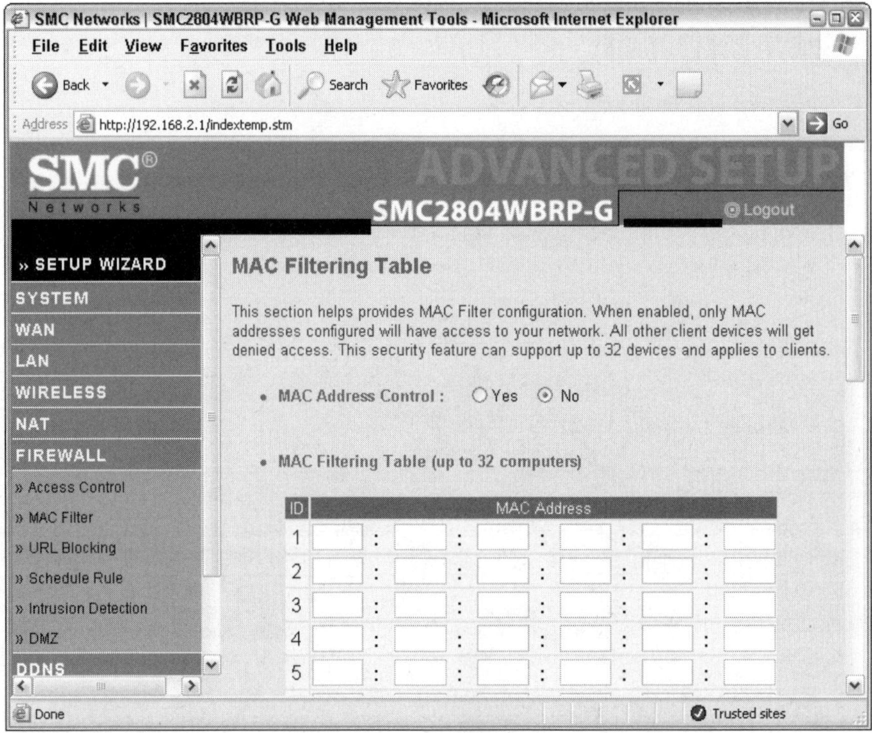

Figure 16-12: The MAC filtering table is used to restrict access to a wireless network.

5. Select the option to enable MAC address control.
6. In the MAC filtering table section, enter the MAC addresses of the wireless network cards used by clients on your network. Be careful to type these addresses correctly (case typically doesn't matter) because client addresses that do not appear in this list will not be able to connect to the access point. After complete, click Save Settings.

Implementing MAC address security helps to keep casual and inexperienced users from being able to connect to and make use of your wireless access point. As such, you should always use this technique to add another layer of protection to your wireless network.

It's also important, however, to understand that MAC addresses can be "spoofed," a technique whereby the burned-in MAC address assigned to a network card is replaced by another. (Some network cards allow you to change their MAC address to any value; others require the use of "spoofing" utilities to do the trick.) On wireless networks that do not use encryption, an experienced user could capture unsecured traffic and then reconfigure their MAC address to one in use on the wireless network. Ultimately, this allows them to bypass MAC address security completely.

Securing Wireless Network Traffic with Encryption

Although a variety of different methods can be used to improve the overall security of a wireless network, no wireless network can truly be considered secure until encryption settings are implemented. In the wireless world, two primary methods are used to encrypt network communications:

- Wired Equivalent Privacy (WEP)
- Wi-Fi Protected Access (WPA)

Both of these wireless encryption techniques are explored in more detail in the following sections.

Wired Equivalent Privacy (WEP)

As part of developing the original 802.11b wireless networking standard, the need for a way to protect and secure wireless networks was already well understood. The solution developed to address the problem was called Wired Equivalent Privacy (WEP). As its name suggests, the idea behind this security scheme was to implement protective measures that would make a wireless network just as a secure as the wired alternatives.

WEP functions by individually encrypting each and every packet sent between devices across a wireless network. It does this using a 64- or 128-bit encryption key stored on all WEP-enabled wireless devices. In some cases, the access point generates the key value, but it can also be configured manually. Ultimately, each device on the WEP-enabled wireless network must have the same encryption key value configured to securely encrypt and decrypt packets sent and received.

Unfortunately, the technique used to secure WEP encryption keys has proven to be flawed. With the correct tools (and enough time), hackers can use a number of popular utilities to capture wireless traffic protected by WEP, crack its encryption key (the same key is used to encrypt all traffic), and ultimately gain access to these "secured" wireless networks.

Note

If you're interested in learning more about the vulnerabilities associated with WEP, an excellent analysis is available online at `www.isaac.cs.berkeley.edu/isaac/wep-faq.html`.

Assuming that WEP is the only encryption option for your wireless devices, use the steps outlined in the following section to configure it on your access point and Windows XP system.

Implementing WEP security

To implement WEP on your wireless network, start by configuring the required settings on your wireless access point, as outlined in the steps below:

1. Click Start → Internet Explorer, or open your preferred Web browser.
2. In the Address box, type **192.168.1.1** or the correct address for your access point make and model. Press Enter.
3. At the logon screen, type your administrative access password. Click the Login button.
4. In the administrative interface, look for a section marked Wireless, Wireless Security, WPA, or similar. On the SMC access point used in this example, the WPA encryption settings are configured from Wireless → WEP, as shown in Figure 16-13.

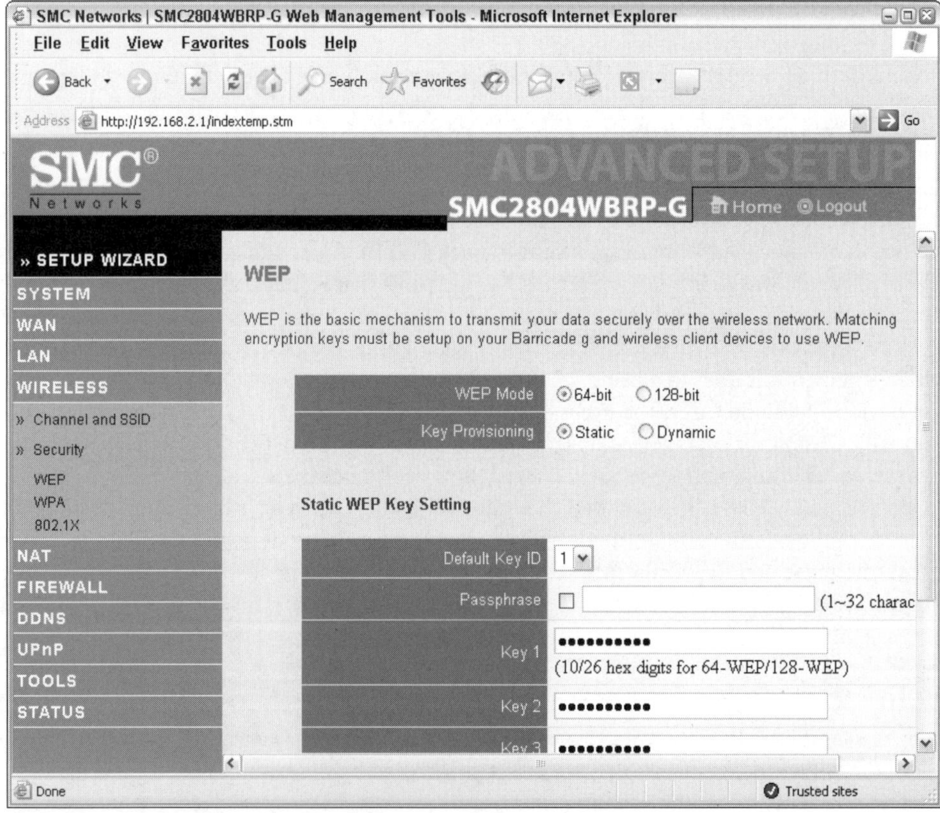

Figure 16-13: Configure WEP security settings on an access point.

5. In the WEP Mode section, select 128-bit.

6. In the Key 1 section, type a 26-character key value, using hexadecimal digits only. Valid hexadecimal characters include letters A through F and the numbers 0 to 9. Write this number down for references purposes because you'll need it to configure WEP settings on Windows XP.
7. Click Save Settings.
8. After WEP settings are configured, look for a setting in the administrative interface that allows you to specify which types of wireless clients should be allowed to connection to the access point. On the SMC access point used in this example, wireless client types are specified from Wireless → Security, as shown in Figure 16-14.

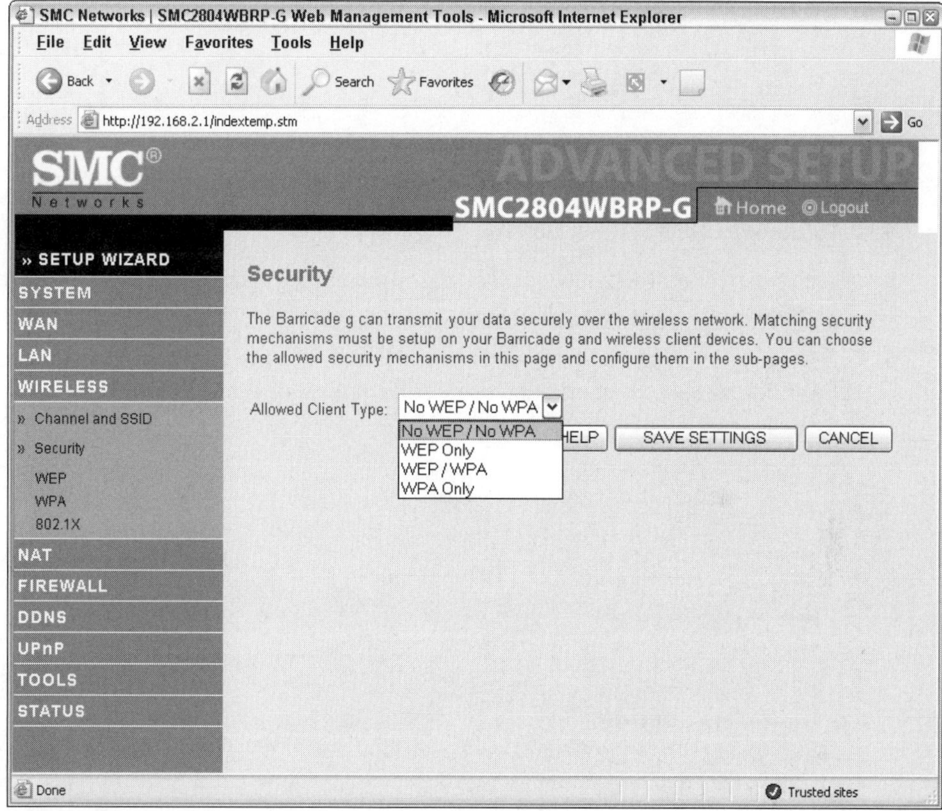

Figure 16-14: Configuring allowed client types on an access point.

9. In the Allowed client types list, select WEP Only or WEP/WPA.
10. Click Save Settings. If you're using a wireless connection to configure your access point, you will probably lose wireless connectivity until the necessary WEP settings are configured on your Windows XP system.

Tip

In additional to the steps outlined in this chapter, it is also possible to configure WEP and WPA settings using the Wireless Networking Setup Wizard included with Windows XP Service Pack 2. This tool can automate the configuration of wireless network devices (including access points) through the use of a USB flash drive. If your access point includes a USB port and supports Windows Connect Now (generally mentioned on the product packaging), you may want to consider using the wizard to configure your wireless security settings. For complete details on using this tool, visit `www.microsoft.com/technet/community/columns/cableguy/cg0604.mspx`.

Follow these steps to configure Windows XP to use WEP encryption:

1. Click Start → Control Panel.
2. Double-click Network Connections.
3. Right-click the icon for your wireless network card and then click Properties.
4. Click the Wireless Networks tab.
5. In the Preferred networks section, click the name of your wireless network and then click Properties.
6. On the Association tab, select Open from the Network Authentication drop-down box, and WEP from the Data encryption drop-down box as shown in Figure 16-15.

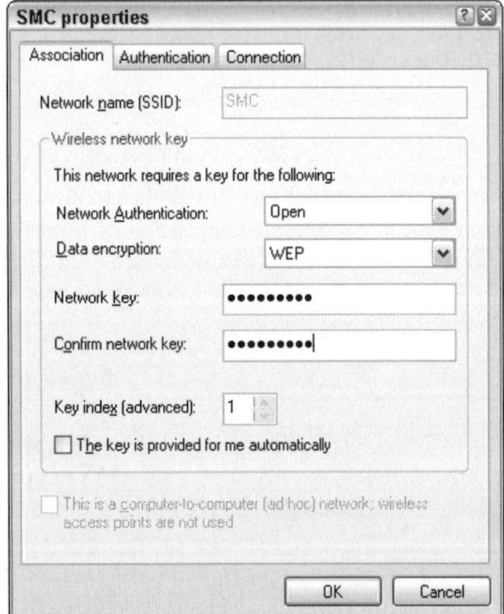

Figure 16-15: Configuring WEP settings on a Windows XP client.

7. Type the same 26-digit key value that you configured on your access point in the Network key and Confirm network key textboxes. If necessary, uncheck the box marked The key is provided to me automatically to enter these values.

8. Click OK to save your settings and then click OK again to close the Properties window for your wireless network connection.

9. Right-click the wireless network connection icon in your system tray and then click View Available Wireless Networks. If WEP is properly configured, the Choose a wireless network list should display your network as a Security-enabled wireless network.

Wi-Fi Protected Access (WPA)

Based on WEP's shortcomings, the Wi-Fi Alliance (the wireless manufacturer's industry group) developed an alternative solution to secure wireless network traffic known as Wi-Fi Protected Access (WPA). Designed as an interim solution while the IEEE's 802.11 working group developed a new wireless security standard, WPA became the defacto standard for securely encrypting traffic on wireless networks.

One of the main benefits of WPA was that it was designed with existing wireless users in mind. Manufacturers of wireless networking equipment could add WPA support to existing devices by supplying new driver files for wireless network cards, and firmware upgrades for access points. As such, almost any wireless device that lacks WPA support can be updated to include it, without the need for users to purchase new hardware. For details on upgrading wireless devices to include WPA support, see the "Gearing Up for WPA" and "Upgrading Router Firmware" sidebars later in this chapter.

WPA addresses WEP's primary vulnerability (the ability to crack the encryption key used) by implementing a number of new security protocols and features. These include:

- 802.1X user and system authentication on networks that include a RADIUS server, and support for pre-shared key authentication on home and small office networks.
- Temporal Key Integrity Protocol (TKIP), a required encryption protocol that changes the encryption keys used to secure each and every frame sent over the wireless network.
- Michael, a new algorithm used to check the integrity of wireless frames and implement a frame counter on WPA networks.

Ultimately, the new protocols and security enhancements implemented by WPA make it the best option for securely encrypting traffic sent over a wireless network. For more details on the exact processes that WPA uses to perform its encryption process, see `www.microsoft.com/technet/community/columns/cableguy/cg1104.mspx`.

Note

In cases where wireless networking devices support both encryption methods, WPA should always be used as the secure alternative. Windows XP and most WEP-only devices can be upgraded to support WPA. In cases where WEP is your only encryption option, however, it should still be used — the protection offered by a vulnerable WEP network is better than using no encryption at all.

Use the steps outlined in the following section to configure WPA security on your access point and Windows XP system.

Gearing Up for WPA

Implementing WPA encryption on a wireless network isn't terribly difficult, but there are a few perquisites that must be met to take advantage of the security it provides:

- The wireless access point must include WPA support.
- The wireless network cards in your Windows XP systems must be using drivers that include WPA support.
- Your Windows XP system must have at least Service Pack 1 and the WPA wireless security update package installed. Systems with Service Pack 2 installed automatically include support for WPA.

To check whether your wireless access point includes WPA support, log on to its administrative interface and review the settings in its wireless security configuration area. If WPA is listed, support is built-in. If WEP is the only wireless security option displayed, you need to download and install a firmware update for your access point, as outlined in the "Upgrading Router Firmware" sidebar.

Most wireless network card manufacturers now ship their products with driver installation packages that already include WPA support, but existing drivers often need to be updated. If you find that WPA configuration options do not appear on your Windows XP system even after installing Service Pack 2, you almost certainly need to update the drivers for your wireless network card.

Begin by determining the exact make and model of your wireless network card. This information can be found in Device Manager, accessible from the Computer Management MMC. To open Computer Management, click Start, right-click My Computer, and then click Manage. Expand Device Manager → Network adapters, right-click your wireless network card, and click Properties. If you click on the Driver tab, the make and model of your wireless network card is listed, along with its current driver version as shown in the following figure.

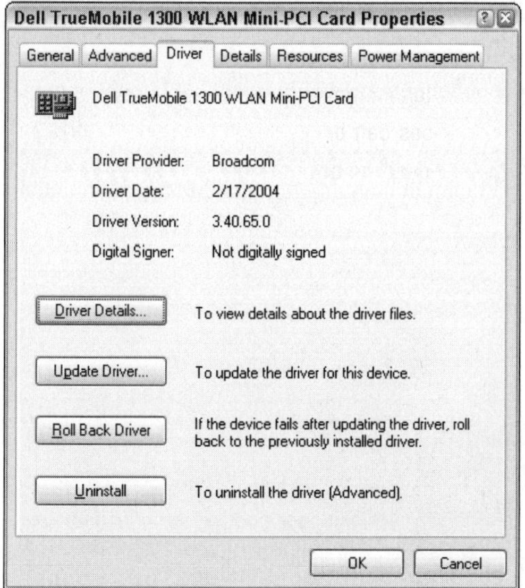

Reviewing driver details for a wireless network card.

With the necessary information in hand, visit the manufacturer's Web site and search for an updated driver for your model that includes WPA support. Download the file and then follow the instructions for installing it as outlined by the manufacturer.

Implementing WPA security

To implement WPA on your wireless network, start by configuring the required settings on your wireless access point, as outlined in the following steps:

1. Click Start → Internet Explorer, or open your preferred Web browser.
2. In the Address box, type **192.168.1.1** or the correct address for your access point make and model. Press Enter.
3. At the logon screen, type your administrative access password and then click the Login button.
4. In the administrative interface, look for a section marked Wireless, Wireless Security, WPA, or similar. On the SMC access point used in this example, the WPA encryption settings are configured from Wireless → WPA, as shown in Figure 16-16.

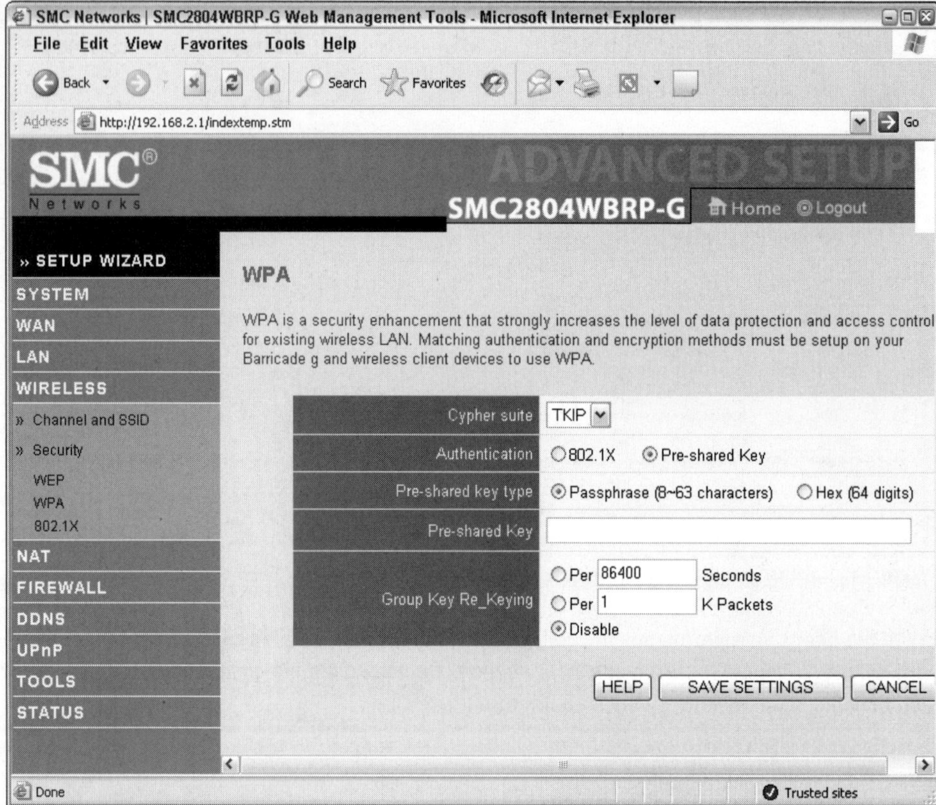

Figure 16-16: Configuring WPA security settings on an access point.

5. In the Cipher suite or protocol drop-down menu, select TKIP.
6. In the Authentication section, select Pre-shared key.
7. In the Pre-shared key type section, select Passphase.
8. In the Pre-shared key textbox, type your passphrase. Follow the same best practices as you would when configuring any strong password.
9. Click Save Settings.
10. After WPA settings are configured, look for a setting in the administrative interface that allows you to specify which types of wireless clients should be allowed to connection to the access point. On the SMC access point used in this example, wireless client types are specified from Wireless→Security.
11. In the Allowed client types list, select WPA Only.

12. Click Save Settings. If you're using a wireless connection to configure your access point, you will probably lose wireless connectivity until the necessary WPA settings are configured on your Windows XP system.

Tip

If you make a mistake when configuring WPA settings and find yourself locked out of your access point, consult the manual supplied with the device. Most access points include a reset button that can be pressed to restore the device to its original factory settings.

Upgrading Router Firmware

If your wireless access point doesn't currently include WPA support, chances are good that it can be added at no cost via a firmware upgrade. Firmware is the code (similar to an operating system) stored on a router that determines its features and capabilities. Manufacturer's regularly post updated firmware files on their Web site for their various access point models.

In some cases, a dedicated utility must be downloaded to perform the upgrade; however, many access points include a built-in tool for updating to the latest firmware version. For example, the SMC access point used in this chapter includes such a tool under Tools → Firmware Upgrade, as shown in the following figure.

Continued

Upgrading Router Firmware (Continued)

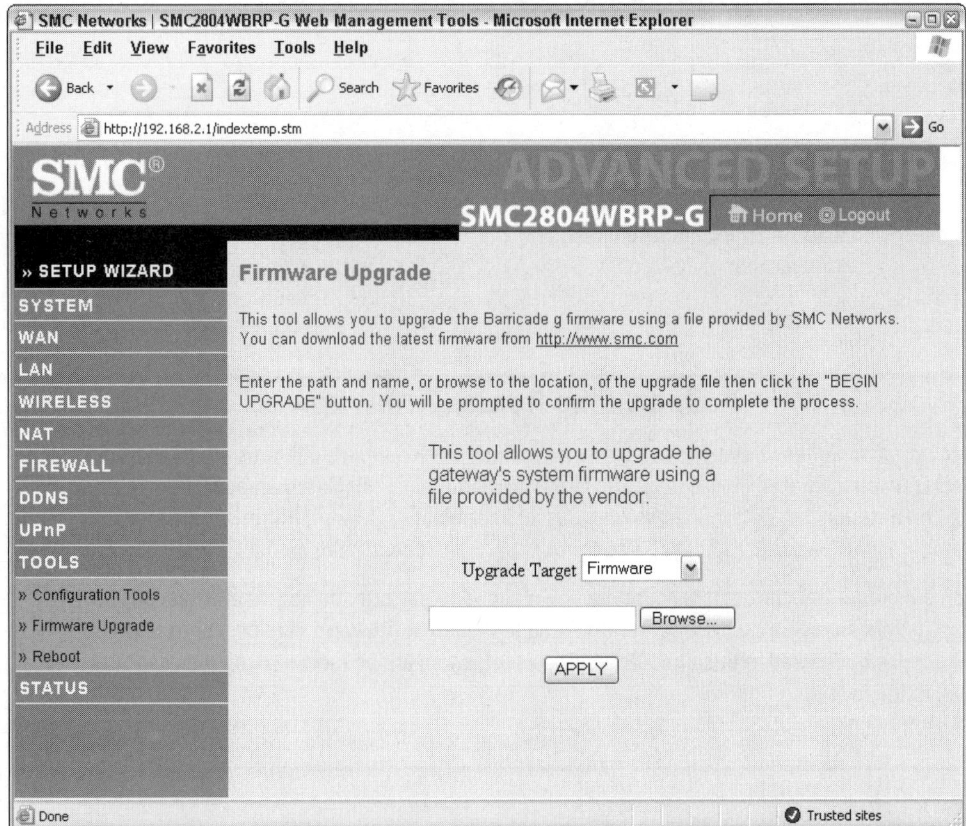

Most wireless routers include a feature that allows you to upgrade the device's firmware.

In this case, you would download the latest firmware version from the manufacturer's Web site and then use this tool to upload it to your access point.

Prior to upgrading your access point's firmware, it's important to ensure that you have its correct make and model number handy, as well as details about its current firmware version. This information can usually be found in the access point's administrative interface in a section named System.

Beyond adding new features, firmware updates are also released for the purpose of addressing known security issues. As a general rule, you should check for firmware updates to your wireless access point at least once every two to three months.

Follow these steps to configure Windows XP to use WPA encryption on your wireless network:

1. Click Start → Control Panel.
2. Double-click Network Connections.
3. Right-click the icon for your wireless network card and then click Properties.
4. Click the Wireless Networks tab.
5. In the Preferred networks section, click the name of your wireless network and then click Properties.
6. On the Association tab, select WPA-PSK from the Network Authentication drop-down box. Select TKIP from the Data encryption drop-down box as shown in Figure 16-17.

Figure 16-17: Configuring WPA security settings on a Windows XP client.

7. Type the same passphrase that you configured on your access point in the Network key and Confirm network key textboxes.
8. Click OK to save your settings and then click OK again to close the Properties window for your wireless network connection.
9. Right-click the wireless network connection icon in your system tray and then click View Available Wireless Networks. If WPA is properly configured, the Choose a wireless network list should display your network as a Security-enabled wireless network (WPA).

Note

The next generation of WPA, known as WPA2 or 802.11i, has recently been standardized and is already being implemented in newer wireless networking devices. WPA2 uses the Advanced Encryption Standard (AES) for data encryption, and the necessary support for this new version is already built into Windows XP. Although many older wireless access points could be upgraded to support WPA via nothing more than a simple firmware update, the same is not necessarily true for WPA2. Newer access points may be able to add WPA2 support by installing new firmware, but many older devices do not have the necessary hardware capabilities to handle AES encryption and need to be replaced. If you're in the market for a new wireless access point, consider a model that includes WPA2 support or can be updated to include it. As the new wireless encryption standard, WPA2 represents an excellent long-term investment in the continued security of your wireless network.

Summary

Wireless LANs offer an unparalleled level of convenience when setting up a home or small office network, but their default configuration settings are inherently insecure and represent a serious security threat. If these settings are left as-is, other users within range can connect to your private network, use your Internet connection, and even change the configuration of your wireless router. Keep the following points in mind when implementing a wireless network:

- Always change the default SSID and administrative passwords used on your wireless access point.
- Disable SSID broadcast on your access point to stop your wireless network from being announced to wireless clients within range.
- Enable MAC address security to control which wireless clients can form an association with your access point.
- Implement WPA security on your wireless network for the highest level of protection possible. If WPA security is not available, use WEP encryption.

Part VII

Appendixes

Appendix A

Reinstalling Windows XP

In the vast majority of cases, a Windows XP system that's been riddled by viruses and malware can be cleaned up and then re-secured using the tools and techniques outlined in this book. In the case of a very severe infestation, however, you might be left with little choice but to reinstall Windows XP and start from scratch. Although reinstalling Windows XP is often considered to be an extreme measure, it's all a matter of perspective — would you rather spend three hours desperately trying to reclaim your existing system (with no guarantees of success), or spend that same time reinstalling your operating system, programs, and then restoring your personal files? The first option might end up being a more interesting journey, but the second gets rid of outstanding issues for good and gives you a chance to start all over again with clean and (this time) properly secured system.

This appendix walks you through the tasks involved with reinstalling a Windows XP system from scratch. The step-by-step instructions outline the standard Windows XP installation process, but important pre- and post-installation tasks are also outlined for reference purposes.

Pre-Installation Tasks

If you jump straight into the process of reinstalling Windows XP without giving anything else a second thought, you'll almost certainly be sorry. When you reinstall Windows XP from scratch, the end result is a sparkling, like-new system — one in which all of your installed programs and personal files are missing, however. For these reasons, it's critically important that you consider the points listed in this section. If you don't, you'll almost certainly lose access to important documents, images, e-mail messages, and even encrypted files along the way.

Prior to performing a clean installation of Windows XP, complete the following tasks:

- Back up all personal files to another computer, external hard drive, or writeable CD/DVD disc. In most cases, this includes the contents of your My Documents folder and other folder locations where you may have used to store documents, images, videos, music files, e-mail messages, address books, and so forth. If multiple users share access to the computer, ensure that their files are backed up as well. For details on backing up personal files on a Windows XP system, see the Windows XP Backup Made Easy article at `www.microsoft.com/windowsxp/using/setup/learnmore/bott_03july14.mspx`.

- Back up any program installation files or hardware drivers that you will require after Windows XP is reinstalled.
- Back up all of your personal certificates (such as those used by EFS or encryption programs), including private keys. If you fail to back up these certificates and private keys, you won't be able to open existing encrypted files or e-mail messages.
- Make note of serial numbers for installed programs if you don't have them written down already.
- Make note of information such as ISP connection details (phone numbers, network settings, and so on) and any other miscellaneous pieces of information that you might require after the Windows XP installation process is complete.
- Gather all necessary CD/DVD discs that you'll require during the installation process before you get started.

Installing Windows XP

As daunting as the process of reinstalling your entire system might seem, the actual Windows XP installation process is probably the easiest part. If you can insert a CD and answer the basic questions posed by the wizard-style installation interface, you'll be just fine. It depends on the speed of your computer, but you can generally expect that it will take anywhere from 45 minutes to 2 hours to reinstall Windows XP start to finish.

Caution

Be sure to complete the tasks outlined in the pre-installation tasks section prior to reinstalling Windows XP. The following steps help you perform a "clean" installation of Windows XP, meaning that all personal files, programs, and other existing settings stored on your hard drive will be lost.

Follow these steps to perform a clean installation of Windows XP:

Note

These instructions assume that you are performing a clean installation of Windows XP using the "full" (not upgrade) version of the product. If you are performing the installation with a Windows XP "upgrade" disc, you will be prompted to supply the CD relating to your previous operating system's full version during the process.

1. Power on your computer and insert your Windows XP installation CD.
2. Restart your computer with the Windows XP CD inserted. When the Press any key to boot from CD message appears, press the spacebar (or any other key). If your computer's BIOS settings have been configured to boot from your hard drive first, you might not see this message. If this is the case, you need to change your computer's BIOS configuration to make your CD/DVD drive the first bootable device checked during the system startup process.
3. At the Welcome to Setup screen, press Enter.
4. At the Windows XP Licensing Agreement screen, press F8.
5. At the Windows XP Setup screen, press the Esc key. This is the option To Continue Installing a Fresh Copy of Windows XP Without Repairing.
6. At the screen where you're prompted to choose an installation partition, select your preferred partition (your former C drive) and click D (to delete the partition). When prompted to confirm the action, press L. After the partition is deleted, select the resulting Unpartitioned space and then press Enter.

Note

Step 6 creates one large partition using your entire hard drive in most cases. You may select the option to create additional partitions on your drive first if that's your preference.

7. Select a file system for the new installation partition from the list of available options. For security purposes, you should choose the Format the partition using the NTFS file system option. Press Enter.
8. The installation process now formats the drive and copy required installation files to it. When prompted, press Enter to reboot your computer. As the computer restarts, do not choose the option to boot from CD — the installation process continues automatically.
9. From this point forward, the installation process simply involves answering a number of different questions that pertain to you and your computer. For example, you will be prompted to supply location and time zone information, your name and organization details, product key information, and so forth. Simply answer the questions as they're asked, and press Next to continue through the process. When complete, you will be prompted to restart the computer — remove your Windows XP CD from the drive and then do so.
10. After the reboot process is complete, you are prompted to activate your copy of Windows XP. You can either activate Windows XP at this point or do so at any point within the following 30 days.

11. Finally, the Windows XP installation process prompts you to create one or more user accounts. As you learned in Chapter 1, all of these accounts are automatically configured as Computer administrators. Create one account for your own administrative use only at this point.

Congratulations — you've successfully reinstalled Windows XP! It's now time to move on to the critically important post-installation tasks, as outlined in the next section.

Post-Installation Tasks

The hard work really begins after the Windows XP installation process is complete. Not only do you have to install of the regular programs that you use on a day-to-day basis, but you also need to restore your personal files and settings and get down to the business of securing Windows XP such that the chances of having to go through this process again in the future (at least for security reasons) are next to nil.

When the Windows XP installation process is finished, complete the following tasks:

- Install your preferred anti-virus program and update it with the latest virus definition files. Run a complete virus scan of your computer.
- Install your preferred anti-spyware program and update it with the latest spyware definition files. Run a complete spyware scan of your computer.
- Install your firewall program, preferably one that includes both inbound and outbound filtering capabilities.
- Visit the Windows Update Web site to download and install all critical Windows XP updates. You might need to make several visits to the Windows Update Web site because some updates require a reboot as part of their installation processes.
- Create limited user accounts for each person who will be using your Windows XP system and ensure that each account is password-protected.
- Have each individual user log on and add a strong password to their user account.
- Restore any files, settings, and certificates that you've backed up, including those belonging to other users. When complete, scan all drives with your anti-virus and anti-spyware programs.
- Install any additional programs that you require for day-to-day use, such as office suites, alternative Web browsers, and so forth.

Appendix B

Helpful Windows XP Security Web Sites

Keeping your Windows XP system properly secured is a little more involved than simply following a series of steps once and then hoping for the best. Keeping any PC secured is more accurately described as an ongoing process — one in which you need to stay abreast of all the latest security threats and then address them accordingly. New security threats (or variations of existing threats) pop up all the time, and as the size and speed of the Internet grows, so too do the number of risks that you and your Windows XP system are likely to encounter.

Thankfully, it's fairly easy to keep informed about all of the latest security risks making the rounds on the Internet and obtain the necessary information to keep your Windows XP system protected. This appendix outlines some of the more useful Windows XP Web sites that are worth visiting regularly in your quest to maintain a clean and secure system.

Windows XP Home Page

The official Windows XP Home Page isn't dedicated to security, but it is a portal to all things Windows XP and worth a visit from time to time. Visit the Windows XP Home Page online at `www.microsoft.com/windowsxp/default.mspx`.

Windows XP Help and Support Page

When you have Windows XP questions and want answers, head to the Windows XP Help and Support Page at `support.microsoft.com/ph/1173`. This page keeps you up to date on all the latest Windows XP news, and the site's Solution Center is your gateway to hundreds of how-to articles, troubleshooting resources, and Windows XP downloads.

Microsoft Security Home Page

The Microsoft Security Home Page is the perfect resource for users who want to stay abreast of all the latest security threats, warnings, and updates related to Windows XP. Accessible at `www.microsoft.com/security/default.mspx`, this site provides a wealth of useful security information in plain English and includes the ability to receive security notifications by e-mail or RSS feeds.

TechNet Security Home Page

If you're of a more technical inclination and find the regular Microsoft Security Home Page a little limiting, check out Microsoft's TechNet Security Home Page at `www.microsoft.com/technet/security/default.mspx`. TechNet is Microsoft's premier resource for IT professionals, but it's also an excellent resource for more advanced Windows XP users who want to dig a little deeper on the security front.

Windows XP Security Guide

The Windows XP Security Guide is a detail-packed document that describes features and recommended settings for securing a Windows XP system running Service Pack 2. This document is especially useful for system administrators who manage networks that include many Windows XP systems, but is also a great resource for advanced users looking for more insight into Windows XP and Service Pack 2. The Windows XP Security Guide can be found on the TechNet Web site at `www.microsoft.com/technet/security/prodtech/windowsxp/secwinxp/default.mspx`.

Windows XP Expert Zone

The Windows XP Expert Zone is an online community for Windows XP users who want to learn more about the operating system's features and capabilities. Although not dedicated to Windows XP security *per se*, many of the site's "experts" write about a wide variety of security-related topics in a simple and jargon-free fashion. To access the Windows XP Expert Zone, visit `www.microsoft.com/technet/security/prodtech/windowsxp/secwinxp/default.mspx`.

PC Magazine Security Watch

Keeping any computer secured is all about staying informed, and when you want the skinny on all of the latest developments in the world of PC and Internet security, head for the PC Magazine Security Watch Web site at `www.pcmag.com/category2/0,1874,12,00.asp`. Here you'll find all of the late-breaking security news with which every PC user should be familiar, along with features, articles, and tips that help you keep your PCs and networks more secure.

The Elder Geek on Windows XP

This site isn't dedicated to Windows XP security alone, but it does include a wide variety of tips, tricks, and articles related to just about every facet of Windows XP. Whether you're looking for step-by-step instructions on performing a particular task or details about a Windows XP component, chances are good that The Elder Geek on Windows XP has what you're looking for. Fire up your Web browser and head to `www.theeldergeek.com` to check it out.

Appendix C

Catalog of Handy Windows XP Security Utilities

To properly secure a Windows XP system to a high level, you need to use the services of a number of different third-party programs. Although there's certainly no shortage of security-related programs available for Windows XP, some are more robust than others. This appendix outlines some of the more popular programs, tools, and utilities that can be used to improve the security of your Windows XP system, grouped according to common functions and features.

Password-Management Programs

Computer security begins and ends with strong passwords. Unfortunately, implementing good passwords means that all of your passwords have to be both complex and unique. Remembering one or two strong passwords may be relatively simple, but remembering 10 to 15 can be next to impossible. Rather than fall into bad password habits (such as using the same password for all of your accounts), you might want to consider employing the services of a password management program that helps you to remember and securely store unique and complex passwords for each and every one of your user accounts. Some of the more popular password management utilities for Windows XP include the following:

- Access Manager (`www.accessmanager.co.uk`)
- Norton Password Manager (`www.symantec.com/passwordmanager/`)
- Password Safe (`www.schneier.com/passsafe.html`)
- Password Depot (`www.password-depot.com`)
- Password Manager XP (`www.cp-lab.com`)

Parental Control Software

The Internet is one of the most amazing resources to ever exist, a source of information on every topic imaginable. For all of its benefits, however, the Internet is also a free-for-all where content such as pornography, hate literature, and other potentially disturbing materials can be accessed by anyone (including children) at the click of a button. This isn't going to change any time soon, so if you want to be sure that family and friends who use your PC cannot access objectionable content, you should consider investing in a parental control (also known as *content filtering*) program. Some of the more popular parental control programs available for Windows XP include the following:

- CYBERsitter (`www.cybersitter.com`)
- NetNanny (`www.netnanny.com`)
- CyberPatrol (`www.cyberpatrol.com`)
- SurfControl (`www.surfcontrol.com`)

Personal Firewall Programs

Every Windows XP system connected to the Internet requires the protection of a firewall, preferably one capable of controlling both inbound and outbound traffic. Some of the more popular firewall packages available for Windows XP include the following:

- Kerio Personal Firewall (`www.kerio.com/kpf_home.html`)
- McAfee Personal Firewall (`www.mcafee.com/myapps/firewall/ov_firewall.asp`)
- Sygate Personal Firewall (`smb.sygate.com/products/spf_standard.htm`)
- Norton Personal Firewall (`www.symantec.com/sabu/nis/npf/`)
- Panda Platinum Internet Security (`www.pandasoftware.com/products/platinum_is2005/`)
- ZoneAlarm (`www.zonealarm.com`)

Anti-Virus Programs

Viruses, worms, and Trojan horses all present a real and constant threat to Windows XP users. To ensure that your Windows XP system is protected from all manner of virus threats, it's critically important to install anti-virus software and keep it updated with the latest virus definition files. Some of the more popular anti-virus programs available for Windows XP include:

- AVG Anti-Virus (`www.grisoft.com`)
- Norton AntiVirus (`www.symantec.com/nav/`)
- McAfee VirusScan (`www.mcafee.com/myapps/vs7/`)
- Sophos Anti-Virus (`www.sophos.com`)
- Nod32 Antivirus System (`www.nod32.com`)
- Kaspersky Anti-Virus (`www.kaspersky.com/personal`)
- Stinger (`vil.nai.com/vil/stinger/`)

Anti-Spyware Utilities

Malware and related spyware threats represent one of the biggest current security threats to all Internet users, including those running Windows XP. With an estimated 80 to 90 percent of all PCs currently infected by some form of malware, removing spyware infections (and preventing them in the first place) is more important that ever. Some of the more popular anti-spyware utilities available for Windows XP include the following:

- Microsoft AntiSpyware (`www.microsoft.com/athome/security/spyware/software/default.mspx`)
- Ad-Aware (`www.lavasoftusa.com/software/adaware/`)
- Spybot Search & Destroy (`security.kolla.de`)
- Webroot SpySweeper (`www.Webroot.com/products/spysweeper/`)
- eTrust PestPatrol (`www.pestpatrol.com`)
- Trend Micro Anti-Spyware (`www.trendmicro.com/en/products/desktop/as/overview.htm`)
- CWShredder (`www.trendmicro.com/cwshredder/`)
- HijackThis (`www.spywareinfo.com/~merijn/`)

Anti-Spam Software

Unsolicited e-mail (also known as spam) probably ranks highest on most users' lists of Internet annoyances. Although the best way to avoid spam is to be careful about exposing your e-mail address to the Internet at large, there may be times when your spam intake is simply overwhelming, and you need a way to keep these junk e-mail messages at bay. Anti-spam software can help to filter incoming e-mail messages so that the number of spam e-mail messages that reach your Inbox is greatly reduced. Some of the more popular anti-spam programs available for Windows XP include the following:

- SpamPal (`www.spampal.org`)
- K9 (`www.keir.net/k9.html`)
- Mailwasher Pro (`www.mailwasher.net`)
- McAfee SpamKiller (`www.spamkiller.com`)
- Spam Bully (`www.spambully.com`)
- Spam Sleuth (`www.bluesquirrel.com`)
- Spamihilator (`www.spamihilator.com`)

E-mail Security Tools

There's no denying that e-mail is one of the most convenient communication methods going, but it's also one of the least secure. By default, every e-mail message that you send or receive is transmitted in plain text, with nothing stopping intermediaries from reading or even altering messages. If you want to ensure that your e-mail messages aren't being read or altered by other users, you need to use e-mail security techniques such as message encryption. If you're concerned about verifying senders' identities and ensuring that other users can be sure that a message they've received is actually from you, it's digital signatures you're after. A number of different programs and techniques can be used secure e-mail communications. These include the following:

- Thawte Personal Email Certificates (`www.thawte.com/email/`)
- CAcert (`www.cacert.org`)
- GeoTrust My Credential (`www.geotrust.com/enterprise_security/mycredentials.htm`)
- Steganos Security Suite (`www.steganos.com`)

File-Encryption Utilities

To secure the contents of your personal and business files with the strongest security possible, you need the protection that only file encryption can provide. Although a number of different file encryption methods and techniques exist, some of the more popular encryption tools for Windows XP include the following:

- Dekart Private Disk (`www.private-disk.net`)
- Folder Lock (`www.newsoftwares.net/folderlock/`)
- Paragon Encrypted Disk (`www.encrypted-disk.com`)
- Blowfish Advanced CS (`bfacs.sourceforge.net`)

Secure Deletion Software

When you delete files using normal methods in Windows XP, they aren't necessarily gone for good. In fact, with the right recovery tools, any user can potentially reclaim deleted files. The only real way to erase files once and for all is through the use of secure deletion software that overwrites the disk space previously occupied by the files. Some of the more popular secure deletion programs that can be used to permanently erase files from a Windows XP system include the following:

- Eraser (`www.heidi.ie/eraser`)
- Destroy (`www.destroy.com.au`)
- Sure Delete (`www.wizard-industries.com/sdel.html`)

Shareware and Freeware Web Sites

The Internet is chocked full of Web sites that allow you to download software for free or on a trial basis. If you can think of a useful program, it probably exists; however, finding the exact tool you're after is often the real challenge. When you're seeking out a program (security-related or otherwise) for Windows XP and you're not sure where to turn, consider turning to the following popular download Web sites:

- PC Magazine Utility Library (`www.pcmag.com/category2/0,1738,2130,00.asp`)
- NONAGS (`www.nonags.com`)
- Download.com (`www.download.com`)
- Tucows Downloads (`www.tucows.com`)

Index

Numerics

A

continued

PC
MAGAZINE
www.pcmag.com

F

G

H

I

K

L

R

PC
MAGAZINE
www.pcmag.com

V

W

X

Y

Z